The Kurds

A Divided Nation in Search of a State

Dedicated to my wife, Judy,
my love and support

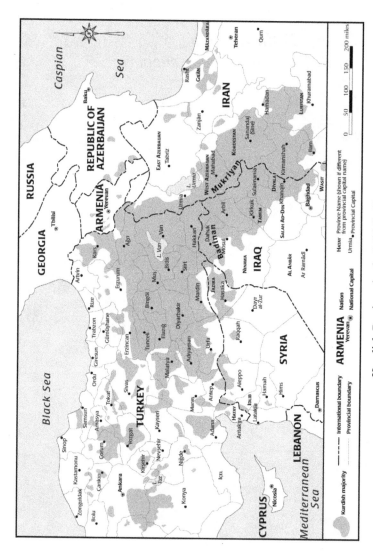

Kurdish Regions in the Middle East

vi

Contents

List of Maps viii

Acronyms and Abbreviations ix

Acknowledgments xiii

Introduction xv

1. Early History 1

2. The Kurds in Turkey: Change and Continuity 25

3. Iraq and the Rise of the Kurdistan
   Regional Government (KRG) 61

4. The Kurds in Syria: A New Dimension 87

5. The Kurds in Iran: Temporarily Quiescent? 133

6. The United States and the Kurds 151

7. ISIS and the Kurds 175

8. Kurdistan Aborning Amidst Continuing Conflict 185

9. Back to Square One? 211

Notes 237

Selected Bibliography 285

Index 299

List of Maps

Map 1: Kurdish Regions in the Middle East vi

Map 2: Demographic Distribution of the
Kurds in the Middle East as of 1996 xvi

Map 3: Liberated Areas of Iraqi Kurdistan 64

Map 4: Map of Kurdish areas of Syria 86

Acronyms and Abbreviations

AI   Amnesty International

AKP   *Adalet ve Kalkinma Partisi* or *AK Partisi*
            (Justice and Development Party) [Turkey]

AQI   Al-Qaeda in Iraq (ISIS precursor)

BDP   *Baris ve Demokrasi Partisi* (Peace and Democracy
            Party) [Turkey]

CHP   *Cumhuriet Halk Partisi* (Republican Peoples Party)
            [Turkey]

CIA   Central Intelligence Agency (USA)

DTP   *Demokratik Toplum Partisi* (Democratic Society
            Party) [Turkey]

EU   European Union

FGM   Female Genital Mutilation

FSA   Free Syrian Army

GAP   *Guneydogu Anadolu Projesi* (Southeast Anatolia
            Project) [Turkey]

HDP   *Halklarin Demokratik Partisi* (Peoples Democratic
            Party [Turkey]

HPG   *Hezen Parastina Gel* (Peoples Defense Force)
            [PKK]

ICG   International Crisis Group

IDP   Internally Displaced Person

IGC	Iraqi Governing Council
IKF	Iraqi Kurdistan Front
INC	Iraqi National Congress
IS	Islamic State, aka ISIS
ISIL	Islamic State of Iraq and the Levant, aka ISIS
ISIS	Islamic State of Iraq and Syria [al-Sham/Levant]
J.K.	*Komalay Jiyanaway Kurd* (Committee for the Revival of the Kurds/Komala) [Iran]
KCK	*Koma Civaken Kurdistan* (Kurdistan Communities Union) [PKK]
KDP	Kurdistan Democratic Party (Iraq)
KDPI	Kurdistan Democratic Party of Iran
KDPS	Kurdish Democratic Party in Syria
KGK	*Kongra Gel* (Kurdistan Peoples Congress), aka KNK [PKK]
KNC	Kurdistan National Congress (KNK)
KNC	Kurdish National Congress of North America
KNC	Kurdish National Council/Coalition (Syria)
KNK	*Kongra Netewiya Kurdistan* (Kurdistan National Congress), aka KGK [PKK]
KRG	Kurdistan Regional Government (Iraq)
MGK	*Milli Guvenlik Kurulu* (National Security Council) [Turkey]
MHP	*Milliyetci Karaket Partisi* (Nationalist Action Party) [Turkey]
MIT	*Milli Istihbarat Teshilati* (National Intelligence Organization) [Turkey]

MP   Member of Parliament

NATO   North Atlantic Treaty Organization

NGO   Nongovernmental Organization

OHAL   *Olağanüstü Hâl Bölge Valiliği* (Governorship of
            Region in State of Emergency) [Turkey]

OPC   Operation Provide Comfort

PJAK   *Parti Jiyani Azadi Kurdistan* (Kurdistan Free Life
            Party) [PKK/Iran]

PKK   *Partiya Karkaren Kurdistan* (Kurdistan Workers
            Party) [Turkey]

PUK   Patriotic Union of Kurdistan (Iraq)

PYD   *Partiya Yekita ya Demokratik* (Democratic Union
            Party) [PKK/Syria]

SDF   Syrian Democratic Forces (PYD)

SNC   Syrian National Council/Coalition

TAK   *Teyrebazen Azadiya Kurdistan* (Kurdistan Freedom
            Falcons/Hawks) [PKK?]

TAL   Transitional Administrative Law (Iraq)

TEV-DEM   *Tevgera Civaka Demokratik* (Movement for a
            Democratic Society/Democratic Popular
            Movement) [PYD]

UAR   United Arab Republic (Egypt and Syria: 1958-1961)

UN   United Nations

YDG-H   Patriotic Revolutionary Youth Movement (PKK)

YPG   *Yekineyen Parastina Gel* (People's Defense Units)
            [PYD/Syria]

YPJ   *Yekineyen Parastina Jin* (Women's Defense Units
            [PYD/Syria]

Acknowledgments

This book is the product of more than 30 years of work on and study of the Kurds. Along the way I have met many people who have made a strong contribution to what I have learned. Phillip Oldham, the president of Tennessee Technological University where I have been teaching since 1972, has strongly supported me in my late career. James Raymondo, the former chairman of the Sociology & Political Science Department at Tennessee Tech in which I have been placed for the past 10 years or so, went out of his way to sustain me and my work. Lori Maxwell, the new chairwoman of my department, has continued this invaluable and much-appreciated support. Angelo Volpe, the former president of Tennessee Technological University, supported me in tough times. Without the support of these people I would not have been able to write this book!

There have also been many scholars/colleagues over the years who have given me good advice and succor when I needed it. At the risk of leaving some very worthy ones out, a partial list in alphabetical order includes: Mohammed M.A. Ahmed, Jack Armistead, Tozun Bahcheli, Marvin Barker, Robert Bell, Ofra Bengio, Michael B. Bishku, Boleslaw Boczek, Hamit Bozarslan, Hans Branscheidt, John Calabrese, Vera Eccarius-Kelly, Nader Entessar, Wil Goodheer, Mehrdad Izady, Joost Jongerden, Anne Joyce, Kemal Karpat, Steve Khleif, Hafeez Malik, Lori Maxwell, Robert Olson, David Romano, Wallace Prescott, Michael Rubin, Seevan Saeed, Eva Savelsberg, Estella Schmid, Paul Semmes, Sanford Silverburg, Gareth Stansfield, Paul Stephenson, Jordi Tejel, Abbas

Vali, Kariane Westrheim, Steve Williams, M. Hakan Yavuz, and Nahro Zagros, among numerous others.

Many Kurdish patriots have also given me the benefit of their advice and backing including, again in alphabetical order, Najmaldin Karim, Bayan Sami Abdul Rahman, Qubad Talabani, and Adem Uzun, among many others. Some of these others whom I would like to mention have not yet made it off the so-called list of terrorists so long maintained for misguided political reasons by various governments including my own. Maybe I can add them in a future edition or another book!

I am also very grateful to Markus Wiener, my publisher, and his most competent, hard-working staff who have given this book actual form and life. Without their technical skills and advice this book would have been impossible. Any unfortunate errors of course, are my responsibility alone.

It would also be appropriate to mention possibly my two best friends over the years, Colonel Joseph Blair and Richard Cooper. Both have given me much good advice and companionship. My son Michael Gunter, daughter Heidi Gunter, and sister Barbara Tierney also have given me strong support. Finally and most importantly I am so thankful and indebted to my wife Judy Gunter of more than 50 years. She has always been most understanding and empathetic even when so seriously ill these past several years.

Michael M. Gunter
October, 15, 2018

Introduction

Kurdistan (the land of the Kurds) straddles the mountainous borders where Turkey, Iran, Iraq, and Syria converge in the Middle East. The approximately 30 million or more Kurds famously constitute the largest nation in the world without its own independent state. The Kurds are a largely Sunni Muslim, Indo-European-speaking people, although there are also Shia, Alevi, and Yezidi Kurds, among others. Thus, the Kurds are quite distinct ethnically from the Turks and Arabs, but they are related to the Iranians, with whom they share the *Newroz* (New Year) holiday at the beginning of spring. No precise figures for the Kurdish population exist, because most Kurds tend to exaggerate their numbers, whereas the states in which they live undercount them for political reasons. In addition, a significant number of Kurds have partially or fully assimilated into the larger Arab, Turkish, or Iranian populations surrounding them. Furthermore, debate continues over whether such groups as the Lurs, Bakhtiyaris, Yezidis, and others are Kurds or not. Thus, there is not even complete agreement on who is a Kurd.

The desire of many Kurds for independence, or at least cultural and even political autonomy, has led to an almost continuous series of Kurdish revolts since the creation of the modern Middle East state system by the Sykes-Picot Agreement during World War I left the Kurds without their own state. On the other hand, the states in which the Kurds live fear that Kurdish demands will threaten and even destroy their territorial integrity. The resulting situation constitutes the Kurdish problem or question.

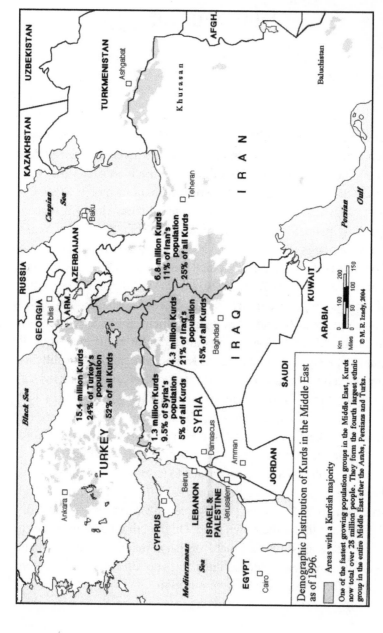

Demographic Distribution of the Kurds in the Middle East as of 1996

Geography

Given various political, economic, and social vicissitudes, the geographic extent of Kurdistan has varied considerably over the centuries. Although semi-independent Kurdish emirates such as Ardalan existed into the middle of the 19th century, there has never been an independent Kurdistan in the modern sense of an independent state. Before World War I, Kurdistan was divided between the Ottoman (mostly) and Persian Empires. Following World War I, Kurdistan was resegmented among five different states. Although only approximations can be cited, Turkey has the largest portion of Kurdistan (43 percent), followed by Iran (31 percent), Iraq (18 percent), Syria (6 percent), and the former Soviet Union (now mainly Armenia and Azerbaijan—2 percent).

Mountains are the most prominent geographic characteristic of landlocked Kurdistan. Indeed, a famous Kurdish proverb explains that "the Kurds have no friends but the mountains." This means that, although their rugged mountainous terrain contributes heavily to the lack of Kurdish unity, these mountains also have defined Kurdish history and culture while protecting the Kurds from being fully conquered or assimilated by the Turks to the north, Iranians to the east, and Arabs to the south and west. The Zagros range constitutes the most important portion of these mountains, running northwest to southeast like a spinal column through much of the land. Portions of the Taurus, Pontus, and Amanus mountains also rise within Kurdistan. On the other hand, significant flat farming areas also exist within Kurdistan. In addition and most important, the Tigris and Euphrates rivers originate in Kurdistan before eventually flowing to the south. The Greater and Lesser Zab rivers also flow through much of Iraqi Kurdistan.

Climate

The climate, especially of Kurdistan's mountains, has been described as bracing, particularly during the winter months. During the summer, however, these areas offer a hospitable retreat from the heat to the immediate south. Whereas northern Kurdistan has the highest average elevation, central Kurdistan enjoys a lower elevation, and thus a warmer, even relatively balmy climate can prevail during the summer. The mean annual temperatures in Kurdistan exhibit great variations, depending on the elevation. Although summers remain pleasantly cool in the mountains, in the lower elevations they can be oppressively hot and humid. Winters in most areas are bitterly cold and snowy.

These climatic contrasts have been sharpened by the loss of the forests that once covered the land but have succumbed to overgrazing, logging for fuel or construction, and the effects of war. In strong contrast to most other parts of the Middle East, much of Kurdistan enjoys adequate and regular rainfall.

Population

As already noted, Kurdistan constitutes the geographical area in the Middle East where the states of Turkey, Iran, Iraq, and Syria converge and in which the vast majority of the people are ethnic Kurds. There are also significant enclaves of Kurds living in the Iranian province of Khorasan east of the Caspian Sea and in central Anatolia. Large numbers of Kurds also live in Turkey's three biggest cities—Istanbul, Ankara, and Izmir—as well as in Iran's capital, Tehran. In addition, Kurds live in Armenia, Azerbaijan, and Turkmenistan, across the border from the Iranian province of Khorasan.

As stated above, no precise figures for the Kurdish population exist because most Kurds tend to exaggerate their numbers, whereas the states in which they live undercount them for political reasons. Nevertheless, a reasonable estimate is that there may be as many as 15 million Kurds in Turkey (20 percent of the population), 8 million in Iran (11 percent), 6 million in Iraq (20 percent), and 2 million in Syria (10 percent). At least 200,000 Kurds also live in parts of the former Soviet Union (some claim as many as 1 million largely assimilated Kurds live there), and recently a Kurdish diaspora of more than 1 million has risen in Western Europe. More than half of this diaspora is concentrated in Germany. Some 30,000 Kurds may live in the United States. Thus, overall there are probably more than 30 million Kurds in the world. (Again, it must be noted, however, that these figures are simply estimates, given the lack of accurate demographic statistics.) Finally, it should be noted that numerous minorities also live in Kurdistan. These minorities include Christian groups such as the Assyrians and Armenians, Turkomans and Turks, Arabs, and Iranians, among others. Accordingly, some have begun speaking of a Kurdistani identity, which would include anyone, not just ethnic Kurds, who lives in Kurdistan.

The Kurds themselves are notoriously divided geographically, politically, linguistically, and tribally. In all of the Kurdish revolts of the 20th century, for example, significant numbers of Kurds have supported the government because of their tribal antipathies for those rebelling. In Iraq, these pro-government Kurds have been derisively referred to as *josh* (little donkeys), while in recent years the Turkish government created a pro-government militia of Kurds called village guards. Thus, their mountains and valleys have divided the Kurds as much as they have ethnically stamped them.

Economy

Although many Kurds were historically nomadic, very few continue to practice such a lifestyle today. Many Kurds now farm and raise livestock. Corn, barley, rice, cotton, and sugar beets are valuable crops. In addition, the best tobacco in Turkey and Iraq is grown in Kurdistan. Animal husbandry (raising of goats, sheep, cows, and buffalo) has been and still is a mainstay. Because of the recent wars, however, most Kurds now live in urban areas. In the southeast of Turkey particularly, this has led to economic squalor. Diyarbakir (Amed in Kurdish), long considered the unofficial capital of the Kurdish areas in Turkey, presently contains well over a million people. Despite repeated proposals of government development aid, the economy of southeastern Turkey remains problematic.

On the other hand, the economy in Iraqi Kurdistan (KRG) has developed dramatically since the fall of the Saddam Hussein regime. Many foreign investors—particularly Turkish—have been attracted to the region, and construction has been booming. Modern stores, homes, and automobiles have proliferated. Two international airports have been constructed and are handling more than 70 flights a week in Irbil and Sulaymaniyah, whose populations are 1.5 million and 800,000, respectively. More than 10 universities are also operating. However, huge discrepancies in wealth have developed, as well as corruption and nepotism. Problems between the KRG and the central government in Baghdad continue regarding access to the rich oil resources and what the land boundary between them should be, among other problems to be discussed below. The ultimate political and resulting security situation also remains a long-term challenge, as illustrated by the so-called Islamic State's (ISIS) attack that drove within 20 miles of Irbil in August 2014 before being stopped.

Blessed with large reserves of water (in the Turkish and Iraqi parts) and oil (in the Iraqi section), Kurdistan has great economic importance and potential. Despite being economically underdeveloped historically, Kurdistan recently has witnessed a tremendous amount of economic, political, and social modernization. Indeed, the economy of the KRG economically surpassed that of the rest of Iraq in the late 1990s due to the oil-for-food program funds it received from the sale of Iraqi oil through the United Nations. Even more, given the security problems to the south, many foreign investors were attracted to the KRG region after 2003. Similar hopes have yet to materialize for the Kurdish areas in Turkey, however, despite the *Guneydogu Anadolu Projesi* (GAP) or Southeast Anatolia Project, for harnessing the Euphrates and Tigris rivers through the construction of gigantic dams. Finally, the Iranian and Syrian portions of Kurdistan still lag profoundly behind other regions in the two countries economically, with the Syrian area also now torn by civil war and its very existence threatened by the so-called Islamic State (ISIS), as illustrated by its horrific attack on Kobane in September-October 2014.

Early History

Introduction

Early Kurdish history melts into the mists of the past and is open to much speculation and debate. However, broadly speaking, there are two main schools of thought on the origins of the nation and nationalism. The primordialists or essentialists argue that the concepts have ancient roots and thus date back to some distant point in history. John Armstrong, for example, argues that nations or nationalities slowly emerged in the premodern period through such processes as symbols, communication, and myth, and thus predate nationalism. Although he admits that nations are created, he maintains that they existed before the rise of nationalism.[1] Anthony D. Smith agrees with the primordialist school when he argues that the origins of the nation lie in the *ethnie*, which contains such attributes as a *mythomoteur* or constitutive political myth of descent, a shared history and culture, a specific territory, and a sense of solidarity.[2]

The constructionists, on the other hand, maintain that nationalism is a recent construction that in effect has invented nations. Ernest Gellner and Benedict Anderson, for example, have argued that states create nations. "Nationalism is not the awakening of nations to self-consciousness: it invents nations where they do not exist"[3]—or as Anderson puts it, "imagines"[4] them through such mechanisms as "print language," which unifies dialects and creates national languages. Massimo d'Azeglio, an Italian nationalist leader during the *Risorgimento*, reputedly exclaimed: "We have made Italy, now we have to make Italians."[5] Eugene Weber has documented the recent process of changing "peasants into Frenchmen." That is, most rural and village inhabitants of France did not think of themselves as members of the French nation as late as 1870 or even up to the eve of World War I.[6]

Primordial Kurdish Nationalism

In their tome entitled *Cradle of Mankind: Life in Eastern Kurdistan*, the Wigrams—two Christian missionaries—wrote that "the country . . . is the very *fons et origo* [fountain and origin] of our Indo-European ancestors. Its tradition connects it with the Garden of Eden, with Noah and with Abraham."[7] Arguably, Kurdistan's documented history goes back to the Neanderthals of Shanidar Cave, an archeological site located on Bradost Mountain in Iraqi Kurdistan and dating from 35,000 to 65,000 years ago. Mehrdad Izady maintains that "the ancestors of modern-day wheat, barley, rye, oats, peas, lentils, alfalfa, and grapes were first domesticated by the ancestors of the modern Kurds shortly before the 9th millennium BC,"[8] and that "the practice of attaching the tribal name to the first name of every pre-modern Kurd has prompted some . . . to suggest that the Kurds were the first ethnic group in the world to use surnames."[9] In the center of Erbil, the current capital of the Kurdistan Region Government of Iraq (KRG), still stands its world-famous Citadel, maybe the longest continuously inhabited site in the world and dating from as far back as 6000 BCE. In 401 BCE the Kardouchoi—whom many view as the ancestors of today's Kurds—famously harassed the retreating Greeks as recorded by Xenophon in the *Anabasis*. Alexander the Great defeated the Persian king Darius III on the plains nearby modern-day Erbil.

Most Kurdish nationalists would be considered primordialists, because they would argue that the origins of their nation and nationalism reach back into time immemorial. Many see themselves as the descendants of the ancient Medes, who overthrew the Assyrian Empire in 612 BCE. They also can recite interesting myths about their origins regarding King Solomon, *jinn*, the blacksmith Kawa who defeated the ruthless ruler Zohhak who had been feeding the brains of young men to two giant serpents' heads growing from his shoulders, and their national holiday *Newroz* celebrating the beginning of spring or the new year. Some believe that the Kardouchoi, who gave Xenophon and his 10,000 such a mauling as they retreated from Persia in 401 BCE, were also the ancestors of the Kurds.

Mehrdad Izady observes that "reconstruction of the Kurdish history is a difficult task," because it "has all too often . . . been written by its hegemons. . . . The Kurds have not been hegemons for over 800 years. The result is that Kurdish contributions to history have been ignored, or worse, appropriated by other peoples."[10] Nevertheless, Izady argues that the period from the 5th century BC through the 6th century AD "marks the homogenization and consolidation of the modern Kurdish national identity. The ethnic designator *Kurd* is established finally, and applied to all segments of the nation."[11]

In examining linguistic and historical data, Vladimir F. Minorsky is more circumspect. He finds that "the Muslim sources and Kurdish traditions do not help us to solve the problem of the origin of the Kurds," but he concludes that "we thus find that about the period of the Arab conquest [mid 7th century] a single ethnic term *Kurd* (plural, *Akrad*) was beginning to be applied to an amalgamation of Iranian or iranicised tribes."[12] Minorsky adds that "we have detailed notices of the Kurds from the time of the Arab conquest onwards. During the five first centuries of the Hidjra, the Kurds frequently played a considerable part in events and often took the initiative in them. Several Kurd dynasties arose at this time."[13] Ahmad Al-Baladhuri's (d. 892) treatise *The Conquests of the Countries*, the earliest book to discuss the traditions of Islamic conquests, related that the Kurds fought alongside the Sassanian Persian Empire against the Muslims in the areas of Mosul and Azerbaijan. After the Islamic conquest, the Kurds continued to rebel whenever the central government declined.[14] Ibn-Jarir Al-Tabari (838-932), possibly the greatest of all early Muslim historians, referred to the Kurds in 17 of the 39 volumes of his work, *The History of Prophets and Kings*, usually known as *The History of Tabari*.[15] He saw the Kurds as a mostly nomadic tribal people who were difficult to control and manifested a strong tendency toward rebellion. Ibn al-Athir (1160-1233) and Ibn Khaldun (1332-1406), two other great Muslim historians, also portrayed the Kurds in a similar light, mentioning them "not in a modern national-ethnic sense, but rather in a sociological sense—as quarrelsome, rebellious pastoral-nomadic tribesmen and feudal dynasties that ruled cities like Dvin, Ganja, Hakkari, and Diyarbakir."[16] "Edith and E. F. Penrose simply observe that "the Kurdish consciousness of separate identity goes back far in history."[17]

The decline of the Islamic Abbasid caliphate centered on Baghdad from the middle of the 9th century onwards led to the rise of several Kurdish dynasties, including the Shaddadid (951-1075), which controlled areas now included in northern Iraq on the border between modern Turkey and Iran; the Hasanwahid (959-1095), which held sway over areas from southeast Azerbaijan to the Shahrizur area in the Zagros Mountains; the Marwanid (984-1083), which was situated around Diyarbakir in what is now modern Turkey; and the Annazid (990-1116), located in the Kermanshah and Shahrizur areas. However, none of these dynasties ever united all of Kurdistan, and one must even be careful about how much they thought of themselves as Kurdish rather than family- and/or tribal-centered. Most of them fell largely due to the arrival of the Turkish tribes and the establishment of their great Seljuk dynasty in the 11th century. The famous Seljuk conqueror Alp Arslan annihilated the Byzantines at the Battle of Malazgird in 1071 and destroyed the Kurdish Shaddadid dynasty in 1075, although a branch of that dynasty continued in Ani on the Armenian border until 1195. In 1083 the last Marwanid fortresses in the area of Jazireh bin Omar (Cizre) in modern southeastern Turkey fell to the Seljuks. The Kurds were slowly forced back into the remote mountainous areas historically associated with them. The Mongol invasion shortly afterward created even greater violence among the Kurds, but its long-term effects were not as permanent.

History also records that Saladin/Salah al-Din (1137-1193) was arguably the greatest and most famous of the Kurds. In 1171, he overthrew the Shiite Fatimid caliphate in Egypt and established the Sunni Ayyubid dynasty that ruled throughout Egypt, Syria, and Iraq. Saladin, of course, gained his greatest fame in the West as the chivalrous Muslim leader who defeated the Christian Crusaders led by the English king Richard the Lion Heart and regained the holy city of Jerusalem for Islam. However, Saladin thought of himself as a Muslim, not a Kurd. The Mamluks replaced the Ayyubids as rulers in Egypt in 1252, although Ayyubid successor proto-states/emirates such as Hasankeyf in modern southeastern Turkey continued to exist on a much lesser scale for hundreds more years.

The Ak Koyunlu (White Sheep) was one of two rival Turkmen federations or dynasties (the other being the Kara Koyunlu or Black Sheep) that ruled parts of Kurdistan during much of the 15th century after the death of the great Mongol conqueror Tamerlane in 1405. However, the Kurds did not play a major role in the armed struggles of the two. In 1476, the able Ak Koyunlu leader Uzun Hasan destroyed his rival Kara Koyunlu federation and eventually extended his power over most of Kurdistan. According to the famous Kurdish history the *Sharafnama* (see below), Uzun Hasan then "took it upon himself to exterminate the leading families of Kurdistan, especially those who had shown themselves devoted to or subjects of the Kara Koyunlu sultans." However, after his death, the Shiite Iranian shah Ismail destroyed the Ak Koyunlu in 1502.

Thus began the long struggle between the Sunni Ottomans and the Shiite Persians, a contest in which the Kurds occupied the borders in between the two great empires. After the Ottoman victory over the Persians in the Battle of Chaldiran in August 1514, the Ottomans took control of most of Kurdistan. The Treaty of Zuhab formally established their border in 1639, although wars continued into the 19th century. Idris Bitlisi (d. 1520) was a highborn Kurdish scholar and diplomat who helped broker important agreements between the Ottoman Empire and Kurdish emirates (see below) when the Ottomans first expanded into Kurdistan in the early 1500s. Possessed with a great deal of excellent political acumen, he was trusted by both sides.

Sultan Selim I (1512-1520) authorized Idris Bitlisi to grant the former ruling Kurdish families prominent positions in the newly conquered territories of parts of Kurdistan and to establish their administrative framework. In return, the Kurds recognized nominal Ottoman suzerainty. Thus, over the years some 16 semiautonomous *Kurd hukumeti* or Kurdish emirates were recognized covering perhaps 30 percent of Kurdistan. Some of these emirates such as Ardalan, Baban, Bitlis, Botan, Hakkari, and Hasankeyf, among many others, lasted into the middle of the 19th century and put the lie to the claim that there never were in effect any independent proto-Kurdish states.

The remaining territory was organized into approximately 20 *sanjaqs* or provincial districts, some under hereditary Kurdish rulers and others directly administered by centrally appointed officials. Most of these Kurdish emirates and some of the hereditary *sanjaqs* were usually, but not always, exempt from taxes or other Ottoman interference. Specifics reflected the balance of forces at any given time. Although neither the central government nor the Kurdish rulers were completely satisfied, Idris Bitlisi's organizational policies proved largely successful.

In 1515, Idris Bitlisi also proved successful in defending Diyarbakir after a siege of one and a half years by the Persians. Subsequently, he captured Mardin and other towns in what is now largely southeastern Turkey. He used substantial numbers of

Kurdish forces in these campaigns. His history, the *Hasht Bihisht* (Eight Paradises), covers the reigns of the eight Ottoman sultans from Othman to Bayezid II and was written in the most elaborate style of Persian.

In 1597, the Kurdish *mir* (prince) Sharaf Khan Bitlisi (1543-1603) published the *Sharafnama*,[18] an erudite history of the semi-independent Kurdish emirates, some of which continued to exist into the middle of the nineteenth century. The first part of this impressive history written in Persian dealt with five Kurdish dynasties that had enjoyed status as royalty or what might be interpreted as independence: the previously mentioned Marwanids of Diyarbakir and Jazireh, the Hasanwayhids of Dinawar and Shahrizur, the Fadluyids of the Great Lur, the princes of Little Lur, and the Ayyubids established by Saladin. The second part of Sharaf Khan's *Sharafnama* went on to list Kurdish dynasties that had had coins struck and the *khutba*[19] recited in their names. These attributes also reflected the equivalent of independence. Many contemporary Kurdish nationalists, therefore, point to the *Sharafnama* as historical documentation of the antiquity of their nation and nationalism.

Evliya Chelebi (1611-1685) was an Ottoman traveler and author who wrote the *Seyahatname* or Book of Travels, one of the most useful sources on the social, political, economic, and cultural life of the Ottoman Empire in the 17th century. In 1655 and 1656, he traveled to many different parts of Kurdistan (in particular Bitlis) and took extensive notes on almost everything he saw. He pointed out how the Kurdish emirates were an important strategic barrier for the Ottomans against the Persians. His descriptions also painted a description of economic and cultural prosperity, urban development, and even relative military power on the part of the Kurdish emirates. Chelebi described also Abdal Khan, the mir of Bitlis as possessing a broad education covering architecture, poetry, medicine, painting, and languages, as well as a library containing thousands of books.

In 1695, Ahmadi Khan published, in the Kurdish dialect of

Kurmanji *Mem u Zin*, a tragic love poem universally hailed as the Kurdish national epic because of its obvious references to Kurdish nationalist beliefs: "If only there were harmony among us, if we were to obey a single one of us, he would reduce to vassalage Turks, Arabs and Persians, all of them. We would perfect our religion, our state, and would educate ourselves in learning and wisdom."[20] In referring to the divisions among the Kurds, Ahmadi Khan, of course, was also identifying the recurring and most important factor stymying Kurdish nationalism today. Thus, elsewhere in his epic, Ahmadi Khan bemoans the results of this Kurdish division: "Look, from the Arabs to the Georgians, the Kurds have become like towers. The Turks and Persians are surrounded by them. The Kurds are on all four corners. Both sides have made the Kurdish people targets for the arrows of fate. They are said to be keys to the borders, each tribe forming a formidable bulwark. Whenever the Ottoman Sea [Ottomans] and Tajik Sea [Persians] flow out and agitate, the Kurds get soaked in blood separating them [the Turks and Persians] like an isthmus."[21] In analyzing Kurdish nationalism in *Mem u Zin*, Ferhad Shakely concludes that Ahmadi Khan "was proud of being a Kurd and thought that the Kurds were a nation like other neighbouring peoples and not inferior."[22]

Amir Hassanpour argues that the *Sharafnama* and *Mem u Zin* mark the historical origin of Kurdish nationalism: "Sharaf Khan's work demonstrates a conscious effort to assert Kurdish statehood."[23] Interestingly, Hassanpour views the development of Kurdish nationalism through a Marxist lens of social classes progressing through what he terms feudal and bourgeois nationalism. He also emphasizes the importance of the Kurdish emirates, some of which existed up to the middle of the 19th century as autonomous political entities. In addition, he refers to the 19th-century Kurdish patriotic poet Haji Qadir Koyi as "next to [Ahmadi] Khan . . . the second apostle of *Kurdayeti* [Kurdish nationalism]."[24]

In Kurdish history and heroic folklore, Dimdim (in Persian

Dumdum) has become a sort of Kurdish Masada. It was at this mountain fortress near the western shore of Lake Urmia that Hatem Beg, the grand vizier of the Safavid Persian shah Abbas the Great, besieged the Baradust *mir* Khan Yakdas from November 1609 to the summer of 1610. When the Persians finally took Dimdim, they found that all its defenders had committed suicide rather than be captured. *Bayti Dimdim* treats the siege of Dimdim as a Kurdish struggle against foreign domination and is considered by many as a national epic, second only to Ahmadi Khan's *Mem u Zin*.

Nevertheless, these protonationalist trends did not develop any further at this time due to Islamic loyalties on the higher level and tribal allegiances on the lower. None of the Kurdish emirates ever accumulated enough power within the overarching Ottoman and Persian empires to impose its sovereignty, promote a common identity, or create a modern state.

Although no records exist of pre-Islamic Kurdish literature and much undoubtedly has been lost because of the ceaseless conflicts that have ravished Kurdistan, it is possible to mention a few important works and authors. In the first place, however, one should note that there have long been Kurdish authors who wrote in Arabic, Persian, and Turkish, while in modern times many Kurds used Western languages. Usage of these other languages obscures the Kurdish origins of this literature. The 13th-century Kurdish historian and biographer Ibn al-Athir wrote in Arabic, while at the beginning of the 16th century Idris Bitlisi's *Hasht Behisht* (The Eight Paradises) traced the early history of the Ottoman sultans in Persian. Melaye Cizri was a famous Sufi poet in the early part of the 17th century who declared, "I am the rose of Eden of Botan; I am the torch of the knights of Kurdistan." His poems remain popular today. Other early Kurdish authors include the famous 14th-century Islamic historian and geographer, Abu al-Fida; the great poet of the Turkish language, Fuduli (d. 1556); Eli Heriri; Mele Ahmed of Bate; and Mir Mihemed of Mukis, surnamed Feqiye Teyran.

KURDISH LANGUAGES AND DIALECTS

The Kurdish languages (or language) belong to the Indo-European language family and are thus distantly related to English and most other European languages. Persian (Farsi), however, is the major language most closely related to Kurdish. On the other hand, despite their close geographic and religious connections, Arabic and Turkish belong to completely separate language families.

The Kurdish language is approximately the 40th in numerical strength among the several thousand languages spoken around the world today. Until very recently, however, it faced what might be termed linguicide or extermination, especially given the official policies in Turkey. However, with the rise of the Internet, the creation of the Kurdistan Regional Government (KRG) in Iraq, and Turkey's evolving more tolerant attitude, it would seem that the Kurdish language is no longer in danger of being destroyed.

Given their geographic and political divisions, there is also a wide variety of Kurdish dialects. To add to the confusion, there are no standard names for these different languages and dialects. In addition, the various Kurdish languages and dialects use three different alphabets: Latin (in Turkey and in most of the Kurdish diaspora), Arabic (in Iraq, Iran, and Syria), and, to a much lesser extent, Cyrillic (in the former Soviet Union and now Russia). Exceptions, of course, exist in this usage of different alphabets.

At the present time, some would argue that there are only two main Kurdish languages or branches of Kurdish. Kurmanji and Sorani may be considered major dialects of one language, belong to the southwestern branch of Iranian languages, and have by far the most speakers. (Others, however, would consider these two to be separate languages.) Gurani and Dimili (Zaza) may be considered dialects of a second language, belong to the northwestern branch of the Iranian languages, and have far fewer speakers. As already noted, there are many different dialects of each one of what may be called the two main Kurdish languages. If one were to compare the Kurdish languages to the Romance languages, the relationship between the two main Kurdish languages might be somewhat analogous to that between French and Italian. To further complicate matters, however, some would consider the southeastern dialects of Kurdish spoken in Iran from Sanandaj to Kirmanshah to be yet another Kurdish language. These southeastern dialects are closer to modern Persian than to Sorani.

This lack of Kurdish language standardization is not unique. In China, for example, Mandarin (the official language) and Cantonese—along with numerous other dialects—continue to coexist. Although the former is recognized as standard German, two principal divisions of the German language still persist as *Hochdeutsch* (High German) and *Plattdeutsch* (Low German). There are also two official forms of Norwegian, *Bokmal* (book language)—also called *Riksmal* (national language)— and *Nynorsk* (New Norwegian)—also known as *Landsmal* (country language). Modern Greek, too, has two different versions, a demotic or popular literary style and a reformed classical style.

Amir Hassanpour's lengthy detailed analysis (*Nationalism and Language in Kurdistan, 1918-1985*) is perhaps the major recent study in English of the Kurdish language, whereas Michael Chyet's new dictionary of more than 800 pages (*Kurdish-English Dictionary/ Ferhenga Kurmanci-Inglizi*) is perhaps the leading work in its field. Finally, it should be noted that most Kurdish nationalists strongly maintain that there is only one Kurdish language, but it has many different dialects.

Under the patronage of the Ardalan court, a number of excellent Kurdish poets also wrote in the Gurani Kurdish language/dialect. This list covers the period from Mulla Muhammad Pareshan in the 15th century to Mulla Abdal Rahim Mawlawi in the 19th century, and also includes Ahmede Texti, Sheikh Mistefa Besarani, Khanay Qubadi, and Mahzuni. Gurani ceased as a court literary language only with the downfall of the Ardalan emirate in the mid-19th century. Its former literary ascendancy is possibly still reflected by the fact that the term *gorani* is the common word for song in the modern Kurdish Sorani language/dialect.

The 19th and early 20th centuries saw so many noteworthy Kurdish authors that it is impossible to list all of them. A partial roll would include the aforementioned Haji Qadir Koyi; the much-adored patriotic journalist, Haji (Piremerd) Tewfiq; the incomparable Kurdish-Syrian scholar, Muhammad Farid Kurd Ali; the vibrant patriotic poet, Sexmus Hesen Cegerxwin; Faiq Abdallah Bakes; Abdallah Mihemed Ziwer; Ahmad Shawki, the Kurdish-Egyptian who was known as the prince of poets; the Kurdish-Egyptian brothers, Muhammad and Mahmud Taymur; and Mihemed Sheikh Abdul Kerim Qani (among many others). In 1898, *Kurdistan*, a journal published in Cairo by a group of Kurdish exiles, proved seminal in the development of Kurdish literature and modern Kurdish nationalism.

In 1839, in an attempt to stem its decline, the Ottoman Empire inaugurated the Tanzimat reforms that centralized control over border regions, among other initiatives. This centralization led to the demise of the last Kurdish emirates, which had possessed many of the characteristics of a state. As a result, religious sheikhs increasingly began to exercise some of the political powers of the former emirate *mirs* or princes. Indeed, many powerful contemporary Kurdish politicians such as the Barzanis and Talabanis owe their original position to forebears who were sheikhs. Another change worthy of mention in the 19th century was the increasing influence of Russia and its geostrategic rival Great Britain in the Kurdistan

area. As the Islamic Ottoman Empire continued to decline, conflicts also arose between the nomadic Islamic Kurds on the one
hand and the more sedentary Christian Armenians and Assyrians
on the other.

Two of the last 19th-century emirates deserve brief mention.
Soran was a declining Kurdish emirate in what is now northern
Iraq, when it experienced a brief revival early in the 19th century.
Under Mir Muhammad Pasha of Rawanduz or Soran (called Miri
Kor or the blind *mir* because of an affliction of the eyes), the emi-
rate of Soran ruthlessly conquered much of what is now northern
Iraq after 1814, only to have it extinguished by the Ottomans in
1834. These events involved much intrigue between the Ottomans,
Persians, Britain, and Russia. Miri Kor was finally invited to
Istanbul and was given many honors, but mysteriously disappeared
(almost certainly murdered by orders of the sultan) on his way back
to Kurdistan. His brother Rasul became governor of Rawanduz
until the *wali* or Ottoman governor of Baghdad expelled him in
1847.

Bedir Khan (1800c.-1868) became the *mir* of the emirate of
Botan (capital Cizre) in what is today southeastern Turkey around
1821. He has been described as brave, charming, pious, ambitious,
and reckless, and is still considered by many Kurds today to be one
of their first nationalists.[25] Under his guidance, Botan grew to en-
compass much of what is today southeastern Turkey and even the
Bahdinan part of northern Iraq. His strict rule made the emirate a
noted place of security. The weakness of the Ottoman Empire at
that time helped lead Badir Khan to strike for what some would
argue was to be an independent Kurdistan. After he committed
bloody massacres of the local Christians—who were being abetted
by the European powers, however—Britain and France forced the
Ottomans to move against Bedir Khan. In 1847, Bedir Khan was
defeated, and his semiautonomous emirate ceased to exist. He was
exiled to Crete, where he defeated a rebellion of the Cretan Greeks.
For this service he was allowed to move to Damascus, where he

finally died in 1868. His descendants continued to play an important role in Ottoman and Kurdish affairs. (See below.)

In 1880, Sheikh Ubeydullah of Nehri led a famous but ultimately unsuccessful revolt that is sometimes said to have been the prototype for subsequent Kurdish nationalist revolts. In a famous letter to the British consul-general in Tabriz, Ubeydullah seemingly made obvious references to some kind of preexisting Kurdish nationalism when he declared that "the Kurdish nation . . . is a people apart. Their religion is different and their laws and customs are distinct. . . . We also are a nation apart. We want our affairs to be in our own hands."[26]

Constructionist Kurdish Nationalism

Despite these primordial or essentialist arguments for the antiquity of Kurdish nationalism, such interpretations can be challenged for a number of very solid reasons. In the first place, of course, the very concept of the nation and nationalism being the focus of one's supreme loyalty is relatively new even in the West, where many would argue that it began to develop only in the latter part of the 18th century and specifically during the French Revolution, which began in 1789.[27] The concept is even newer in the Middle East. Turkish, Iranian, and even Arab nationalism largely emerged only after World War I, following the demise of the multinational Ottoman Empire and its emphasis on Islam as the supreme focus of one's loyalty. Martin van Bruinessen, for example, disputes the oft-made claim that Ahmadi Khan's seventeenth-century epic *Mem u Zin* was a precursor of modern Kurdish nationalism. He argues that neither the political nor the socioeconomic prerequisites existed in seventeenth-century Kurdistan for any notion of the nation to exist, because tribes were the main collectivity with which the Kurds identified. "In general, people did not identify themselves as ethnic groups or nations in the way that people nowadays do."[28]

Hugh Seton-Watson analyzes the rise of what he calls "official nationalism" in such multinational states as Russia and Hungary during the second half of the 19th century: "The leaders of the most powerful nations . . . impose[d] their nationality on all their subjects—of whatever religion, language or culture. . . . As they saw it . . . they were strengthening their state by creating within it a single homogeneous nation."[29] Russification in the Russian Empire under Alexander III and Nicholas II imagined a nation without diversity, and subsequently became the model for many of the new states in the Middle East such as Turkey.

Denise Natali illustrates how "in both the Ottoman and Qajar [Persian] Empires the absence of an exclusive official nationalist project based on ethnicity prevented *Kurdayeti* [Kurdish nationalism] from becoming salient or highly ethnicized."[30] Following World War I, however, "different forms of Kurdayeti have evolved in Iraq, Turkey, and Iran as a function of the political space in each state."[31] Hakan Ozoglu aptly demonstrates how Kurdish nationalism began to emerge in Turkey only after the Ottoman Empire collapsed and the Kurdish notables had to seek a new identity. "Kurdish nationalism appeared to be the only viable choice for Kurds in the absence of a functioning ideology such as Ottomanism. It was a result of a desperate search for identity after Ottomanism failed."[32] Thus, "Kurdish nationalism . . . was not a cause of [the Ottoman] Empire's disintegration, but rather the result of it."[33]

M. Hakan Yavuz elaborates on the modern origins of Kurdish nationalism in Turkey when he declares: "The state's [Turkey's] policies are the determinant factors in the evolution and modulation of . . . Kurdish ethno-nationalism. The major reason for the politicization of Kurdish cultural identity is the shift from multi-ethnic, multi-cultural realities of the Ottoman Empire to the nation-state model."[34] The Kemalist reforms, which aimed to create a modern Turkish nation-state "resulted in the construction of Kurdish ethno-nationalism."[35] Yavuz identifies five stages in the modern development of Kurdish nationalism in Turkey: (1) the impact of the

Ottoman Empire's centralization policies from 1878 to 1924; (2) the reaction of the Kurdish tribes to the nation-building project of Mustafa Kemal (Ataturk) from 1925 to 1961; (3) the secularization of Kurdish identity within the framework of the broader leftist movement in Turkey from 1962 to 1983; (4) the Kurdistan Workers Party (PKK) insurgency from 1984 to 1998; and (5) the period following the arrest of the PKK leader, Abdullah (Apo) Ocalan in 1999. Throughout his analysis, Yavuz emphasizes that "the major difference between Turkish and Kurdish nationalism is the presence of the state. . . . Since Kurdish nationalism in Turkey, Iraq, and Iran evolved in response to modernizing nation-states, it constantly stresses its ethnic 'difference,' sometimes even evoking racism to historicize itself."[36]

Hamit Bozarslan basically agrees with Yavuz's analysis when he argues that two significant factors preventing Kurdish nationalism from exerting significant influence from 1919 to 1921 were "the ideal of Islamic fraternity, and the fear of the establishment of an Armenian state."[37] However, "the proclamation of the Kemalist Republic in 1923 meant the end of . . . the Ottoman tacit contract between centre and peripheries [and] . . . to a large extent explains the . . . traditional [Kurdish] dignitaries . . . participation in the subsequent revolts."[38]

Similarly in Iraq, Kurdish nationalism began to develop only after World War I in response to the attempts to build a modern Arab state that would permit no more than a minimal amount of Kurdish autonomy.[39] Thus, the revolts of Sheikh Mahmud Barzinji in the 1920s and Mulla Mustafa Barzani beginning in the 1930s were mainly tribal affairs, at times opposed by more Kurdish *josh* (literally, little donkeys or Kurds who supported the Iraqi government in Baghdad) than supported. In discussing the revolts of Sheikh Mahmud Barzinji, for example, David McDowall argues that "he had little in common with today's Kurdish leaders. Both the vocabulary and style are quite different. It is significant that Shaykh Mahmud did not waste his time appealing to nationalist sentiment. He was a sayyid (literally a reputed descendant of Muhammed), and the language his constituency understood was the language of Islam. In 1919 he appealed for a *jihad*, not a national liberation struggle. Furthermore, his style was to use kin and tribal allies, and his aim was the establishment of a personal fiefdom."[40]

Only in the 1960s did the Kurdish movement in Iraq begin to take on the characteristics of a genuine nationalist movement. Following the destruction of the Mahabad Republic of Kurdistan in Iran in 1946 (see below), the famous Iraqi Kurdish leader Mulla Mustafa Barzani's retreat to the Soviet Union subsequently became epic in the rise of modern Kurdish nationalism: "We marched for fifty-two days. In the high mountain passes the late spring snow was six to twelve feet deep. We fought nine encounters, lost four killed and had seven wounded."[41] Even so, to his dying day, Barzani never fully exceeded the bounds of tribal chieftain. In part, this helps to explain his bitter disputes with Ibrahim Ahmad and Ahmad's son-in-law, Jalal Talabani.

Saddam Hussein's genocidal attempts to reduce the Kurds in the 1970s and 1980s had the opposite effect of fostering Kurdish nationalism. Iraq's defeat in the Gulf War of 1991 spawned a de facto Kurdish state in northern Iraq, in which an increasingly strong sense of Iraqi Kurdish nationalism began to grow within a Kurdish-ruled state.[42] Social and economic factors also played important roles in the development of Kurdish nationalism in Iraq. The oil industry, construction of major dams, cement and tobacco factories, and agricultural mechanization all created greater wealth and helped move people out of their smaller traditional valleys into the larger urban world. In the first decade of the 21st century, Iraqi Kurdish nationalism has become the most highly developed form of Kurdish nationalism among the entire Kurdish people, but clearly its origins are mainly modern, dating only to the events described briefly above.

Farideh Koohi-Kamali also has demonstrated the modern origins of Kurdish nationalism in Iran. Only with the structural changes in their traditional nomadic, tribal society and economy brought on by the Pahlavi monarchy beginning in the 1920s did the Kurds in Iran begin to see themselves as a community with a homogeneous ethnic identity possessed with a sense of Kurdish nationalism.[43] Even though Iran spawned the short-lived and tiny Mahabad Republic of Kurdistan in 1946,[44] however, Kurdish nationalism in Iran has not developed to the same degree as it has in Turkey and Iraq.

Until the civil war began in 2011, even more so was this true in Syria. Unlike the Kurds in Turkey, Iraq, and Iran, those in Syria were divided into three separate areas and had no mountains for a possible guerrilla safe house. Only the civil war suddenly created the prerequisites for autonomy, as will be analyzed below. Earlier, Nelida Fuccaro showed how the continuing importance of tribal and religious loyalties had impeded the spread of Kurdish nationalism in Syria and also opened it up to intervention and manipulation by competing Arab nationalist forces in that state, even refusing to grant citizenship to some of them.[45]

The Bedir Khan brothers' (Tureyya, Kamuran, and Celadet) attempt to develop or invent Kurdish nationalism in the 1920s and 1930s also aptly illustrates its modern origins. The three brothers were grandsons of the famous Bedir Khan of Botan, whose powerful emirate was only destroyed by the Ottomans in 1847. The three brothers grappled with many problems, including the ambivalent nature of the Kurdish relationship with the Turks and the primitive state of affairs in Kurdistan. As Martin Strohmeier notes, "All Kurds were deeply if variously enmeshed in social, ideological, economic and personal relations with the Turks. . . . These bonds hampered the development of a self-assertive, robust and distinct Kurdish identity."[46] Indeed, even today, Murat Somer has shown how "Turks and Kurds do not constitute monolithic group categories with historically fixed identities."[47]

In addition, the Kurdish "language was a shambles, not fit for education or literature; their culture was backward, and their history was a mystery."[48] Furthermore, "a language-factor potentially more divisive than dialects was the problem presented by Turkish speakers among the Kurds."[49] Indeed, even today the PKK has wrestled with this problem by having to maintain both Turkish- and Kurdish-language schools for its cadres. Ocalan himself struggles with this problem as he speaks Turkish better than Kurdish, only learning to use the latter later in life. The Russian tsar's court faced an analogous problem in 1812 when most of its members spoke French during the Napoleonic invasion.

Following World War I and the subsequent rush to create nation-states in the Middle East, the Kurds had no one to counter the appeal to Muslim loyalty of Mustafa Kemal (Ataturk). Kurdish leaders such as Muhammad Sherif Pasha—who attempted to win a Kurdish state by cooperating with the Armenian delegation at the Paris Peace Conference in 1919—appeared to be traitors willing to compromise Kurdish positions. "The making of their (Turkish) nation was to depend on the unmaking of any plans the Kurds had had for their own nation."[50]

After the failure of the Sheikh Said and Ararat rebellions in the 1920s, the Bedir Khan brothers broke completely with their residual Turkish loyalties and sought to develop, with French support in Syria, a full-blown Kurdish nationalism. In *Les Massacres Kurds en Turquie* and *The Case of Kurdistan against Turkey*—both published by Tureyya Bedir Khan in 1928—"the Turks are portrayed as having pursued throughout the whole of their co-existence with the Kurds and other races the aims of extermination and assimilation. . . . The Turks, descendants of Attila and Jingiz Khan, are an unchanging entity, barbaric and evil by nature."[51] Although Bedir Khan's writings were propagandistic and contained simplistic, misleading, and distorted analyses of Kurdish and Turkish history, they still maintain an important influence on the subsequent development of Kurdish nationalism and its analysis.

Celadet Bedir Khan was elected the first president of Khoybun, a transnational Kurdish party created in 1927 by Kurdish intellectuals living in exile in Syria. The party sought to establish a strong

Kurdish national liberation movement with a trained fighting force that would not depend on the traditional tribal leaders and helped instigate the unsuccessful Ararat uprising of the Kurds in 1927-1930. Subsequently, Celadet Bedir Khan devoted himself to literary work and helped to develop a Kurdish alphabet in Latin characters. During his final years in the 1960s, he served as a spokesman for Mulla Mustafa Barzani, the famous Iraqi Kurdish leader.

In 1937, Kamuran Bedir Khan published *Der Adler [Eagle] von Kurdistan*, a formalistic and forgotten attempt to write an epic novel to promote the Kurdish cause on the magnitude of Franz Werfel's classic, *The Forty Days of Musa Dagh* for the Armenians. Bedir Khan attempted to forge an imagined Kurdish nation that illustrated its heroism, patriotism, reverence for the land, identification with the mountains, pride in the language and heritage, beauty of the folktales and songs, strong and patriotic women, and overall Kurdish solidarity. He even sought to assert that the Kurds' true religion was Zoroastrianism and that the biblical Garden of Eden had a Kurdish counterpart in the legend of the Thousand Lakes (Bingol). Proverbs such as "Lion, put your faith in your paws" demonstrated how the Kurds relied on their own strength and did not merely await divine aid. Kamuran Bedir Khan's effort to produce a Kurdish national epic, however, proved inconsequential and failed to stir Kurdish nationalism. The large majority of the Kurds had not yet imbued enough sense of Kurdish nationalism to part with other Muslims.

Segueing into the Future

That the origins of Kurdish nationalism lie mainly (although not completely) in modern times in no way impugns either its current existence or legitimacy. Indeed its modern origins are not unique. Arab, Turkish, and Iranian nationalisms are only slightly older, whereas those of the European nations—where the concept of nationalism was born—are also relatively new.

It is true, of course, that Kurdish nationalism—compared with that of its immediate neighbors in Turkey, the Arab world, and Iran—has been stunted and divided. In addition, this chapter has shown that Kurdish nationalism largely developed in the 20th century as a stateless ethnic reaction against the repressive "official state nationalisms" of Turkey, Iraq, Iran, and Syria. Martin van Bruinessen has commented on how "the sort of 'nation building' policies that were so successfully implemented in the earlier period appear to have the reverse result in the present. . . . Since the 1970s . . . repressive measures directed at the expression of Kurdish nationalist sentiment have had the effect of strengthening rather than eliminating it."[52] Moreover, referring specifically to the Kurds, Murat Somer recently noted how "people can have multiple and mixed conceptions of their identities, whereby ethnicity has to compete with other sources of belonging, such as national, supranational, and regional identities."[53] These problems and differences in Kurdish nationalism, however, do not negate its existence, which continues to develop and mature.

Recently, for example, the development of transnational space has led "to externally based opportunity structures such as diasporic networks, international nongovernmental organizations, host-country democratic systems, and advanced telecommunication systems that provide new forms of support or constraint to Kurdish nationalist projects."[54] In Iraq, "the creation of a protected, autonomous region encouraged the transfer of people, ideas, and resources to Iraqi Kurdistan, all of which helped advance the notion of Kurdish self-rule."[55] In Turkey, "access to European Union institutions has reinforced ties to the international network of human-rights organizations and created a new legal political arena for Kurdish nationalist claims . . . a 'juridicization' of Kurdayeti at the international level"[56] not present even in Iraq.

Indeed, in the 21st century, newly empowered Kurdish nationalism bids fair to challenge the future of such states as Turkey, Iraq, Iran, and Syria. In northern Iraq particularly, Kurdish nationalism has flourished since the creation of a de facto Kurdish state there following the defeat of Iraq in the 1991 Gulf War. Under the protection of a no-fly zone enforced against the government of Saddam Hussein until his fall in 2003, an entire Kurdish generation was raised under a Kurdish-run administration and learned to speak only Kurdish, not Arabic. In addition, a Kurdish civil society began to emerge, with dozens of newspapers, magazines, and television and radio stations using the Kurdish language and representing a broad spectrum of opinion. The Kurds enjoyed freedoms impossible to imagine in the rest of Iraq. Furthermore, an increasingly influential and, in part, highly educated diaspora of more than 1 million Kurds in the West has provided a reservoir of support for the Kurdish nationalism developing in this de facto state.

The US war that removed Saddam Hussein from power in 2003 has furthered the development of Kurdish nationalism in Iraq.[57] At the expense of its inveterate opponent Turkey, Iraqi Kurdish nationalism became an even closer US ally than anyone could have possibly expected. This ironic situation was brought about by Turkey's refusing to allow the United States to use its territory as a base for a northern front to attack Iraq in March 2003. The Iraqi Kurds were suddenly thrust into the role of US ally, a novel position they eagerly and successfully assumed. Although the postwar insurgency turned many sections of Arab Iraq into a very dangerous place, the Kurdish area of Iraq served as a relatively peaceful haven and Kurdish nationalism as the staunchest supporter of the United States. In return, the United States–supported interim constitution for Iraq has given the Kurds an enormous power over their future in Iraq.

As of 2015, Iraqi Kurdish nationalism is in a uniquely powerful position, given its virtual veto power over future developments in Iraq. If the Arabs will not agree to a democratic federal Iraq that satisfies the goals of Kurdish nationalism, the Kurds will simply continue administering themselves as they have since 1991. Indeed, two unofficial referenda held in 2004 and 2005 almost unanimously opted for Kurdish independence. Geopolitical realities, of course, currently prohibit independence, but who can accurately predict what the future will bring if a democratic federal Iraq proves impossible to create? Kurdish nationalism in Iraq may come to be seen as having the right—in the name of stability that also would benefit the United States, Turkey, and other neighboring states—to move toward independence.

What is more, given the fact that greater Kurdistan contains a sizable amount of the oil in the Middle East as well as the water, Kurdish nationalism clearly will impact the region's and, therefore, the world's future. To begin to come to grips with these consequences, therefore, other states and nations must grant the legitimacy of Kurdish nationalism. Once this legitimacy is admitted, then stable and just solutions to the problems it entails may be found. Kurdish national self-determination need not necessarily destroy the territorial integrity of the states the Kurds now inhabit. Various forms of autonomy, federalism, and even simple but genuine democracy may satisfy the just demands of Kurdish nationalism. From this perspective, the solution would lie in the application of modern standards of human rights for the Kurdish nation. Such a denouement need not offer a zero-sum result, but rather would more likely lead to a win/win solution for all those nationalisms involved.

Given its growth in four separate states, however, Kurdish nationalism will continue to develop at different rates and ways. Thus, the following four separate chapters will examine modern Kurdish nationalism in each one of these states—Turkey, Iraq, Syria, and Iran—even though this division is somewhat artificial, because increasingly Kurdish developments in one state affect the Kurds in the other states. This is particularly true of the Iraqi Kurds and, increasingly we will see too, of the Turkish and Syrian Kurds. On the other hand, for the time being this interaction is less so of the Iranian Kurds.

The Kurds in Turkey: Change and Continuity

Introduction

More than half of the Kurds in the world live in Turkey. However, they are anything but homogeneous in their goals, ranging from those who seek assimilation into the broader Turkish society to those seeking outright independence. Most of them probably would like to remain in Turkey but with guaranteed political, social, and cultural rights as Kurds.

Over the years, two overarching, seemingly contradictory themes involving change and continuity have characterized Turkey's policy toward the Kurds. During Ottoman times (1261-1923) and even into the early Republican days (1923-), the Kurds were granted a type of separate status befitting their unique ethnic identity. However, around the time of the Sheikh Said Rebellion in 1925, Kemalist Turkey abruptly cancelled this policy and instead initiated one of denial, assimilation, and force. Indeed, even in Turkish foreign policy, the Saadabad Treaty of 1937 with Iran and Iraq as well as the Baghdad Pact in 1955 with those two states plus Great Britain and Pakistan had in part the purpose of mutual co-operation in keeping the potentially volatile Kurdish issue quiet. The fear was that the Kurds would potentially challenge Turkey's territorial integrity and divide the state.

Only gradually, beginning in the 1970s and 1980s, when this position of denial, assimilation, and the fist had clearly failed, did Turkey cautiously and incrementally begin again reversing its policy and granting the Kurds some type of recognition. Turgut Ozal's domestic and external proposals for Kurdish rights in the 1980s—although followed by Suleyman Demirel, Tansu Ciller, Bulent Ecevit, and Ahmet Sezer's sterile return to what was essentially denialism—adumbrated Recep Tayyip Erdogan's domestic Kurdish Opening and the present peace process between the state and the *Partiya Karkaren Kurdistan* (PKK) or Kurdistan Workers Party, as well as its external de facto alliance with the Kurdistan Regional Government (KRG) in Iraq and are the most recent manifestations of what is once again the state's changing policy.

However, behind this policy of change remains one of continuity, in which the state continues to see the Kurdish problem as one of security, whereas the Kurds view it as one of achieving human rights and democracy. Thus, Turkey basically offers today's changes to maintain state security and its territorial integrity, not to implement change for the primary sake of Kurdish rights and democracy. The sudden explosion of the Kurdish problem in Syria because of the anarchy the civil war has created there since 2011 has presented Turkey with a whole new dimension of the Kurdish security problem at the same time that Turkey is supposedly trying to implement change in its Kurdish dealings. The purpose of this chapter is to analyze Turkey's Kurdish policy in light of these two seemingly contradictory, but related themes.

Ottoman Times

During Ottoman times, the state always recognized the separate Kurdish existence and even referred to their historical homeland as *Kurdistan,* a geographical term that went down the memory hole in modern Turkey in favor of the designation *eastern Turkey* or simply *the East*. However, the term *Kurdistan* had presented no problem for the multi-national Ottoman Empire, especially since the Kurds were largely fellow Sunni Muslims, had only a very stunted sense of separate nationalism, and were still living in a largely premodern, undeveloped condition. What sense of identification the Kurds had was owed on the larger dimension to Islam and on the smaller level to the tribes.[1]

In 1891, Ottoman sultan Abdul Hamid II created the *Hamidiye*, a modern pro-government Kurdish cavalry that proved to be an important stage in the emergence of Kurdish nationalism.[2] Nevertheless, most of the Kurds supported the Ottomans in World War I and Mustafa Kemal (Ataturk) during the Turkish War of Independence following that conflict.

During World War I, one of US President Woodrow Wilson's Fourteen Points (Number 12) declared that the non-Turkish minorities of the Ottoman Empire should be granted the right of "autonomous development." The stillborn Treaty of Sevres, signed in August 1920, provided for "local autonomy for the predominantly Kurdish area." (Article 62) and in Article 64 even looked forward to the possibility that "the Kurdish peoples" might be granted "independence from Turkey." Turkey's quick revival under Ataturk— ironically enough with considerable Kurdish help, as the Turks played well on the theme of Islamic unity—altered the entire situation. The subsequent and definitive Treaty of Lausanne in July 1923 recognized the modern Republic of Turkey without any special provisions for the Turkish Kurds. The path was open to change state policy toward denial, assimilation, and the fist.

The Kemalist Change of Denial and Assimilation

When Mustafa Kemal first began to create the new Republic of Turkey, it was not clear what constituted a Turk.[3] Indeed, in appealing for unity against the Greek and Armenian invaders imme-

diately after World War I, Ismet (Inonu) Ataturk's famous lieutenant and eventual successor—initially spoke of the new state as
being a "homeland for Kurds and Turks."[4] Kurdish troops played
an indispensable role in the overall Nationalist victory. The Nationalist parliament in Ankara included some 75 Kurdish deputies.
For a while Mustafa Kemal apparently even toyed with the idea of
meaningful Kurdish autonomy in the new state. The minutes of the
Amasya interview and the proceedings of the Erzurum and Sivas
congresses in 1919, as well as two other occurrences in 1922 and
1923, make this clear.[5] Kurdish autonomy, however, proved to be
the road not taken.

Shortly after the Nationalist victory, a series of steps were taken
in an attempt to eliminate the Kurdish presence in the new Republic of Turkey through legal proclamation and gradual assimilation.
On March 3, 1924, for example, a decree banned all Kurdish
schools, organizations, and publications, as well as religious fra-
ternities and *medressehs* (Islamic religious schools), which were
the last source of education for most Kurds. The Sheikh Said rebellion[6] in 1925 sealed this determination. In an attempt to dilute
and assimilate the Kurdish population, Kurdish deportations to the
west were initiated. Only the sheer impossibility of fully carrying
out such a task prevented its fulfillment. The Kurdish areas in the
southeast were declared a military zone forbidden to foreigners
until 1965. In 1928, the entire civil and military administration of
the Kurdish provinces in the east was placed under an Inspector-
General of the East. Subsequently, regimes of martial law, state of
siege, and state of emergency complete with a supra-governor were
instated. Given the Kemalist insistence on a unitary framework
for the Turkish government, these special measures were ironic,
because they in effect placed the Kurdish provinces under a special
administration.

After another major Kurdish rebellion around Mount Ararat was
finally crushed in 1930, new further deportations followed. Law
No. 2510 in June 1934 sought to disperse the Kurdish population

to areas where it would constitute no more than 5 percent of the total. It was even suggested that Kurdish children be sent to boarding schools where they would speak exclusively in Turkish. Only the lack of state resources and the sheer size of the growing Kurdish population defeated the intention. Nevertheless, an extreme form of Turkish nationalism with its associated historical myths developed that had no place for Kurdish ethnic awareness.

The Turkish Historical Thesis claimed that all the world's civilizations had been founded by the Turks, whereas the so-called Sun Language Theory held that all languages derived from one original tongue spoken in central Asia. Turkish, the closest extant descendant of this primeval language, was the source from which all other languages had developed. Isolated in their mountain fastnesses, the Kurds had simply forgotten their mother tongue. The Kurdish language supposedly contained fewer than approximately 800 words and thus was not a real language. Indeed, the very word "Kurd" was declared to be nothing more than a corruption of the crunching sound (kirt, kart, or kurt) one made while walking through the snow-covered mountains in the southeast. The much-abused and criticized appellation "Mountain Turks" when referring to the ethnic Kurds in Turkey served as a code term for these actions.

During the 1960s, Turkish president Cemal Gursel lauded a book written by Sherif Firat that claimed that the Kurds were Turkish in origin, and he helped to popularize the phrase "spit in the face of he who calls you a Kurd" as a way to make the word "Kurd" an insult.[7] At the same time, Law No. 1587 furthered the process of changing Kurdish names, "which hurt public opinion and are not suitable for our national culture, moral values, traditions and customs," into Turkish names. As recently as 1995, the Turkish government suddenly announced that the Kurdish new year's holiday *Newroz* was in fact a Turkish holiday commemorating the day that the Turks first left their ancestral Asian homeland, Ergenekon. The day was renamed *"Nevruz"* as the letter "w" was not in the Turkish alphabet.

A year later, the Turkish media launched a campaign to "prove" that the traditional Kurdish colors of green, red, and yellow were actually those of certain crack Ottoman regiments. This concern with color recalled another attempt to change traffic lights in some southeastern cities of Turkey such as Batman by replacing the supposed Kurdish green with blue. An assessment by the US Central Intelligence Agency concluded: "In the early years of the Turkish Republic, the government responded . . . by ruthlessly . . . attempting, albeit unsuccessfully, to eliminate all manifestation of Kurdish culture and nationalism."[8]

The new Turkish Constitution written in 1982 attempted to continue and revitalize the policy of denying the existence of the Kurds in Turkey. Publications began to appear claiming that the Kurds were really Turks and that there was not a separate Kurdish language. Efforts to illustrate otherwise were said to be simply fabrications of Western intelligence services and separatist groups seeking to divide Turkey.[9] When several ethnic Kurdish members of parliament (MPs) from the Social Democratic Populist Party (SHP) voted in favor of the Minority Languages report of the Council of Europe in 1988, they were accused of having joined certain hostile European states in a conspiracy to create a Kurdish minority in Turkey where one did not exist. This situation was essentially replayed as recently as 2005, when Professors Baskin Oran and Ibrahim Ozden Kaboglu were prosecuted for simply arguing in a report regarding European Union (EU) harmonization laws and commissioned by the prime minister's own office, that "Turk" is an identity of only one ethnic group and that Turkey also includes other ethnic groups such as "Kurds."[10]

To be fair to Ataturk and his associates, their ultimate purpose, of course, was to achieve unity and modernization by mobilizing the population in Anatolia behind a territorial and civic-determined national identity.[11] However, many Kurds perceived this attempt to be at the expense of their own religious, traditional, and ethnic identity. Indeed, a case can be made that Kemalist Turkey's policy of attempted assimilation toward the Kurds actually made them more aware of their latent ethnic identity. M. Hakan Yavuz, as noted earlier, elaborated on the modern origins of Kurdish Nationalism in Turkey when he declared: "The state's [Turkey's] policies are the determinant factors in the evolution and modulation of . . . Kurdish ethno-nationalism. The major reason for the politicization of Kurdish cultural identity is the shift from multi-ethnic, multicultural realities of the Ottoman Empire to the nation-state model."[12] The Kemalist reforms, which aimed to create a modern Turkish nation-state "resulted in the construction of Kurdish ethnonationalism."[13] Hamit Bozarslan basically agreed with Yavuz's analysis when he argued that "the proclamation of the Kemalist Republic in 1923 meant the end of . . . the Ottoman tacit contact between centre and peripheries [and] . . . to a large extent explains the . . . traditional [Kurdish] dignitaries . . . participation in the subsequent revolts."[14]

It is true, of course, that, since the Republic of Turkey was established in 1923, many ethnic Kurds who were willing to identify as being Turkish were readily admitted into the ruling elite. Abdulmelik Firat (1934-2009), the grandson of Sheikh Said, was a good example. Many other ethnic Kurds served as MPs, cabinet ministers, city mayors, state prosecutors, directors of state enterprises, and the like. They did so, however, only by denying their Kurdish ethnic heritage. Those who refused to do so were penalized, as was the case of the 55 Kurdish tribal chiefs exiled to western Turkey after the military coup in 1960[15] and Serafettin Elci, who served as Minister of Public Works in the government of Bulent Ecevit in the late 1970s. Elci was sentenced to two years and three months in prison for "making Kurdish and secessionist propaganda." He had declared: "I am a Kurd. There are Kurds in Turkey."[16]

The PKK Insurgency

Beginning in the 1970s, an increasingly significant portion of Turkey's population of ethnic Kurds has actively demanded cultural, linguistic, and political rights as Kurds. Until recently, however, the government ruthlessly suppressed these demands for fear that they would lead to the breakup of the state itself. This official refusal to brook any moderate Kurdish opposition helped encourage extremism and the creation of the *Partiya Karkaren Kurdistan* (PKK) or Kurdistan Workers Party, headed by Abdullah (Apo) Ocalan on November 27, 1978. In August 1984, the PKK officially launched its insurgency that by early 2015 had resulted in more than 40,000 deaths, as many as 3,000 villages partially or completely destroyed, and during the 1990s some 3 million people internally displaced.[17] (However, given the current cease-fire and negotiations that began in 2013 between Turkey and the PKK, there have been no combat deaths from fighting since March 2013.) Thus, the PKK insurgency represented the nightmare of Turkey's security policy toward the Kurds and the necessity to institute a policy of change.

For a short period in the early 1990s, Ocalan actually seemed close to achieving a certain degree of military success. In the end, however, he overextended himself, while the Turkish military spared no excesses in containing him. Slowly but steadily, the Turkish military marginalized the PKK's military threat. Ocalan's ill-advised decision in August 1995 to also attack Massoud Barzani's Kurdistan Democratic Party (KDP) in northern Iraq because of its support for Turkey further sapped his strength. The final blow came when Turkey threatened to go to war against Syria in October 1998 unless Damascus expelled Ocalan from his longtime sanctuary in that country.

Ocalan fled to Italy, where US pressure on behalf of its North Atlantic Treaty Organization (NATO) ally Turkey pressured Italy and others to reject Ocalan as a terrorist undeserving of political asylum or negotiation. Indeed, for years the United States had given Turkey intelligence training and weapons to battle against what it saw as the "bad" Kurds of Turkey, while ironically supporting the "good" Kurds of Iraq against Saddam Hussein. With US and possibly Israeli aid, Ocalan was finally captured in Kenya on February 16, 1999, flown back to Turkey for a sensational trial, and sentenced to death for treason.

However, instead of making a hard-line appeal for renewed struggle during his trial, Ocalan issued a remarkable statement that called for the implementation of true democracy to solve the Kurdish problem within the existing borders of a unitary Turkey. He also ordered his guerrillas to evacuate Turkey to demonstrate his sincerity. Thus, far from ending Turkey's Kurdish problem, Ocalan's capture began a process of implicit bargaining between the state and many of its citizens of Kurdish ethnic heritage as represented by the officially illegal PKK and various legal pro-Kurdish parties such as the *Baris ve Demokrasi Partisi* (BDP), or Peace and Democracy Party, which was created after the *Demokratik Toplum Partisi* (DTP), or Democratic Society Party, was banned on December 11, 2009, but was subsequently merged into the more inclusive *Halklarin Demokratik Partisi* (HDP), or Peoples Democratic Party, in April 2014 . Since the 1990s, these legal pro-Kurdish parties have elected numerous mayors in the Kurdish areas during the local elections, most recently held on 30 March 2014, and Kurds also gained representation in the Turkish parliament running as independents.[18]

In the past decade, Turkey's potential candidacy for membership in the EU has entered the picture.[19] If implemented, EU membership would fulfill Ataturk's ultimate hope for a strong, united, and democratic Turkey joined to the West. However, until Turkey successfully implemented the Copenhagen Criteria of minority rights for its Kurdish ethnic population and suspended Ocalan's death sentence to conform with EU standards, which banned capital punishment, it was clear that Turkey's long-treasured candidacy would be only a pipe dream. As some have noted, Turkey's road to the EU lies through Diyarbakir, the unofficial capital of Turkish Kurdistan.

However, arguing that Turkey had not implemented the necessary reforms, the PKK ended the cease-fire it had implemented after Ocalan's capture and renewed low-level fighting in June 2004. In addition, opposition to Turkish membership in the EU began to grow in such EU members as France, Germany, and Austria, among others. In November 2002, Recep Tayyip Erdogan's *Adalet ve Kalkinma Partisi* (AKP), or Justice and Development Party, with its roots in Islamic politics, won an overwhelming victory, which it added to in elections held in July 2007 and again in June 2011. In August 2014, Erdogan was elected president, the first time that office was elected by a popular vote instead of by the parliament. The next parliamentary election is scheduled for June 2015. As of this writing—and despite the Gezi Park demonstrations of June 2013 against perceived authoritarian AKP rule, followed by accusations in December 2013 of massive AKP corruption—Erdogan's AKP seems well-positioned to triumph again.

Beginning in 2005, the *Koma Civaken Kurdistan* (KCK), or Union of Kurdistan Communities began to operate as the umbrella organization bringing together the PKK and numerous other related Kurdish groups in Turkey as well as in other states in the Middle East and Western Europe. Under the leadership of first Murat Karayilan and since July 2013 Cemil Bayik, approximately 5,000 PKK guerrillas remained entrenched in the Qandil Mountains straddling the border between northern Iraq and Iran.

Among many promising new legal leaders, Osman Baydemir was elected mayor of Diyarbakir in 2004 and quickly emerged as one of the most successful young ethnic Kurdish politicians in Turkey. Baydemir also carried his message of achieving Kurdish rights peacefully in his travels to Europe and the United States, but he was constantly in danger of being arrested for his activities. He left office following the local election in March 2014, but he will surely remain a potent force in the years to come. The off-again, on-again Ilisu Dam project on the Tigris River was touted by the government as a way to help modernize the southeast's agriculture, while opponents denounced the project as a way literally to drown the Kurdish historical presence in the area. ROJ TV, a Kurdish television station in Denmark connected to the PKK, stoked Kurdish self-awareness throughout Turkey, the Middle East, and Europe. Leyla Zana—a Kurdish leader elected to the Turkish parliament in 1991 but imprisoned in 1994 for her nonviolent support of the Kurdish cause—was finally released in 2004 after her case had become a cause célébre for Kurdish human rights. On 30 June 2012, Zana actually met with Turkish prime minister Erdogan and expressed her confidence in his ability to solve the Kurdish problem.[20] Currently, she also once again holds a seat in the Turkish parliament.

Turgut Ozal's Initiatives

When he first came to power, Turgut Ozal continued Turkey's traditional policy of denial, assimilation, and the fist toward the Kurds. For example, in April 1985 he instituted the village guards system of civilian, pro-government Kurdish militia to supplement the state's military and divide the Kurds. Then in the summer of 1987, he also established a system of emergency rule (OHAL) with a regional governor for most of the Kurdish areas in the southeast. The PKK and other critics of official state policy have long considered both measures prime examples of official state repression.

Perhaps because of his Islamic proclivities and their stress on religious equality and/or his earlier studies and work in the United States, Ozal began to change his stance and advocate imaginative reforms after he became president in 1989. Possibly too as president, he began to see himself as more above the everyday fray of politics and a spokesman for all citizens of Turkey and thus charged to take the longer-term view of the future of the body politic. On the other hand, in his previous task as a more partisan prime minister he might have seen himself as simply heading the ruling party or coalition.

If so, however, in September 1989, while still prime minister, Ozal hinted at a reassessment in his cryptic response to a question about the existence of a Kurdish minority in Turkey: "If in the first years of the Republic, during the single-party period, the State committed mistakes on this matter [of the Kurds], it is necessary to recognise these."[21] In April 1990, he gave further hints of a new Kurdish policy at the meeting of the Turkish Industrialists' and Businessmen's Association (TUSIAD). At this time he let it be known that the government was "engaged in a quest for a serious model for solving the Kurdish problem in a manner that goes beyond police measures."[22]

At about the same time, Abdullah (Apo) Ocalan, the leader of the PKK, told two Turkish reporters: "Let us declare a cease-fire and sit at the negotiating table. If Turkey abandons its oppressive policy in the region, then we will refrain from violence. . . . In fact, separating the region from Turkey immediately is out of the question. Our people need Turkey and we cannot separate, at least, not for another 40 years."[23]

Ozal was not the only Turkish politician seeking new concepts. In the summer of 1990, the SHP (which was at that time the main opposition party) issued a comprehensive policy report on the Kurdish question that went far beyond anything ever before offered by a mainstream Turkish party. Describing the ban on the use of the mother tongue as "primitive" and a "tool of assimilation," the document called for "the abolition of all restrictions on the use of the mother tongue, the enshrinement of the right of citizens to speak, write and teach their own language and use it in daily life and in various cultural activities and the establishment by the state of research centres and institutes undertaking research into different cultures and languages."[24] Shortly before his death in a car accident on 5 February 1993, Adnan Kahveci, a state minister and close aide to Ozal, went so far as to warn that Turkey was headed for a civil war if a democratic solution was not found.[25]

Why did some Turkish authorities begin to reassess their historic position? Certainly, the growing PKK insurgency was one reason. Repetitive "groupthink"[26] on handling this situation appeared to be stuck, while thoughtful new measures might offer a way out of the growing quandary. The exploding ethnic Kurdish population relative to the slower-growing demographics of the ethnic Turks themselves represented another reason.

According to one study, by 1990 some 13.7 million Kurds were living in Turkey, a figure that constituted 24.1 percent of the total Turkish population.[27] Furthermore, "if present demographic trends hold, as they are likely to, in about two generations' time the Kurds will also replace the Turks as the largest ethnic group in Turkey herself, re-establishing an Indo-European language (Kurdish) as the principal language in that land." Corroborating these figures, a report drawn up by the National Security Council (MGK) Secretariat in Turkey and released at the end of 1996 after Ozal had been dead for more than three years, declared that "the Kurdish people will make up 40 percent of the population in the year 2010. That they will increase to make up more than 50 percent of the population in the year 2025 is a possibility."[28]

However, Ozal himself believed that as ethnic Kurds moved west they tended to assimilate and that already "60 percent of the Kurds live west of Ankara."[29] In addition, Servet Mutlu has disputed these large population figures for the Kurds by concluding that as of 1996 there were only slightly more than 7 million Kurds living in Turkey, which constituted only 12.60 percent of the country's total population, "far lower than the 12.5 million to 15 million claimed by some."[30] Mixed marriages and partial assimilation may account for these demographic discrepancies. And although the year 2010 has now come and gone, not even ardent Kurdish nationalists would claim that the Kurds have come to constitute 40 percent of the population of Turkey, as the MGK had supposedly predicted back in the 1990s.

In addition, the results of the Gulf War in 1991 stimulated Ozal's new thinking. Suddenly a nascent Kurdish entity appeared on Turkey's southeastern border and demanded attention. On 8 March 1991 Turkey broke its long-standing policy against negotiating with any Kurdish groups when Ambassador Tugay Ozceri, undersecretary of the foreign ministry, met in Ankara with Jalal Talabani, the leader of the Iraqi Kurdish Patriotic Union of Kurdistan (PUK) and Mohsin Dizai, a representative of Massoud Barzani, the leader of the other main Iraqi Kurdish group, the Kurdistan Democratic Party (KDP). A second meeting between Ozceri and Dizai occurred on 22 March 1991. In his typical mercurial style, Talabani concluded "that a new page had been turned in relations between Turkey and the Kurds of Iraq."[31]

For the first meeting, the two Iraqi Kurds arrived together in Istanbul on a flight from Damascus and were immediately flown to Ankara's military airport by personnel of the National Intelligence Organization (MIT). After it was over, Talabani declared that, for the Iraqi Kurds, "the most significant result . . . was Turkey's lifting its objection to the establishment of direct relations between the Kurdish front in Iraq and the United States."[32] He stated that he had assured the Turkish officials that the Kurds did not want to establish an independent state in northern Iraq and then explained that "Turkey has for years been putting forth effective and significant obstacles to the struggle we have been waging in northern Iraq. We wanted to explain our goals and eliminate Turkey's opposition. . . . We were received with understanding."[33]

Ozal's bold gesture toward the Iraqi Kurds soon evolved to the point that Turkey actually issued Turkish diplomatic passports to Talabani and Barzani to facilitate their travel abroad. At one point, Talabani even suggested that the Iraqi Kurds might want to be annexed by Turkey.[34] By inviting the Iraqi Kurdish leaders to Ankara, Ozal also might have been seeking another way in which to deflate the PKK insurgency in Turkey. Being seen as trying to help their ethnic kin in northern Iraq might be well received by the Turkish

Kurds. It might illustrate to the ethnic Kurds in Turkey that the Turkish state was not necessarily hostile to the Kurds in general, but only to the violence of the PKK.

Ozal's actions created a furor in Turkey. To some he was simply being realistic in seeking to build reasonable relations with those who looked likely to establish an autonomous Kurdish region on Turkey's border. Better to be seen by this fledgling entity as a friend and protector than an inveterate enemy. To others, however, Ozal was dangerously opening up a Pandora's box of troubles that would come back to threaten Turkish territorial integrity. If the Turkish president could countenance some sort of federal solution for the Iraqi Kurds, might he not also be contemplating one for the ethnic Kurds in Turkey? Indeed Ozal was soon to shock his compatriots by declaring that he was willing to discuss a federal system if only to oppose it.[35] In another break from the past, Ozal revealed that his grandmother had been of Kurdish origin.[36] He went on to explain that Turkey was being prevented from progressing by a series of taboos and that he intended to challenge them.[37]

Turgut Ozal also played a seminal role in the establishment of a safe haven for the Iraqi Kurds in their northern Iraqi homeland. Following the defeat of Saddam Hussein in February 1991, the Iraqi Kurds spontaneously rebelled, only to be crushed by Iraq's still formidable forces. The failed rebellion quickly led to a human tragedy of incredible proportions, as 1.5 million Kurdish refugees fled to the Iranian border while another half million fled to the Turkish border. There they joined some 30,000 Iraqi Kurdish refugees remaining in Turkey from the 1988 exodus following the end of the Iran-Iraq war.

These new refugees threatened to overwhelm their hosts. In response, Ozal called on all states to join together as they had in the war against Iraq that had just been concluded. He added that "otherwise, a new dispute will be created in the Middle East and that a problem threatening peace and stability will be created."[38] Elaborating, he argued that "even the most perfect organization cannot cope with such an influx within such a short period. . . . It is impossible for any country to solve a problem of such proportions by itself."

The resulting "safe havens" in northern Iraq in time morphed into the KRG of today. United Nations Security Council Resolution 688 of 5 April 1991 gave a certain amount of legal sanction for this action when it condemned "the repression of the Iraqi civilian population . . . in Kurdish populated areas, the consequences of which threaten international peace and security in the region" and demanded "that Iraq . . . immediately end this repression." It was the first time in its almost half century of existence that the world organization had so explicitly addressed the Kurdish question. Turkish willingness to allow the United States to enforce Operation Provide Comfort and the no-fly zone over northern Iraq from bases in southeastern Turkey provided the military protection necessary for the fledgling KRG to begin to develop.

However, Turkey was caught between a rock and a hard place because, by allowing Operation Provide Comfort to continue, it was in effect encouraging nascent Iraqi Kurdish statehood. To abandon the force, however, would simply lead it to regroup elsewhere and strip Ankara of any influence whatsoever over the course of events, much as would later occur after Turkey's decision not to join the United States in its invasion of Iraq in 2003. At best, some argued, "Turkey appears to have been selling support for the multilateral force against silence on its own Kurdish question."[39] Therefore, Turkey repeatedly allowed the Operation to be renewed at six-month intervals. Ankara, however, added the provision that the territorial integrity of Iraq must be respected. This meant, of course, that Turkey continued to oppose the creation of a Kurdish state in northern Iraq. The entire situation illustrated the complicated interplay between Turkey's policies of change and continuity toward the Kurds.

For their part, the Iraqi Kurds felt dependent on Turkey. Hoshyar Zebari, a KDP spokesman and later the foreign minister of the post-

Saddam Hussein government in Iraq, explained: "Turkey is our lifeline to the West and the whole world in our fight against Saddam Husayn. We are able to secure allied air protection and international aid through Turkey's cooperation. If Poised Hammer [Provide Comfort] is withdrawn, Saddam's units will again reign in this region and we will lose everything."[40] By 2015, of course, Saddam Hussein was long gone, but Turkey's indispensable role for the Iraqi Kurds' survival continued.

As a result of Ozal's innovative diplomacy, Jalal Talabani (later to become president of post-Saddam Hussein Iraq) ironically concluded: "Turkey must be considered a country friendly to the Kurds."[41] By the time he met with Ozal's prime minister Suleyman Demirel in June 1992, the Turkish prime minister was referring to the Iraqi Kurdish leader as "my dear brother Talabani,"[42] while the Iraqi Kurdish leader declared that "the people in northern Iraq will never forget the help of the Turkish Government and people in their difficult days." Following Ozal's sudden death on 17 April 1993, however, Demirel as the new president decided to reverse Ozal's initiatives toward the Iraqi Kurds and permitted relations with them to deteriorate. As a result, one might argue that Turkey lost its ability to influence the development of events in northern Iraq, which it otherwise might have had if Ozal's policies had been maintained.

Domestically, Ozal also partially repealed Law 2932, under which the military government had banned the usage of the Kurdish language in 1983. Ozal now allowed the language to be used in everyday conversation and folkloric music recordings. However, using Kurdish in official agencies, publishing, or teaching would still be a crime. Asked when Kurdish could be used in newspapers, audiocassettes, radio broadcasts, and schools, Ozal replied: "In the future the use of the written language may also be allowed, but everything has its time."[43] Metin Gurdere, the assistant leader of Ozal's Motherland Party (ANAP), added that further liberalization "would depend on developments that will take place in Turkey."[44]

Events moved quickly under Ozal, and within the following year he was suggesting that the GAP Television Network should carry 60- or 90-minute programs in Kurdish and that the appropriate schools should even teach in that language: "What would happen if we do it? We should not be afraid of this at all."[45] Years later, after Ozal had been long dead, the well-known Turkish journalist Cengiz Candar revealed how Ozal had once warned him not to write about the need for Kurdish language TV and education. Six months later, however, Ozal himself came out with just such proposals. When the two next met, Ozal told Candar that "who says it and when it is said matters. If you had suggested this six months ago, the military would have been all over you. But when I, the president, suggest it six months later, it might have better traction."[46]

Response   The response of many influential Turkish politicians demonstrates how Ozal's modest proposals to begin to change his country's historic position on the Kurdish question were very controversial because they seemingly threatened Turkish security. Suleyman Demirel, who as noted above succeeded Ozal as president following his death in 1993, declared, for example, that "this move is an attempt at dividing the country. . . . This is the greatest harm you can inflict on Turkey."[47] Others expressed themselves even more forcefully. Oltan Sungurlu, the minister of justice, exclaimed: "What language is that? I do not know of such a language."[48] Alpaslan Pehlivanli, the chairman of the justice committee in the Turkish parliament, asserted: "If the word 'language' now in the bill stays in, we will have admitted that the Kurds are a nation. . . . If it passes this way, tomorrow there will be cafes where Kurdish folk songs are sung, theaters where Kurdish films are shown, and coffee houses where Kurdish is spoken. If this is not separatism, what is?"[49]

Other Turkish leaders, however, seemed to cautiously approve of Ozal's initiative.[50] Erdal Inonu, the leader of the SHP, said that it was a positive step and that he was pleased that the government finally had accepted a policy that was originally his. Husamettin

Cindoruk, the speaker of the Turkish parliament, declared that Ozal's initiative was an "end of a constitutional embarrassment." Even former president Kenan Evren, who had led the military takeover in 1980 and had been the architect of the laws reinforcing the prohibition of the use of Kurdish and especially Law 2932, expressed his guarded support, "as long as this does not enter the schools or appear on placards during demonstrations." Many years later, Evren even implicitly supported Ozal's language reform when the general mused that his original ban "was not a proper step to be taken on the path toward modernization and democratization."[51]

A number of news reporters also reacted with cautious approval to the Ozal language initiative. The late Mehmet Ali Birand, long one of Turkey's most distinguished journalists, noted how this step would improve Turkey's image in Europe.[52] Ertugrul Ozkok of *Hurriyet*, who sometimes served in effect as an unofficial spokesman for Ozal, found the president's move "the first positive consequence of the [1991 Gulf] war." Oktay Eksi, also from *Hurriyet*, declared that "we must thus acknowledge with satisfaction the ANAP's initiative, or rather, Turgut Ozal's, to abolish this shameful prohibition of a language."

Even more cautiously, Ugur Mumcu, the famous leftist journalist who was notoriously assassinated in January 1993, pointed out that there were still various other laws concerning separatist propaganda that could be used against the Turkish Kurds and their supporters. He also recalled that the political parties law still prohibited parties from asserting that any minorities existed in the country, with the exception of the non-Muslim ones, specifically defined by the Treaty of Lausanne in 1923. Mumcu explained Ozal's initiative in terms of the 1991 Gulf War and the need to preempt the possible creation of a Kurdish state in northern Iraq.

Kendal Nezan, a leading Kurdish dissident who has long headed the Institut Kurde de Paris, reacted to Ozal's initiative more favorably: "The bill is a positive step towards finding a peaceful, democratic, and civilized solution to the Kurdish problem in Turkey. Turgut Ozal is the first statesman . . . to accept and recognize the Kurdish presence in Turkey."[53] Abdullah Ocalan, the leader of the PKK, concurred with Nezan's assessment: "To tell the truth, I did not expect him [Ozal] to display such courage. . . . In this context, he shamed us. . . . He has taken an important step."[54] At approximately the same time, the PKK leader also announced that his organization "might opt for a diplomatic-political solution" and was ready to hold "conditional" negotiations with Turkey.[55] Ocalan added that the PKK no longer sought independence, just "free political expression" for Turkey's Kurds.

Abortive Cease-fire   In the second half of February 1993, Jalal Talabani, the Iraqi Kurdish leader and frequent foe of the PKK, nevertheless met with Abdullah Ocalan in Syria to discuss Ozal's initiatives and how to react to them. Following this meeting, Talabani presented Ozal, on 8 March 1993, Ocalan's proposal for a cease-fire: "I am giving up the armed struggle. I will wage a political struggle in the future. . . . Turkish officials can hold talks with Kurdish deputies in the National Assembly. We agree to live within Turkey's existing borders if the necessary democratic conditions are created to allow us to do so."[56] Then on 17 March 1993, Ocalan followed up this message with a formal declaration of "unilateral and unconditional"[57] cease-fire at a press conference in the Bekaa valley town of Zahlah, some six miles from the Syrian border. Symbolically, the PKK leader doffed his guerrilla fatigues and put on a suit and tie for the occasion.

During his press conference, Ocalan made some of the following conciliatory points. The Kurds in Turkey "want peace, dialogue, and free political action within the framework of a democratic state." He explained that "we are not working to partition Turkey. We are demanding the Kurds' human rights (cultural, political, and so on) in the framework of one homeland." After praising Talabani's role "in bringing this initiative to fruition," the PKK leader then stressed that "we want guarantees, because we cannot be betrayed, as happened with our historic leaders like Shaykh Said and the Badrakhaniyyin."[58]

A truly historic opportunity, the cease-fire failed for two basic reasons: (1) the continuing security attitude of the Turkish authorities, who interpreted Ocalan's move as a sign of weakness and therefore their chance to finish his movement off, rather than as a way to achieve a permanent solution to the Kurdish question; and (2) the sudden death of Ozal, the Turkish leader who was probably most receptive to some type of compromise that might have ended the struggle.

Apparently, the Turkish authorities believed that the PKK's back had been broken the previous October during their joint operation with the Iraqi Kurds in northern Iraq. Thus, when Ocalan announced his cease-fire, "all were agreed that the PKK was in a position of weakness."[59] Although there were offers of partial amnesty and an end to the state of emergency in the southeast, "Ankara's response . . . had never gone further than words. While the PKK ceased its raids, reports of mystery killings, torture and the burning of villages in the region persisted."[60] Furthermore, "the State authorities have chosen to act as if they believed that the PKK would refrain from terrorism unconditionally and simply allow itself to be mopped up by the security forces."

While the cease-fire hung in the balance, the sudden death of President Turgut Ozal on 17 April 1993 dealt it a fatal blow by removing the Turkish official most receptive to bold, imaginative thinking on the issue. Citing "very senior sources within the security apparatus,"[61] for example, Ismet G. Imset claimed that, if Ozal had lived, "everything would have been different. A major reform package would have been underway and even the hawks [hard-liners] would have fallen in line."

Apparently, an important meeting of the National Security Council (MGK)—until Erdogan's reforms after he became prime minister in 2003, the military body that decided security matters in Turkey—had been scheduled for a week after Ozal's death. The president had ordered a special group within the MGK to be set up "to seek political solutions to the crisis, to brainstorm and produce ideas, and to carry them out." In the words of one official, "it would have been [just] short of a revolution." After Ozal unexpectedly died, however, the meeting was postponed. For several weeks Turkish policy drifted until Suleyman Demirel finally emerged as the new president and Tansu Ciller as the new prime minister. When the MGK meeting Ozal had originally planned was finally held, Demirel, who was unwilling to take bold steps, was now in charge. "What happened is that Ozal was a momentum, a political one, that was thrusting us out of a vicious cycle. Now, we have fallen back into orbit again. We are part of the vicious cycle," declared a senior officer.

During an interview at the end of 1993, Jalal Talabani agreed with this interpretation when he argued that, "in the past, when I acted as a mediator, there was a good person like Ozal," and that "Ozal was making [an] enormous effort for this problem. Ozal's death was a great loss for democracy and peace."[62] Even before Ozal's death, Ocalan himself seemed to have had similar beliefs. In an interview with a Turkish newspaper, the PKK leader was asked, "How do you assess Turkish politicians?"[63] He cautiously responded that Ozal "seems to be open to progress. He seems to be open to change. He has confirmed this in his statements and in the concepts he has put forward." Following Ozal's death, Ocalan even declared that "a solution to the problem could have been reached had the late President Ozal lived."[64] The PKK leader also claimed that Talabani had told him that Ozal had intended "to put some radical changes on Turkey's agenda." More than a decade would go by of sterile minimalist reform policies before Erdogan took up the mantle of true reform again in 2005.

The Continuity of Security and Its Consequences

The present (1982) constitution instituted by the military after its successful coup in 1980 contained a number of specific provisions that sought to limit even speaking or writing in Kurdish. Its preamble, for example, declared: "The determination that no protection shall be afforded to thoughts or opinions contrary to Turkish national interests, the principle of the existence of Turkey as an indivisible entity." Two articles banned the spoken and written usage of the Kurdish language without specifically naming it.

Although restrictions on the usage of the Kurdish language were eased following the Gulf War in 1991, Article 8 of the Anti-Terrorism Law that entered into force in April 1991 made it possible to consider academics, intellectuals, and journalists speaking up peacefully for Kurdish rights to be engaging in terrorist acts. Similarly, under Article 312 of the Turkish Penal Code, mere verbal or written support for Kurdish rights could lead one to be charged with "provoking hatred or animosity between groups of different race, religion, region, or social class." Despite harmonization efforts of the EU, a new Article 301 that took effect in June 2005 made it a crime to denigrate "Turkishness," a provision that made it possible for extreme nationalists and statists to accuse writers, scholars, and intellectuals such as Nobel Prize–winning Orhan Pamuk of treason and subversion. Thus, although many partial reforms have occurred in recent years, as of this writing early in 2015, the promised new, more democratic and civilian constitution has yet to be written.[65]

PERSONAL OBSERVATION

In March 1998, I was invited by Abdullah Ocalan, the leader of the PKK, to visit him in his safe house in

Syria. After obtaining a Syrian visa in London, I flew to Cairo and then on to Damascus, where I was met at the airport by a PKK member. He took me to a hotel, where I rested for several hours before someone else came to take me to an apartment in Damascus, where I first met the then secretive Ocalan. He smiled broadly when we met, but we had to speak through an interpreter, whose command of English was not very good. Ocalan spoke in Turkish and told me that this was his first and working language, although he had spoken Kurdish when he was young and was trying to relearn it now. We did manage to share numerous personal stories, which brought us closer together. Both of our mothers, for example, had recently died, and Ocalan expressed genuine sympathy about my recent loss. Several other people then joined us for a large meal.

The next day I was picked up at the hotel and driven to a PKK military camp that was a short distance outside of Damascus. Ocalan and others greeted me. We walked around the large compound, and Ocalan allowed me to take several photographs of him alone and the two of us together. He was particularly interested in somehow gaining support from the United States.

While we were eating outside, a bumblebee settled on his hand, causing him to muse how it was both sweet with its honey but bitter with its sting. He then drew an analogy between the bee and what life itself brought. After more talks and another very filling meal, interrupted on several occasions by his cell phone calls, he invited me to play volleyball. Several hundred PKK guerrillas watched as we competed in a friendly game. At one time Ocalan went up for a dunk but his shot was just out of bounds. Silence prevailed for a second or so, as nobody wanted to make the call against him. I clearly saw that it was out, since I was standing exactly opposite Ocalan and his shot had landed very near my feet. Over the years as a tennis player I had been in similar situations and had experienced many bad calls. Although he was obviously competitive, however, Ocalan quickly broke the uncertainty and called his own shot out. I was impressed that a man who was supposed to be a megalomaniac, and clearly had the power to do whatever he wanted in this situation, still opted to make the close call against himself. I think that this particular incident spoke positively about his real character.

Erdogan's Reforms

In August 2005, Prime Minister Erdogan declared that Turkey had a "Kurdish problem," had made "grave mistakes" in the past, and now needed "more democracy to solve the problem."[66] Never before had a Turkish leader made so explicit a statement regarding the Kurdish problem. As progressive Islamists, however, the AKP was increasingly opposed by the reactionary Kemalist establishment, which included Turkey's influential military, fearful of losing their long-held privileged positions.[67]

This situation eventually led to the crisis of 2007 over the election of the AKP's Abdullah Gul as Turkey's new president. The AKP triumphed in this struggle by winning an enormous electoral victory on 22 July 2007 (even slightly outpolling the pro-Kurdish DTP in the southeast) and then electing Gul as president. Gradually the AKP began to reduce the political influence of Turkey's military and secretive Deep State,[68] which was opposed to Turkey's democratization and Kurdish rights.

Rise and Fall of the Kurdish Opening

During the summer and fall of 2009, the continuing and often violent Kurdish problem in Turkey seemed on the verge of a solution when the ruling AKP government of Prime Minister Recep Tayyip Erdogan and President Abdullah Gul announced a Kurdish Opening or Initiative (aka as the Democratic Opening/Initiative). Stressing the policy of change and reform, Gul declared that "the biggest problem of Turkey is the Kurdish question" and that "there is an opportunity [to solve it] and it should not be missed."[69] Erdogan asked: "If Turkey had not spent its energy, budget, peace and young people on [combating] terrorism, if Turkey had not spent the last 25 years in conflict, where would we be today?"[70] Even the insurgent PKK, still led ultimately by its imprisoned leader Abdullah Ocalan, itself briefly took Turkey's Kurdish Opening seriously.[71] For a fleeting moment optimism ran rampant.

Problems

However, it soon became evident that the AKP government had not thought out its Kurdish Opening very well and then proved rather inept in trying to implement it. Specific proposals were lacking. Furthermore, despite AKP appeals to support its Kurdish Opening, all three of the parliamentary opposition parties declined. Indeed, the *Cumhuriet Halk Partisi* (CHP) or Republican Peoples Party (Kemalists or Nationalists) accused the AKP of "separatism, cowing to the goals of the terrorist PKK, violating the Constitution, causing fratricide and/or ethnic polarization between Kurds and Turks, being an agent of foreign states, and even betraying the country,"[72] while the *Milliyetci Hareket Partisi* (MHP) or Nationalist Action Party (Ultra Turkish Nationalists) "declared AKP to be dangerous and accused it of treason and weakness."[73] Even the pro-Kurdish DTP failed to be engaged, because it declined to condemn the PKK as the AKP government had demanded. Erdogan too began to fear that any perceived concessions to the Kurds would hurt his Turkish nationalist base and future presidential hopes.

Then on December 11, 2009—as mentioned above—the Constitutional Court, after mulling over the issue for more than two years, suddenly banned the pro-Kurdish DTP because of its close association with the PKK. Although the BDP quickly took the DTP's place, coming when it did, the state-ordered banning of the pro-Kurdish DTP could not have come at a worse time and put the kiss of death to the Kurdish Opening. In addition, more than 1,000 BDP and other Kurdish notables were placed under arrest for their supposed support of the PKK—yet another body blow to the Kurdish Opening. Soon the entire country was ablaze from the fury that had arisen, and the Kurdish Opening seemed closed.

Although the AKP won practically 50 percent of the popular vote or 326 seats while the BDP and its allies won a record 36 seats in the parliamentary elections held on June 12, 2011, further problems soon arose, and hopes for a renewed and more successful Kurdish Opening quickly foundered. The newly elected BDP MPs began to boycott parliament in protest over the jailing of five of their elected colleagues, while a sixth (the well-known Hatip Dicle) was stripped of his seat for "terrorism" offenses. Newly reelected Prime Minister Erdogan seemingly turned his back on an earlier promise to seek consensus on the drafting of a new constitution that would help solve the Kurdish problem, broke off contact with the BDP, and continued to declare that the Kurdish problem had been solved and only a PKK problem remained. Once again Turkey was falling back on its continuity policy of security in regard to the Kurds. However, how could the new AKP government begin to solve the Kurdish problem when it refused to deal with its main interlocutor?

Moreover, others took the security thesis even further and argued that the ultimate problem was the inherent ethnic Turkish inability to accept the fact that Turkey should be considered a multiethnic state in which the Kurds have similar constitutional rights as co-stakeholders with the Turks. Moreover, during 2011 and 2012, more leading intellectuals were rounded up for alleged affiliations with the KCK/PKK, whose proposals for democratic autonomy seemed to suggest an alternative government. Many of those arrested were also affiliated with the BDP.

These arrests pointed to serious problems. First, there was the nature of the crimes, which alleged no violence. Mere "association" was enough for one to be counted as a terrorist. In addition, the connections were tenuous. As Human Rights Watch noted, these arrests seemed less aimed at addressing terror than at attacking "legal pro-Kurdish political organizations."[74] Second, the arrests came at a time when Turkey was planning to develop a new constitution. The silencing of pro-Kurdish voices as constitutional debates went forward was counterproductive for Turkey's future. Finally, there was the way suspects were treated. Virtually all were subject to pretrial detentions, effectively denying them freedom without any proof that they had committed a crime. Although precise figures are unavailable, Human Rights Watch declared that several thousand were on trial and another 605 in pretrial detention on KCK/PKK-related charges.[75]

Despite this myriad of problems, contacts between the government and the PKK continued, with the result that in 2013 a formal cease-fire was proclaimed and negotiations of a sort began. However, the great optimism that these events aroused quickly receded, and the peace process began to stall. It is to these current events that this chapter will now turn.

The Interplay between Static Security and Dynamic Change: The Stalled Peace Process

Peace can be a relative concept. Prime Minister Recep Tayyip Erdogan is first and foremost an adept politician. Thus, his main purpose appears to be to maintain and even expand his electoral mandate as Turkey enters its next electoral cycle in 2014-15. In so doing, he has many opposing constituencies to appease and satisfy. If he goes too far in satisfying the Kurds, he will surely alienate other, maybe even more important elements of the electorate. As a result, he seems to have treated the mere agreement to begin the peace process as the goal itself, rather than as a part of a process to address the root causes of the conflict. Once again the continuity policy of security had to be balanced against that of change. His so-called democratic package released on 30 September 2013 failed to implement any of the reforms the Kurds were looking for. Gone were the earlier hopes of a new, more democratic Turkish constitution. Instead, Erdogan seemed more interested in women's head scarves.

Where then do we now stand? Should Turkey pursue the policy of security or change? The government seems uncertain. Thus, on the one hand, while urging Erdogan to move faster and further, the Kurds also should remember that he has arguably done much more to begin trying to change Turkish policy and solve the Kurdish issue than all his predecessors combined. In addition, the Kurds should recall Erdogan's bold declaration when the peace process began that, "if drinking poison hemlock is necessary, we can also drink it to bring peace and welfare to this country."[76]

However, from June 30 to July 5, 2013, the People's Congress of Kurdistan (Kongra-Gel), a PKK affiliated body, held its 9th General Assembly and declared that the first stage of the peace process had been completed by the PKK withdrawals from Turkey.[77] Thus, it was now time for the Turkish state and government to take concrete steps and make the required legal arrangements for the second stage of the peace process by presenting a democratization package of legal reforms. Instead, the Turkish government was constructing new military posts and dams, increasing the number of village guards, and failing to ensure the connection between the PKK head Abdullah Ocalan and democratic circles. Thus, concluded the Congress, the Turkish government was raising doubts about the peace process and creating the risk of a deadlock and failure.

In line with the gender equality principle, the Kongra-Gel assembly also elected Cemil Bayik and Bese Hozat as the co-chairs of the *Koma Civaken Kurdistan* (KCK) or Kurdistan Communities

Union to succeed Murat Karayilan who, however, supposedly was appointed as the new leader of the *Hezen Parastina Gel* (HPG) or People's Defense Forces.[78] At the time there was much speculation about what these new appointments might mean for the peace process, with some thinking that Bayik would be more hawkish than the supposedly more moderate Karayilan.[79] However, it soon became clear that the reshuffling of leaders did not represent a policy change, but merely a procedural organizational restructuring. Ocalan, for example, was reelected the *serok* or president of the KCK/PKK, and it was inconceivable that the switch of cochairs between Karayilan and Bayik could have occurred without his approval. Thus, the leadership change probably did not signal a repudiation of the peace process.

By September 2013, however, there were more signs that "the peace process has become bogged down and neither party is prepared to risk an initiative."[80] Erdogan accused the PKK of "not keeping its promises" and asserted that only 20 percent of its guerrillas in Turkey had moved back over the border, most of them simply being children, invalids, and elderly people. Although the PKK had not released any official numbers, one of their spokesmen declared that "about 500" people had reached northern Iraq since the withdrawal process had started on May 15, 2013. This figure of 500 was close to that of 20 percent cited by the prime minister. If so, this was good news for the peace process, as it was not easy for the PKK to evacuate Turkey without running into a firefight with government troops. That no such conflict had occurred also might be viewed as a positive sign and a credit to both sides. Indeed, as already noted, as of early 2015, nobody had been killed in an armed clash since the peace process had officially commenced in March 2013.

On the other hand, the new KCK cochair Bayik had already announced that, "if the government fails to take action by Sept. 1 [2013], the cease-fire between Turkey and the PKK will be broken."[81] The PKK claimed that it was living up to its part of the peace process by evacuating its militants from Turkey, but that the government was failing to reciprocate by presenting its promised democratization package of legal reforms. Thus, a few days later, the KCK Executive Council Presidency announced that the PKK had halted its withdrawal from Turkey, and it accused Ankara of not living up to the agreement to implement democracy and a solution to the Kurdish problem.[82] Nevertheless, Bayik added that the PKK would continue the cease-fire.[83]

When the peace process began, the Kurds expected the government to take the following steps to facilitate matters: (1) release from prison the approximately 5,000 KCK nonviolent activists being held on terrorism charges; (2) improve Ocalan's prison conditions to facilitate his ability to pursue peace; (3) introduce mother-tongue education for the Kurds; (4) reduce the 10 percent electoral threshold for parliament that made it very difficult for pro-Kurdish parties to win seats in the Turkish parliament; (5) expand the boundaries for civil liberties regarding organizing, assembly, and speech; (6) delist the PKK from the terrorism list since the government was now engaging it in a peace process.

Although a report in May 2014 indicated that Erdogan has promised that Ocalan would be moved from his isolated island prison on Imrali to some form of more lenient house arrest, among other concessions, in return for Kurdish support for his presidential ambitions,[84] as of the end of May 2014, the government had not taken any of these steps. Instead Erdogan's democratization package, announced on September 30, 2013, merely granted the following rights: (1) established private schools for Kurdish-language education; (2) restored the Kurdish village names that had been changed into Turkish; (3) permitted the use of the letters X, Q, and W of the Kurdish alphabet on signposts and identification cards; (4) granted freedom for political campaigning in Kurdish; (5) abolished the student's daily vow of allegiance that began, "I am a Turk."

The Kurds were not satisfied with these provisions and also objected to their unilateral formulation, which negated their desire to commence equal negotiations with the government. The PKK wanted the government's mere dialogue with Ocalan to segue into real, in-depth negotiations in which specific proposals for a solution of the Kurdish problem were discussed. As Selahattin Demirtas, the cochair of the pro-Kurdish BDP explained: "If you prepare the package without consulting us, we will not link it to the [peace] process. If we hear about this package for the first time from the mouth of the prime minister, then it will remain as your package."[85]

In addition, the PKK wanted Ocalan's prison conditions to be improved so that some of the BDP parliamentarians who wished to meet with him would not be arbitrarily vetoed by the government. The BDP, for example, stated that the government had prevented the delivery of letters from the PKK fighters in Kandil to Ocalan. Indeed, the death of Nelson Mandela in December 2013 reminded one of how the South African peace process was moved forward successfully by the government's releasing Mandela from prison, where he had been held on terrorism charges for some 27 years.

Along these lines, Ocalan had three more requests: (1) the right to have external contacts in addition to his meetings with the BDP and the government; (2) some sort of a neutral third-party observer or facilitator to monitor the negotiations as occurred in the earlier (2009-11), but secret Oslo talks between the government and PKK (given the long-standing struggle and resulting level of mistrust between the two sides, the peace process inevitably will continue to founder without some neutral facilitator to bring them together and transparently serve as a witness and encourager) and (3) the government should offer serious proposals and solutions. As Ocalan cautiously concluded, "While I maintain my belief in the [peace] process I expect the government to take a more positive initiative on negotiations."[86]

Instead, the government seemed to be flirting with the idea of shutting Ocalan and the PKK out of the peace process and instead somehow negotiating with Massoud Barzani, the president of the KRG in northern Iraq, who had become Turkey's de facto Kurdish ally in recent years. Indeed, in June 2014, Turkey actually announced that it now would recognize the KRG's independence if Iraq split up, which seemed increasingly possible after the Sunni Islamic extremist organization the Islamic State of Iraq and Syria (ISIS) captured Mosul and effectively divided Iraq into separate Sunni and Shia parts plus the KRG. Previously, Turkey's policy had been exactly the opposite; it would have gone to war to prevent KRG independence that might have served as an unwanted model for Turkey's Kurds.[87]

Subsequently, on 16-17 November 2013, Erdogan and Barzani met in Diyarbakir, Turkey. Here Erdogan seemingly sought to leverage his energy and other economic and political dealings with Barzani to seek the Kurdish vote in the upcoming cycle of Turkish elections that began in 2014. The Turkish prime minister went so far as to encourage Barzani to establish a new, more moderate Kurdish party in Turkey with more Islamic characteristics than the secular and nationalist PKK.[88] By using the ancient technique of divide and rule, Erdogan appeared to be seeking to split and weaken the Kurdish movement and to make it more applicable to his wishes, not only in regard to the current peace process, but also in the many other avenues of Middle Eastern politics dealing with energy resources and the continuing civil war in Syria. In other words Erdogan was seeking to marry the seemingly contradictory policy of security continuity to changing reform. However, to the extent that Erdogan was trying to use Barzani to marginalize the PKK, the Turkish-Kurdish peace process would fail because the PKK was the main Kurdish party in Turkey, not Barzani's Iraqi KDP.

Other Factors

The continuing civil war in Syria interjected the security continuity dimension as a further factor into the problems of the peace process. De facto Kurdish autonomy just across the Turkish border in Hasaka (Jazira) province played havoc with Turkey's fears regarding what it perceived as the PKK threat. The problem was even greater because the leading Kurdish party in Syria was the *Partiya Yekitiya Demokrat* (PYD) or Democrat Union Party, an affiliate of the PKK. In effect, this meant that, even though the PKK was supposed to be withdrawing across the border into Iraq's Qandil Mountains, it now had extended its cross-border presence next to Turkey by several hundred miles in Syria. In addition, this new Syrian position granted the PKK a type of strategic depth that added to its influence.

At first, Turkey reacted to this situation by bitterly opposing the PYD politically and diplomatically and also covertly supporting armed Jihadists/Salafists groups such as Jablat al-Nusra which was affiliated with al-Qaeda, and the even more extremist Islamic State in Iraq and Syria (ISIS), which even al-Qaeda had disowned. These Salafists/Jihadists looked upon both the Assad regime and the secular Kurds as *Takfiri* or apostates. Bitter fighting broke out between them and the Syrian Kurds, largely led by the PKK-affiliated PYD. Soon Turkey found itself in the unenviable position of seemingly siding with al-Qaeda-affiliated Salafists/Jihadists fanatics against secular, even pro-Western Syrian Kurds. This became all the more apparent when Turkey disdained to join the United States-led coalition against ISIS during the bitter fighting in Kobane, Syria, during September-October 2014. (See below in the chapter on the Islamic State of Iraq and Syria or ISIS.)

Thus, on July 25, 2013, amid reports that the PYD was about to declare Kurdish autonomy in Syria, Turkey sought to implement the change policy of Kurdish recognition and publicly invited Salih Muslim, the cochair of the PYD, to Istanbul for talks. Indeed one report claimed that the PYD already had produced a constitution for the Syrian Kurdish regions.[89] Under its provisions, Syria would become a democratic parliamentary federal system; Western (Syrian) Kurdistan—aka Rojava or the direction from where the sun sets—with Qamishli as its capital, would be one of the federal or autonomous self-ruling regions making its own internal decisions. Kurdish and Arabic would be its official languages, and self-ruling units would protect the Syrian borders from foreign intervention.

Then on November 12, 2013, the PYD moved yet another step toward some type of autonomy by declaring provisional self-rule in areas under its control and announced that it had formed a constituent assembly with the view toward creating a transitional government. Elections would be held within three months. However, both Turkey and the KRG responded negatively to what they perceived as change threatening their security. Barzani, for example, declared that "this is clearly an unilateral . . . act which disregards the other Kurdish parties."[90] Thus, it remained to be seen what the future held for Kurdish autonomy within what seemed to be the crumbling remains of the now-failing Syrian state.

However, if the stalled Turkish-Kurdish peace process could be revived and brought to a successful conclusion, the Syrian Kurds might seek to become associated in some manner with Turkey. After all, the PYD of Salih Muslim is closely associated with the PKK and is by far the strongest Syrian Kurdish party. If its elder brother the PKK and elder statesman Abdullah Ocalan accept Turkey, the PYD and Salih Muslim might see fit to follow in their footsteps instead of risking life in a broken Syria. Turkey would not only continue to become more democratic and thus acceptable to Kurdish nationalists, but also offer the Kurds in Syria the 16th largest state economy in the world. In the end, no matter what they do, the landlocked Kurds in Syria would obviously require good relations with Turkey to enjoy any chance for economic success.

Furthermore, if Turkey joined the European Union (EU), as it has been formally seeking to do so since 2005, the Syrian Kurds would suddenly become part of this most advanced economic bloc that also offers considerable political protection to its members. The PKK model, instead of Barzani's KDP/KRG, would have led ironically to a successful moderate future. Moreover, Turkish EU membership would also offer Barzani's KRG close ties with the EU, given the de facto alliance between Turkey and the KRG. Even more, of course, the Kurds in Turkey would also enter the EU by definition.

A strong and democratic Turkey might offer the vast majority of the Kurds in the world an incredibly bright future. For their part, the Kurds ironically would offer Turkey the Kemalist security it has always sought to the detriment of the Kurds, but now with the support and cooperation of the Kurds, because it would now be to the benefit of the Kurds! What just a decade ago might have seemed counterfactual, would have become reality. The seemingly contradictory policies of change and continuity would be harmonized. However, as of this writing early in 2015, Turkey's EU accession is stalled and seems increasingly unlikely. Indeed, the AKP lost its parliamentary majority in the elections held on June 7, 2015, mainly because the pro-Kurdish HDP won enough votes to enter parliament. By the end of July 2015, heavy fighting between Turkey and the PKK had resumed and their peace process ended.

— 3 —

Iraq and the Rise of the Kurdistan Regional Government (KRG)

Introduction

Kurdish history in Iraq has led to the most successful Kurdish state building in modern times. Not only has the Kurdistan Regional Government (KRG)—first established in 1992 and then officially recognized by the new Iraqi constitution after the fall of Saddam Hussein in 2003—offered the Kurds in Iraq their own self-government, this protostate has served as the nearest approximation for a real home for Kurds throughout the world. How did this occur?

Following World War I, the British artificially created Iraq[1] out of the former Ottoman *vilayets* (provinces) of Mosul, Baghdad, and Basra. This new state[2] consisted of a numerical but politically repressed Shiite Arab majority of perhaps 60 percent of the population, a ruling Sunni Arab minority of perhaps 20 percent, and the Kurds, who constituted perhaps another 20 percent. Other much smaller minorities included the Turkomans and Assyrians, among others. The new state became a British mandate under the League of Nations, while Faisal I, a Hashemite ally of the British during World War I, was made the king. Although it was understood that the Kurds were to negotiate their future position in the oil-rich state, from the beginning the Kurds were in an almost constant state of revolt because their supposed rights were not implemented.[3]

Officially the Kurds in Iraq were not considered to be under colonial rule, as that concept came to be developed under the League of Nations and subsequently under the United Nations system of classifications of mandate, and then trusteeship and non-self-governing territories.[4] Nevertheless, it might be said that the Kurds in Iraq have suffered under a form of sequential triple colonialism over the past century: first, the Ottoman Empire until 1918, then the British until 1932, and subsequently the Arabs, once Iraq gained its independence.[5] Indeed the Baathist regime that came to power in postcolonial Iraq in 1968[6] eventually employed genocidal tactics against the Kurds during the notorious Anfal campaign and chemical attack against the city of Halabja in March 1988. The purpose of this chapter is to analyze late-blooming Kurdish nationalism as it developed in Iraq largely as a reaction to Arab nationalism in that state. What factors long inhibited Kurdish nationalism in postcolonial Iraq but eventually led to a series of revolts, genocidal response, and finally—since 1991 and 2003 with the defeats of Saddam Hussein—to the establishment of the Kurdistan Regional Government (KRG) in Iraq, a de facto autonomous state? This chapter will be based on extensive on-site fieldwork and interviews as well as a detailed perusal of the existing scholarly literature.[7]

Birth of Modern Iraq

During World War I, one of US President Woodrow Wilson's Fourteen Points (Number 12) declared that the non-Turkish minorities of the Ottoman Empire should be granted the right of "autonomous development." The stillborn Treaty of Sevres, signed in August 1920, provided for "local autonomy for the predominantly Kurdish area" (Article 62) and in Article 64 even looked forward to the possibility that "the Kurdish peoples" might be granted "independence from Turkey."

The definitive Treaty of Lausanne, in July 1923, brought on by Turkey's quick revival under Ataturk—ironically enough with considerable Kurdish help, as the Turks played well on the theme of Islamic unity—altered the entire situation. As for the Kurds in Iraq, the British decided that their new mandate would be more viable by including the oil-rich Kurdish *vilayet* of Mosul rather than granting the Kurds a separate administration. Thus, the Treaty of Lausanne made no mention of the Kurds, condemning them to a de facto colonial existence in Iraq as well as in Turkey, Iran, and Syria.

As a result, the Kurds were in an almost constant state of revolt.[8] Even though the British established a local Kurdish leader, Sheikh Mahmud Barzinji of Sulaymaniya, as their governor over the Iraqi Kurds in 1919, for example, he immediately began the first of several rebellions, even proclaiming himself king of Kurdistan. The British Royal Air Force (RAF) successfully bombed the sheikh's forces and put down his repeated uprisings.

On the other hand, both the British and Iraqi governments issued a number of statements that theoretically recognized and guaranteed some Kurdish rights. On December 24, 1922, for example, an Anglo-Iraqi Joint Declaration to the Council of the League of Nations clearly recognized "the right of the Kurds who live within the frontiers of Iraq to establish a Government within those frontiers" and also to "send responsible delegates to negotiate their future economic and political relations."[9]

Indeed, it was not until 1926 that the League Council formally recognized the incorporation of Mosul into Iraq. Before then Turkey had continued to claim the area.[10] The International Commission of Inquiry established by the Council also required that "the desire of the Kurds that the administrators, magistrates and teachers in their country be drawn from their own ranks, and adopt Kurdish as the official language in all their activities, will be taken into account."[11] Although Baghdad issued a "Local Languages Law," these pledges to the Kurds were not included in the Anglo-Iraqi Treaty of 1930, which granted Iraq its independence in 1932.

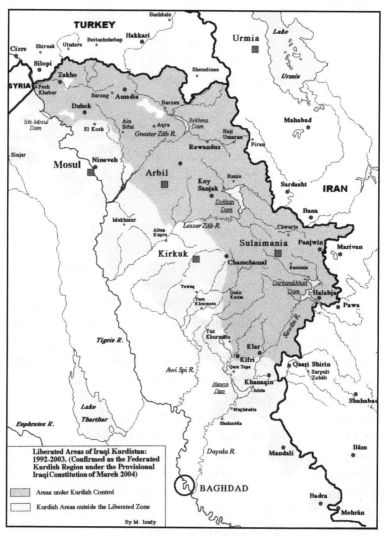

Liberated Areas of Iraqi Kurdistan

On the other hand, Stephen H. Longrigg, an authority on Iraqi history, argued that, "in adopting a hesitant attitude to Kurdish claims, the Iraq Government was not always unreasonable. These claims were at times frankly separatist." Longrigg explained that "the fear existed, in addition, that privileges granted to the Kurds would be demanded immediately by the Shi'is of the Euphrates." Thus, he concluded that, as a result, "the Kurds . . . represented a profoundly unsatisfactory and even a menacing element in the national life [of Iraq]."[12]

Meanwhile, the only serious opposition to the British imposition of Faisal I as king of Iraq occurred in the Kurdish regions. Most of the negative votes came from Kirkuk, while Sulaymaniya did not even participate in the referendum that approved it. Indeed, Sheikh Mahmud styled himself king of Kurdistan in part to show his opposition to Faisal becoming king of Iraq. However, it would be a mistake to see the activities of the sheikh as exercises of Kurdish nationalism. In discussing the revolts of Sheikh Mahmud Barzinji, as noted above, David McDowall argues that "he had little in common with today's Kurdish leaders. Both the vocabulary and style are quite different. It is significant that Shaykh Mahmud did not waste his time appealing to nationalist sentiment. He was a sayyid [literally a reputed descendant of Muhammed], and the language his constituency understood was the language of Islam. In 1919 he appealed for a *jihad*, not a national liberation struggle. Furthermore, his style was to use kin and tribal allies and his aim was the establishment of a personal fiefdom."[13]

With the final defeat of Sheikh Mahmud in the spring of 1931, Mulla Mustafa Barzani (1903-1979) began to emerge as the leader almost synonymous with the Kurdish movement and the nascent nationalism in Iraq. Despite his eventual wide appeal, however, Barzani remained ultimately a traditional, tribal leader. For many years, this situation would prove to be the ultimate weakness of Kurdish national aspirations in Iraq. Even today its divisive effects still forestall complete Kurdish unity in the KRG.

Mulla Mustafa Barzani

The eponymous home of the Barzanis, Barzan is a remote old mountainous and economically marginal village in the upper regions of what is today northern Iraq, just south of the present Turkish border on the edge of Mt. Shirin and on the left (eastern) bank of the Great Zab River. In his famous *Sharafnama*, Sharaf Khan Bitlisi called it Baziran and listed it as a possession of the mirs of Bahdinan. During the 1840s, Sheikh Abdul Rahman—sometimes called Tajuddin—(a disciple of the Naqshbandi sufi order established in Kurdistan by Maulana Khalid) settled in Barzan and thus became the first Barzani of today's famous family and tribe. Barzan soon began to serve as a sort of utopian society in which refugees were welcomed.

Since Barzan was located next to the powerful Zebari tribe's territory, however, much fighting took place between the two. The sheikhs of Barzan became noted for their religious authority and martial prowess. Nevertheless, the village itself was destroyed by the government 16 times during the fighting between it and the Barzanis, but it has been rebuilt since 1991. The legendary Mulla Mustafa Barzani is buried here in a simple grave, while a nearby cemetery contains the remains of some of the Barzanis killed by the Saddam Hussein regime.

Mulla Mustafa Barzani was arguably the most famous Kurdish leader of the twentieth century. His name became virtually synonymous with the Kurdish nationalist movement in Iraq, while his fame made him a legendary hero for Kurds everywhere. He was a natural leader, inspired emotional loyalty, and was physically strong and brave. Because of the stunted development of Kurdish nationalism, however, in some ways Barzani, as noted above, never exceeded the bounds of tribal chieftain. Some of his Kurdish opponents called him feudal and reactionary. Nevertheless, his career helped mightily to foster a Iraqi Kurdish nationalism that continues to grow in the 21stt century.

Mulla Mustafa and his mother were imprisoned by the Ottomans when he was an infant, and his elder brother Sheikh Abdul Salam II was executed by the Ottomans for supposedly supporting the Russians in World War I. Barzani eventually had three wives, 10 sons, and several daughters. Hamayl, his third wife, was a member of the Barzani tribe's hereditary Zebari enemy. She came to wield considerable power behind the scenes and is the mother of Massoud Barzani, the current Barzani, Kurdistan Democratic Party (KDP) leader, and president of the KRG.

Mulla Mustafa first emerged in the early 1930s when, with his elder brother Sheikh Ahmed Barzani, he opposed a plan to settle Assyrians in Barzani tribal land. Fighting erupted, but eventually the Barzani brothers surrendered and were imprisoned. During World War II, Barzani escaped from house arrest, and he soon renewed his opposition to the government and various pro-government tribes. Despite early successes, Barzani was eventually forced across the frontier into Iran, where he became a general in the short-lived Mahabad Republic of Kurdistan.[14] He also became the leader of the new Kurdish (later Kurdistan) Democratic Party (KDP), founded in Iraq on August 16, 1946.

With the fall of the Mahabad Republic in late 1946, Barzani was forced into an epic retreat with some of his best fighters to the Soviet Union, where he became known by some as the "Red Mulla." However, he did not become a communist. With the fall of the Iraqi monarchy in 1958, Barzani returned to Iraq, where he quickly regained his former tribal prominence.

Barzani's rise to prominence after his return to Iraq from exile in the Soviet Union in 1958 is not easy to fully explain unless one appreciates the contemporary roots of Kurdish nationalism in Iraq. As late as 1957, for example, no less an astute observer of affairs than C. J. Edmonds, who had been a British Political Officer in Iraq during the 1920s and also had written a number of useful analyses of the Iraqi Kurds, mentioned Barzani only in passing as a "fugitive rebel from Iraq,"[15] and concluded that "with every year that passes any concerted armed revolt becomes more improbable."

How wrong could anybody be? Two years later, although now realizing that "the event which perhaps more than any other has caught the popular imagination is the return of Mulla Mustafa,"[16] Edmonds could only argue that "it is difficult to explain this rapid build-up into a national all-Iraqi figure . . . otherwise than as the work of a well-organized chain of communist propagandists long established throughout Iraq." Again how wrong could any analyst be? Given subsequent developments, Edmonds's lack of foresight stemmed from his understandable failure to predict the contemporary rise of Kurdish nationalism in Iraq as a reaction to the excesses of postcolonial Iraqi Arab nationalism.

Thus, only in the 1960s did the Kurdish movement in Iraq begin to take on the characteristics of a genuine nationalist movement. Following the destruction of the Mahabad Republic of Kurdistan in Iran in 1946, in which, as noted above, Barzani had been one of commanding generals, Barzani's retreat to the Soviet Union subsequently became epic in the rise of modern Kurdish nationalism in Iraq: "We marched for fifty-two days. In the high mountain passes the late spring snow was six to twelve feet deep. We fought nine encounters, lost four killed and had seven wounded."[17] Even so, to his dying day, Barzani never fully exceeded the bounds of tribal chieftain. In part, this helps to explain his bitter disputes with Ibrahim Ahmad and Ahmad's son-in-law, Jalal Talabani.[18]

By 1961, Barzani was in full revolt against the government. Given the weakness of the Iraqi government in those days, Barzani was able to achieve considerable success and maintain a de facto independence for many years. During his long period of ascendancy, Barzani mastered the art of guerrilla warfare in his mountainous homeland. Barzani also battled against and defeated the forces of the KDP-Politburo led by two former associates, Ibrahim Ahmad and his son-in-law Jalal Talabani. By the late 1960s, Barzani was the undisputed leader of the Iraqi Kurds.

The March Manifesto (1970) reached with the Iraqi government, now led by the Baath Party and increasingly by Saddam Hussein, held out the promise of real autonomy for the Kurds. In the end, however, neither side really wanted a compromise. The growing strength of the Baathist government and the treachery of the United States and Iran in withdrawing their support that Barzani had naively come to rely on, finally enabled the Iraqi government to quickly win the new round of fighting that began in 1974 and ended in March 1975 with Barzani's total defeat. Broken and in ill health, Barzani eventually went into exile in the United States, where he died in March 1979.[19] He was initially buried in Iran, but in 1993 he was reinterred in his Kurdish homeland (the town of Barzan) amid much emotional demonstration on the part of all Iraqi Kurds.

Although he was not a religious figure, throughout most of his career Barzani was known by the religious title "Mulla." The origins of so doing are obscure, although one close observer said that it came from a maternal uncle. Be that as it may, the name "Mulla" was a proper name and not a title. Today most Kurdish writers prefer not to use the word because of its religious implications, but during his lifetime he was almost always known by this name.

Although Iraq technically became sovereign in 1932, it was not until the Hashemite monarchy was overthrown by a bloody coup on July 14, 1958, that the state really became independent. Article 23 of the new provisional constitution of Iraq gave the Kurds a theoretical recognition they had never before received in any other state when it declared: "The Kurds and the Arabs are partners within this nation. The Constitution guarantees their rights within the framework of the Iraqi Republic." Despite earlier hopes for reconciliation, however, hostilities between the government and the Kurds, as noted above, again commenced in September 1961 and raged intermittently throughout the 1960s.

General Abdul Karim Kassem ruled from 1958 until he himself was overthrown and killed on February 8, 1963.[20] The Baath Party briefly came to power for nine months and then permanently achieved power by two separate coups in July 1968. As already noted, Saddam Hussein negotiated the March (1970) Manifesto with Mulla Mustafa Barzani that would have allowed a considerable amount of Kurdish autonomy. In the end, however, neither side was able to trust the other's ultimate intentions, and the fighting resumed in 1974. The status of the oil-rich city and area of Kirkuk was one of the major disagreements. Under the terms of the Algiers Agreement between Iran and Iraq, Iran ceased its support for Barzani, and by March 1975 he had collapsed. The Iraqi government then attempted to solve the Kurdish problem by destroying more than 3,000 Kurdish villages, exiling some 500,000 Kurds to the south, and establishing a Kurd-free buffer zone on the borders of northern Iraq. Guerrilla warfare, however, resumed by the late 1970s.

The Iran-Iraq War during the 1980s offered new opportunities and dangers for the Iraqi Kurds, who ended up supporting Iran. The Iraqi Kurdistan Front of the Kurdistan Democratic Party (KDP) and the Patriotic Union of Kurdistan (PUK), along with most of the other smaller Kurdish parties, held out the hope for Kurdish unity. In retribution for the Kurdish support for Iran, Saddam Hussein unleashed chemical weapons against the Kurds at Halabja and during his genocidal Anfal campaign. These criminal attempts to reduce the Kurds in the 1970s and 1980s,[21] however, had the opposite effect of fostering further Kurdish nationalism in Iraq.

Saddam Hussein's annexation of Kuwait in August 1990 led to the first Gulf War in 1991. Iraq's quick defeat, the failed Kurdish and Shiite uprisings at the end of the war, and the horrific Kurdish refugee flight to the borders ultimately led to intervention by the United States in the form of a no-fly zone over the north of Iraq. This response allowed the Kurds to establish a precariously situated, unrecognized de facto state that increasingly prospered despite vicious Kurdish infighting between Massoud Barzani's KDP and Jalal Talabani's PUK during the mid-1990s.[22] By 2002, Saddam Hussein's Iraq had increasingly become a failed, pariah, and rogue state. In addition, despite adamant Turkish, Iranian, and Syrian opposition to Kurdish statehood, the United States–enforced no-fly zone, and United Nations money from Iraq's share of renewed Iraqi oil sales, allowed the Iraqi Kurds to prosper and begin to construct a civil society.

Social and economic factors also played important roles in the development of Kurdish nationalism in Iraq. The oil industry, construction of major dams, cement and tobacco factories, and agricultural mechanization all created greater wealth and helped move people out of their smaller traditional valleys into the larger urban world. In the first decade of the 21st century, Iraqi Kurdish nationalism has become the most highly developed form of Kurdish nationalism among the entire Kurdish people, but clearly its origins are mainly contemporary, dating only to the events described briefly above.

The KRG in Iraq

The Kurdistan Regional Government (KRG) refers to the Kurdish self-government that has administered the Kurdish region in northern Iraq since 1992. With the adoption of the new Iraqi constitution in October 2005, the KRG has gone on to gain constitutional legitimacy as a constituent state in a democratic federal Iraq.[23] As of early 2014, the KRG consisted of the three provinces of Irbil, Sulaymaniya, and Dohuk, with a combined population of approximately 6 million. In deference to those who died in the chemical attack in March 1988, Halabja was constituted as a fourth province at the end of that year.

For the first time ever, most Iraqi Kurds now think of their government in Irbil, not the one in Baghdad, when the concept of government is broached. Thus, as of 2015, the Iraqi Kurds not only possess their most powerful regional government since the creation of Iraq following World War I, but also play a very prominent role in the Iraqi government in Baghdad, including the posts of president (Jalal Talabani, followed by Fuad Masum in 2014), until August 2009 deputy prime minister (Barham Salih), until 2014 foreign minister and now finance minister and deputy prime minister (Hoshyar Zebari), and several other cabinet positions. This dual governmental role stands in marked contrast to the situation that existed before the events of 1991 and 2003, when the Kurds were treated as second-class citizens and worse.

Nevertheless, enormous problems remain, and in a sense the Kurdish postcolonial struggle in Iraq continues.[24] For example, the actual division of power between the Iraqi government and the KRG remains in dispute. These contested powers include the ownership of natural resources (mainly oil) and the control of the revenues flowing from them, the role of the KRG army or *peshmergas*, and the final status of oil-rich Kirkuk,[25] as well as several other disputed territories such as Sinjar and Khanaqin, among others.

The ultimate question, therefore, is for how long this new unique Kurdish position of strength will last. Many Arabs resent the Kurdish claims to autonomy as a challenge to the Arab patrimony, and a federal state for the Iraqi Kurds within Iraq as merely a prelude to secession. Indeed, unofficial referenda held in February 2004 and again in January 2005 almost unanimously called for independence despite the opposition of the main Kurdish leaders, who argued that independence would not be practical, given strong regional opposition. In the summer of 2008, Kurdish and Arab Iraqi forces came close to actual blows over territorial disputes in Khanaqin. When the Kurdish parliament unilaterally approved a new constitution for the KRG in June 2009, Baghdad denounced the move as tantamount to secession. As a result, the Kurds put their new constitution on hold.

Evolution of the KRG

Before proceeding any further with this analysis of the KRG, how-ever, it would be useful to review the immediate events that led to its creation. As already noted, after the Gulf War of 1991 and the failure of the ensuing Kurdish uprising in March 1991, the mass flight of Kurdish refugees to the mountains and borders of Iran and Turkey forced the United States to launch Operation Provide Com-fort (OPC). OPC created a safe haven and maintained a no-fly zone to encourage the refugees to return to their homes by protecting them from further attacks by the Iraqi government. In addition, the unprecedented United Nations Security Resolution 688 of April 5, 1991 gave the fledgling KRG support by condemning "the repres-sion of the Iraqi civilian population . . . in Kurdish populated areas" and demanding "that Iraq . . . immediately end this repression."

On May 19, 1992, elections in the protected Kurdish region re-sulted in a virtual dead heat between Massoud Barzani's Kurdistan Democratic Party (KDP) and Jalal Talabani's Patriotic Union of Kurdistan (PUK), both for the position of supreme leader (presi-dent) and parliament. A number of other parties also competed, but none of them met the qualification of receiving 7 percent of the vote to enter parliament. The KDP and the PUK decided not to pur-sue the selection of a president and to share power equally in par-liament, which met for the first time in Irbil on June 4, 1992. An executive with Fuad Masum as the prime minister was established on July 4, 1992.

At its inception, the KRG was handicapped by the refusal of the surrounding states of Turkey, Iran, and Syria (not to mention Sad-dam Hussein's Iraq) to countenance the concept of any type of Kur-dish administration or state. All of these states feared the precedent it would set for their own restless Kurds. In addition, the KRG suf-fered from immense economic problems and a seeming paralysis of decision making because of power being shared equally between the KDP and the PUK, as well as Barzani's and Talabani's decision not to participate in the administration.

PERSONAL OBSERVATION

In August 1993, shortly after the original creation of the KRG, I traveled there at the invitation of Barzani's KDP and Talabani's PUK to attend the KDP congress and to visit various people and places. I was to meet numerous then obscure people who later became famous as leaders of the KRG. Barham Salih made some of my travel arrangements and met me several times while I was there. He later became the prime minister of the KRG. Dr. Najmaldin O. Karim, a prominent Kurdish-American neurosurgeon in Washington, DC, served as my travel companion from the United States and back, as well as acting as my guide while I was in Kurdistan. He not only seemed to know almost everybody and everything, but also commanded everybody's respect. He later moved back to Kurdistan and became the much-admired governor of his home province and city Kirkuk. While he and I were in Irbil, we accidentally met his father. It was a very emotional experience, as the two had not seen each other for maybe a quarter of a century.

Traveling to the Iraqi Kurdish region was not easy. First we flew to Istanbul and then on to Diyarbakir in southeastern Turkey, from where we hired a taxi to take us to the KRG border approximately 100 miles away. When we arrived we walked across the border, going through Turkish and then Kurdish customs officials and being greeted by a trilingual "Welcome to Kurdistan" sign. Once across the border we were met by Kurdish friends driving an all-purpose Toyota van, which proved indispensable in navigating the still very primitive roads to Irbil. At one time we literally had to exit the vehicle and push it across some then shallow river. What a contrast with more recent trips to the region for which I flew on a regularly scheduled jet airliner from Vienna to Irbil's modern airport, boasting the sixth largest runway in the world!

The highlight of my trip in 1993 was attending the important KDP congress that was meeting to consider the recent important developments. From where I stood I could clearly see Massoud Banzani and Jalal Talabani sitting next to each other, frequently engaging in what seemed to be amicable conversation. The sight made me feel confident in future intra-Kurdish cooperation. How disappointed I was when in less than a year a bloody four-year-long civil war broke out between the two!

Another highlight of the KDP congress I always will remember is when the then arguably dean of Kurdish academic studies Ismet Cheriff Vanly was greeted by the more than 1,000 in attendance with an incredibly loud and long-lasting applause. No scholar would have ever been honored in such a manner in the West! Obviously, the Kurds knew and appreciated their scholars much more than Westerners did theirs. I too was allowed to address the multitude, but for only 30 seconds. Still the entire experience made me feel that my arduous trip had been worthwhile.

A few days later, while talking with some Kurds near a small woods, a figure wearing a large brimmed hat approached from behind some trees. It turned out to be Vanly himself. We spoke only briefly, but he remembered our meeting a decade later when we met again at a Kurdish conference in Amsterdam in 2003. One of Vanly's dreams was to produce an Encyclopedia Kurdistania as all great nations do, but he never lived to fulfill this wish. However, he did live to see more Kurdish rights won than anyone would have ever imagined when first we met at the KDP congress in 1993. Vanly, who had somehow survived being shot at point-blank range through the head by an agent of Saddam Hussein, finally died in 2011 shortly before his eighty-seventh birthday.

While in Kurdistan in 1993, Dr. Karim also introduced me to Massoud Barzani, Jalal Talabani, Nechirvan Idris Barzani, and Hoshyar Zebari, among a number of others. All four of the above, of course, later became major figures in the KRG.

In December 1993, fighting first broke out between the PUK and the Islamic Movement of Kurdistan. Then, on May 1, 1994, the PUK and the KDP began a bloody on-again, off-again civil war that took more than 3,000 lives, caused untold suffering and destruction, and threatened the very existence of the KRG. The KDP-PUK fighting led to the creation of two rump governments or administrations: the KDP's in Irbil and the PUK's in Sulaymaniya. Only one parliament, however, continued to meet in Irbil. After repeated attempts by the United States—as well as on other occasions Britain, Iran and Turkey—the United States finally managed to broker a cease-fire in September 1998.

On 7 May 2006, the two separate KRG administrations were finally unified with Massoud Barzani (already serving as the president since June 12, 2005) as the president and his nephew Nechirvan Idris Barzani as the prime minister. It was agreed that the PUK would hold the later position in the future. Jalal Talabani eventually became the largely ceremonial president of Iraq. As of 2015, approximately 6 million people live under the KRG, including perhaps 100,000-200,000 Turkomans and 50,000 Assyrians. Given recent developments, probably more than 80 percent of the population is now urban and only 20 percent is rural. Irbil has some 1.5 million people and Sulaymaniya maybe 800,000.

However, the Kurdish people remained frustrated at the lack of services, transparency, women's and youth's rights, institutionalization, and, of course, the continuing nepotism and corruption. Nawshirwan Mustafa—who resigned from his post as the number-two man in the PUK in December 2006 and eventually set up his own political party (*Gorran* or Change Party) to contest the July 25, 2009, elections—charged that both the KDP and the PUK received $35 million a month as part of the funds transferred to the KRG by the central government in Baghdad, but did not have to account for it.[26] Senior leaders of both parties hid their ownership of large companies by funneling tens of millions of dollars through mid-level party members or reliable friends. Both the Barzanis and the Talabanis had small groups that were running everything for them. The PUK, for example, owned Nokan, a conglomerate in Sulaymaniya, with interests in construction, trade, and food. Steps also were needed to be taken to separate the interests of the two ruling parties (the KDP and the PUK) from those of the KRG.

Despite claims that the KRG is business friendly, huge economic problems also remain. For example, there is no banking, taxing, insurance, or postal system. The public payroll gobbles up three-quarters of the budget, and, as discussed above, crony capitalism and nepotism thrive. The government is still unable to provide regular electricity and affordable fuel. As many as 900,000 people are internally displaced. Honor killing of women and female genital mutilation (circumcision) remain a problem, but attempts are being made to control them.

Nevertheless, over the past several years the economic situation in the KRG has improved dramatically, as the region was spared the horrific civil war that engulfed Arab Iraq to the south after the fall of Saddam Hussein in 2003. What is more, the Kurds now receive 17 percent of the Iraqi national budget. Earlier the KRG was receiving 13 percent of Iraq's funds originally allocated from the oil the United Nations allowed Iraq to sell under UN Security Council Resolution 986 of April 14, 1995. From 1997 to 2001, the United Nations oil-for-food program also had pumped approximately $4.6 billion into the KRG. Despite some serious inefficiencies, most Kurds are now better off than are Iraqis under the administration in Baghdad. Trade over the border with Turkey in particular has also been profitable; new roads are being built;

refugees are being resettled; food supplies are adequate; water and electricity are available; and shops are full of refrigerators from Turkey, and even potato chips from Europe. Nongovernmental organizations contribute to all of this with literacy and community-building organizations not addressed by the United Nations.

A civil society is also emerging, with dozens of newspapers, magazines, and television and radio stations representing a broad spectrum of opinion. People have freedoms impossible to imagine in the rest of Iraq. In addition to the KDP and the PUK, there are numerous other much smaller political parties, and criticism of the government is tolerated. The entire region under the KRG has at least 10 hospitals. Better medical training, however, is needed, and some medical specialties such as neurosurgery and plastic surgery are lacking. The electricity is still sometimes turned off, but hospitals have their own generators. The incidence of cancer is high, probably because of the Iraqi usage of chemical weapons in the past and the current lack of chemotherapy. Most services require only a nominal fee.

There also are at least 10 separate universities now operating: Salahaddin, the University of Kurdistan (Hawler), and Isik in Irbil; Sulaymaniya and the American University in Sulaymaniya; Koy Sanjaq; Soran; and Dohuk, among others. However, essential infrastructure is still not complete. Primary and secondary schools have proliferated and are contributing to Kurdish state building.[27] The future of the KRG is, of course, very uncertain. Protection from Baghdad and, since 2014 even more ISIS, is the ultimate concern, but the KRG has continued to prosper despite the US withdrawal from Iraq at the end of 2011. Since 2009, the KRG also has been able to improve political relations with Turkey.

In June 2009, as previously mentioned, the KRG parliament suddenly approved a new constitution for the region and called for it to be ratified during the Kurdish regional elections scheduled to be held on July 25, 2009. Although this constitution declared that it adhered to the federal Iraqi constitution, defined Kurdistan as a region within Iraq, recognized the rights of all ethnic groups and their religions living within the region, provided for women to receive 30 percent of the membership in the KRG parliament and non-Kurdish ethnic groups 10 percent, and supposedly declared that it respected the will of the people of Kirkuk and the surrounding areas; it was criticized for granting too much power to the KRG president, unilaterally claiming Kirkuk, and being submitted for ratification too quickly. As a result, the Kurdish leadership decided not to try to have the document ratified during the elections held on July 25, 2009.

The elections for a president and new parliament proceeded, however. Approximately 78 percent of 2.5 million eligible voters participated. Massoud Barzani was reelected president with a large majority of almost 70 percent of the popular vote. Four years earlier he had simply been elected president by the KRG parliament. More dramatically perhaps was the strong showing of Nawshirwan Mustafa's *Gorran* or Change Party] which garnered approximately 24 percent of the vote and gained 25 seats in the parliament, largely at the expense of the PUK. The joint KDP/PUK Kurdistani List won only 57 percent of the vote and saw its seats in parliament fall from 78 to 59 out of the 100 elected seats, which did not count 11 additional seats reserved for various minorities. The Service and Reform coalition of four small leftist and Islamic parties garnered almost 13 percent of the vote and gained 13 seats in the new parliament. Despite his party's relatively poor showing, Barham Salih, the main PUK candidate, eventually was chosen to be the new KRG prime minister, replacing Nechirvan Idris Barzani, who returned to the post, however, in 2012.

Recent KRG Developments

The KRG currently has many of the trappings of an independent state: its own president, prime minister, and parliament; its own flag and national anthem; its own army that even prevents Baghdad's army from entering the Kurdish region; its own international airports and educational system in which few any more even bother to learn Arabic; and even its own stamp entered into the passports of visitors.

However, many wondered what would happen to the KRG once the remaining US troops were withdrawn from Iraq at the end of 2011. Earlier the KRG and Baghdad had already come perilously close to blows over Kirkuk and their disputed internal border often referred to as "the trigger line," Khanaqin in 2008 being a prime example. Despite the US withdrawal, however, the KRG has continued to prosper by gaining increased significance as a type of strategic depth for Turkey against Baghdad and Tehran, and a safe haven for American operations in the region.[28]

In the meanwhile, moreover, the Iraqi Kurds have had their own Kurdish Spring, first when the anticorruption *Gorran* (Change) Party split the long-entrenched Patriotic Union of Kurdistan (PUK) in the KRG elections held on July 25, 2009, and subsequently when violent demonstrations broke out in Sulaymaniya, the KRG's second largest city, on February 17, 2011, and continued until forcibly curtailed by the KRG leadership on April 19, 2011.

Most of the demonstrators were protesting against corruption, nepotism, and the lack of effective services such as jobs and electricity. Intellectuals and journalists also protested against limitations on speech and the press as well as daily harassment. Among all there was a deep anger against the Barzani's Kurdistan Democratic Party (KDP) and Talabani's Patriotic Union of Kurdistan (PUK) family domination over society and government.[29]

Unlike the objects of the Arab Spring demonstrators, however, the KRG had just been democratically elected in July 2009 and thus was not so readily able to be denounced as illegitimate. The KRG also was able to prevent demonstrations from breaking out in Irbil, its capital and largest city, by closing the universities, sending the students home, and banning large gatherings. Nevertheless, the anti-KRG demonstrations that did occur constituted a serious wake-up call that all was not well with the KRG. As Barham Salih, the KRG prime minister from 2009 to 2012, declared: "We must do better. Our citizens demand better, and they deserve better."[30]

Barzani Hints at Independence

In return for vague promises to support the KRG's agenda regarding the disputed city and province of Kirkuk as well as oil revenues, the Kurds played a major role in helping Nouri al-Maliki form his new, second Iraqi government in Baghdad at the end of 2010. At a KDP conference in Irbil to help patch Maliki's new coalition together and at which Maliki was in attendance, KRG president Massoud Barzani declared that the Iraqi Kurdish region had the right of self-determination.[31] Such a right usually implies independence, although it could also lead to the type of self-chosen autonomy the Kurds already exercised.

However, as soon as Maliki assumed power again and against the backdrop of the final US troop withdrawal at the end of 2011, relations between Baghdad and the KRG began to deteriorate. Solutions to the perennial issues of Kirkuk and the sharing of oil revenues[32] proved elusive. In addition, since Maliki was unable to complete his new cabinet, he personally also assumed control of several leading ministries, leading to charges of nascent dictatorship. Then in January 2012, Maliki issued a warrant for the arrest of Vice President Tariq al-Hashemi, the highest ranking Sunni in his Shiite-dominated government, on charges of having led death squads against Shiites during the civil war that had followed Saddam Hussein's demise. Hashemi denied the charges and fled to the Kurdish region, where he was granted protection. US Senator John McCain, who had been the unsuccessful Republican candidate against US President Barack Obama in 2008, noted the rising tensions and declared that "the situation in Iraq is unraveling. . . . Iraq will likely break up which would eventually lead to the formation of three different states."[33] Although Obama's vice president

Joseph Biden would not have liked to have been reminded of it, McCain's three-state solution was similar to what he had earlier adumbrated, but now opposed.[34]

In a flurry of activity, Barzani journeyed to the United States, Turkey, and Europe for well-publicized meetings. His talks in Turkey were especially noteworthy, given how relations between the two sides had improved so dramatically in the past few years. Turkey was now taking the KRG's side in disputes with Baghdad. Turkish Prime Minister Recep Tayyip Erdogan accused Maliki of fanning tensions in Iraq with the Kurds, while Maliki denounced Turkey for its "flagrant interference in Iraqi internal affairs."[35] The following month, Nechirvan Barzani, once again KRG prime minister, also journeyed to Turkey for yet another high-level Turkish-KRG meeting. With such Turkish support, some speculated that the KRG might indeed be emboldened to secede from a crumbling Iraq.[36]

Back in Irbil, Barzani suggested that Baghdad might use the 18 F-16 fighter jets it was scheduled to purchase from the United States to once again subject the Kurds.[37] The KRG president demanded that Maliki agree on sharing power with his political opponents by September 2012, "or else the Kurds could consider breaking away from Baghdad." There was a "very dangerous political crisis in the country," and unless the impasse was broken "voters in the Kurdish region may consider a referendum for a state independent of Iraq."[38] Barzani also supported an Iraqi parliamentary motion to remove Maliki from office. Jalal Talabani, Barzani's old Kurdish nemesis and now president of Iraq, however, successfully opposed the motion to remove Maliki.

In November 2012, a sudden new crisis erupted as tensions mounted over the formation of Baghdad's Dijla Operations Command, a new military formation that was to operate in the area over which both Baghdad and the KRG claimed jurisdiction. Troops from the two sides faced off in what one report declared was "a crisis that . . . could erupt into a full-blown war,"[39] before tensions were defused. How often, however, could Baghdad and the KRG keep dodging the bullet?

Despite Barzani's bellicosity, most observers felt that he was really maneuvering for position in post-US–occupied Iraq. Premature Kurdish independence that would be seen as destroying Iraq would be opposed by not only the United States, but all the KRG's regional neighbors. What is more, the KRG continued to enjoy as a federal state within Iraq most of the advantages of independence without its disadvantages. It would be far better for the Iraqi Kurds to be seen as doing their utmost to keep Iraq united. Only if the Kurds' best efforts failed and Iraq still split apart, would the Kurds then be seen as having had independence forced on them and therefore justified. Patience and astute diplomacy remained the main call words.

On December 18, 2012, Jalal Talabani, the longtime leader of the Patriotic Union of Kurdistan (PUK) and also currently the president of Iraq, suffered a debilitating stroke. Mam Jalal, as he affectionately was called, had worked successfully to help keep Iraq united and had also just met with Iraqi prime minister al-Maliki in an attempt to ease tensions between the KRG and Baghdad over the territories disputed between them and the disposition of the oil reserves. What would the removal of Talabani's calming and astute abilities mean? In the event, both President Massoud Barzani and Prime Minister Nechirvan Barzani soon met with Maliki in Baghdad. Although no solutions to the basic underlying problems were reached, they were able temporarily to defuse tensions.

On September 21, 2013, the KRG held its fourth parliamentary elections. Barzani's KDP gained 37.70 per cent of the vote, which earned it 38 seats, a gain of 8 from the previous election in 2009. Nawshirwan Mustafa's *Gorran* (Change) Party replaced the incapacitated Talabani's PUK (now headed during the election by Barham Salih) as the second largest party by winning 24.21 per cent of the vote and 24 seats in parliament, which, however, was a loss of 1 seat from its showing in 2009. The PUK was the big loser, garnering only 17.80 per cent of the vote and just 18 seats, a loss of 11 from the previous election. The two Islamic parties won slightly more than 15 per cent of the vote, which gained them 16 seats, an increase of 6. The Turkomans, Assyrian, and Armenian minorities had 5, 5, and 1 seats reserved for them in the 111-seat parliament. Despite the rule limiting the KRG president to only two four-year terms, Massoud Barzani had already had his term extended a month earlier for another two years, while his nephew Nechirvan Barzani remained the prime minister. However, new problems soon broke out and, throughout most of 2014, Baghdad withheld the 17 percent of the Iraqi budget that was supposed to go to the KRG. This caused a financial crisis in the KRG, but was finally solved when the two sides were forced to work together again to combat the existential ISIS threat that began in June 2014. (See below.)

Regarding the continuing civil war in Syria and what it meant for the Kurds who lived there, Massoud Barzani continued to play an active role. Seeking to mediate while also being buttressed by the support of his de facto allies Turkey and the United States, Barzani also sought to call a pan-Kurdish conference in Irbil that would include all of the Kurds in Turkey, Syria, and Iran. This gathering would certainly seek to provide guidance and leverage for the pan-Kurdish future. As of this writing in early 2015, however, the pan-Kurdish conference has been postponed three times amid pan-Kurdish differences over how to allocate representation to the different Kurdish groups, among other points.

In the summer of 2014 major new opportunities but also existential crises suddenly emerged when ISIS took Mosul and drove the now largely Shiite government in Baghdad out of both that city and several other areas. The Kurds quickly took advantage of Baghdad's collapse by occupying Kirkuk and in effect implementing Article 140 of the Iraqi constitution regarding the future of that long-disputed area. KRG president Massoud Barzani declared that the time had come to consider declaring independence.[40] However, in August 2014, ISIS suddenly struck the KRG and drove within 20 miles of Irbil before US air support and supplies saved the day. Nevertheless, it was obvious that the KRG was not ready for independence. These traumatic events concerning ISIS will be discussed more thoroughly below in a separate chapter on ISIS.

PERSONAL OBSERVATION

Barely a month after ISIS almost captured Irbil in August 2014, I journeyed to the city to give the commencement address at the invitation of Soran University, which was located further on near the Iranian and Turkish borders. At first I was nervous about the situation regarding ISIS, as all flights into the Irbil airport had been canceled when ISIS had first attacked. However, on arriving at the end of September, I quickly saw that the situation had been stabilized and life had returned to normal in the city. Indeed, my first evening there I took a short walk through Irbil with my hosts and mingled with large crowds going peacefully about their business. Even more impressive, given the depredations of ISIS, were the Christian crosses prominently displayed on windows throughout Ankawa, the Christian section of Irbil. It seemed strange that barely 50 miles away were modern-day religious fanatics who would literally like to crucify these very Christians living peacefully with the Kurds! Within downtown Irbil also stood the 7,000-year-old citadel that many believe might be the oldest continually inhabited settlement in the world. My visit allowed me to interview several people with firsthand experience fighting against ISIS, so when I returned I was able to give several interviews to National Public Radio (NPR) and British Broadcasting Corporation (BBC), among others, as well as to write the chapter on ISIS in this book.

Kurdish areas of Syria

The Kurds in Syria:
A New Dimension

Background

Although an ancient land, the modern state of Syria dates only from the French mandate established in 1920. The earlier concept of Greater Syria (*Bilad al-Sham*) had been a much larger one that also included today's Lebanon, Jordan, and what was then known as Palestine, which is today's Israel, the West Bank, and the Gaza strip. Indeed some Arab nationalists would even include modern Iraq, so that Greater Syria would denote the united fertile crescent. This chapter on of the Kurds in Syria largely begins with the French mandate, as any earlier mention of Syria could easily be misleading. In addition, because there were no separate states of Turkey, Iraq, and Syria until the collapse of the Ottoman Empire after World War I, the Kurds in those future states simply lived in the Ottoman Empire. The concept of the Kurds in Syria could not be meaningful until the French mandate was created, and even later after failed Kurdish uprisings during the 1920s in Turkey forced many Kurds to leave that country for Syria.

Among pan-Kurdish nationalists, Syrian Kurdistan is often referred to as *Western Kurdistan* or *Rojava* (the direction of the setting sun). Since this region contains the country's most fertile areas and is also home to most of its oil reserves, the Kurdish-populated areas of Syria are a prize well worth struggling over.[1]

During the past century it might be said that the Kurds in Syria—as those in Iraq—also have suffered under a form of sequential triple colonialism: First, the Ottoman Empire until 1918, then the French until 1946,[2] and subsequently the Arabs once Syria had gained its independence. Furthermore, after it came to power in 1963, the now moribund Baathist Party proved even more hostile toward the Kurds. However, this heritage has not been completely negative, as the Ottomans in many ways reserved priority for their Muslim subjects, of whom the Kurds constituted a part, and on occasion the French actually showed favoritism toward such minorities as the Kurds in order to rule the Sunni Arab majority. Thus, it might be argued that assimilationist and denialist Arab colonialism has most exploited the Kurds in Syria.

Kurdish Roots in Syria

As testimony to Kurdish roots in Syria, the huge Crusader castle Krak des Chevaliers in the Alawite Mountains between Homs and Tartus is called in Arabic Hisn al-Akrad or Castle of the Kurds. Salah al-Din (Saladin), the most famous Kurd of all, is buried in the great mosque in Damascus. Kurd Dagh or Kurdish Mountain northwest of Aleppo (also referred to as Afrin after its main city) remains one of the three distinct and separate Kurdish areas in Syria, whereas Kobane (Ain al-Arab) in the north-central area of Syria and Hasaka (Hesice) or Jazira (Island, in reference to its lying between the Euphrates and Tigris Rivers) in the northeastern part of Syria constitute the other two separate and distinct Kurdish areas in Syria. Kurd Dagh and Kobane are contiguous with Kurdish-populated areas in Turkey, while part of Hasaka (Jazira) borders Kurdish areas in both Turkey and Iraq in the area the French called le Bec de Canard or Duck's Beak in reference to its relatively long, narrow shape that juts between Turkey and Iraq. Indeed, Cizre, once the capital of the Kurdish emirate of Botan and now situated in Turkey, lies only some 20 miles from the Syrian border. Qamishli—with a population of 184,231, according to the 2004 census, but now much larger—is the largest Kurdish city in Syria and is often considered the de facto capital of Western (Syrian) Kurdistan. It borders on the Turkish city of Nusaybin in the province of Hasaka (Jazira). In addition, perhaps 20 percent of the Kurds in Syria also live in the predominantly Kurdish quarters of Aleppo (Sheikh Maqsood, Ashrafiya, and Shar) and Damascus (Zorava [aka Wadi al-Mashari], Jabal al-Riz], and Rukn al-Din).

Almost all of the Syrian Kurds speak the Kurdish language/dialect of Kurmanji. Many have relatives in Turkey as the present international border was only drawn following World War I, largely along the lines fashioned by the secretive British-French Sykes-Picot Agreement of 1916, which became a byword for British-French imperialist control of the Middle East and manipulation of the Kurds.

Many Kurds living in the Syrian province of Hasaka (Jazira) originally fled to the region from Turkey following the failure of the Sheikh Said Rebellion in 1925 and subsequent Kurdish uprisings in Turkey.[3] As Wadie Jwaideh has pointed out, developments in Turkey had a profound influence on the Kurdish situation in Syria. This was true both for the urban Kurdish population and the rural tribes. "The newly drawn frontier line did not mean much at the time to the Kurdish tribesmen in the northern frontier regions of the country, for although the new frontier in many cases placed members of the same tribe under two different administrations, French and Turkish, it separated but did not actually sever the two segments."[4] However, this situation regarding the Turkish origin of some Syrian Kurds provided the Syrian rationale for the disenfranchisement of many of these Kurds in modern Syria, which began with the French mandate under the League of Nations following World War I and the removal of the short-lived rule of Faisal as king. After much acrimony, a French-Turkish agreement arbitrarily made the Baghdad railway line that ran between Mosul in Iraq and Aleppo in Syria the present border between most of Turkey and Syria after it crossed the Iraqi-Syrian boundary. Indeed, even today many Kurds in Turkey and Syria who live on either side of the border do not refer to themselves as coming from those states. Rather, for the Kurds of Turkey, Syria is *Bin Xhet* or below the line, and for the Kurds of Syria, Turkey is *Ser Xhet* or above the line.

Although the League of Nations concept of mandates began as simply the old hag of colonialism putting on a fig leaf and calling itself a mandate, in time it began to develop as a genuine pathway to independence. Thus, the British mandate of Iraq technically won its freedom as early as 1932, whereas Syria achieved it in 1946. Under the French mandate, underdeveloped and nascent Kurdish national identity was not deemed the threat that more mature Arab identity held. Thus, the Kurds in Syria enjoyed many political and cultural rights, as illustrated by the rise of a modest civil society consisting of political and social organizations, the legality of the Kurdish language and publications, and Kurdish recruitment into both the governmental administration and the military. A number of Kurdish tribes and aghas (landlords) also supported French rule because decentralization did not seem to challenge their traditional authority. On the other hand, it is also true that some Kurds joined uprisings or rebellions against the French mandate. During the 1930s these Kurds lobbied for an autonomous government in part as a reaction to the French attempt to settle Sunni Arabs in the area and as a result of the traditional Kurdish disdain for centralized government.

Compared with that in Iraq and Turkey, however, a sense of Kurdish national identity developed more slowly in Syria in part because of the divisions between tribes, and aghas (landlords) who were usually not motivated by nationalist concerns. Urban and rural Kurdish divisions also inhibited Kurdish national awareness; domestic leaders continued to arise from urban and merchant families whose origin stemmed from the Ottoman period and who thus possessed minimal Kurdish identity. Indeed, many urban Kurds were almost entirely Arabicized, Muhammad Kurd Ali (1876-1953), a noted intellectual, and Khalid Bakdash (1912-1995), who became the leader of the Syrian Communist Party during the 1930s, being primary examples. Rural Kurds living in the Jazira and Kurd Dagh had little in common with such urbanites, especially given their strong socio-economic differences. Furthermore, given how new the ideas of Syrian nationalism and statehood were, most Kurds who were motivated by their Kurdish identity at first thought of themselves less as Syrian Kurds and more as members of the wider pan-Kurdish nation. On the other hand, Sheikh Ahmad Kuftaru (1921-2004) made no attempt to hide his Kurdish origins, serving in Damascus as the grand mufti of Syria for 40 years until his death, by "being a very popular spiritual leader among the Kurds and Sunni Arabs at the same time, . . . rejecting the idea of political Islam," and acting as "an intermediary between the state and the Syrian Kurds."[5]

Among the most prominent leaders of the Syrian Kurds during the French mandate era were the Bedir Khan brothers (Thurayya, Jaladet, and Kamuran) who originally came from Cizre in Turkey. The brothers were grandsons of the famous Bedir Khan Beg (1800c.-1868), the last *mir* of the Kurdish emirate of Botan in what is today southeastern Turkey. Thus, his grandsons were of princely descent. Each grandson became a famous Kurdish intellectual in the cause of Kurdish nationalism and was also a noted figure in Kurdish literature.

Jaladet Bedir Khan (1893-1951), for example, helped to develop a Kurdish alphabet with Latin letters, while Kamuran Bedir Khan (1895-1978) became an author, editor, and professor teaching Kurdish at the Ecole des Langues Orientales in Paris, where today's prominent scholar of Kurdish literature Joyce Blau was one of his students. During the 1960s Kamuran also served as a spokesman for Mulla Mustafa Barzani, the famous Iraqi Kurdish nationalist/ tribal leader, at the United Nations. Thurayya Bedir Khan (1883-

1938) published a bilingual Kurdish-Turkish journal in Istanbul called *Kurdistan* after the young Turk coup in 1908 and was one of the original members of the transnational Kurdish political party Khoybun (literally, Be Yourself, or Independence) that was formed in Bhamdoun, Lebanon, in October 1927 by Kurdish intellectuals of aristocratic background and living in exile.

Khoybun had the close cooperation of the Armenian nationalist Dashnak Party and also enjoyed some initial support from France, particularly in the Jazira area where the French needed strong local backing to implement their own rule. Jaladet Bedir Khan served as Khoybun's first president, along with several other prominent figures. Khoybun's permanent headquarters were established in Aleppo, Syria, with French acquiescence.

Khoybun sought to establish a strong Kurdish national liberation movement with a trained fighting force that would not depend on the traditional tribal leaders although Hajo Agha, who originally had been expelled from Turkey in 1926 and was the leader of the powerful Heverkan tribal confederation of some 20 separate tribes, was also an important leader. Osman Sabri (1905-1993), who later created the first Kurdish party in Syria, the Kurdish Democratic Party in 1957, also hailed from tribal origins and had fled from Turkey. He too played an important role in Khoybun.

Most famously perhaps, Khoybun instigated the unsuccessful Ararat rebellion of the Kurds in Turkey from 1927 to 1930 under the military leadership of General Ihsan Nuri Pasha, a former commander in the Ottoman army and Kurdish negotiator during the peace conferences after World War I. Eventually, however, Iran helped Turkey crush the rebellion, while France tightened its restriction on the party in response to Turkish pressure.

Although Khoybun failed to achieve its immediate goals in Syria or Turkey, its nationalist ideology had a permanent effect on many Kurds in Syria by bringing them into belated contact with nationalist concepts already widespread among the Arabs and Turks. Thus, the Kurdish nation was cast in a primordial light as dating back to some distant point in history and merely in need of having its ancient national identity revived. Although such an essentialist view was largely a myth, Khoybun did play a constructivist role by helping to begin the process of creating or inventing Kurdish nationalism.[6] However, the failure of Khoybun's armed struggle led most Kurds in Syria to abandon it in time in favor of political and cultural activity.

Indeed, such activities had already begun before the defeat of Khoybun. In 1928, for example, five Kurds were elected to the Syrian parliament, where they lobbied for Kurdish being made the official language of the Kurdish areas in Syria and the creation of a Kurdish educational system. This proposal failed to be implemented because of the lack of qualified instructors and adequate pedagogical materials. The French also turned down a demand by these same Kurdish parliamentarians for Kurdish administrative autonomy, with the argument that the Kurds did not constitute a religious minority like the Alawites and the Druzes and because the Kurdish areas were not contiguous. A proposal to create a Kurdish humanitarian and charitable organization in Jazira failed as well.

However, Sexmus Hesen Cegerxwin (1903-1984) proved a vibrant and popular patriotic poet and Jaladet Bedir Khan established *Hawar* (The Call), a monthly journal to promote popular literature and teaching materials in Kurdish. Hajo Agha of the Heverkan tribal confederation also played a significant role in *Hawar*, publishing an article in it that was important in promoting Kurdish education among tribal leaders. He also distributed books in Kurdish to visitors at his home in Jazira, strongly encouraged the teaching of the language, and, despite his continuing tribal ties, displayed a Kurdish flag in front of his home.

In addition to treating social and cultural issues, *Hawar* also dealt with Kurdish linguistics, grammar and dialects as well as introducing a Latin script for the Kurdish language. Although *Hawar* ran only from 1932 to 1937, when the French authorities banned it, the journal played an important role in the unification of Kurdish dialects and the creation of a standardized Kurdish language. By opening up a serious dialogue among the different elements in Syrian Kurdish society, *Hawar* contributed importantly to a sense of Kurdish identity. Nevertheless, widespread Kurdish identity among Kurds in Syria remained barely nascent.

Therefore, at this point it would be useful to turn to an analysis of the failed antecedents (approximately up to 1938) of contemporary Kurdish nationalism by Martin Strohmeier. Following the failure of the Sheikh Said and Ararat rebellions in the 1920s, the Bedir Khan brothers broke completely with their residual Turkish loyalties and sought to develop, with French support in Syria, a full-blown Kurdish nationalism. In *Les Massacres Kurdes en Turquie* and *The Case of Kurdistan against Turkey* "the Turks are portrayed as having pursued throughout the whole of their co-existence with the Kurds and other races the aims of extermination and assimilation. . . . The Turks, descendants of Attila and Jingiz Khan, are an unchanging entity, barbaric and evil by nature."[7] Although "propagandistic in its simplistic, misleading, and distorted interpretations of Kurdish and Turkish history," (p. 111), "Thurayya's "[Bedir Khan's] publications had a tremendous influence on later writings on the Kurds. . . . The statistics on deportations and losses contained in his booklets as well as his equally propagandist versions of historical events were integrated into many subsequent accounts of the Kurdish national struggle" (p. 114).

On the other hand, Strohmeier concludes that, for "the progress of Kurdish identity-building as manifested in nationalist writing, we must regard [Thurayya's] . . . publications as being of seminal importance" (pp. 100-101). In addition, Bedir Khan cites the Turkish newspaper *Vakit* at length to illustrate "that the Turkish government never regarded the Said Rebellion as essentially a religious revolt [as it always claimed] and was aware that the leaders had used religion as a screen" (p. 108) for their Kurdish nationalist purposes. Nevertheless, despite these early attempts to foster a beginning sense of Kurdish nationalism, the more nationally conscious Sunni Arab majority led to the Franco-Syrian treaty of 1936 that resulted in Syrian independence as an Arab state immediately following World War II. It is to this situation that we now will turn.

Syrian Independence

During World War II, the universal promises of the Atlantic Charter regarding national self-determination initially stirred Kurdish hopes. Although Jaladet Bedir Khan was in contact with foreign representatives in Damascus while his brother Kamuran acted as a quasi Kurdish ambassador in Paris, however, the Kurds were unable to have their interests brought up when the United Nations was created in 1945 because they lacked representation as a state. (Indeed, it was not until April 1991 that the United Nations even specifically mentioned the Kurds, when, as a result of Saddam Hussein's defeat, it passed Security Council Resolution 688, which condemned "the repression of the Iraqi civilian population . . . in Kurdish populated areas.")

The first two decades of Syrian independence proved tumultuous, as numerous military coups and attempts occurred. Two short-ruling leaders of coups in 1949 actually involved principals of Kurdish origin, Colonels Husni Zaim and Adib al-Shishakli, both of whom also had as their top aide men of similar ethnic roots, Muhsen Barazi and Fawzi Selo. However, neither Zaim nor al-Shishakli emphasized his Kurdish background, spoke Kurdish, or advocated Kurdish interests. Rather both were urban, Arabic speakers who aroused little identification from the larger Kurdish population. Indeed, al-Shishakli proclaimed that Syria was a unified Arab-Muslim state, began the process of banning Kurdish organizations, dress, and signs, and even argued that demands for minority privileges amounted to treason. Kurds began to be seen as hired agents for foreign enemies of Arab nationalism.

Egypt's staunchly Arab nationalist leader Gamal Abdul Nasser actually ruled a joint entity with Syria called the United Arab Republic (UAR) from 1958 until 1961, but this period proved only a prelude to the assault against Kurdish interests that took place once Baathism came to power in the 1960s. As Jordi Tejel concluded: "From the end of the 1950s, the Syrian army would experience several purges during which Kurdish officers were expelled from it, and the military academies and the police force both closed their doors to young Kurds."[8]

The creation of the Kurdish Democratic Party in Syria (KDPS) in 1957—one of whose founders was Osman Sabri—also served as a pretext for strong measures against the Kurds. The KDPS simply asked for democracy in Syria and that the Kurds be recognized as an ethnic group. The new party also pointed to the dearth of economic progress in the Kurdish areas of Syria and how Kurds were being discriminated against for positions in the police and military. In response, the government arrested Kurdish leaders and banned Kurdish publications. In addition, although the facts were never verified, the Kurds have always thought that the hostile government was responsible for a fire that killed 283 Kurdish children in a movie theater in Amuda on November 13, 1960.[9] Thus, along with the Syrian Kurds' strategy of dissimulation or pretending to be part of the Syrian state,[10] the state's legal actions against the Kurds eventually helped lead to their becoming virtually an invisible or forgotten people, the thesis of the following section.

The Forgotten

The situation regarding the Turkish origin of some of the Syrian Kurds described above provided the Syrian government's rationale for the disenfranchisement of many of these Kurds in modern Syria. Never mind the fact that before the Sykes-Picot Agreement artificially separated the Kurds of the Ottoman Empire into three separate states after World War I (Turkey, Iraq, and Syria) all of these Kurds had lived within a single border.

Thus, following an exceptional census in 1962, Decree 93 classified some 120,000 Kurds, which at that time represented about 20 percent of the Kurdish population in Syria, as *ajanib,* or foreigners who could not vote, own property, or work in government jobs. They were issued red identity cards stating that they were not Syrian citizens. Their number has now risen to more than 300,000 since the status of *ajanib* was inherited. Some 75,000 other Syrian Kurds were also known as *maktoumeen,* or unregistered/concealed. As such, they had virtually no civil rights and thus were even worse off than the *ajanib.* For at time they were able to get unofficial "white papers" testifying to their identity from local authorities, but even this practice has now been discontinued. Their number has also grown over the years. "The lack of nationality and identity documents means that stateless Kurds, for all practical purposes, are rendered non-existent. . . . It is like being buried alive, said one man."[11]

Given the arbitrary manner in which the Syrian government established these categories, siblings from the same family and born in the same Syrian village could be listed differently. Fathers might be classified as *ajanib*, while their children remained citizens. One man asserted: "The grave of my grandfather is here in Syria; our family has been here for over 100 years, but we lost our nationality in 1962."[12] Even such Kurdish notables as General Tawfiq Nizam al-Din, once the general head of staff of the Syrian army, were deprived of their Syrian citizenship and condemned to live in a legal vacuum. They were unable to travel legally domestically or abroad (which required a passport or domestic identification card), own property, enter into a legally recognized marriage, obtain food subsidies, and vote or hold elected or appointed office.

Although Kurdish children were supposed to possess the right to primary education—albeit not in their Kurdish mother tongue—statelessness made this very difficult for those seeking to enroll in secondary schools and universities. Those who managed still found it impossible to gain employment in their trained field. *Maktoumeen* children were not given diplomas from secondary schools, which prevented them from enrolling in a university. Thus, some took to using the names of relatives who did possess Syrian nationality to attend. A young man listed as a *maktoum* earned the highest grades in his class, but, because he was not permitted to obtain a diploma upon graduation, he was unable to apply for entrance into a university.

Although *ajanib* can obtain a driver's license and cash checks, they are not allowed to have bank accounts or to receive a commercial driver's license. One *maktoum* man told how he received paychecks or signed contracts to work using the name of a friend who possessed Syrian nationality. Many others reported how companies exploited them because of their stateless situation. Public health service was also unavailable, thus forcing stateless Kurds to pay much higher costs for private services or more likely simply go without. More imaginative stateless Kurds used the identity cards of friends who still held citizenship.

Stateless Kurds who are married are considered single—which presents problems for their children and even prevents them from sharing a room in a hotel. Without nationality, Kurds are prohibited from owning property or registering a car or business. Again some register using the names of friends or relatives, an arrangement that depends on the good faith of the legal person. Despite promises to solve these problems, little was done until the civil war that began in March 2011 forced the government to reassess its attitude toward the Kurds, a situation that will be considered below.

After the nationalist, supposedly pan-Arab Baath Party came to power in 1963,[13] the Arab nationalist plan to reduce the Kurds was furthered by the creation of an Arab Belt (*al-Hizam al-Arabi*) to expropriate the Kurds from their lands along the border with Turkey and Iraq and to repopulate the area with "loyal" Arabs. (In September 1956, the discovery of oil in the region [Qarachok and

Remilan] also probably served as a motivation.) This Arab Belt was to be 6-9 miles wide and to extend some 170 miles along the Turkish border from Ras al-Ayn (Serekaniye in Kurdish) in Jazira province to the Iraqi border in the east. The dispossessed Kurds were forced either to leave Syria for Lebanon or to move into the Syrian interior. The evacuated Kurdish regions were then given Arab names in an effort to Arabize them and to further the assimilation of any remaining Kurds who had already become deprived of education. The plan was put into operation only in 1973 because of technical problems and further Arabization was finally halted in 1976 although not reversed.

In 1967, schoolbooks began omitting the mention of the Kurdish existence. A decree issued in 1977 further attempted to cleanse the Kurdish historic presence in Syria by providing for dropping non-Arabic place names. Thus, Kobane became Ain al-Arab, Serekaniye was changed to Ras al-Ayn, while Derek became Al-Malikiyah, etc. (Kurdish place names suffered even more in Turkey.) Two Decrees in 1989 (1865/S/24 and1865/S/24) prohibited the use of Kurdish in the workplace and during marriage ceremonies and festivities. Another government decree (No. 122) in September 1992 prohibited the registration of children with Kurdish first names, a policy that already had been implemented unofficially for many years. In May 2000, Resolution 768 provided that Kurdish cultural centers, bookshops, and similar activities involving the selling of cassettes, videos, and discs in the Kurdish language also be banned. More recently, on September 10, 2008, Decree 49 amended Statute 41 of October 26, 2004, that had regulated the ownership, sale, and lease of land in border regions. The Kurds saw this new decree as a tightening of the earlier Arab Belt policies that sought to dispossess them of their property.

Although these measures were not always enforced and bribes also could help Kurds sometimes get around them, the mere existence of such regulations spoke to the state's hostility. Indeed, some have suspected that, in return for giving the Kurdistan Workers

Party (PKK) of Turkey sanctuary in Syria for many years, the PKK kept the lid on Syrian Kurdish unrest. (This situation involving the PKK will be analyzed below.) As a result of all these legal provisions, little was heard about the Kurds in Syria, compared with their co-nationals in other states of the Middle East. The Kurds in Syria, in effect, had become forgotten.

In addition, Articles 10, 11, 15, and 20 of the Baath Party's constitution provided for an exclusive Arab nationalism that made any other political or even social groups not sharing this belief illegal. (Article I of the Syrian constitution mirrors these provisions by proclaiming: "The people of the Syrian Arab Region are part of the Arab Nation, who work and struggle to achieve all-embracing unity." In addition, Article 8 outlaws any other political party but the ruling Baathists and their coalition partners.) Although Michel Aflaq, one of the Baath Party founders who was ironically a Christian, recognized that there were ethnic minorities within the Arab nation, he argued that the Kurds would want to remain within the Arab purview, because being part of such a vast nation would assure their welfare. Thus, the Kurds might be tolerated as long as they accepted the Baathist concept of Arab nationalism.

In practice, however, the Baathists came to view the Kurds as a foreign group that was a menace to the Arab nation. Even more, of course, after he came to power in November 1970, Hafez al-Assad reduced the supposedly pan-Arab Baath Party to a mere facade for his own Alawite family's personal property. Thus, as mentioned above and as a result of all these legal provisions and political initiatives, little was heard about the Kurds in Syria, compared with their co-nationals in other states of the Middle East. As stated above, the Kurds in Syria, in effect, had become forgotten.

M. Talab Hilal Manuscript

The theoretical justification for these harsh, discriminatory measures was a clandestine treatise written and then published by Lieutenant Muhammad Talab Hilal, the chief of the Syrian security police in the province of Hasaka (Jazira), on November 12, 1963. The title of his manual translated into English as *National, Political, and Social Study of the Province of Jazira*. A look at some of this book's main points would be very enlightening as to why many Kurds in Syria feel alienated toward that state.[14]

- The bells of alarm in Jazira call on Arab conscience to save this region, purify it and rid it of the dirt and historical refuse [the Kurds] of history in order to preserve the riches of this Arab territory (p. 2).

- People such as the Kurds—who have no history, civilization, language, or ethnic origin—are prone to committing violence and destruction, as are all mountain people (pp. 4-5).

- The Kurdish question advanced by them has become a malignant tumor on the side of the Arab nation and must be removed (p. 6).

- They [the Kurds] are supported by the imperialists since the goals of these Middle East outlaws are similar to their goals (p. 12).

- The imperialists are trying to legitimize the Kurdish question as they legitimized that of the state of Israel (p. 14).

- The Kurdish question is the most dangerous threat to the Arab nation, especially Jazira and northern Iraq. It is evolving as the Zionist movement did before Israel was established. The Jazira Kurds tried to prevent the Syrian army from intervening on behalf of the Arab state of Iraq against [Mulla Mustafa] Barzani (p. 24).

- The Kurds of Turkey live north of the Kurdish belt of Syria. The Kurds of both countries are blood brothers, and many of their tribes are spread all over Turkey, Syria, and Iraq. They are ready on horsebacks at the frontiers for the realization of their golden dream of the Kurdish homeland, Kurdistan (pp. 24-26).

- Despite their differences, the Jazira Kurdish tribes are united and inspired by one idea, which is the Kurdish race. This one desire has given them the strength to pursue their national dream of a Kurdish homeland (pp. 26-28).

- The Kurds differ from the Arabs ethnically, psychologically, and physiologically (no page numbers listed).

- Although they do not speak an acceptable form of Arabic, the majority of the Muslim ulamas [religious leaders] in the Hasaka province are Kurds; they are conspiring to create their nation under the guise of religion (pp. 38-40).

To excise this threat of what he termed "a malignant tumor on the side of the Arab nation," Muhammed Talab Hilal recommended the creation of an Arab Belt—as mentioned above, extending some 200 miles along the Syrian-Turkish border and having a depth of 6-9 miles—in which all Kurds would be removed and replaced by Arab settlers. The Kurds would have their lands confiscated, be stripped of their citizenship, have their employment opportunities restricted, and be denied public social services, medical treatment, and schooling. Further justification for such drastic action included the ignorant claim that the Kurds "have no history, civilization, language, or ethnic origin," while also representing a threat to the Arab nation analogous to that of the Zionist movement in Israel.

Although it is correct that many (but not all) Kurds do dream of an independent Kurdistan and, as already noted above, some came to Syria from Turkey after the failed uprisings of the 1920s, the Hilal treatise ignores the fact that, as mentioned above, the borders between Turkey and Syria that now divide the Kurds were established only following World War I and thus artificially separated the Kurds similarly as many Arab nationalists have argued they also artificially separated the Arabs. In truth, Kurdish and Arab tribes had contested the Hasaka region for hundreds of years, and around the beginning of the 20th century this struggle had climaxed in a bitter conflict between Ibrahim Pasha's Kurdish Milli confederation and the powerful Arab Shammar tribe. After their arrival, the then French authorities had favored the Kurds as a way to strengthen their claims to the area. Indeed, the Terrier Plan (named for Captain Pierre Terrier) was a French proposal in the 1920s to encourage the Kurdish nationalists to concentrate their political ambitions only on Jazira (Hasaka) province and not seek to tie this with other Kurdish enclaves in Mandatory Syria.[15] In addition, the French also allowed the pan-Kurdish nationalist party, Khoybun [Independence], to operate out of Syria for several years after its creation in 1927.[16]

Even more, of course, the Kurds who had come from Turkey and were now living in Syria had been living there since the 1920s when they had been issued identity cards by the then French authorities. Thus, these Kurds were already Syrian citizens when that state became independent in 1946. Stripping them of their citizenship was a clear violation of international law regarding nationality rights in cases of state succession as well as such international legally binding human-rights doctrines as the Universal Declaration of Human Rights, International Covenant on Civil and Political Rights, Convention on the Rights of the Child, and International Convention on the Elimination of All Forms of Racial Discrimination.[17]

Kurdish Political Parties

Ironically, one might argue that the weak and fractured Kurdish political party system in Syria is another reason why the Kurds in that state were forgotten until the civil war led to their sudden emergence in July 2012. Although Khoybun, created in 1927 as a transnational Kurdish party, had lingered on until 1944, its main target had been Turkey, from where many of its members had originally come. In addition, Khoybun had focused its attention on France and Syrian nationalists, and did not see itself as a Kurdish party in Syria with a Kurdish nationalist agenda that focused mainly on Syria. Its brief-lived successor, the Kurdish League (1945-46) continued this position so as not to antagonize the authorities in Damascus.

Ironically, so many Syrian Kurds were involved with the Syrian Communist Party (SCP) during the 1930s and 1940s—seeing communism as their best strategy against Arab nationalism—that is was called the "Kurdish Party."[18] Its leader, Khalid Bakdash, was also a Kurd from Hayy al-Akrad or the Kurdish quarter in Damascus. Although some saw Bakdash as an example of an Arabized Kurd, he maintained social and political relations with Kurdish nationalists such as Rewshen Bedir Khan, the widow of Jaladet Bedir Khan, and was also able to speak Kurdish.

Thus, it was not until June 14, 1957, that the first modern Kurdish political party was formed, the Kurdish Democratic Party in Syria (KDPS). Even so, the KDPS maintained a Syrian national agenda that did not call for the liberation of a Syrian Kurdistan. Rather, it was concerned with the improvement of Kurdish socioeconomic conditions. Indeed, it is revealing that none of the numerous Kurdish parties currently use the sensitive term *Kurdistan* in their names for fear that it might incite government fears of secession. Such concerns have never troubled the Kurdish parties in Turkey, Iraq, or Iran.

Nevertheless, it was the growth of a chauvinistic Arab nationalism as well as the conclusion that Kurdish rights would not be protected by the SCP that helped lead to its formation. The previously mentioned Osman Sabri is often listed as the founder of the KDPS, although in truth this title should be shared with a number of others who in time were to split the party. The young Jalal Talabani, who often found refuge in Damascus during those days, also played an important role in the party's creation, as the Syrian Kurds were closely following the development of Kurdish nationalism in neighboring Iraq and thus were clearly influenced by such transnational events. Indeed the KDPS served as a propaganda outlet for the Kurdistan Democratic Party (KDP) in Iraq, to which Talabani still belonged and whose then leader, Mulla Mustafa Barzani, he then greatly admired and still served.

Despite this pedigree of Kurdish nationalism, Syrian political parties have never taken up arms against the government as have Kurdish parties in Iraq, Turkey, and Iran. Indeed, even during the Syrian civil war that began in 2011, the myriad of Kurdish parties hesitated to join the opposition and preferred to follow a third or middle road between the government and the opposition, as will be analyzed in a later chapter. The main reason for this strategic line was probably their greater perceived weakness, compared with their regional kin, and their lack of any accessible mountains to serve as a sanctuary.[19]

Whether because of or in spite of the Kurdish hesitancy to take it on directly, the Syrian government, newly split from Nasser's UAR and determined to maintain and build its Arab identity, renamed the state the Syrian **Arab** Republic (emphasis added) and accused the Syrian Kurds of supporting Barzani's Kurdish uprising in neighboring Iraq. Osman Sabri and Nureddin Zaza were among 32 leading members of the KDPS who were arrested in September 1962. These arrests helped Hamid Haj Darwish, a young law student, become the new leader. He too was arrested in 1965 but was released after 10 months. Other Kurds accused him of collusion with the government, a petard that has become common among the Syrian Kurdish parties.

The first formal split of the KDPS occurred in 1965, and it was split even more in 1970 between supporters of Osman Sabri on the one hand and Hamid Darwish and Nureddin Zaza on the other. Sabri wanted to continue a stronger struggle for Kurdish rights, while Darwish and Zaza argued for a softer approach. Sabri's faction kept the name Kurdish Democratic Party in Syria and became known as *el-Party* [the Party], while Darwish's faction took the name Kurdish Democratic Progressive Party in Syria. Sabri's leftist faction consisted of teachers, students, and former communists, whereas Darwish's rightist group contained notables such as urban merchants, professionals, religious leaders, and landowners. On the transnational/regional level, the former sided with Barzani's then-perceived more militant group, while the later identified with the then-seen more accommodating Talabani. The latter would later form his own Iraqi Kurdish party, the Patriotic Union of Kurdistan (PUK), which he formally declared in Damascus on June 1, 1975, after Barzani's collapse in his war against Baghdad.

Over the years a host of small political parties emerged, with more than 10 now claiming to be heirs to the original KDPS and perhaps another 5 also in existence, with each division and new nomenclature adding to the confusion and party transience. Indeed, there are even two completely separate parties using exactly the same name. Several different coalitions also exist, but with the breakout of the Syrian civil war in 2011, it was clear that the PKK-affiliated Democratic Union Party (PYD)—created only in 2003 —had suddenly emerged as by far the strongest, while the bewildering array of others loosely constituted the so-called Kurdish National Coalition (KNC).

This perplexing disunity was caused by links to different Kurdish parties outside of Syria as well as personal and traditional ties of loyalty to families and tribes. Although tactical differences were usually more important, ideological differences over such issues as the nature and scale of political activity have also contributed to this divisive milieu. Moderate/rightists favored dialogue with the government, while leftists were more inclined to favor demonstrations and similar activist approaches.[20] In addition, Jordi Tejel argues that the government's policy of selective/partial alliance or "collusive transactions" with some parties have alienated and split them from others.[21]

The situation was all the more damning for the Syrian parties, because the new kingpin PYD was not fully even a Syrian entity, given its PKK roots. All of this will be analyzed in greater detail below, but at this point it should simply be reiterated that the fractured, transient, and even obscure nature of the Syrian political parties[22] (with the exception of today's PYD, of course!) contributed to what, until the Syrian civil war broke out, was the forgotten character of the Kurds in Syria.

Prelude to Autonomy

In addition to the Syrian civil war, which broke out in March 2011, two other events served as catalyst preludes to the unexpected autonomy that suddenly was thrust on the Kurds in Syria on July 19, 2012: the Qamishli uprising (*Serhildan*) in March 2004 and the assassinations of Sheikh Mashouq Khasnawi in June 2005 and Mishaal al-Tammo on October 7, 2011.

The Qamishli Uprising (Serhildan)

On March 12, 2004, a riot broke out at a football (soccer) game in Qamishli between fans of the local Kurdish team and Sunni Arab fans of the opposing team from Dayr al-Zur to the south, eventually leading to further demonstrations throughout Kurdish areas of the country, including the Kurdish quarters of Hama, Aleppo, and Damascus. Rioters destroyed statues of Hafeez Assad as well as a number of government structures, and the security forces responded by at first killing six Kurds and eventually as many as 30-50 while arresting more than 2,000. Hundreds of others were injured.

On the second day, Qamishli witnessed thousands of people turning out for the procession to the cemetery where the six victims of the first day of riots were buried. Security forces again fired into the crowd, which led to Kurdish attacks against government buildings, the railroad station, and the toppling of Hafeez Assad's statues. The latter action was a powerful symbolic act against the regime reminiscent of what had happened to the statue of Saddam Hussein in Baghdad less than one year earlier, as well as a strong statement in a state where the ruling family was supposed to be inviolable. Word quickly spread to other Kurdish communities in Syria, including Kurdish quarters in the major cities via cell phones, and the riots escalated.

These unprecedented demonstrations and riots were not planned by the Kurdish parties, who feared a backlash and counseled restraint, but were spontaneous popular outbursts that continued until March 25 when the regime's forces finally prevailed. However, the *Serhildan* or Uprising still led to a newly found Kurdish self-awareness and pride that marked a definite turning point in the Kurdish existence within Syria and was, therefore, a momentous event around which the Kurds could subsequently rally. For the first time in the history of the Kurds in Syria, a protest movement had united all the Kurds, as well as eliciting support from the Kurds in Turkey and Iraq. Indeed, one year later, as mentioned above, Massoud Barzani, the president of the Kurdistan Regional Government (KRG), called on the Syrian government to grant the Kurds in Syria their democratic rights, a first for him, given the implicit understanding that forbade foreign Kurdish criticism of Damascus in return for sanctuary.

According to Kurdish sources, the supporters of the visiting Sunni Arab team started the initial riots by chanting insults against the Iraqi Kurdish leaders Barzani and Talabani, while flaunting portraits of Saddam Hussein. Kurdish fans responded by chanting praises of US President George W. Bush. Arab supporters used knives, stones, and sticks, thus escalating the clashes onto the streets of Qamishli.

However, other sources claimed that, at a match in Dayr al-Zur two weeks earlier, some Kurdish fans had provoked the Sunni Arab fans by cursing Saddam Hussein and showing support for the recently promulgated Transnational Administrative Law or draft constitution for post-Saddam Iraq that formally recognized the Kurdistan Regional Government (KRG). In addition, of course, *Newroz*, the Kurdish New Year's Day celebration, also falls in March and often acts as a catalyst for protests. Further reports indicated, therefore, that the regime was in a state of high alert and had mobilized security forces. If so, however, why did the state then allow the second football match in Qamishli even to be held?

In June 2005, yet another event galvanized the Kurds in Syria and led to further demonstrations: the disappearance and murder of Sheikh Mashouq Khasnawi. Khasnawi was a Kurdish Sufi leader who had demanded justice and political reform for the Kurds. Although the regime claimed that he had been killed by a criminal gang, many Kurds believed that the state had perpetrated the deed. Large demonstrations consisting of as many as 25,000 people chanting slogans for Kurdish autonomy were held at his funeral in Qamishli, resulting in the security forces killing several more protesters. Sheikh Khasnawi quickly became a new iconic symbol of martyrdom in the emerging Syrian Kurdish nationalist narrative. The prelude was set for a more powerful and emboldened Kurdish identity and initiatives.

The Syrian Civil War

It is difficult to write conclusively about an ongoing event such as the Syrian civil war, which began in March 2011 as a struggle over socioeconomic conditions and a fight for democracy, but quickly metastasized into a regional and even global proxy conflict. The resulting violence and deaths led both sides to the security dilemma conclusion that they would be safe only if the other were eradicated. Thus, a popular uprising against a dictator had become entangled with a life-or-death domestic sectarian struggle that now raged between Sunnis and Alawites; a proxy regional conflict between Shiite Iran, Iraq, and Hezbollah against Sunni Turkey, Saudi Arabia, and Qatar; and on the international plane, a renewal of the Cold War struggle between the United States and its NATO allies against Russia and China. There was also an element of the absurd involved, with al-Qaeda–affiliated groups such as Jabhat al-Nusra or Al-Nusra Front and the Islamic State of Iraq and Syria (ISIS)— also formerly known as al-Qaeda of Iraq, but by the end of 2013 split from al-Qaeda—supposedly being allied with the democratic Syrian opposition, thus enabling Assad and his supporters to be able to claim that they were defending secular values prized in the West against Islamic terrorist groups.

By the April 2015, more than 200,000 persons had been killed, many more had been injured, and over 2 million had become refugees who had crossed the borders into Turkey, Lebanon, Jordan, and Iraq. Meanwhile within Syria there were at least 2 million Internally Displaced Persons (IDPs), roughly 8 million more in need of humanitarian aid, and one third of the housing stock damaged or destroyed.[23] By July 2013, according to one respected source, the Syrian economy had shrunk 35 percent since the civil war had begun, unemployment had increased fivefold, the Syrian currency had decreased to one sixth of its earlier value, while the public sector had lost $15 billion.[24] For a long time, it seemed to most observers that the Assad regime's days were numbered. After all the Arab Spring had already washed away the dictators in Tunisia, Egypt, and Libya. Practically every week seemed to bring new advances for the rebels to the extent that on July 19, 2012, the regime suddenly decided virtually to abandon the Kurdish areas of

Syria in the north along the Turkish border in a desperate effort to consolidate and husband its remaining resources to retain what it still held. As we have already seen, this decision enabled the Kurds to emerge out of nowhere and assume a de facto autonomy that will be analyzed below.

However, the viewpoint that the Assad regime was ready to collapse was probably misleading. For one thing, in contrast to the other regimes that had fallen, Damascus was able to mobilize civil servants, trade unionists, business groups, Islamists, and other supporters such as Baath Party members as well as minorities and pro-regime nationalists. YouTube videos of victorious opposition fighters capturing military strong points and weapons gave the false impression that the regime was on the ropes. As the rebellion continues well into a fifth year, however, it has become clear that the reality is that no one is winning a quick victory. The Syrian civil war will more likely play out as did the extended civil war in Lebanon and the continuing fighting in Iraq.

How has the regime managed to hold on? Strong support from Iran, Hezbollah, Russia and to a lesser extent (now Shiite) Iraq is probably the main factor, especially when countered against the lesser support, especially in troops and heavy equipment, the opposition has been receiving from the United States and its NATO allies, Turkey, Qatar, Saudi Arabia, and the United Arab Emirates.

Iran has been key to the regime's survival. The two have had a strategic alliance since the Islamic Republic first came to power. As soon as the Syrian civil war began, Iran sent arms, technical support, and its Revolutionary Guards to protect its only Arab ally and also to keep supply lines open to its Shiite ally Hezbollah in neighboring Lebanon.[25] Despite its own economic problems created by Western-imposed sanctions, Iran also granted Syria a $1 billion import credit line in January 2013. Iraq too has sent Shiite militants to help Assad, while also permitting Iranian planes to ship military supplies to Syria over Iraqi airspace.[26] The Iraqi foreign minister, Hoshyar Zibari, who ironically happened to be a Kurd, said that there was nothing he could do to stop it.

At the end of April 2013, Hassan Nasrallah, the leader of the powerful Shiite party/militia Hezbollah in Lebanon, reversed his earlier pronouncements on the subject and declared that his militia would aid Syria "with its full organizational might" and would not allow it to "fall into the hands of America, Israel or *takfiri* groups," the latter a reference to such al-Qaeda affiliated Sunni fundamentalist organizations as al-Nusra.[27] A few months earlier, Hezbollah fighters had already helped to turn the tide of struggle for Qusayr, a town near the Lebanese-Syrian border some 20 miles south of Homs. Along with Iran, Hezbollah too has proven a staunch ally of the Assad regime.

Many think that Russia has been Assad's greatest supporter.[28] Indeed, Russia has had a strong relationship with Syria since the 1950s. In 2010, Russian exports to Assad's regime were more than $1.1 billion, while its investments were almost $20 billion. Russia's only military base in the Mediterranean is at the Syrian port of Tartus. By supporting Syria, Russia also counters what it views as unrestricted United States/NATO influence in the Middle East. Therefore, on three occasions, Russia has used its veto in the UN Security Council to prevent an anti-Assad resolution. Some have also explained Russia's support as necessary to stop Islamist revolutions before they reach the Caucasus and other Muslim areas of Russia, which has already suffered greatly from past events in Chechnya. Thus, Syria has obtained most of its military equipment such as tanks, missiles, and antiaircraft missile batteries from Russia. Russian suppliers have upgraded Syria's air defense systems since the civil war broke out and even manned some of them.

In addition to Assad's foreign supporters, his opposition is fractured to the extent that some of its elements battle each other as well as Damascus. The so-called Free Syrian Army (FSA) is nothing of the sort, merely a notional concept of several different often conflicting groups. The new National Coalition for Syrian Revolutionary and Opposition Forces that was created on November 12,

2012, in Doha, Qatar, has proven to be splintered as thoroughly as was the Syrian National Council (SNC) it replaced. When Moaz al-Khatib, the new Coalition's president announced his willingness to meet with Assad in February 2013, his hardline associates rejected his proposal even before the regime did: "The opposition didn't even give us time to reject Moaz," joked a regime supporter.[29]

At times, the opposition has proven radical, criminal, and even incompetent, as well as riddled by fundamentalist groups openly allied with al-Qaeda and by 2014 the even more radical ISIS. One YouTube video showed an opposition soldier eating the heart and liver of a dead Syrian army soldier, a disgusting act of cannibalism not well calculated to win over more moderate support of, for instance, the minorities and members of the urban elite who might have otherwise turned against the regime.[30] On March 24, al-Khatib, the moderate leader of the Syrian National Coalition, resigned, declaring that, since the Coalition was controlled by foreign powers such as Saudi Arabia and Qatar, it had lost the ability to decide for itself. His successor has had a similar lack of success.

What is more, the regime's strategy of pulling back from exposed outposts has enabled it to enjoy more defensible interior lines. Well into its fifth year, the opposition has been able to capture only two of 16 provincial capitals in Syria, Raqqah in the east, which of course serves as the capital of ISIS, and Idlid in the northwest, which fell to al-Nusra in March 2015. In addition, with the counter-insurgency help of Hezbollah and Iranian advisers, the regime has restructured its forces by training a militia of 60,000 called the National Defense Force to protect positions that earlier tied down the regular army, which is now freed to launch counterattacks. Basically, however, the regime is concentrating on retaining strategic areas and not trying to recapture the entire country and overwhelm the opposition, a scenario that appears to be well beyond its capacity.[31]

In addition, the opposition—which consists of a huge *lumpen* underclass that has been subjected to such extreme forms of regime violence that it believes (probably with good reason) that surrender would lead to its death—is not likely to give up short of suffering a total defeat and even then would probably continue the conflict on a lesser guerrilla level. Similarly, the regime's supporters also feel that it is either kill or be killed. Thus, it appears that the Syrian civil war will continue well into the future. If so, Syria is likely to descend into the ranks of a failed state consisting of pockets of various embattled militias and statelets. And the longer this takes, the more likely Kurdish autonomy will become regularized and therefore institutionalized. However, before turning to this situation, one more prelude to it will be analyzed.

Mishaal Tammo's Assassination

As the civil war in Syria grew, Mishaal Tammo (1957-2011), the widely respected 53-year-old leader (speaker) of the Syrian "Kurdish Future Movement" and also a member of the executive committee of what was then the recently formed, broadly based opposition Syrian National Council (SNC), was assassinated in Qamishli, Syria, on October 7, 2011. His wife and one of his six children were also injured in the attack. Tammo was attending a political meeting when the attack occurred. The assassination obviously held implications for the developing situation in Syria, especially for the Kurds. Who was responsible and why did they do it? What were the implications?

Following Tammo's assassination, 50,000 demonstrators took to the streets in Qamishli for his funeral. It was perhaps the largest demonstration in the Kurdish areas since the Arab Spring uprising against Assad had begun in March 2011. Security forces killed six of the demonstrators. Other large demonstrations took place in the suburbs of Aleppo, Latakia, and Hasaka. Smaller protests were held before the Syrian embassies in Berlin, Vienna, London, and

Syria's permanent mission to the United Nations in Geneva. Other protests in sympathy for Tammo were staged in Britain, France, and the Netherlands, leading to speculation that a real turning point had been reached in favor of Kurdish unity in Syria and support for the uprising against the regime. Ironically, therefore, the embattled Assad government had only recently rescinded the notorious Decree 93 passed in 1962, which had denied citizenship to approximately 120,000 Kurdish *ajanib* (stateless) and another 75,000 Syrian Kurds known as *maktoumeen* (concealed). As the famous French scholar Alexis de Tocqueville once observed, revolutions seldom start when things are at their worst, but rather when they are getting better.

In the event, Mishaal Tammo's assassination did not lead to an immediate Syrian Kurdish unity as such but would probably occur only as a gradual process. However, one still must conclude that his assassination served as a prelude that enabled the Kurds to seize the opportunity that soon was presented to them when the embattled Assad regime decided to precipitously pull its troops out of the Kurdish areas in the country's north in order to better defend what it still possessed to the south.

Autonomy

From being merely a sleepy unimportant backwater in the Kurdish struggle, Syria has suddenly graduated to being not only a burgeoning center of newly empowered Kurdish nationalism, but even more importantly a major flash point in the regional geopolitical situation. How did this occur?

As mentioned above, the Arab Spring revolt that broke out against the long-ruling Assad family in March 2011 quickly involved not only the many different groups within Syria, but also most of the surrounding states and parties, as each perceived the Syrian outcome as potentially bearing a most important impact on its own future. Turkey feared that the violence would spill over its borders[32] and further inflame its own Kurdish problems, especially as the PKK-affiliate *Partiya Yekitiya Demokratic* (PYD) or Democratic Union Party headed by Salih Muslim (Mohammed) in Syria began to gain influence. The Syrian civil war was beginning to blur the border artificially dividing the Kurds since the end of World War I.

To meet this threat, Turkey supported the oppositional Syrian National Council (SNC), recreated after November 2012 as the National Coalition of Syrian Revolutionary and Opposition Forces or simply Syrian National Coalition. However, such Turkish support scared the Kurds in Syria away from backing the opposition, as Turkey clearly had no interest in empowering the Syrian Kurds in a post-Assad Syria. The PYD especially argued this point. Furthermore, the Syrian Kurds did not trust any prospective Sunni Arab government that might succeed Assad to grant or protect Kurdish rights. As Salih Muslim told this author, "the mentality of Arabs cannot accept the Kurds as a nation."[33] For this reason most Kurdish parties including the PYD chose not to join either the SNC or its Coalition successor.

Shiite Iran, of course, felt its very future threatened if its main ally in the Middle East went down. Similarly, newly Shiite-ruled Iraq also felt a need to support Alawite- (a sect akin to the Shiites) ruled Syria. Lebanon's nonstate, but still very influential (Shiite) Hezbollah also supported Assad. The Sunni-ruled Kurdistan Regional Government (KRG) in Iraq, however, opposed Assad, whose earlier anti-Kurdish record had been abysmal. The KRG's support for the Syrian opposition allied it with its new ally Turkey but against the Kurdistan Workers Party (PKK) and its related Syrian affiliate the PYD, which in part implicitly supported Assad since they feared Turkish control of the Syrian opposition. Thus, even the Kurds in Syria were divided among themselves between the much stronger PYD and its various affiliates, such as the People's Council of Western Kurdistan (PCWK) and the Kurdish National Council (KNC), which consisted of most of the other 12-15 odd Kurdish parties in Syria. Such Kurdish divisions in Syria, however, were not novel.

Nevertheless, in July 2012 KRG president Massoud Barzani managed to patch together a tenuous umbrella Supreme Kurdish Council out of the various Syrian Kurdish groups at a gathering held in Irbil. At the same time Barzani sought to further extend his influence among the Syrian Kurds by providing military training to some 600-2,000 who had fled to his jurisdiction from Syria.[34] Sunni-ruled states such as Saudi Arabia and Jordan also supported the Syrian opposition. As for Lebanon, the gallows humor had it that this notoriously divided state so closely connected to Syria was not being mentioned yet because it already had a bye into the final apocalypse. Israel, with an obvious interest in the Syrian outcome, probably also possessed a bye into the finals.

Outside the region, the United States and the EU cautiously supported the opposition, while Russia and China continued to support and even supply Assad because they did not want to set an unfortunate precedent for the international community to intervene in a state for human rights violations that might come back to haunt them for their own misdeeds. Russia also supported Assad as a way to prevent perceived United States/NATO domination in the Middle East,[35] among other reasons discussed above. The result was that not only was international cooperation on what to do about the Syrian situation impossible to achieve, but even more the whole affair had the potential to escalate into a regional war.

The Rise of Salih Muslim and the PYD

Salih Muslim (born in 1951, married with five children, a chemical engineer, and fluent in English) became active in the Kurdish movement during the 1970s while he was an engineering student at Istanbul Technical University and due to the influence of Mulla

Mustafa Barzani's revolt in Iraq. Upon graduation, Salih Muslim worked as an engineer in Saudi Arabia, returning to Syria only in the 1990s. In 1998, he joined the well-established Kurdistan Democratic Party of Syria, but he quit in 2003 because of what he saw as its lack of success. He then joined the newly created *Partiya Yekitiya Demokratic* (PYD) or Democratic Union Party that had been created in 2003—largely from the remnants of the PKK that Hafez Assad had expelled from Syria in October 1998—and became a member of its executive council.

Dr. Fuad Omar (born in Damascus in 1962), however, was chosen as the new party's first leader at its second conference and served in this role until 2010. Although Fuad Omar claimed to accept the militant philosophy of Abdullah Ocalan's PKK, he also incongruously maintained that "we do not believe in violence and solving issues through military means."[36] Nevertheless, by 2008, Fuad Omar had been sentenced to prison and was living in exile in Belgium.

Thus, Salih Muslim became the *serok* or president of the PYD only in 2010, despite being in prison for 2 or 3 months every year since 2003. However, he was soon forced to flee from his Syrian home to Iraqi Kurdistan, where he lived in a camp maintained by the PYD and PKK. For whatever reasons, the Assad regime allowed him to return to Syria in April 2011 just after the civil war broke out. He quickly became the most visible spokesman of the rejuvenated PYD. On June 16, 2012, he was reelected as PYD's cochair at its extraordinary fifth party congress, while a woman, Asia Abdullah, was chosen as the other cochair. However, Salih Muslim remained the party's primary representative.

Salih Muslim currently plays a complicated, but potentially important role in the Syrian uprising against Bashar Assad that has been raging since March 2011. Some argue that in effect Salih Muslim's PYD has become *Shabiha* (thuggish militiamen of Assad) unlike the other 12-15 or so odd Kurdish groups in Syria.[37] Indeed, as mentioned above, Assad's late father Hafez Assad

(d. 2000) long granted the PKK a virtual alliance and safe house in Syria until Turkey's threat to go to war in 1998 forced Assad to sign the Adana Agreement under which Syria finally expelled the PKK.

However, once Turkey began supporting the Syrian Arab Spring uprising against Assad in 2011, the Syrian regime apparently began playing the PKK card again against Turkey by inviting Salih Muslim back and allowing him to operate relatively freely.[38] Assad had already sought to appease the Syrian Kurds—who at maybe 2.2 million constitute the largest ethnic minority in Syria—by lifting long-running restrictions against them. In this newly found role Salih Muslim has strongly opposed Turkish influence on the opposition Syrian National Council (SNC), its successor the National Coalition of Syrian Revolutionary and Opposition Forces, and the Kurdish National Council (KNC), regarding them as lackeys of Turkey and other outside forces.[39] Indeed, he once went so far as to state that Turkey, the supporter of the SNC, was a greater enemy than Assad.[40]

As a result, the PYD was the only Syrian Kurdish party that boycotted the 11-party KNC opposition conference held in the KRG capital of Irbil in January 2012 under the auspices of KRG president Massoud Barzani. As already noted, Barzani has been working closely with Turkey in recent years to improve the economic and political position of the KRG and also, at the behest of Turkey, pressuring the PKK to come to a settlement with Turkey. Thus, the PKK, as the enemy of Turkey, has not been on good terms with Barzani. This is all the more so, given Salih Muslim's position that Barzani supports the KNC, which is supported by Turkey to the detriment of the true interests of the Syrian Kurds. Accordingly, Salih Muslim declared: "We see that this effort by the Kurdistan President [Barzani] for reconciliation in Syria will lead to the disintegration of [the] Syrian Kurds."[41] These strained ties between the PYD and Barzani's KRG are not likely to improve in the near future.

The following month (February 2012), Salih Muslim also declined to attend the SNC's Friends of Syria conference held in Tunisia that brought together representatives of some 60 states and numerous Syrian opposition groups. Thus, Salih Muslim's actions have served to further fracture Kurdish unity in Syria and to oppose Turkish aid to the Syrian opposition, actions that have helped Assad continue to survive. Salih Muslim's dealings have also made it more difficult for the United States and other Western states to effectively support the Syrian opposition. However, Salih Muslim denies any support for Assad and can point to members of his PYD being detained by the Syrian regime and his own denunciations of the regime.[42] Thus, the alliance between Salih Muslim's PYD and Assad is more implicit and only partial.

With its military wing the *Yekineyen Parastina Gel* (YPG),[43] or Peoples Defense Units, and its female affiliate the *Yekineyen Parastina Jin* (YPJ), or Women's Defense Units, the PYD has become the largest, best-armed, and most-disciplined Syrian Kurdish party. One of the PYD's weaknesses, however, might be the traditional PKK inclination his PYD has inherited to either be the unchallenged leader of the Kurds and thus reluctant to join in any alliance of equals or to go it alone. Indeed, the so-called Supreme Kurdish Council Barzani tenuously had patched together between the PYD and the KNC in July 2012 seemed to be unraveling by October 2012. Furthermore, at the end of October 2012, 30 people were reported killed in Aleppo as a result of fighting between the PYD and the Free Syrian Army (FSA), the supposed military arm of the SNC.[44]

This supposed Kurdish fighting against the Free Syrian Army (FSA)—with a few exceptions—was really against Salafists[45] or Jihadists, who were Sunni Muslim extremists waging a violent struggle to achieve an ideal Islamic society and were only loosely connected to the FSA, which itself was becoming more of merely a loosely coordinated umbrella collection of even hostile groups. Increasingly, one was hearing now more about individual militias and brigades as being Assad's opposition instead of the military FSA and the political SNC. Even so, however, to a large extent the PYD saw the FSA as Turkey's hireling army, whereas the FSA viewed the PYD as a proxy for the Assad regime. The creation of the National Coalition of Syrian Revolutionary and Opposition Forces in November 2012 to replace the moribund SNC did not solve these difficulties. Even more, however, conflict among the Syrian Kurds themselves threatened, given the divisions between the PYD and the KNC.[46]

Intra-Kurdish Fighting

Even before the Syrian civil war and current intra-Kurdish infighting, the Syrian Kurdish Democratic Concord Party (SKDCP) or *Wifaq* had split from the PYD in 2004. This schism soon led to violence. Kamal Shahin, the new party's founder and a former PYD leader, was murdered by PKK militants on February 17, 2005, and Kamuran Muhammad was murdered in August 2005. Nadeem Yusif managed to escape a similar fate in September 2005. Kamal Shahin's assassins were apprehended and sentenced in Sulaymaniya in Iraqi Kurdistan. The PYD accused *Wifaq* members of collaborating with Damascus against them.[47] *Rekeftin* (Reconciliation), led by Fawzi Shingali, represented another small party that split from the PYD in 2004. It still exists but plays only a very marginal role.

Further intra-Kurdish fighting involving the PYD occurred in March and April 2013. The PYD claimed the right to hold a monopoly on the use of force and that no rival militias would be allowed. However, the Jabhat al-Akrad [a Kurdish unit headed by Haji Ahmed Kurdi in the FSA], Salah al-Din Brigade [mainly from Afrin], and Mishaal Tammo Battalion [consisting of army defectors], were small, additional Kurdish militias loosely associated with the FSA and also battling the Salafists.[48] The Kurdistan Democratic Party (KDP) of Massoud Barzani accused the PYD of being involved in killings, arrests, and kidnappings of members of other Kurdish parties.[49] On May 18, 2013 the PYD's *Asayesh* or security forces arrested 74 members of the Democratic Party of Syria, who had undergone training in the KRG by the KDP. Then at the end of June the PYD killed at least six other Kurds and injured many more in the city of Amuda, just west of Qamishli. The PYD also detained dozens more and burned down youth and cultural centers of the rival Kurdish Yekiti and Azadi parties.

Kurdish opponents of the PYD chanted: "He who kills his people is a traitor." The opposing Kurdish KNC charged that the PYD was trying to impose its authority on Kurds who did not want to accept it and even accused the PYD of working with the Assad regime by protecting landing sites in nearby Kobane used by the regime's helicopters. Even the US State Department condemned the PYD's actions. Less than two weeks later, a group of Kurdish intellectuals held another anti-PYD protest in Qamishli; the PYD responded with sticks and knives.[50] In August 2013, Siamend Hajo, an employee of the independent KurdWatch in Berlin, who had been closely covering the PYD, was threatened with death for his criticism of its human rights abuses.[51]

Despite these problems, Salih Muslim responded via email to this author that "I would like to state that the Kurdish Forces (YPG and Asayish) are in [a] self defence position [and] they never attacked the others."[52] In a wide-ranging interview he held earlier in November 2011,[53] Salih Muslim blamed Turkey for spreading rumors that he was behind several recent assassinations of various other Kurdish leaders in Syria, such as Mishaal Tammo, who, as analyzed above, was assassinated in October 2011.

Salih Muslim, however, readily did admit that "we apply Apo's [the imprisoned PKK leader Abdullah Ocalan] philosophy and ideology to Syria." The PYD leader continued by declaring that "we have put forth a project: 'democratic autonomy.'" This term, of course, comes right out of Ocalan's latest books published in

English.[54] Salih Muslim elaborated that "we as the Kurdish Freedom Movement . . . reject classical models like federalism, confederalism, self-government, and autonomy," explaining that "our goal is the formation of a new Kurdish society, the formation of a free person, a person with free will. . . . The point is to renew society from the bottom up."[55]

Salih Muslim also demanded "the constitutional recognition of the Kurds as a second ethnicity in Syria." Although this demand might make Assad think twice about his tactical ally, Salih Muslim further claimed that "the PYD has opened Kurdish cultural centers and language schools. . . . We are profiting from the unrest." However, he also criticized the opposition Syrian National Council for signing an agreement with Turkey: "We consider anyone who does not publicly take a stand against the Turkish position to be one of Turkey's henchmen."[56] In a later text conversation,[57] Salih Muslim cited the cryptic proverb that "a wise enemy is better than an ignorant friend" to explain how the Assad regime viewed him and why the PYD sometimes seemed to be cooperating with the Syrian regime.

To explain the PYD's newfound strength, Azad Muhiyuddin, a member of the Movement of the Youth in the West (apparently an allusion to the Kurds living in Syria constituting Western Kurdistan) said that "they [the PYD] have taken on the conflicts that the [other Kurdish] parties [in Syria] have been waging for more than forty years. . . . The PYD is trying to show the people that it represents the interests of the Kurds. . . . They offer numerous services and are active in social welfare. . . . Thus the people are joining those who do things for them.[58] Even more important to explain the relative strength of the PYD, of course, is that it is armed while the KNC is still largely not.

Although it is difficult to see clearly through the complexity that is Syria today, Salih Muslim's PYD is likely to continue to grow in strength within the multifaceted Kurdish movement in Syria, because the other Kurdish parties are so divided and therefore weak. In addition, Salih Muslim has the proven organizational skills of the PKK behind him. If Turkey were to intervene in Syria, it would face the possibility of the PYD leading vigorous Kurdish opposition as part of those Syrian nationalists who inevitably would oppose such outside interference. The same would apply to any intervention from Barzani's KRG. Finally, Salih Muslim also has positioned himself in the morass of Syrian politics so as to have connections with both the Assad regime and its opposition. Thus, if either side ultimately wins in Syria, Salih Muslim's PYD is likely to still be standing.

De Facto Syrian Kurdish Autonomy

Although the immediate active momentum from the Qamishli (*Serhildan*) uprising in March 2004 soon petered out, newly formed youth groups independent from the traditional political parties as well as local coordination committees (LCCs) continued the spirit of discontent. These included the Kurdish Youth Movement, the Union of Kurdish Youth Coordination, the Kurdish Youth Union, and the Avahi Union, among others. These youth committees established a nonhierarchical, democratic administrative structure that proved viable.

During its third party congress in 2007, the PYD established a Central Coordinating Committee (CCC) as a governing body with 11 members (increased to 24 in August 2012 during the fourth party congress) with political, youth, cultural, and women's departments, among others. The CCC also coordinated the work of People's Local Committees (PLCs) or local governance bodies. Equally important, the PYD also established its own militia, the YPG that was mentioned above. Thus, even before the civil war broke out in March 2011, the PYD had begun to project an image as concerned and able, compared with other Kurdish parties.

Then on July 19, 2012, as previously noted, the Assad regime suddenly pulled most of its troops and authority out of the Kurdish regions of northeastern Syria, which lie just below Turkey's southern border, to concentrate on holding its position in the heartland of the country.[59] Kobane (Ayn al-Arab) proved to be the first city occupied by the PYD, followed in short order by Amuda and Afrin the following day. On July 21, YPG forces took Derik (al-Malikyah) and a day later Serekaniye (Ras al-Ayn) and Dirbesi (al-Darbasiyah). By the beginning of August 2012, PYD forces occupied most Kurdish cities, with the exception of Qamishli and Hasaka, which, however, also had considerable numbers of Arabs, among other groups residing there. The speed with which all this occurred led to speculation that there was an agreement between the regime and the PYD. Indeed, on April 7, 2011, Decree 49 already had granted long-sought-for citizenship to the *ajanib.*

This situation, of course, allowed the emerging PYD governmental structures greater room to grow. De facto PYD autonomy continued to develop after the civil war had begun when, on December 12, 2011, the PYD created the Peoples Council of Western Kurdistan (PCWK) as an elected local assembly of 320 members with executive and legislative branches to provide social services and a modicum of authority in places undergoing anarchy and violence because of the civil war. The PCWK has local representatives such as mayors throughout Syrian Kurdistan, including the Kurdish quarter in Aleppo, to carry out the work of municipalities instead of the Assad regime. In addition, the PYD confusingly formed local, self-organized civilian structures under the label of the *Tevgera Civaka Demokratik* (TEV-DEM), or the Movement for a Democratic Society and also known as the Democratic Popular Movement. Also still operating in September 2013, the Supreme Kurdish Council was yet another entity that supposedly sought to achieve administrative coordination between the PYD and the other Kurdish parties. All this seemingly overlapping and bewildering proliferation of institutional forms, however, gave the PYD an enormous edge over the other political parties in organizational strength and effectiveness.

In addition, these various bodies the PYD has created in Syria to supposedly begin implementing grassroots democracy only pretend to include the local population; in practice they decide little. The PKK leadership in the Qandil Mountains and Abdullah Ocalan in Imrali are the ones who really rule through various PKK/PYD commanders responsible for different areas. For example, as of September 2013, Shahin Cello from Kobane was reportedly the commander-in-chief of all military units of the PYD/YPG in Syria. Formerly, he was a member of the PKK central committee and a leading PKK operative in Europe.[60] Nevertheless, this proliferation of governmental institutions led to comparisons with how the KRG had been initially created back in 1991. Initially strongest in Afrin (Kurd Dagh) in the west, the PYD also now began to show strength in the far eastern province of Hasaka or Jazira.

The resulting Syrian Kurdish autonomy caused great apprehension in Turkey, because suddenly PKK flags were flying just across its southern border with Syria; what had been just 500 miles of border with Kurdistan (the KRG) had overnight metastasized into one of 750 miles. A second or even pan-Kurdish state seemed possible. Ankara feared that this newly won Kurdish Syrian position would serve as an unwanted model for Turkey's own disaffected Kurds and the PKK. Turkey also feared that the Syrian Kurdish autonomous area bordering the KRG might seek to unite with the KRG and form for Turkey the nightmare of a pan-Kurdish state. Thus, Turkey hoped that its influence over the Syrian opposition and the KRG would help to control pan-Kurdish ambitions.

The earliest incidents of Kurdish-FSA (actually Salafists or Sunni Muslim extremists) fighting actually had already occurred at the end of June and the beginning of July 2012 in the city of Afrin in the northeastern area of the country known as Kurd Dagh. By October 2012, fighting between the two sides was continuing in the west and also began in Serekaniye. Confusingly, regime air strikes also took place here at the same time. In addition, PYD clashes occurred against other Kurdish groups, particularly the

Yekiti party. However, at this point, the analysis will turn to the al-Qaeda–affiliated Jabhat al-Nusra and its struggle against the regime, which, however, also involves the Kurds.

Jabhat al-Nusra

Jabhat al-Nusra (The Victory or Liberation Front) in general grew out of the Jihadist/Salafist radical Islamic movements spawned by al-Qaeda, and specifically out of Abu Musab al-Zarqawi's al-Qaeda in Iraq (AQI) force that fought the United States in Iraq during its horrific civil war following the overthrow of Saddam Hussein. Ironically, the Assad regime had helped to sponsor AQI as a way to confront the United States, so when its immediate successors turned on Assad in his hour of need it was a classic case of blowback. (The US support for Jihadist groups in Afghanistan during the 1980s also led to blowback against the United States on the part of the Taliban and al-Qaeda after September 2011.)

Joined by Jihadists from other countries in the Middle East (especially Saudi Arabia, Libya, Tunisia, Egypt, Jordan, Lebanon, and Iraq, among others), Europe (Britain, France, and Belgium, among others), and even—in smaller numbers—the Caucasus (Chechnya), south Asia, and North America, these radicals entered the porous borders of Syria through border gates from Turkey (Tel Abyad/Gire Spi) and Iraq (Tel Kochar) to announce al-Nusra's creation on January 23, 2012. Its leader, Abu Mohammad al-Golani, swore allegiance to al-Qaeda's leader, Ayman al-Zawahiri,[61] but offered only cooperation with the Islamic State of Iraq and al-Sham [Syria] (ISIS), which will be analyzed in a separate chapter below, given its subsequent importance. Despite several other Jihadists and secular organizations, al-Nusra quickly earned a reputation for being one of the most militarily effective of all the anti-Assad rebel groups. The United States, the United Kingdom, Australia, and the United Nations, among others, responded by officially stamping al-Nusra as a terrorist organization.

Al-Nusra's reputed goal was to overthrow the infidel (Alawite) Assad regime—which it viewed as *takfiri* or apostates to Islam—and to create a pan-Islamic state under sharia law and a new Sunni caliphate. These militants also saw their fellow Sunni brothers being slaughtered by the Assad regime and victory in Syria as a base for eventually retaking al-Quds (Jerusalem) and the al-Aqsa Mosque. They quickly combined their battlefield prowess with providing social services that enabled them to win over some of the local population whose territory they seized.

The new organization contained a hierarchy of religious bodies, with a small *majlis or shura* (council) at the top. Each region also had its own emir, commander, and/or sheikh. It referred to the United States and Israel as its enemies and, in contrast to its supposed secular allies in the FSA, warned against Western intervention in Syria.

Al-Nusra was estimated to have approximately 5000 members with a structure that varied across Syria. Most of the new organization's fighting was against the regime; in Aleppo and Hasaka, where it also fell into conflict with the Kurds, it was organized into conventional military lines of units divided into brigades and regiments. Although al-Nusra supposedly constituted part of the FSA, in practice it operated largely independently and seemed bent on eventually hijacking what had started out as a democratic, secular revolution. Secularists, for example, accused al-Nusra of committing numerous atrocities against captured fighters and civilians, but the Jihadists/Salafists retorted that they did not target civilians, and they actually brought medical supplies to those places they occupied. However, one FSA leader declared that "we are not fighting Bashar al-Assad to go from living in an autocratic to religious prison."[62] Thus, one could easily foresee al-Nusra turning against its supposed secular allies in the FSA when the opportunity presented itself.

Fighting vs. Kurds

Although historically there have been ultra-Islamic Kurdish sufi orders, there is an old maxim that, compared with a nonbeliever, a Kurd is a good Muslim. This is largely true because Kurds have mostly seen Muslim Arabs deny Kurdish rights. In other words, most Kurds are more nationalist and secular than religious and are thus not prone to adopt Salafist positions.

The earliest incidents of Kurdish fighting against Jihadist/ Salafist groups such as al-Nusra actually occurred before the regime even pulled its troops out of most Kurdish cities on July 19, 2012. Thus, at the end of June and the beginning of July 2012 in the city of Afrin, in the northwestern area of the country known as Kurd Dagh, and also in the Kurdish neighborhood of Ashrafieh in Aleppo, hostilities had already broken out as al-Nusra came into contact with the local, secular-minded Kurds. The latter saw the Jihadists/Salafists as thugs acting on behalf of neighboring Turkey, which was seeking to quash Kurdish influence in northern Syria and to allay its fears of a breakaway Kurdish state on its southern border, while the former viewed the Kurds as de facto allies of the despised Assad regime and *takfiri* or apostates to Islam. By October 2012, fierce fighting between the two sides was also occurring in the west, where it began in Serekaniye, Syria's northernmost city,[63] and continued until a tenuous cease-fire occurred in February 2013. Clashes also took place in Tel Abyad (Gire Spi), Qamishli, and Tel Tamr, also near the Turkish border, as well as in the city of Hasaka.

In areas under their control, al-Nusra and other Jihadists/ Salafists hastened to impose their reactionary vision of Islam, including enforcing fasting, threatening women to wear the hijab (head scarf), kidnapping civilians, and enforcing shariah (Islamic law) without considering the local diversity and cultures of the Kurds with whom they were interacting. Indeed the Jihadists/ Salafists had particular difficulties with women, seeking to isolate them socially and politically. The Egyptian Salafist Abu Islam even issued fatwas justifying raping women in Tahrir Square as a punishment for their unveiling themselves. These religious fanatics "consider women to be sex objects that are a permanent threat to society."[64] Salafists also pillaged and looted Kurdish towns and villages, torturing, raping, and killing.

Events quickened on July 16, 2013, when al-Nusra attacked PYD female fighters in Serekaniye. Fierce fighting that cost mostly Jihadist/Salafist lives drove al-Nusra out of the city bordering Turkey. Most observers saw this as a major victory for the PYD, and it was. However, for al-Nusra the Kurdish fighting was simply a lesser battle within the larger one against the regime taking place in the west around Aleppo. In addition, Jihadist/Salafist militants occupied the provincial capital of Raqqah to the south and battled to the east of Qamishli, where al-Nusra seized many of Syria's oil wells that were of great importance.

If al-Nusra were to prevail, it might be in a position to establish a self-sustaining autonomous al-Qaeda statelet, which would surely represent blowback onto Turkey and thus might cause it to reconsider its immediate position regarding whom to support and oppose in Syria. However, to the west around the Kurdish city of Afrin, the Jihadists/Salafists and Turkey continued to impose a suffocating blockade against the Kurds. Similarly, Barzani's Kurdistan Democratic Party (KDP) in the far east also continued to keep the border closed with Hasaka province where the Kurds lived. On July 30, 2013, Isa Hisso, a prominent member of the PYD, was assassinated in Qamishli. Some suspected the Jihadists/Salafists, but others blamed the regime.

By mid-August 2013 the YPG/YPJ was battling Jihadists/ Salafists on five separate fronts in the provinces of Raqqah, Aleppo, and Hasaka. Furthermore, of course, by 2014 ISIS had become an even greater threat to the Syrian Kurds, as illustrated by the horrific battle for Kobane. As already noted, ISIS will be analyzed in a subsequent chapter. Given all these pressures, the PYD called on the international community for support against their Jihadist/Salafist foes.

Salih Muslim Negotiates with Turkey

On July 25, 2013, amid reports that the PYD was about to declare Kurdish autonomy in Syria, Turkey publicly invited Salih Muslim to Istanbul for talks. Indeed, one report claimed that the PYD already had produced a constitution for the Syrian Kurdish regions. Under its provisions, Syria would become a democratic parliamentary federal system; Western Kurdistan, with Qamishli as its capital, would be one of the federal or autonomous self-ruling regions making its own internal decisions. Kurdish and Arabic would be its official languages, and self-ruling units would protect the Syrian borders from foreign intervention. This Kurdish government would be headed by a man or a woman with 21 ministers appointed by the parliament. Among these ministries would be Finance, Judiciary, Tourism and Environment, Human Rights, Culture, Electricity, and Defense, among others. However, Salih Muslim quickly pulled back from this constitutional proclamation, claiming that it was premature and that other viewpoints still had to be consulted.[65]

The PYD leader hastened to assure Turkey that his party's call for a local administration for Syria's Kurdish regions did not mean that it was seeking independence that would threaten Turkey: "Our thought is to establish a provisional council of 40 to 50—maybe a hundred people." He added that "this council will comprise Kurds, Syriacs, Arabs and Turkmens," and was simply a necessary ad hoc device to help alleviate the war-torn situation until the end of the civil war would allow more permanent arrangements. "Kurds will need to have a status in the new order in Syria. But what's in question now is a provisional arrangement. . . . It's not about making a constitution." [66]Nevertheless, in January 2014, the PYD declared autonomous self-rule and further developed its nascent local governmental units in the three Kurdish provinces or cantons along the lines of PKK leader Ocalan's concepts of democratic autonomy or bottom-up rule.[67] This novel concept supposedly provided a way to supersede the traditional state, which was seen as inherently oppressive by allowing Kurds, Arabs, Christians, and others all to participate in their local self-government. Democratic autonomy also stressed gender equality and ecological concerns.[68]

The Kurds in Iran:
Temporarily Quiescent?

Introduction

Unlike the Arabs and the Turks, the Persians are closely related to the Kurds. This ethnic affinity at times has probably served to moderate Kurdish national demands in Iran. Nevertheless, as one of the four main states (Turkey, Iraq, and Syria are the other three) in which historical Kurdistan lies, the Kurds in Iran and its predecessor the Persian Empire have always pursued their separate identity in one form or another. Thus, Iran too has played a most prominent role in Kurdish affairs. Much of the competition between the Ottoman Empire and the Persian Safavid dynasty (1502-1736), for example, took place on their Kurdish frontiers. Turkish-Iranian rivalry in Kurdistan continues today for influence over the Kurdistan Regional Government (KRG) in northern Iraq.

A significant number of Iranian Kurds live in the northwestern province of Kordestan, the only province in all pan-Kurdistan that bears this name. Sanandaj (Sinna) is the capital of Kordestan and the general name of the district around it. The population is largely Sunni Kurdish. Sheikhs of the Islamic Naqshbandi Sufi order have traditionally been influential, although earlier the *mirs* of Ardalan were Shiite, possibly because of their former connections to the Ahl-i Haqq, an ancient indigenous Kurdish religion that today

133

shares some tenets with the Shiites and heterodox Alevis. Most Kurds in the region speak the so-called southeastern dialects of Kurdish, which are closer to modern Persian than Sorani. Just to the west, however, there are Gurani speakers.

The Kurds in Iran also live in four other Iranian provinces: Western Azerbaijan, Kirmanshah, Hamadin, and Ilam. In addition, there is a community of Kurds in the northern part of Khorasan province in northeastern Iran that was forcefully relocated there during the eighteenth century to disperse and thus better control the ethnic and religious composition of the Persian Empire. Finally, in recent decades many Kurds have also moved to Tehran to seek better employment and living opportunities. Currently, Iran contains some 8 million Kurds, who account for approximately 11 percent of its entire population.

In recent years Iran has received large numbers of Kurdish refugees from Iraq, especially after the failed Iraqi Kurdish revolts in 1975 and 1991. However, despite their ethnic affinity with Persians and with a few exceptions, Kurds (unlike the Turkic Azeris) have been barred from high levels of power in Iran, and human rights violations are systematically carried out against them. In January 2009, for example, Human Rights Watch documented how Iranian authorities use security laws, press laws, and other legislation to arrest and prosecute Iranian Kurds solely for trying to exercise their right to freedom of expression and association. The government has closed Persian- and Kurdish-language newspapers and journals, banned books, and punished publishers, journalists, and writers for opposing and criticizing government policies.[1]

Amnesty International also expressed concern over the treatment of ethnic Kurdish prisoners of conscience. Kurdish representatives have testified how ethnic Kurds are denied education in their own language. Kurds are not allowed to give their children certain Kurdish names; Sunni Muslims—which most Kurds are— face discrimination because of their religion; women's rights are denied; and economic opportunities are bleak.[2] In June 2012, the

US assistant secretary of state for democracy, human rights, and labor, Michael Posner, denounced continuing negative trends in Iran toward its Kurdish population: "Intolerance, of dissent . . . ; free speech restricted; internet freedom restricted; political participation severely circumscribed; unfair trials; amputations; floggings; lots of death penalty. . . . So it is a very grim picture."[3]

History

Sheikh Ubeydullah

In 1880, Sheikh Ubeydullah of Nehri—a devout and highly revered religious leader—led possibly the most significant Kurdish revolt of the nineteenth century in the area along the Ottoman-Persian border. This ultimately unsuccessful uprising is sometimes said to have been the prototype for subsequent Kurdish revolts in the twentieth century. Explaining his actions, Sheikh Ubeydullah famously wrote the consul-general of Great Britain in Tabriz that "the Kurdish nation . . . is a people apart. . . . We also are a nation apart. We want our affairs to be in our own hands."[4] Indeed, in his seminal work on Kurdish studies, Wadie Jwaideh concluded concerning the sheikh that "as the old parochial interests of a local leader gave way to a more comprehensive concern for the welfare of a whole nation, the idea of a united and independent Kurdistan took shape and came to dominate his thinking."[5]

After his two sons had already commenced attacks within the Persian Empire—apparently because of the poor way the Persian government had been treating local tribal leaders who acknowledged Sheikh Ubeydullah's religious authority—Ubeydullah himself crossed the border from the Ottoman Empire into Persia. After initial success, however, Ubeydullah's tribal forces broke up before a determined Persian counterattack bent on exacting retribution for the heavy loss of life and destruction of property the sheikh's invasion had caused.

However, the Ottomans dealt rather leniently with Ubeydullah, simply exiling him first to Istanbul, and then, after his escape in 1882, to the Hijaz, where he died in 1883. This leniency was because Sheikh Ubeydullah probably had the sultan's tacit consent to prevent the emergence of any Christian Armenian state and to prevent the encroachment of Western reforms into the sultan's eastern domains. Earlier, Sheikh Ubeydullah had been appointed commander of the Kurdish tribal forces in the Russo-Turkish War of 1877-78. As a member of the Naqshbandi Sufi order, he not only would defend Sunni Islam against the Christians and Shiite Persians, but also would support the Ottoman Empire.

Thus, in retrospect, Sheikh Ubeydullah's uprising was more of a large Kurdish tribal revolt partially manipulated by the Ottomans to contain Western pressures for reform that might threaten their empire. On the other hand, Sheikh Ubeydullah clearly sought an autonomous domain similar to that enjoyed earlier by the Kurdish emirates. Thus, his revolt did indeed bear some seeds of emerging Kurdish nationalism.

Simko

From 1918 until 1922, Ismail Agha Simko led another significant Kurdish tribal revolt in Iranian Kurdistan and even established an autonomous government until he was defeated and eventually assassinated by the government. Simko was considered by many as a notorious Iranian Kurdish adventurer and tribal chief par excellence. For some others, however, he was a nascent Kurdish nationalist who established an autonomous Kurdish government in the area south and west of Lake Urmia in northwestern Iran for much of the period from 1918 to 1922. To do so, he created a strong army, which for several years proved superior to government troops and on numerous occasions actually defeated them. For a short period Simko even formed a cross-border alliance with Sheikh Taha of Nehri in Turkish Kurdistan and was in contact with other Kurdish nationalist leaders in Iraq and Turkey.

Simko exploited the instability of the frontier region at the end of World War I to build his power. At one time or another, he took aid from Russia and the Soviet Union, Turkey, Great Britain, and Iran. In March 1918, Simko also treacherously killed his guest, the Assyrian leader Mar Shimun. (The Assyrians had fled from their mountainous home in Hakkari in Turkey and settled in the region claimed by Simko.) By February 1920, however, Iranian government forces temporarily defeated Simko, chased him into exile, but then gave him clemency. Soon Simko was building an even greater force. He was at the height of his power in 1921 and even published a newspaper in Sawdj-Bulak (Mahabad).

Many Kurds feared and disliked Simko, however, and on 9 August 1922, he also was dealt a sharp defeat by the Iranian government from which he never really recovered. He spent his remaining years trying to regain his former position, moving from Iraq to Turkey, while mending fences with Sheikh Taha of Nehri and Sheikh Mahmud Barzinji in Iraq. In the spring of 1925 Simko returned to Iran and replaced Amr Khan, his rival, as the chief of the Abdui Shikak tribe. Soon he was again in open rebellion. When half of his troops defected to Amr Khan, however, Reza Shah Pahlavi's more modern Iranian government troops easily defeated him. In 1930, the government tricked him into returning to Iran and killed him in an ambush.

Simko's main strength and weakness was the Kurdish tribal system. While he was in ascendance, the tribes gave him a great deal of support, which, however, quickly melted away as soon as he was defeated. Moreover, even in victory tribal support proved tenuous, because tribal members tended to return home with their loot after a victorious campaign. In retrospect, Simko had neither clear nationalist goals nor any political party organizational base to support him. He remained at heart a tribal leader who had little but disdain for urban livers and sedentary nontribal peasants. In the end Simko was defeated by the modernizing government of Reza

Shah Pahlavi, which successfully sought to break tribal power and centralize the state. Nevertheless, after Abdul Rahman Ghassemlou and Qazi Muhammad, Simko was probably the best-known Iranian Kurdish leader during the twentieth century. However, like the first two, Simko also ended up being assassinated by the Iranian government.

Modernization

In the 1920s, the Iranian government began new policies that ended the traditional tribal nomadic economy based on herding.[6] This was largely accomplished by dislocating and resettling Kurdish tribes and exiling their leaders. As the Kurdish society became part of Iran's developing market economy, further changes occurred in the social and political structure. Subsequently, Muhammad Reza Shah Pahlavi's land reform in 1966 proved very significant in this process.

Mahabad Republic of Kurdistan[7]

Mahabad acquired its current name during the 1920s in the time of Reza Shah Pahlavi. Previously it was known as Sawadj or Sawdj-Bulak. The city has long boasted a purer Kurdish culture and more intense Kurdish nationalism than the larger cities of Urmia (Rezaiya) to the north and Sanandaj to the south, both of which have important non-Kurdish minorities. Thus, Mahabad has earned the premier role in the development of Iranian Kurdish nationalism.

From 1942 to 1945 Komala (committee) was the name of a political party Iranian Kurds formed in September 1942 in Mahabad, Iran. Its complete name in Kurdish was *Komalay Jiyanaway Kurd* (J. K.), or Committee for the Revival of the Kurds, so the party has also been referred to as simply J. K. Abdal Rahman Zabihi was appointed party secretary. Some Iraqi and Turkish Kurds were also represented in Komala. Indeed, Mir Haji, a close associate of Mulla Mustafa Barzani and the representative of the Iraqi Kurdish Hiwa (Hope) Party, was present at Komala's first meeting.

Komala's pan-Kurdish aspirations were made clear by the motto and title of its journal *Nishtiman* (Motherland), which declared "Long live greater Kurdistan." Indeed, the famous three-borders meeting (*Peyamiani sei Sanowar*) of Kurdish delegates from Iraq, Turkey, and Iran was held on Mt. Dalanpar in August 1944 where the borders of their three states met. Komala's activities eventually led to the short-lived Mahabad Republic of Kurdistan in 1946.

Komala looked to the Soviet Union for guidance and emphasized language and social rights. In April 1945, Qazi Muhammad, a highly respected cleric and the unquestioned Kurdish leader in the city of Mahabad, was invited to become Komala's new president. In September 1945, Qazi Muhammad dissolved Komala and absorbed its membership into the new Kurdish Democratic Party, later called the Kurdistan Democratic Party of Iran (KDPI). This new party was apparently created on Soviet advice. (A quarter of a century later, a completely new and different Iranian Kurdish party also, and therefore confusingly, called Komala was formed.)

Also known as the Democratic Republic of Kurdistan, the Mahabad Republic of Kurdistan in northwestern Iran became a rump Kurdish state that was proclaimed on 22 January 1946, received considerable aid from the Soviet Union, but collapsed by December 1946. During its brief tenure, schools in the Mahabad Republic began to teach in Kurdish, while scholars also began to translate texts into that language. A printing press provided by the Soviet Union produced a daily newspaper and the famous monthly journal called *Nishtiman* (Motherland). Limited amounts of Soviet military aid also arrived.

There is debate over whether Qazi Muhammad actually sought complete independence or simply autonomy. During its brief existence, the miniscule entity extended no further than the small cities of Mahabad, Bukan, Naqada, and Ushnaviya in a part of what is now the Iranian province of Western Azerbaijan. Thus, not even all of Iranian Kurdistan supported the experiment, let alone the Kurds in other states. On the other hand, the Mahabad Republic had pan-Kurdish ambitions and attracted such non-Iranian Kurds as Mulla Mustafa Barzani, who served as one of the republic's generals. There also can be no doubt that the Mahabad Republic became a symbol of forlorn Kurdish nationalism and statehood in the 20th century. However, the Mahabad Republic collapsed because of Iran's vigorous response, the Soviet Union's unwillingness to offer more support, and the usual Kurdish divisions. Its much revered leader Qazi Muhammad was hanged on March 31, 1947, and the KDPI he headed virtually ceased to exist.

Aftermath

The Kurdish national movement in Iran lost most of its impetus following the demise of the Mahabad Republic in 1946. Since then, Iraq and Turkey have seen much more Kurdish national activity than Iran. Nevertheless, a lesser Kurdish movement has repeatedly risen up in Iran. During the late 1940s and the early 1950s, the KDPI cooperated closely with the Tudeh or Iranian Communist Party. When the Shah returned to power in 1953, however, he was able to close down most of this activity.

In the 1960s, the Iranian Kurds at first tended to cooperate with the much more successful Kurdish movement in Iraq headed by Mulla Mustafa Barzani. In the late 1960s, some young KDPI members launched a guerrilla war against Tehran, but they failed completely. Relations between the Iraqi and Iranian Kurds soured, because Barzani apparently aided Iran in suppressing the Iranian Kurds, even to the extent of executing or handing over more than 40 KDPI fighters to Iran.[8] In return, Barzani received aid from Iran.

During the late 1970s period of the Islamic revolution in Iran, there were two main Iranian Kurdish parties, the more moderate and flexible KDPI and the more radical, Marxist Komala. Both had explicitly secular programs, and for a while they controlled most of Iranian Kurdistan. The KDPI goal was "autonomy for Kurdistan, democracy for Iran."[9] Sheikh Izziddin Husseini, an unconventional Sunni cleric, also played an important role as a mediator and unifying force. However, Ayatollah Ruhollah Khomeini, the new revolutionary Iranian leader, had little patience for the Kurdish demands and declared holy war against them on August 19, 1979. His agent, the Ayatollah Sadiq (Sadegh) Khalkhali sentenced hundreds of Kurds to execution after summary trials.

The Iranian Kurds were not united, and their attempt at armed rebellion had completely failed by 1983. Armed remnants, however, continued to shelter in northern Iraq. However, fighting broke out between the KDPI and the Komala in 1985. Hundreds died in this intra-Kurdish bloodletting. Further divisions occurred among the Iranian Kurds in 2006. As of 2015, the KDPI continues to shelter in the small village of Azadi in Koya township of the Erbil governorate of the KRG between Erbil and Sulaymaniya, while Komala has been reduced to being active only in exile in Los Angeles, California.

Although neither the KDPI nor Komala is currently active militarily in Iran, some have argued that the United States would like to use them to overthrow the present Iranian regime.[10] In 2006, top KDPI and Komala leaders such as KDPI head Mostafa Hejri visited Washington to meet with middle-level US State Department and intelligence officials. Hejri made it clear that, although he would accept US financial aid, he opposed US military attacks against Iran as being counterproductive. On the other hand, Komala declared that it neither opposed nor supported such attacks. In August 2012 the KDPI and Komala, once bitter enemies, reached a strategic agreement calling for federalism in Iran to undo the national oppression suffered by the Kurds. In addition, the divided KDPI began reunification talks in December 2012.

PERSONAL OBSERVATION

In October 2012, before speaking at a large academic conference in Erbil, I took the afternoon off to visit Mostafa Hejri, the longtime leader of the KDPI. A member of that party drove us some 60 miles east to the small town of Azadi in the township of Koya in the Erbil governorate. There the KRG had permitted the KDPI to establish a small, but fully functioning community of Iranian Kurds complete with its own modest hospital, children's school, radio and television broadcasting facilities, numerous homes, and who knows what else. Armed guards were also present in the village of perhaps 300.

Mostafa Hejri welcomed me and my academic friend Joost Jongerden into his comfortable home, where we at first sat awkwardly around a large room with several of his associates. The difficult attempt at conversation was broken only when somehow the subject of Persian literature came up. Mostafa Hejri, it turned out, had studied it earlier at Tehran University and greatly admired it. Joost Jongerden and I knew just enough to begin a lively conversation with our host that eventually segued into other topics concerning Kurdish history, politics, economics, and culture, among others. Our host also shared information about recently successful initiatives to reunify his long-fractured KDPI, as well as to bring harmony between it and its longtime Marxist rival Komala.

Mostafa Hejri spoke good English so long as we talked slowly and distinctly. He also was a handsome man, who told us that he exercised regularly and did not smoke, a curse to which many Kurds are enslaved. Eventually an excellent Kurdish lunch appeared, over which the conversation continued. Finally we left our host for a tour of Azadi.

At the school we spoke briefly to a class and watched others play volleyball. We also visited the modest hospital and radio/TV facilities, where we conversed with a number of others. In several places we saw photos of the martyred KDPI leaders Abdul Rahman Ghassemlou and Sadiq Sharafkindi. In total we spent perhaps five hours at Azadi. This visit enabled me to learn something about the Kurds of Iran at first hand to match my admittedly larger knowledge of those in Turkey, Iraq, and later in Syria.

Thus, over the years my trips to Kurdistan and later Europe have enabled me to meet the main Kurdish leaders in all four states of the Middle East in which the Kurds live: Abdullah Ocalan of the PKK, Massoud Barzani of the KDP, Jalal Talabani of the PUK, and in Belgium on a number of recent occasions Salih Muslim of the PYD in Syria. Salih Muslim and Mostafa Hejri spoke English the best. Jalal Talabani also communicated well in the language. Although I was told that he could speak and understand English, Massoud Barzani spoke only through an interpreter. Abdullah Ocalan did not speak English; Turkish was his working language, although he told me that he also knew Kurdish.

Iran-Iraq War (1980-88)

In September 1980, Saddam Hussein's Iraq invaded Iran in the mistaken belief that Iran had been fatally weakened by its Islamic revolution. After initial Iraqi successes, the war bogged down into a long stalemate, and thus created potential opportunities and dangers for the Kurdish national movements in both Iraq and Iran. Both countries attempted to use each other's Kurds as fifth columns against the other. For their part, the Kurds attempted to win their national rights by supporting the enemy of the state in which they lived. Thus, the war set loose forces that enabled the

Kurds to become more important international actors than they previously had been.

In Iraq, Massoud Barzani's Kurdistan Democratic Party (KDP) supported Iran from the very beginning. Jalal Talabani's Patriotic Union of Kurdistan (PUK), however, played a much more careful role, even for a while seeking to reach an understanding with Baghdad through the good offices of the KDPI. It was not until 1987 that the KDP and the PUK were able to bury the hatchet and—with Iran's help—to announce in principle the creation of the Iraqi Kurdistan Front. This front became the seed of the de facto state of Kurdistan in northern Iraq following the Gulf War in 1991 and later the Kurdistan Regional Government (KRG).

The Iraqi Kurdish support for Iran, however, helped lead to Iraq's use of chemical weapons against them in Halabja in March 1988 and the associated genocidal Anfal campaign to kill as many as 180,000 of them. At the war's end, the Kurds were definitely much worse off than they had been before the start of the war. On the other hand, the Iran-Iraq War also served to internationalize the Kurdish issue. The Gulf War three years later furthered this situation for the Iraqi Kurds, but the Iranian Kurds remained in a weakened position. In addition, on July 13, 1989, Iran treacherously assassinated the much-admired KDPI leader Abdul Rahman Ghassemlou in Vienna while supposedly negotiating with him[11] and then his successor Sadiq Sharafkindi on September 17, 1992, at the Mykonos Restaurant in Berlin. These assassinations, along with the military defeats in the early 1980s, greatly demoralized the Kurdish nationalists in Iran, guerrilla elements of which now live in exile across the border in the area ruled by the KRG. Mostafa Hejri became the new KDPI leader and remains so.

During the Kurdistan Workers Party (PKK) rebellion in Turkey (1984-99), Turkey at times accused Iran of giving aid and sanctuary to the PKK. In 1996, Iran overtly supported Talabani's PUK in its struggle against Barzani's KDP for supremacy in northern Iraq, while Turkey supported the KDP. Since then, Turkey and Iran have varied their support, but always with the purpose of trying to prevent the creation of an actual Kurdish state that might act as a powerful magnet to their own Kurds.

Recent Developments

Many Iranian Kurds supported reformist Mohammad Khatami when he was elected president of Iran in May 1997.[12] While Khatami was president there was even a Kurdish list (party) in the Iranian parliament (Majlis), and its members wore Kurdish clothes. Khatami appointed Abdollah Ramazanzadeh, a Shiite Kurd, as the first governor general of Iranian Kurdistan. In turn, Ramazanzadeh appointed a number of Sunni Kurds to important governmental positions.

However, Khatami proved too weak to stand up against the hard-liners. In April 2001, Ramazanzadeh was accused of libelous statements against the powerful watchdog body, the Council of Guardians, for objecting to the nullification of the Majlis votes in two Kurdish cities. A non-Kurd succeeded him. During the same year, several legislators from the Kurdish provinces resigned from the Majlis, accusing the government of discrimination. The situation continued to deteriorate when over half of the Kurdish members of the Majlis were prevented from participating in the February 2004 elections. As a result, more than 70 percent of the Kurds boycotted the elections and civil unrest occurred in several Kurdish cities.

Many Kurds also boycotted the election of hard-line Mahmoud Ahmadinejad, who was elected president of Iran on June 24, 2005. Only 25 percent of those eligible voted in the decisive second round of the June 2005 presidential elections in Kordestan province. Even fewer Kurds voted in other provinces. This compared with a national turnout of more than 60 percent and would seemingly be indicative of Kurdish alienation from the Iranian political system.[13] Ahmadinejad also immediately rebuked Kurdish appeals to place qualified Kurds in his new administration. As a result most Iranian Kurds boycotted the subsequent, disputed presidential election held on June 12, 2009. In July 2009, many Iranian Kurds also participated in a general strike to mark the twentieth anniversary of the assassination of Abdul Rahman Ghassemlou, which some accused Ahmadinejad of having played a role in perpetrating.[14] Although there were some 18 Kurds among the 290 members of the Majlis as of September 2009, they were not allowed to form a Kurdish list.

The creation of the KRG in northern Iraq and its institutionalization after the Gulf War in 2003—as well as the inauguration of Massoud Barzani in June 2005 as its president—also have influenced the neighboring Iranian Kurds to demand changes. In July 2005, thousands of Iranian Kurds protested in Mahabad, the unofficial capital of Iranian Kurdistan, as well as in numerous other cities. The Iranian government responded with a state of de facto martial law and deployed large numbers of security forces.

On 9 July 2005, Iranian troops killed Shivan Qadiri, a young Kurdish leader, and dragged his body through the streets. The government claimed that Qadiri had organized the destruction of ballots in three voting centers in the recent elections that had resulted in Mahmoud Ahmadinejad winning the presidency. Thousands of Iranian Kurds launched protests in Mahabad, the unofficial capital of Iranian Kurdistan, as well as in Sanandaj, Sardasht, Ushnaviya, Divandareh, Baneh, Sinne, Bukan, and Saqqez, among others.[15] The Iranian government, again, responded with a state of de facto martial law and deployed large numbers of security forces. A number of deaths were reported on both sides. Further Kurdish demonstrations in protest against a death sentence handed down for the July unrest occurred in Mahabad at the end of October 2005. In addition, on February 16, 2007, the anniversary of Abdullah Ocalan's capture in 1999, large demonstrations and mass meetings occurred in Iranian Kurdistan. They led to three deaths and hundreds of detentions. These events served as a reminder to the Iranian authorities that they still had a volatile Kurdish problem.

Parti Jiyani Azadi Kurdistan

The *Parti Jiyani Azadi Kurdistan* (PJAK, or sometimes PEJAK) or Free (Independent) Life Party of Kurdistan, is a new Iranian Kurdish party that held its first congress on March 25, 2004, and is closely associated with the PKK. The PJAK supposedly is led by Abdul Rahman Haji Ahmadi, who had previously been a member of the PKK and currently resides in Europe. As of 2015, fighters of both the PKK and PJAK are located in the Qandil Mountains that straddle the border between the KRG and Iran, with PKK fighters on the western side and PJAK fighters on the southern side.

The exact origin of the PJAK is disputed.[16] However, according to its members, the party's beginnings may be traced back to 1997 to a peaceful student-based human rights movement that was inspired by the successes of the Iraqi Kurds and the PKK. In 1999, following a series of Iranian government crackdowns, the group's leaders moved to the safety of the Qandil Mountains on the border of Iran and Iraqi Kurdistan. Here, the group adopted many of the political and military ideas of the imprisoned PKK leader, whom they already admired. Veteran PKK fighters of Iranian origin also moved into the group's ranks.

The PJAK advocates replacing Iran's theocratic leadership with a democratic, federal system that would grant autonomy not only to the Kurds, but also to the Azeri, Beluchi, and Arab regions of Iran. Women also play a major role in the party and constitute as many as 45 percent of its some 3,000 fighters. (In addition, PJAK claims that it has thousands of activists within Iran.) PJAK also claims that it resorts to military actions only in reaction to violent Iranian government acts, such as those surrounding the government's killing in July 2015 of Shivan Qadiri, a young Kurdish leader, whose body was dragged through the streets, as previously noted. Thousands of Iranian Kurds launched protests in Mahabad and other cities as a result.

Although the PJAK shares PKK facilities such as hospitals, remains within the PKK's defensive perimeter in the Qandil Mountains, and shares many of the PKK's goals as well as supposedly being coordinated by the *Koma Civaken Kurdistan* (KCK), or Kurdistan Communities Union, whose Executive Council is currently chaired by the PKK military leader Cemil Bayik, the PJAK also maintains its own administrative structure. This includes a Congress, Head of the Party (Abdul Rahman Haji Ahmedi), Assembly, and General Coordination [Leadership Council]. Other PJAK bodies are the Union of Women of Eastern [Iranian] Kurdistan (YJRK), Union of the Youth of Eastern Kurdistan (YCRK), Democratic Press Union (YRD), and Political and Diplomatic Committee. Gulistan Dogan heads the important women's branch of the PJAK, which, as previously noted, supplies perhaps 45 percent of the party's fighters, yet another similarity with its PKK ally. Dogan is also a member of PJAK's seven-member Leadership Council.

Some sources have claimed that the PJAK was receiving surreptitious US backing as a way for the United States to counter Iranian ambitions in the Middle East.[17] Although this has been denied, earlier it was known that the United States was supporting the Mujahedin-e Khalq, an Iranian opposition group that was officially classified as a terrorist organization by the US State Department. However, in February 2009, the US Treasury Department blacklisted the PJAK in an effort to appease its Turkish ally. This US designation under Executive Order 13224 was not as politically significant, however, as being termed a terrorist organization and placed on the list of Foreign Terrorist Organizations as is the PKK. Under the current listing, the United States has frozen the PJAK's assets and prohibited US citizens from doing business with it.

After relatively large-scale clashes between the PJAK and Iran in the summer of 2011, the two sides announced a cease-fire, and, in October 2011, KRG president Massoud Barzani declared that the PJAK would terminate its armed actions.[18] However, low-level fighting continues, and Iran has hanged several captured PJAK members. Nevertheless, the PJAK has largely maintained the cease-fire, while declaring that it was going to send militants to join the PKK in the Kurds' Syrian struggle.[19] Given the divisions that prevailed until at least recently within the KDPI and the decline of Komala, opportunity spaces for PJAK have clearly opened up and been utilized.

Iran's New President

On June 14, 2013, Hassan Rouhani—a supposed reformist and moderate with a doctorate in law from the University of Glasgow—was elected as the new president of Iran. In sharp contrast to his predecessor, Mahmoud Ahmadinejad, Rouhani received 71 percent of the votes in the Kurdish areas of Iran.[20] Many Kurds had hoped that the new president would address their main concerns, which included their impoverishment, lack of civil liberties, imprisonment of numerous activists, many of whom were under the risk of execution, limited cultural rights, denial of education in the mother tongue, and disproportionate Kurdish student rejection into higher education by the notorious *gozinesh* or selection process, among many other issues.[21] In addition, there was also a hope that Rouhani would choose a Sunni Kurd to be one of his cabinet members as well as the new governor of Kurdistan.

However, so far Rouhani has disappointed on all fronts. Indeed, since his election more Kurdish political prisoners have been executed. There also are about 400 Kurdish political prisoners, with 60 of them on death row. Life sentences have been handed out to 15.[22] Abdulsalm Gulnawaz, the preacher of the Omar Mosque in Sardashat, was also stripped of his post and sentenced to six years in prison for being a member of an outlawed Sunni organization founded by the late but still influential Kurdish religious thinker Ahmed Muftizadeh. In addition, Gulnawaz was accused of spreading propaganda against the regime, preaching in favor of the KDPI, and inciting division between Shiites and Sunnis.[23] Abdullah Muhtadi, the secretary-general of Komala, concluded that "Rouhani comes from a security background and therefore, he will never look at the Kurdish question from a cultural or political perspective."[24] If this assessment is correct, the presently quiescent Kurdish situation in Iran will not continue indefinitely.

New Clashes

In May 2015, clashes erupted between Kurds and Iranian security forces in Mahabad after Farinaz Khosrovani, a 27-year-old female hotel worker committed suicide trying to avoid being raped by an Iranian intelligence agent. Angry crowds demonstrated against what they claimed was Tehran's discriminatory treatment of its Kurdish population. Soon thousands of Iranian Kurds were demonstrating in the streets of more than 10 Iranian Kurdish cities. According to Alessandria Masi, "buildings are burning, protesters are bloodied, law enforcement vehicles are destroyed, hundreds of young men and women have been arrested and there is no end in sight." More than a dozen people were reported killed or injured. Demonstrations were also held in front of Iranian embassies in several European cities, including Vienna, Paris, and London. At the same time, small-scale clashes broke out between KDPI and PKK guerrillas on the Iraqi-Iranian border when the KDPI sought to show solidarity with the rioters in Iran by moving some forces up to the border from their base within the KRG. Apparently the PKK resented KDPI forces enterting what the PKK viewed as its area. How long would Iran's potential Kurdish problem remain quiescent?

The United States
and the Kurds

Overview

The United States has come to affect the Kurdish situation perhaps more than any other state. For example, the US invasion of Iraq and the overthrow of Saddam Hussein in 2003 led directly to the present autonomy of the Kurdistan Regional Government (KRG) in Iraq, while also helping to open the gates of hell to the ~~onslaught~~ of the Islamic State of Iraq and Syria (ISIS) against the Kurds in both Iraq and Syria.

However, the United States does not really have any grand foreign policy strategy toward the Kurds, because they live in four separate states (Turkey, Iraq, Iran, and Syria), each one of which requires its own separate considerations. What is more, the states in which the Kurds live usually are more important for US foreign policy. The Kurds cause problems for the United States when it deals with these more important states. Nevertheless, given its interest in Middle East stability as well as human rights, the United States has come to accept that it does owe the Kurds a certain amount of attention and even protection. This has been true especially in Iraq, given how the Iraqi Kurds supported the United States in the 2003 war against Saddam Hussein when others such as Turkey did not. Indeed, as just noted, the virtually independent KRG largely owes its very existence to the United States.

Despite its support for the Iraqi Kurds, however, the United States opposes independence for the Iraqi Kurds, because US leaders think that this would lead to the partition and end of Iraq and thus lead to greater instability in the Middle East. The United States' position on this point is all the more adamant, given the attitudes of the leaders of other states such as Turkey, Iran, and the various Arab governments, all of which oppose Kurdish independence as a threat to their own territorial integrity. The United States tentatively does support the KRG as a way to maintain the political unity of Iraq and to satisfy the Kurds. This position, of course, can be inherently contradictory and is a very fine line to implement successfully, especially given the new de facto Turkish-KRG alliance.

Many observers emphasize how much the Iraqi Kurds love the Americans. This needs to be qualified, because the Kurds remember that they earlier were twice betrayed by the United States, in 1975 and again in 1991, and therefore might be again. Indeed, some Kurds began to fear the worst when the Baker-Hamilton *Iraq Study Group Report* (December 2006) suggested that the hard-won Kurdish federal state might have to be sacrificed to the perceived need for a reestablished centralized Iraqi state.[1] Fortunately for the Kurds, the report's recommendations were not adopted by the United States, but their mere consideration illustrated how tenuous future US support might be.

On the other hand, US Secretary of Defense Robert Gates acknowledged in a meeting on December 11, 2010, with KRG President Massoud Barzani that Kurdish cooperation is indispensable for the successful implementation of security and strategic framework agreements between the United States and Iraq and is essential for a unified and peaceful Iraq.[2] Even more importantly, the US Obama administration a few days later publicly committed itself to broker disputes between the KRG and the Baghdad government and also to help resolve the Kirkuk issue, since the Kurds had agreed to accept the new Iraqi election law that slightly reduced the number of seats the KRG would have in the new Iraqi parliament that was elected in March 2010.[3] When ISIS suddenly attacked the KRG in August 2014 and drove to within 20 miles of its capital, Erbil, the United States quickly responded with just enough air strikes to save the Kurdish day. On the other hand, Turkey, supposedly the KRG's best regional ally, chose to do nothing.

Thus, the United States sees the KRG as a friend and a de facto ally, but not as important an ally as Turkey or even the Shiite government in Iraq. Therefore, the message is clear. The KRG must get along with Turkey and Baghdad or else, in a showdown between either of these two states and the KRG, the KRG might not be able to count on US support. Fortunately for the Iraqi Kurds, Turkey's supposed zero problems with its neighbors' foreign policy means that Turkey is beginning to accept the KRG politically as a friend rather than a security threat, as had been the earlier view. Clearly, however, the Kurdish question holds only a minor position in the national security of the United States and the democratization process it pursues in the Middle East.

Given its relatively weak hand, compared with Turkey and the Baghdad government, therefore, the KRG lobby in the United States has made a positive impression and achieved successes. Qubad Talabani, the KRG representative in the United States until 2012, made a good impact and was able to gain much goodwill for the Kurds. Unfortunately for the KRG, it then left the position vacant until January 2015, when Bayan Sami Abdul Rahman, formerly the able KRG representative in London, finally assumed the post.

On the other hand, rightly or wrongly, the Turkish Kurds are often perceived in the United States as too closely tied to the Kurdistan Workers Party (PKK), which the United States considers to be a terrorist organization. As a result, the cause of the Turkish Kurds in the United States has not prospered as well as that of their brothers and sisters to the south. This is all the more true, given the long-standing US alliance with Turkey. The United States has paid even less attention to the Kurds in Iran, although they might someday serve as a potential ally against the Islamic government in much the same way as the Iraqi Kurds did against Saddam Hussein's Iraq. As for the Kurds in Syria, they were clearly off the radar until Kurdish autonomy occurred in July 2012. Even subsequently, however, the United States has shown little interest in the Kurds of Syria, because of its vision of a united Syria contributing to stability as well as its deference to Turkish sensitivities, which viewed the Syrian Kurds as largely an extension of the PKK. On the other hand, the Syrian Kurds are keenly aware of the United States' all-important role and would dearly like to win its support.

With this brief overview and its caveats in mind, the purpose of this chapter is to analyze what might be viewed as the six stages of American foreign policy toward the Kurds.[4] The first three of these stages, involving Woodrow Wilson's promises, Mulla Mustafa Barzani's era, and the 1991 US war against Iraq, have been completed, whereas as of this writing the last three, concerning the KRG in Iraq since 2003, Turkey and the PKK, and Syria and the existential ISIS threat, are a continuing process. Thus, a survey of US policy toward the Kurds is necessary in order to understand recent developments in Kurdish history and politics.

First Stage

American foreign policy involvement with the Kurds dates back to World War I and President Woodrow Wilson's famous Fourteen Points, the twelfth of which concerned a forlorn promise of "autonomy" for "the other nationalities [of the Ottoman Empire] which are now under Turkish rule."[5] Resurgent Kemalist Turkey's successful struggle to regain its territorial integrity[6] and British Iraq's decision to maintain control over the oil-rich Kurdish region of northern Iraq known as the Mosul *vilayet*, however, ended nascent Kurdish hopes for independence or even some type of autonomy.[7] The first brief Wilsonian stage or prelude to American foreign policy toward the Kurds had ended.

Second Stage

A half century passed before American foreign policy again became involved with the Kurds. Because of the North Atlantic Treaty Organization (NATO), the United States supported the position of the Turkish government on the Kurdish issue in that state. This was to deny Kurdish demands for minority rights, as they might escalate into further demands that would threaten Turkish territorial integrity.[8] Thus, the Kurds who supported the PKK in Turkey became "bad Kurds" from the point of view of American foreign policy.[9]

In Iraq, however, in what might be called the second or Mulla Mustafa Barzani stage in American foreign policy toward the Kurds, the United States encouraged and to a certain extent even supported Barzani's revolt against Iraq during the early 1970s.[10] Thus, the Iraqi Kurds became the "good Kurds" from the point of view of American foreign policy. The United States pursued this policy for several reasons: (1) as a favor to its then-ally the shah-ruled Iran; (2) as a ploy during the Cold War, as Iraq was seen as an ally of the Soviet Union; (3) as a means to relieve pressure on Israel so that Iraq would not join some future Arab attack on the Jewish state; and (4) as a means to possibly satisfy its own need for Middle East oil, since Barzani had promised that the United States could look to a friend in OPEC [Oil Producing and Exporting Countries] once oil-rich Kurdistan had achieved independence.

Accordingly, US President Richard Nixon and his national security advisor and later secretary of state, Henry Kissinger, first encouraged the Iraqi Kurds to revolt against Baghdad, but then with their ally Iran double-crossed the Kurds when the Shah decided to make a deal with Saddam Hussein. To rationalize US actions, Kissinger argued that the "benefit of Nixon's Kurdish decision was apparent in just over a year: Only one Iraqi division was available to participate in the October 1973 Middle East War."[11] Cynically, he also declaimed that "covert action should not be confused with missionary work."[12]

Barzani himself died a broken man four years later in US exile as an unwanted ward of the CIA.[13] Years later Jonathan Randal argued that Barzani's son and eventual successor, Massoud Barzani, had "never forgotten Kissinger's treachery in 1975, had never totally recovered from the humiliation of his years of enforced exile, which he blamed on the United States . . . [and] never stopped worrying about American constancy."[14] Massoud Barzani himself explained that "we have had bitter experience with the U.S. government. . . . In 1975 . . . it changed its alliances purely in its own interest at the expense of our people's suffering and plight."[15]

More than a quarter of a century later, Kissinger revisited what the United States had done under his stewardship and explained that "saving the [Iraqi] Kurds [in 1975] would have required the opening of a new front in inhospitable mountains close to the Soviet border."[16] Thus, "we did not have the option of overt support in a war so logistically difficult, so remote, and so incomprehensible to the American public." Moreover, "the Shah had made the decision, and we had neither the plausible arguments nor strategies to dissuade him." Kissinger then concluded: "As a case study, the Kurdish tragedy provides material for a variety of conclusions: the need to clarify objectives at the outset; the importance of relating goals to available means; the need to review an operation periodically; and the importance of coherence among allies." In other words the Iraqi Kurds had played the role of dispensable pawns for American foreign policy.

Third Stage

The third stage of American foreign policy toward the Kurds began with the Gulf War in 1991 and lasted until the US attack on Iraq in March 2003. This third stage led to the creation of the Kurdistan Regional Government (KRG), the closest approximation of an independent Kurdish state in modern times. As the Iraqi military was being ousted from Kuwait, US president George H. W. Bush encouraged "the Iraqi people to take matters into their own hands—to force Saddam Hussein, the dictator, to step aside.[17] Despite initial successes, however, neither the Iraqi Shiites nor the Kurds proved able to cope with Saddam Hussein's stronger military. As Saddam Hussein began to put the Kurdish rebellion down, the two Iraqi Kurdish leaders—Massoud Barzani of the Kurdistan Democratic Party (KDP) and Jalal Talabani of the Patriotic Union of Kurdistan (PUK)—appealed to Bush for help by reminding him: "You personally called upon the Iraqi people to rise up against Saddam Hussein's brutal dictatorship."[18]

For a variety of reasons, however, the United States decided not to intervene in the internal Iraqi strife. Doing so could lead, it was feared, to an unwanted, protracted US occupation that would be politically unpopular in the United States, to an unstable government in Iraq, or even "Lebanonization" of the country and destabilization of the Middle East. Furthermore, the United States also concluded that Saddam Hussein could win. To support the Kurds against him might require an unwanted, permanent American commitment. Possibly too, the memory of overstepping itself in the Korean War, by trying to totally replace the North Korean regime after initially liberating South Korea, also influenced American thinking. In addition, Kurdish success in Iraq might provoke Kurdish uprisings in Turkey, Syria, or Iran, states whose cooperation the US leaders thought that they needed. (All of these problems, of course, came back to haunt the United States after its second war against Saddam Hussein in 2003 under the second President

Bush.) A US Senate Foreign Relations staff report, written by Peter Galbraith and issued a month after Saddam Hussein had put down the rebellion, confirmed that the United States "continued to see the opposition in caricature" and feared that the Kurds would seek a separate state and that the Shiites wanted an Iranian-style republic.[19]

Once it became clear that the United States was not going to in-tervene in 1991, the uneven struggle turned into a rout, and ap-proximately 1.5 million Kurdish refugees fled to the Iranian and Turkish frontiers, where they faced death from the hostile climate and lack of provisions. This refugee dilemma quickly created a disastrous political problem for everyone involved, including the United States, Turkey, and Iran. Thus, after much soul-searching, the United States reversed itself and took several steps to protect the Kurds. United Nations Security Council Resolution 688 of April 5, 1991, condemned "the repression of the Iraqi civilian pop-ulation . . . in Kurdish populated areas" and demanded "that Iraq . . . immediately end this repression." Under the aegis of Operation Provide Comfort (OPC) and a no-fly zone imposed against Bagh-dad, the Kurds were able to return to their homes in northern Iraq, where they began to build a fledgling de facto state and govern-ment, which soon became today's KRG. The current Syrian refugee problem—which also involves a substantial number of Syrian Kurds—is a partial reminder of how this earlier tragedy that then redounded into a virtual Kurdish state might also develop pos-itively for the Syrian Kurds. The continuance of OPC became a major political issue in Turkey, however, because many Turks be-lieved that it was facilitating the vacuum of authority in northern Iraq that enabled the PKK to enjoy sanctuaries there. Some even argued that OPC was the opening salvo of a new Treaty of Sevres (1920) that would lead to the creation of a Kurdish state in northern Iraq as almost occurred following World War I. Thus, went the ar-gument, Turkey was facilitating its own demise by housing OPC. (This argument, of course, became even more relevant during the next stage of American foreign policy toward the Kurds that began in 2003.)

To abandon OPC, however, would alienate Washington and would strip Ankara of important influence over the course of events. OPC, for example, enabled Turkey to launch military strikes into Iraqi Kurdistan against the PKK at almost any time. If the United States refused to allow such Turkish incursions, Turkey could threaten to withdraw its permission for OPC. Although it might have seemed ironic that an operation that was supposed to protect the Iraqi Kurds was allowing Turkey to attack the Turkish Kurds, as well as to inflict collateral damage on the host Iraqi Kurds, such was the logic of the Kurdish imbroglio and part of the dilemma for American foreign policy. Similar dilemmas exist for the United States today concerning Syria, as support for the opposition would involve al-Qaeda–affiliated groups that also are fighting against the Syrian Kurds. However, US support for the Democratic Union Party (PYD), which is the strongest Syrian Kurdish party, would alienate Turkey, because such aid would be for a group affiliated with the PKK, which both Turkey and the United States deem a terrorist organization.

Moreover, in May 1994, the two main Iraqi Kurdish parties—Barzani's KDP and Talabani's PUK—fell into a civil war that immensely complicated American foreign policy toward them. How could the United States help and protect the Iraqi Kurds when they were busy killing themselves? In late January 1995, US President Bill Clinton sent a message to both Barzani and Talabani in which he warned: "We will no longer cooperate with the other countries to maintain security in the region if the clashes continue."[20]

The situation was then allowed to drift, with the United States declining to try harder to effect a cease-fire between the Iraqi Kurds or to contribute a mere $2 million to an international mediation force that might have forestalled the next round of fighting.[21] In August 1996, a sudden renewal of the intra-Kurdish struggle seemed likely to result in a PUK victory, given that it had received arms from Iran. Desperate, Barzani did the unthinkable and invited Saddam Hussein in to help him against Talabani.

How could the United States enforce the no-fly zone against Saddam Hussein when the very people it was supposed to be protecting had invited Saddam Hussein in? Halfheartedly, the United States responded by bombing a few meaningless targets south of Baghdad. Saddam Hussein used the few hours he had to capture and execute some 96 Iraqis who had defected to the United States-financed Iraqi opposition, the Iraqi National Congress (INC). A senior INC official claimed that "in two hours, the Iraqi opposition [had] lost its entire infrastructure,"[22] while a US official concluded, "[O]ur entire covert program has gone to hell."[23]

New peace initiatives early the next year, however, finally led to significant developments and renewed attempts by the United States to bring the Iraqi Kurds together. Following a successful high-level meeting at the end of August 1998 between KDP officials and Talabani, in early September 1998 first Barzani and then Talabani journeyed to Washington. After separate individual meetings with US State Department officials, the two Iraqi Kurdish leaders finally met personally for the first time since the summer of 1994, when their civil war had begun. After two days of lengthy sessions, they reached a tentative agreement to end their fighting permanently and to establish peace.

In announcing this pact, US Secretary of State Madeleine Albright also made general promises of American support for the Iraqi Kurds—contingent on their continuing unity—by declaring, "the United States will decide how and when to respond to Baghdad's actions based on the threat they pose to Iraq's neighbors, to regional security, to vital U.S. interests and to the Iraqi people, including those in the north."[24] President Clinton repeated Albright's lukewarm assurances in letters to Congress on November 6, 1998, and again on May 19, 1999.[25] Although these pronouncements did not constitute an ironclad agreement of protection, they were—in contrast to Nixon's and Kissigner's covert and unkept promises of a quarter of a century earlier—public declarations. Thus, they could not and have not been so cavalierly ignored, particularly after the Iraqi Kurds supported the United States in its war to overthrow Saddam Hussein in 2003. Subsequently, of course, the United States has had to walk a fine line as mediator between the new Baghdad government and the KRG, both of which it largely created. The United States also walks a delicate line in Syria today between nuanced support for the opposition that will not benefit Jihadi groups such as ISIS that are tacitly and covertly supported by US ally Turkey, which seeks to restrain by these means the Syrian Kurds who, however, are largely secular and pro-Western. Would Solomon himself know how to respond?

Fourth Stage

The fourth stage of American foreign policy toward the Kurds began with the US war to remove Saddam Hussein from power in March 2003 and continues to the present (2015). This most recent period might also be called the de facto United States-KRG alliance stage. Until this fourth stage, Turkey's opposition to the Kurdish identity, and Turkey's strong strategic alliance with the United States since the days of the Truman Doctrine that was first promulgated in 1947 had arguably been two of the main reasons for the inability of the Kurds to create any type of independent state in the modern Middle East that began to develop after World War I. Although the United States had always paid lip service to the idea of Kurdish rights, whenever it was necessary to make a choice the United States always backed its strategic NATO ally Turkey when it came to the Kurdish issue.

Only when the United States perceived the Iraqi Kurds to be a useful foil against Saddam Hussein did Washington begin to take a partially pro-Kurdish position, at least toward the Iraqi Kurds. However, this US support for the Iraqi Kurds did not prohibit

Turkey from unilaterally intervening into northern Iraq in pursuit of the PKK during the 1980s and 1990s. However, US support for the developing KRG, the disagreements over sanctions against Saddam Hussein's Iraq, and the future of Iraq itself gradually helped begin to fray the long-standing United States-Turkish alliance.

The US war to remove Saddam Hussein from power in 2003 furthered this process and even partially reversed alliance partners. For the first time since the creation of Iraq, the Iraqi Kurds now had a powerful ally in the United States. This ironic situation was brought about by Turkey's refusal to allow the United States to use its territory as a base for a northern front to attack Saddam Hussein's Iraq in March 2003 during the second Gulf War. Courtesy of Turkey, the Iraqi Kurds suddenly were thrust into the role of US ally, a novel position they eagerly and successfully assumed. Quickly, the Iraqi Kurds occupied the oil-rich Kirkuk and Mosul areas—which would have been unthinkable encroachments on Turkish red lines had Turkey anchored the northern front. What is more, Turkey had no choice but to acquiesce in the Iraqi Kurdish moves.

The new situation was further illustrated in July 2003, when the United States apprehended 11 Turkish commandos in the Iraqi Kurdish city of Sulaymaniya who were apparently seeking to carry out acts intended to destabilize the de facto Kurdish government and state in northern Iraq. Previously, as the strategic ally of the United States, Turkey had had carte blanche to do practically anything it wanted to in northern Iraq. No longer was this true. The "Sulaymaniya incident" caused what one high-ranking Turkish general called the "worst crisis of confidence"[26] in United States-Turkish relations since the creation of the NATO alliance. It also illustrated how the United States was willing to protect the Iraqi Kurds from unwanted Turkish interference. What is more, Washington now began to reject Turkish proposals that either the United States eliminate the PKK guerrillas holed up in northern Iraq or permit the Turkish army to do so. Previously, the Turkish army had entered northern Iraq any time it desired in pursuit of the PKK.

Accordingly, many observers now stress how the Iraqi Kurds love the Americans. Yes, but. Although the United States is currently widely popular in the KRG, it is with a background caveat reminding all that they were betrayed twice before by the United States, in 1975 and again in 1991, as mentioned above. Indeed, as already mentioned, some Kurds began to fear the worst when the Iraq Study Group Report—coauthored by former US Secretary of State James A. Baker III and former US representative Lee H. Hamilton and released in December 2006—suggested that the hard-won KRG federal state might have to be sacrificed to the perceived need for a reestablished centralized Iraqi state.[27] Fortunately for the KRG, US President George W. Bush did not adopt these recommendations, but their mere broaching showed how tenuous future US support might be.

Nevertheless, the KRG leadership maintains that it received renewed US guarantees of protection in December 2009. At a meeting in Irbil between KRG President Massoud Barzani and US Secretary of Defense Robert Gates, the latter assured the Iraqi Kurds by declaring: "We recognize the concerns that you have about the future of your people and we will help you to ensure a prosperous and peaceful Iraq. We will not abandon you."[28] In addition, Gates made the following three commitments: (1) to use US influence to ensure that the outstanding disputes between the KRG and the Iraqi government, including the Kirkuk dispute and other disputed areas and the sharing of oil revenues, are resolved based on the Iraqi Constitution and Article 140 regarding the future of Kirkuk; (2) to continue with US military efforts with the peshmerga (KRG defense forces) as well as with the Iraqi army and security forces within the framework of US joint security architecture; and (3) to offer US support and assistance for a census to be conducted in Iraq the following year.[29]

A few days later, the Obama administration gave the Iraqi Kurds what they maintained was an "historic"[30] commitment when it promised to broker disputes between them and the Baghdad government as well as to give support for resolving the vexing issue of oil-rich Kirkuk.[31] This US support was in return for the Iraqi Kurds' agreeing to accept a new election law that would give them a few fewer seats in the new Iraqi parliament that was elected on March 7, 2010. The delicate Baghdad-Irbil balance has continued despite the US troop withdrawal from Iraq at the end of 2011. This has required the KRG leadership to practice particularly astute diplomacy to survive.

Fifth (PKK) Stage

Commencing a decade earlier and then overlapping the third and fourth stages analyzed above is what might be called the fifth or PKK stage of American foreign policy toward the Kurds. In contrast to its support for the "good" Iraqi Kurds and despite Turkish conspiracy theories to the contrary,[32] the United States has very strongly opposed the "bad" Kurds of the PKK. Turkey's longtime and continuing geostrategically important position as a US NATO ally is clearly the main reason for this situation. Other explanations include the US fear of Islamic extremism and Turkey's alliance with Israel, which, however, is currently on hold. As a constitutionally secular state, Turkey is seen as a bastion against Islamic extremism, whereas support for Israel remains a given for American foreign policy.

Although it continues to criticize Turkey in its annual human rights country reports,[33] the United States has also maintained that the PKK are "terrorists" who "frequently kill noncombatants, and target village officials, village guards, teachers and other perceived representatives of the state."[34] "The PKK are terrorists. Turkey is going after terrorists. The PKK are indiscriminately killing their own people. They are not supported by the majority of Kurds."[35]

Other US officials claim that they have compiled a thick dossier on the PKK that includes murder, drug trafficking, extortion, robbery, and trafficking in illegal immigrants.[36] The US State Department has also long had the PKK on its list of terrorist organizations, but not the KDP or PUK of the Iraqi Kurds.[37]

US support for Turkey on the Kurdish issue was amply illustrated by the help it gave Turkey to capture Abdullah Ocalan, the leader of the PKK. When Turkey forced Syria to finally expel Ocalan from his longtime sanctuary in that country in October 1998, the United States backed Turkey by sending a strongly worded letter to Syria regarding the situation.[38] After a short, surreptitious stay in Russia, Ocalan arrived in Italy, where for a brief period it looked as if he might be able to turn his military defeat into a political victory by having the European Union try him and thus also try Turkey.

Although the Italians and other Europeans such as the Germans initially appeared sympathetic, at this point the United States weighed in heavily by denouncing Ocalan in the strongest of terms as a terrorist. The United States also pressured Italy—and any other state that was tempted to offer the PKK leader asylum and a platform from which to negotiate—to instead extradite him to Turkey for trial. An editorial from the US State Department broadcast by the Voice of America (VOA) declared: "It is neither U.S. practice nor policy to provide an international platform from which terrorists can expound their views or try to justify their criminal actions. No one should doubt our views on Ocalan; the United States considers him a terrorist who should be brought to justice for his crimes."[39]

As he flew from country to country, James Foley, the US State Department representative, seemingly mocked Ocalan by joking: "I'd hate to be the pilot of that small plane."[40] Desperate, Ocalan finally allowed the Greeks to take him to their embassy in Nairobi, Kenya, where US intelligence agents had inundated the country following the US embassy bombing there the previous summer. At this point American animus toward the PKK leader entered its final stage by providing Turkey with the technical intelligence to pinpoint his whereabouts and capture him. Mark Parris, the US ambassador to Turkey, approvingly spoke of "Ocalan's rendition,"[41] an archaic term referring to the surrender of a fugitive slave.

Although the US war to overthrow Saddam Hussein in 2003 brought new tensions between the United States and Turkey over the Kurdish issue, more recently the United States has continued to support its longtime Turkish ally against the PKK, now ensconced in the Qandil Mountains of the KRG. Late in 2007, for example, the United States began giving Turkey "actionable intelligence"[42] on the PKK's location. Then in February 2008, Turkey, armed with this intelligence, launched its first military incursion into northern Iraq against the PKK since the 1990s. As in earlier times, the United States did not object despite its de facto alliance with the KRG. In February 2010, US Secretary of Defense Robert Gates indicated that the United States was seeking to determine whether it could offer Turkey even more help with equipment and intelligence to combat the PKK.[43] Moreover, when Turkey finally began negotiating with the PKK early in 2013, the United States proved pleased to support the peace process. Turkey's much greater gravitas and value as a US ally had inevitably reasserted itself.

Sixth (Syrian) Stage

The sixth or Syrian stage of American foreign policy toward the Kurds stems from the Syrian civil war. The United States had long viewed Syria with caution and often with hostility as a radical Arab state sponsor of international terrorism and an implacable foe of Israel. This position was formalized by the Syria Accountability and Lebanese Sovereignty Restoration Act (SALSRA) that Congress passed on December 12, 2003. The stated purpose of this act was to end what the United States saw as Syrian support for terrorism and illegal presence in Lebanon, to stop Syria's development of weapons of mass destruction that included chemical weapons, and to halt Syria's illegal importation of Iraqi oil and shipments of military items to anti-US forces in Iraq. Ironically, however, SALSRA did not address Syrian violation of human rights

As of this writing in April 2015, the United States had the following priorities in Syria: (1) respond successfully to the regime's probable chemical attack against elements of the opposition on August 21, 2013, and any other such attacks; (2) protect Israel; (3) oppose Iran; (4) curb ISIS as well as such al-Qaeda affiliates as al-Nusra and other Jihadi extremists; and (5) maintain Syrian unity.[44]

On August 21, 2013, the Syrian regime apparently used chemical weapons against the opposition in Ghouta, an eastern suburb of Damascus, killing anywhere from 500 to 1,400 people, the numbers varying according to US intelligence reports made public. Whereas the Assad regime had long had a great deal of innocent blood on its hands and now probably was guilty of using chemical weapons, this was not a sufficient reason for the United States and its Western allies to bomb Syria. Indeed, the United States had neither an intelligent entry nor exit plan if it did so.

In the first place, however, it was not yet even certain that the Syrian regime actually had used these weapons. US intelligence on these matters has erred and lied to the world before. For example, in 1998 the United States bombed a pharmaceutical plant in Sudan, claiming that Sudan had supplied al-Qaeda with chemical weapons that had been used in its attacks on US embassies in Kenya and Tanzania. Later, however, it learned that the intelligence supposedly implicating Sudan was incorrect. Similarly, in the run-up to the war that toppled Saddam Hussein in 2003 and the murders and repercussions of which are still being felt more than a decade later, the United States falsely claimed that it had incontrovertible intelligence that Iraq possessed weapons of mass destruction, which justified attacking. It turned out that US intelligence was wrong or simply lied to justify going to war.

Given such an uncertain track record, why should one be so certain that the US intelligence was correct this time about Syrian chemical weapons? And even if it were correct, did this justify bombing just because the Syrian regime had crossed a red line drawn by the United States, which then would lose face if it did not retaliate? Furthermore, some have even claimed that the Syrian opposition was the real culprit, because it wanted to get the United States to topple the Assad regime, which it could not do itself. As both the United Nations and Russia demanded, positive proof was called for before one could expect the international community to go down this road again.

The United States justified its possible attack against Syria on the grounds that the Assad regime had violated international law by using chemical weapons. However, using napalm in Vietnam had not bothered the United States when it was the one using such weapons. More recently, the United States simply ignored Saddam Hussein's use of chemical weapons against the Kurds in Halabja on March 16, 1988, because in those days Saddam was its ally. Does anyone believe that the United States would have made all this fuss about chemical weapons if it had been the opposition in Syria that had used them?

It is patently illegal under international law for the United States to bomb Syria unless authorized to do so by the United Nations Security Council or in immediate self-defense. Neither applied to the reputed Syrian use of chemical weapons. The legal way for the United States to respond to this crisis was to negotiate with Russia to bring the Security Council on board. After all, the United Nations was constituted in the first place not to take military action unless all five permanent members of the Security Council concurred. Otherwise, the United Nations would simply become the tool of one great power or the other, not the arm of international justice. By not acting in this case, the United Nations might be wiser than the United States, although President Barack Obama and his supporters initially did not want to hear this. Without UN action, the United States might have sought Arab League support. However, by bombing without such international approval, it would be the United States that was violating international law, not the Assad regime.

Furthermore, if the United States bombed, it ran the risk of escalating the Syrian civil war into a regional and even an international war that might involve Russia and Iran and inevitably might bring in Israel, which of course has long possessed nuclear weapons, the legality of which was questionable, but which the United States never mentioned because Israel was its ally. Despite assurances that it would conduct only precise surgical strikes, the resulting so-called collateral damage that would inevitably kill innocent civilians if the United States bombed Syria was yet another reason not to do it. What is more, the Assad regime would surely have sought to retaliate in some way if bombed. Tit-for-tat bombings could soon escalate into a much larger war that nobody with a sound mind would want.

In addition, if the United States had succeeded in bombing Assad into surrender, it might have led to an even worse situation from the point of view of US national interest, because some of the most powerful elements of the Syrian opposition, as noted above, were affiliated with al-Qaeda or worse, ISIS being the prime example. US action against Assad could bring about the law of unintended consequences. If ISIS or a small al-Qaeda state actually came to power in a post-Assad splintered Syria, suddenly the United States would have to exercise real self-defense against Syria similar to what occurred when the United States armed Islamist elements in Afghanistan in the 1980s, only to suffer blowback on September 11. Furthermore, how would the KRG in Iraq like suddenly to have ISIS or an al-Qaeda statelet as a next-door neighbor, which of course is exactly what occurred in 2014?

Furthermore, if the United States with its British and French allies struck Syria, it would have looked as if Western imperialism was again rearing its ugly head in the Middle East. These countries might then have opened the gates of hell and brought on themselves even more unwanted blowback from a union of Arab nationalists with Islamic Jihadists and Salafists. Had the United States learned nothing about how to proceed intelligently in international affairs? How many more American lives had to be needlessly lost, not to mention the thousands of others who might now have to die if a new war were to commence, before the United States learned that there were more intelligent ways to handle these matters?

However, the major problem for the United States was that it had not offered any valid strategy for what it would be trying to accomplish by bombing Syria other than somehow supposedly punishing the Assad regime for using chemical weapons. Obama had already ruled out regime change. However, without really degrading Assad's assets, how would such a mere pinprick US attack do anything but arouse his anger and determination to fight on and even to retaliate against the United States and maybe Israel?

Even worse than not having a good explanation for what it was trying to accomplish, the United States also lacked a valid exit strategy for what it was proposing to do. Once the United States bombed Syria, escalation was likely that would draw the United States further into a new quagmire. To what would that supposedly lead? Without either an intelligent entry or exit strategy, bombing Syria had all the earmarks of starting a disastrous dumb war, something Obama was supposedly smart enough to avoid.

Fortunately, the British Parliament promptly voted not to support the United States. This was a truly amazing action, given how powerful the British prime minister had become and how much the parliament had declined in the past century. Showing that he still could learn quickly, US President Obama picked up on what the British Parliament did and managed to wiggle out of the trap he had set for himself by drawing his red line on chemical weapons. Throwing the decision on what to do into the hands of the US Congress at least created the possibility of keeping some presidential credibility without having to start bombing. It also offered Obama the opportunity to share the blame with Congress if the bombing backfired or even turned disastrous. In the short run, this would be good for the president and the United States.

However, in letting the US Congress make the final decision, Obama was potentially giving up the power to decide on war and peace, which was one of his greatest assets. He might soon regret this loss of power since he was negotiating Iran's nuclear weapons, which posed a much more serious threat to US national security than Syria's use of chemical weapons. North Korea's nuclear ambitions offered similar problems. Egypt's new military regime that had removed President Mohammed Morsi in July 2013 also continued to ignore US calls for peace after killing more than 600 protesters. Iraq's continuing sectarian killings and Afghanistan's shaky future as US troops pulled out also represented potentially deadly problems for the United States in the near future for which the president might want the authority to move quickly without congressional deliberation and approval.

The history of the past century aptly demonstrates that Congress by definition is a deliberative body and is ill cut out to make sudden decisions on how to react to military crises. This is precisely why, despite what the US Constitution still asserts about Congress declaring war, it is really the president who now does, because only he can make the quick decisions that are so absolutely crucial in the modern world. Thus, in gaining a short-term solution to his redline problem with Syria, Obama might have been creating a long-term problem for his own effectiveness as president.

As for protecting Israel, bombing Syria to punish Assad might cause him to retaliate against Israel, as Saddam Hussein did in 1991 when he came under US attack. Israel, of course, can take care of itself, but any time the Jewish state comes under attack from an Arab opponent there is the immediate risk of an all-out regional war or worse. Thus, protecting Israel might best be done by not bombing Syria.

Similarly, for opposing Iran, curbing al-Qaeda, and even maintaining Syria's unity, US bombing might force Iran's hand to more overtly defend its all-important and only Arab ally, Assad. On the other hand, it might also be true that doing nothing about Assad's probable use of chemical weapons might lead Iran to conclude that the United States would do nothing seriously about Iran building nuclear weapons. However, there were other ways to send a message to Iran than simply bombing Syria.

Furthermore, if US bombing led to Assad's overthrow, such al-Qaeda–affiliated groups as Jablat al-Nusra as well as ISIS, among others, might have a better chance to craft some sort of long-term institutional power out of the ruins of a splintered Syria. Again, bombing Syria in retaliation for its probable use of chemical weapons might work against all five of the US priorities listed above in that beleaguered state.

Finally, there were other ways for Obama to make a statement without bombing Syria or falling back on Congress. Covert operations famously reinstated the United States–friendly Shah of Iran in 1953 and even earlier supported Husni Zaim's military coup in Syria in 1949, overthrew the supposedly pro-communist Arbenz regime in Guatemala in 1954, and who knows what else over the years. Similarly, clandestine actions might be able to accomplish whatever the US leaders thought that it had to do in Syria without risking as much blowback.[45] Arming selected opposition groups such as the Syrian Kurds that were secularly inclined, tougher smart sanctions, encouraging more defections from Assad's entourage, and more vigorous diplomacy to bring Russia and Iran on board were all possibilities that needed to be examined.

In this event, the United States apparently found a way out of its chemical weapons dilemma in Syria, by taking up a Russian suggestion to have Assad surrender his arsenal to international control and destruction. Although many in the United States and the Syrian opposition criticized Obama's UN option as feckless, the UN route not only avoided most of the pitfalls of the United States unilaterally bombing Syria, but also provided a legal diplomatic strategy.

On the other hand, by opposing Kurdish autonomy in Syria as leading to secessionism and to please its NATO ally Turkey, the United States might find itself weakening a secular Kurdish ally that was successfully combating ISIS. This was so even in the case where, as of this writing, the United States had hesitated to give heavy military equipment to the opposition, fearing that it would fall into anti-Western, Jihadist/Salafist hands. However, by remaining aloof, the United States in effect ironically favored the Assad regime, which its ally Turkey opposed but its enemy Iran supported.

In July 2013, however, the United States did see fit to denounce the PKK-affiliated PYD for clashes in the town of Amuda, in which the PYD had killed several Kurds from other parties. Once again, by denouncing the strongest Kurdish party battling ISIS, the United States ironically was implicitly supporting ISIS! The PYD itself replied that it had to defend itself against ISIS and other Jihadi groups.[46] Probably in deference to its Turkish ally, the United States has also opposed the PYD's plans to establish some kind of Kurdish administration in the areas of Syria they now dominate.

However, the PYD claims that it has been in hopeful contact with the United States over the issue.[47] Indeed, its cochair Salih Muslim has appealed to both the United States and Europe to support the Kurds against their common Jihadi enemies in the Syrian civil war.[48] "I want the American public and the entire world to know that we are trying to stop these jihadist groups, and we want them to stand with us. These people attack innocent civilians and kill children, women and old people simply because they are Kurds." The PYD leader furthered claimed that the Jihadists "issue fatwas that raping Kurdish women and looting their properties is legitimate, after you kill their husbands" and added that "this is what happened in Tal Abyad recently. . . . [and] in the Tal Arn and Tal Hasel towns of Aleppo."

Continuing, Salih Muslim asserted that "unfortunately, the United States and Europe have not done anything yet . . . [and] have not even condemned atrocities against civilian Kurds. . . . They do not even send us humanitarian aid!" Salih Muslim went on to complain that "everybody in Syria received international aid, but not us, the Kurds! On the contrary, we are under an embargo from all around." The PYD leader added that "I have applied twice for a visa to travel to the United States, but they did yet not respond to my request." He also said that "I do not know either why American officials are not willing to meet with us, and he declared that "we have never had any animosity against America and the American people." Warming to his task, Salih Muslim even proclaimed that "we see our future in Western democracy," because "the United States is the cradle of democracy and the American people support freedom for everyone. . . . There is no doubt that the interests of the American people are not contrary to ours."

The US opposition to the Syrian Kurds began to change only after ISIS attacked the KRG in August 2014 and the Syrian Kurdish city of Kobane the following month. Indeed, US air support for the beleaguered Syrian Kurds in Kobane proved indispensable for the eventual Kurdish victory, and heralded the possibility of further US support, as will be analyzed in the next chapter, on ISIS.

ISIS and the Kurds

Introduction

The rise of the Kurdistan Regional Government (KRG) in northern Iraq, the ongoing Kurdistan Workers Party (PKK) insurgency and now peace negotiations with the Turkish government, and the sudden emergence of the Kurds in Syria because of its civil war have empowered the Kurds and challenged the artificial borders of the Middle East that were established after World War I by the notorious Sykes-Picot Agreement.[1] However, it also is now necessary to analyze the rise of the Islamic State in Iraq and Syria (ISIS) [also known as ISIL, the *Daesh* (a derogatory Arabic acronym), or the Islamic State (IS)] as one of the other main tipping points changing the Middle East political map and the existential threat it has posed to the Kurds in Iraq and Syria.

Indeed, both ISIS and the Syrian Kurds (PYD) and the PKK in Turkey (but not the KRG in Iraq) claim to be post-state entities that supersede the concept of the Westphalian state. ISIS purports to have established a trans-state caliphate, whereas the Syrian Kurds and the PKK claim to have instituted PKK leader Abdullah Ocalan's philosophy of democratic autonomy, or bottom-up rule, largely cut loose from the concept of what Ocalan saw as the traditional oppressive nation-state.[2] What has caused the traditional state and with it the Middle East political map to weaken and potentially change so much?

From the present perspective, it appears that there is a wide range of political, sociological, economic, and military factors, among others. However, the bottom line is the virtual collapse of the traditional state system in Syria and Iraq because of their civil wars, with the resulting absence of its previous legitimacy.[3] As the prestigious British weekly *The Economist* recently concluded: "Across the Middle East non-state actors increasingly set the agenda, challenging governments, overthrowing them or prompting them to retrench behind increasingly repressive controls."[4] Some have even argued that only two and a half states remain in the region: Turkey, Iran, and Egypt as the fractional digit.

In addition to the artificiality of the remaining states, other factors are also at work. Frequently, the region's weak, sometimes minority-dominated governments fail to integrate their populations within any sense of inclusive nationality. At the same time important political ideologies such as Arab nationality, political Islam, Jihadism,[5] and Salafism[6] transcend existing state borders. Existing state governments also frequently fail to provide public services, such as functioning courts, schools, or hospitals. These failures prompt citizens to look to nonstate religious groups and charities for the services that successful states are supposed to provide. Furthermore, the civil wars in former Iraq and Syria have resulted in horrendous internally displaced persons (IDPs) problems and even more international refugee problems for Turkey, Lebanon, Jordan, and the KRG in Iraq, among others. These IDP and refugee problems have strongly contributed to the destabilization of the existing state system and will likely result in large populations being permanently relocated.

Tribal loyalties too have been reactivated and rejuvenated to the extent that one now can refer to tribes as well as even gas stations with flags, instead of states with flags. In addition, the age-old Sunni-Shia split has further torn Iraq and Syria apart and is bidding to do so to other regional states such as Libya and Yemen, among others. Indeed, the Sunni-Shia division bids to rearrange the entire

Middle Eastern map.[7] Thus, the seemingly mad violence and power of ISIS is largely a symptom of the collapsed state system. In the past, stronger states would have quickly prevented ISIS' rise.

Rise of ISIS

There are, of course, a number of additional specific factors that should be mentioned. Although Turkey denies it, its earlier tacit support of ISIS, which allowed Jihadists from all over the world to transit its territory and cross into Syria, has been well documented.[8] Turkey's motivation was to enable the Syrian opposition to defeat Assad and increasingly too the Syrian Kurds, who had declared a thinly disguised PKK protostate on the southern Turkish border. In addition, Chechnya, long since radicalized by Islamic ferment and struggle, has been one of many important contributors to this Jihadist traffic.[9]

These Jihadists, who sought to recapture the lost glories of a resplendent Islam, were bolstered by others whose truer motivations were more a sense of adventure and excitement all the way to the pathologically sick and criminal who reveled in approved thrill killings, rape, and the chance for wealth. Drugs have even been used to convince converts to launch suicide attacks with the promise of immediate entrance into a paradise that would offer them worldly delights.[10] The beheading of their enemies is the most infamous of ISIS's actions. The group interprets some verses in the Quran (especially in Al-Anfal and Muhammad) to justify this deed. The Surah Muhammad, for example, in verse 47:4 states: "So when you meet those who disbelieve [in battle], strike [their] necks until, when you have inflicted slaughter upon them, and then secure their bonds."

Paradoxically, even some Kurds have joined ISIS for either sheer adventure or ideological reasons dealing with anti-Americanism/Westernism or whatever perceived grievance they bore.

However, the total number of Kurds is low and should not be over-emphasized. Still, that odd individuals have been recruited warns against facile explanatory factors for the strength of ISIS. Clearly there is much that we simply do not know about the organization.[11] Nevertheless, clearly relevant to our understanding is the strict and uncompromising Wahabi Islamic doctrine prevalent in Saudi Arabia, as well as finances from sympathizers in such states as Saudi Arabia, Qatar, and the United Arab Emirates, among others.[12]

Even more important, however, is the Baathist connection, or what might be termed the revenge of Saddam Hussein. Indeed, 19 out of the top 20 positions in the ISIS cabinet were recently held by former Baathists who were middle-level party members when Saddam Hussein fell in 2003. Thus, a detailed recent report emphasized "the pervasive role played by members of Iraq's former Baathist army in an organization more typically associated with flamboyant foreign jihadists. . . . Almost all of the leaders of the Islamic State are former Iraqi officers, including the members of its shadowy military and security committees, and the majority of its emirs and princes."[13] These former Baathists have given ISIS their military expertise and access to the smuggling networks they developed to bypass the UN sanctions in the 1990s. Although its mere foot soldiers are largely foreign Jihadists/Salafists, Hassan Hassan, the coauthor of a book on ISIS,[14] concludes that it "is a homegrown Iraqi insurgency, and it is organic to Iraq."[15]

Although initially the Baathist secularist ideology would seem at odds with ISIS's strict interpretation of Islamic law, the two overlap in many respects, especially in their reliance on fear and torture. Furthermore, during his last decade in power, Saddam Hussein had cynically begun to rely increasingly on Islamic motifs to justify his rule. His supposedly elite Fedayeen units were even pictured marching in black masks and perpetrating beheadings. Thus, these former Baathists look on the foreign Jihadists who have joined ISIS with a Leninist mind-set that they are useful idiots who can be used to regain power. Islam is simply a useful tool for this purpose. On the other hand, some have argued the opposite, that the Jihadists are really using the unemployed former Baathists desperate for jobs. As for its apparently mindless violence, some have argued that actually ISIS "does not think so differently from the founders of many modern nation-states, who sought a congruence between state and culture as an assumed condition for a viable polity."[16]

The United States, of course, inadvertently helped what has now morphed into ISIS by destroying Saddam Hussein, who had kept a lid on the Islamists, and then disbanding the Iraqi army and Baathist party. Such policies that were poorly envisioned by the United States put several hundred thousand armed men on the street and deprived many others capable of running the state's infrastructure of a job and pension for their future. ISIS offered these former Baathist/Sunni rulers an opportunity to regain their lost dignity and former positions of power. In addition, lax policies allowed many of ISIS's current leaders to escape from earlier US detention centers in Iraq.[17] The list includes the caliph himself, Abu Bakr al-Baghdadi—who spent almost five years imprisoned at Camp Bucca in southern Iraq—as well as Abu Muslim al-Turkmani, Abu Louay, Abu Kassem, Abu Jurnas, Abu Shema, and Abu Suja, among others. In prison these extremists were held side by side with those less radical, allowing US coalition prisons in Iraq to become recruitment centers and even training grounds for ISIS recruits. Moderates who objected to being radicalized were harassed or worse through so-called Sharia courts that spread through the prisons. Limited resources to evaluate the prisoners effectively helped obscure what was occurring. Eventually, even prisoners with strong evidence against them were released because of the weaknesses of the Iraqi court system and the refusal of the United States to share classified information. In addition, some of the most extreme radicals who had been sentenced to death were freed by successful ISIS attacks on what were now Iraqi prisons after the United States withdrew from Iraq at the end of 2011.

Thus, from its past travails, ISIS's leadership has clearly learned much about how to survive to fight successfully another day. The organization then burgeoned because of its perceived success, dynamism, and sense of destiny. The Mosul victory in June 2014 enforced these attributes by bringing vast amounts of captured finances[18] and bringing some of the latest US military equipment into the organization's grasp. Although ISIS now seemed to be the enemy of everybody and had become the specific target of a hastily constructed US alliance, its opponents' strength was much less than the sum of their parts due to their mutual hatreds and lack of unity. The United States, for example, forgot Winston Churchill's positive reference to the devil when Nazi Germany attacked the Soviet Union and its own wartime alliance with Joseph Stalin, and refused to admit Iran to its anti-ISIS coalition, even though the Shia state was clearly one of the most effective potential opponents of Sunni ISIS. For the time being at least, ISIS could mobilize the maximum possibility of its strength, while its myriad opponents were divided and unable to strike back in unison.

Thus, when ISIS suddenly struck the KRG on 3 August 2014, its vaunted military or peshmerga found themselves outgunned because of inferior military equipment and initially without allies. Since the KRG was still not yet independent, American aid could legally be given only through Baghdad, which hesitated to give too much lest the Kurds use it to become independent. Only after an emergency appeal from KRG President Massoud Barzani for immediate US aid[19] to stem the ISIS tide that had driven within a mere 20 miles of its capital, Erbil, with its 1.5 million inhabitants, was ISIS brought to a halt by US air power in the Iraqi Kurdish region. However, the present US proclamation that it will not commit US "boots on the ground" obviously encourages ISIS leaders to believe that it can eventually triumph because of its enemies' lack of total commitment, continuing weaknesses, and disunity. On the other hand, ISIS's attacks on the two rival Kurdish groups in Iraq (KRG) and Syria (PYD/PKK) have served to bring them together. Indeed, a new agreement between the two Kurdish rivals was announced in Dohuk on October 25, 2014.[20] In addition, ISIS's attack on the Syrian Kurds in Kobane elicited nascent US support for the PYD, to the chagrin of Turkey.[21]

The collapse of the poorly conceived Geneva II process for peace in Syria in January 2014 amply illustrates the bankruptcy of US foreign policy when it ignores these new realities in the Middle East, especially the rise of ISIS and of the Syrian Kurds, as well as the importance of Iran. Thus, the United States decided not to invite either the Syrian Kurds or Iran to Geneva II. How could one possibly believe that a formula for peace could be found when two of the main participants in the Syrian struggle were not even invited to the peace talks? Indeed, one might well argue that the Syrian Kurds controlled more territory, were far more unified, and apparently were more democratic and secular than any other opposition group that was invited!

Furthermore, the important role the PKK played in helping roll back ISIS and save the lives of thousands of Yezidi Kurds in Sinjar (Shingal) threatened with ISIS's genocidal campaign in August 2014 further illustrates the changing Middle East political map. When the Kurds rallied against ISIS in front of Erbil with US air support in August 2014, it was not just the KRG peshmerga, but also the battle-hardened PKK militants from the Qandil Mountains in northern Iraq, and the Democratic Union Party (PYD)/PKK fighters from Rojava (Syrian Kurdistan) who were closely associated with the PKK, who helped save the day. One month later it was again the PYD/PKK who successfully used US air support to beat back ISIS's attack on Kobane in Syria. The US aid to the PKK-related PYD showed how the changing political map in the Middle East was also making for strange bed fellows. The ISIS threat created even stranger associates by bringing US air power together with Iranian ground forces to recapture Amerli, an Iraqi city near the Iranian border, from ISIS in August 2014 and more recently in the Iraqi Shiite and Iranian drive to recapture Tikrit from ISIS in March 2015.

Turkey

At the same time Turkey will surely come to rue its earlier support for Jihadists in Syria. ISIS blowback against Turkey in 2014 led to its holding 49 Turks captured when it overran Mosul in June 2014 and only released after three months, as well as ISIS threats to attack targets in Turkey if possible. However, this did not prevent Turkey from passively watching ISIS try to destroy the Syrian Kurds holed up in Kobane just across the Turkish border during the vicious fighting for that city in September-October 2014. Again the collapse of the traditional state system in Syria and Iraq has made for strange and confused bed fellows as the parties involved groped for new ways to understand the changing situation.

Now, of course, Turkey had good reasons not to support the Syrian Kurds in the battle for Kobane. As Turkey saw it, support for the Syrian Kurds would be tantamount to supporting the PKK, a terrorist enemy that had been trying to dismember Turkey for more than 30 years. Aid for the PYD would simply make the PKK, and its tacit ally, Assad, stronger. In addition, why should Turkey get involved when the United States would not do any more? It suited Turkey that ISIS and the Kurds—two enemies—were weakening themselves by slugging it out with each other. Instead, Turkey wanted to create a buffer zone between itself and the Syrian fighting to keep ISIS out, to absorb some of the refugees currently taxing Turkey, and from where anti-Assad forces could strike Assad from a safe house. Turkey saw Kurdish threats and Assad as greater problems than ISIS.

Conclusion

In conclusion, why has ISIS chosen to attack the Kurds? Although it is not possible to delve into its mind, the following are some probable reasons: (1) in Syria, the Kurds occupy crucial territory that ISIS believes necessary for it to connect areas it already possesses and also to connect with the Turkish border and the outside world to facilitate movement such as oil sales and communications; (2) in Iraq, the Kurds have been historical enemies of the Baathists; (3) the Kurds supported the United States in its invasion of Iraq and the overthrow of Saddam Hussein's Sunni rule in 2003; (4) in June 2014 the Kurds quickly occupied the disputed territories around Kirkuk when ISIS pushed Baghdad out of the Mosul area; and (5) finally, the Kurds may not be seen as good Muslims, given their support for the Yezidi Kurds, Christians, and other minorities.

The rise of ISIS and the Kurds make it clear that this situation will call for a new paradigm to classify and understand the changing geopolitical reality of the Middle East. Turkey and the United States have been slow to comprehend this fact, as illustrated by their continuing insistence on trying to maintain the artificiality of what should be called former Iraq as well as former Syria. Neither state any more comes close to meeting Max Weber's famous definition of a state as being that entity which commands a monopoly on the legitimate use of force within its territory. Instead, new types of entities are being born before our very eyes, and ironically the two bitter enemies, the Kurds and ISIS, are the two main beneficiaries of this situation. A variety of political, sociological, and economic factors are operating in addition to the more visible military ones. The United States has also been slow to understand and fully implement Carl von Clausewitz's famous understanding that war is often politics by other means. In other words, US military action must be used wisely in conjunction with intelligent political and diplomatic policies that conform to the new geopolitical realities of the collapsed state systems in Syria and Iraq and the resulting changing political map of the Middle East.

Kurdistan Aborning Amidst Continuing Conflict

By 2017, Kurdish geopolitical realities had reached the stage where one might speak about Kurdistan aborning amidst all the continuing conflict. Given its different stages of development in Iraq, Syria, Turkey, and Iran, of course, one had to view this as a sequenced or cascading process that was pursuing different paths in each state. The purpose of this chapter is to analyze and intelligently speculate about this developing process, first, in Turkey; then, Syria; and finally, Iraq. Iran will be omitted given the present stagnant Kurdish situation there.

The Collapse of the Turkish-PKK Peace Process

The collapse of the Turkish-Kurdish peace process[1] in July 2015 and renewed fighting seemingly pushed the situation back to square one. What led to this failure? Despite progress toward a resolution, the two sides proved unable to bridge the enormous gap between them. On the one hand the government of Turkish president Recep Tayyip Erdogan's Justice and Development Party (AKP) was unwilling to actually negotiate with Abdullah Ocalan, the imprisoned leader of the Kurdistan Workers Party (PKK).

Instead, the government believed it could simply list the conditions for peace and have them accepted with minimal concessions. The old Kemalist penchant for maintaining a unitary ethnic Turkish state remained. Tellingly, for example, the government rejected a neutral third-party observer or facilitator who might have encouraged and recorded the talks while even making suggestions when the process reached impasses. The failure of the minimal Dolmabahce consensus—an attempt in March 2015 to establish a monitoring committee to oversee the failing peace process—and simmering Kurdish anger over the Turkish government's failure to support the Syrian Kurdish struggle in Kobane that raged from September 2014 until January 2015 proved to be two heavy blows to the peace process. Erdogan's AKP losing its majority in the June 7, 2015 parliamentary elections, largely due to the pro-Kurdish Peoples Democratic Party (HDP) exceeding the 10 percent threshold and entering parliament as a party instead of mere independents as before, proved to be the final blow as the HDP's new seats cost the AKP a majority.

On the other hand, Selahattin Demirtas, the co-chair of the HDP, also made a strategic error by declaring that Erdogan would never achieve his ambition of becoming a powerful executive president when the Kurdish leader, possibly alluding to the required three repetitions of the traditional Islamic formula for divorce, three times declared: "Mr. Recep Tayyip Erdogan, you will never be able to be the head of the nation as long as the HDP exists and as long as the HDP people are on this soil. . . . We will not make you the president."[2] This unwise stand against Erdogan's ambitions clearly helped provoke the Turkish leader's anti-Kurdish reaction.

In addition, on July 30, 2015, a suicide bomber from the Islamic State of Iraq and Syria (ISIS)—who was a Turkish national who might also have been an ethnic Kurd—killed more than 30 people at a Kurdish political rally held in the Turkish city of Surac near the Syrian border. Blaming the Turkish state, the PKK reacted by killing two policemen in the town of Ceylanpinar, even though there was no strong proof of the state's culpability. This ill-advised PKK action also helped fuel the state's belligerent response.

Furthermore, the PKK's attempts to institute democratic autonomy or grass-roots, local governing structures of decentralization throughout much of southeastern Anatolia seemed to the government Kurdish independence disguised. Indeed, a month before the peace process even formally began in March 2013, the PKK formed the Patriotic Revolutionary Youth Movement (YDG-H). This new organization grew quickly into an armed, urban youth militia that enticed government security forces into street battles in numerous southeastern cities. When the Turkish army entered Nusaybin (the twin city of Syria's Qamishli) after the PKK Ankara car bombings in February 2016, it was stunned by the extent of the PKK network of underground tunnels, which allowed snipers to move about the city secretly and effectively[3] and employ a new strategy of a *hendek* (trenches) style urban warfare.[4] As the International Crisis Group concluded: "Divergent understandings and irreconcilable expectations coupled with the lack of a concrete roadmap made the [peace] process fragile."[5] Thus, a genuine resolution of the Kurdish issue proved beyond reach despite the veneer of a peace process. Once heavy fighting resumed, several southeastern cities such as the Sur district of Diyarbakir, and most of Nusaybin, Cizre. Silopi, and Yuksekova, among others, were reduced to ruins.

Resumed Fighting Amidst New Conditions

However, despite the resumption of fighting, the Turkish-Kurdish peace process has not returned to square one for a number of reasons. Compared to the days when the very word "Kurd" constituted a four-letter word in the Kemalist lexicon and denial of a Kurdish ethnic problem prevailed, the Kurdish issue now has been institutionalized within Turkish domestic politics and furthermore regionalized—indeed, internationalized. Despite the current impasse, official Turkish talks with Ocalan, the PKK, and the legal pro-Kurdish Peoples Democratic Party (HDP) have given the Kurdish issue, in general, and the PKK, specifically, a permanent legitimacy that would have been inconceivable even a decade ago. In spite of the resumed fighting, the Turkish-Kurdish relationship has moved far beyond square one.

Moreover, regionally and internationally the Kurdish issue in Turkey—as well as in Iraq and now, of course, Syria (but not Iran)—has achieved a major new permanency that also would have been unfathomable a mere decade ago. Thus, Turkey—its political and economic future still bright in the long-run despite short-term domestic and regional instability—must continue to recognize and contend with the expanding Kurdish issue. Domestically this has led to a situation where even such esteemed Turkish scholars as M. Hakan Yavuz and Nihat Ali Ozcan have recently suggested that Kurdish autonomy be considered as a solution: "for the first time, some Turks are thinking about separating from the Kurdish minority,"[6] and that even "a Kurdish state seems to be inevitable, given the current political fragmentation throughout the Middle East."[7]

However, how Kurdish autonomy might be implemented in Turkey, when the majority of ethnic Kurds no longer live in their historic southeastern homeland or probably do not even want autonomy as distinguished from full democracy, remains uncertain. Thus, a solution to the Kurdish problem in Turkey along the lines of autonomy or even independence might simply create new problems despite any genuine Turkish government goodwill in facilitating such policies!

Former Turkish prime minister Ahmet Davutoglu's once touted policies of zero problems with neighbors and strategic depth have instead metastasized into ones of huge problems with neighbors and strategic quagmire. As noted earlier, the U.S invasion of Iraq and overthrow of Saddam Hussein in 2003 is one major background reason for this dilemma. Without the late dictator's strong hand, in the opinion of some, Iraq has largely been shattered into its sectarian and ethnic parts and has come to exist largely in the minds of the United States.[8] The resulting instability led to countless problems for Turkey such as space for the rise of the Kurdistan Regional Government (KRG) in Iraq[9] as well as ISIS.[10] More recently the Syrian civil war also helped give rise to ISIS as well as the institutionalization of Rojava (Western or Syrian Kurdistan) as a second de facto autonomous Kurdish state (and in this second case one closely linked to the PKK).[11] Within the horrific Syrian civil war raging just below Turkey's southern borders, ISIS and Rojava, two dynamic non-state actors, created a dilemma of new realities that cannot be ignored or imagined away by the now moribund Sykes-Picot Agreement of 1916. Moreover, on all of these new problems, including its early call for the demise of Bashar al-Assad's Syrian regime, Turkey has arguably come down on what seems the wrong or at least losing side.

In a well-documented, misguided attempt to facilitate the overthrow of Assad and restore stability to its southern Syrian neighbor, Turkey, as noted above, allowed jihadists from all over the world to transit its territory and cross into Syria.[12] Turkey also hoped to reduce or even eliminate the threat it perceived in the rise of Rojava, which Turkey saw as a proto-PKK state that would transform its success against ISIS into a contiguous Kurdish-dominated territory along its southern border. Thus, Turkey sat by passively watching ISIS try to destroy the Syrian Kurds holed up just across the Turkish border in Kobane during the vicious fighting for that city from September 2014-January 2015. As Turkey perceived matters, support for the Syrian Kurds in Kobane would be tantamount to aiding the PKK, a terrorist enemy that had been trying to dismember Turkey for more than 30 years. As Erdogan explained: "For us [the] PKK is what IS [ISIS] is."[13] As previously pointed out, why should Turkey get involved when the United States, its superpower NATO ally, would not do more? It suited Turkey that ISIS and the Syrian Kurds were weakening each other by slugging it out while Turkey sat idle.

Furthermore, many Turks felt betrayed that by giving the Syrian Kurds air support against ISIS, their American NATO ally was strengthening Syrian Kurdish attempts to gain autonomy that could encourage separatism among Kurds in Turkey as well as to seize Arab lands near the Turkish border.[14] On June 15, 2015, for example, Syrian Kurdish forces—led by the PKK's closely associated Democratic Union Party (PYD) and its militia the Peoples Defense Units (YPG) and women's branch YPJ—took control of the Syrian border town of Tal Abyad and supposedly forced its non-Kurdish population to flee to Turkey where a burgeoning refugee population was destabilizing Turkey and now exceeded 2 million.

However, the Syrian Kurds strongly objected to such reports as being inaccurate and unjust.[15] Amnesty International (AI), an NGO that plays an important role in protecting the rights of the individual against government suppression, released a partial and distorted report on supposed Syrian Kurdish abuses alleges forced Syrian Kurdish displacement and home demolitions. It does not do justice to the PYD's efforts to protect not only Kurds but also Arabs against the depredations of ISIS. For example, the YPG has pointed out that many of the villagers AI spoke to were interviewed in their villages of origin, thus contradicting claims that they had been ethnically cleansed. In addition, it is possible that some of these Arab refugees AI interviewed simply were fleeing the YPG advance because of their past collaboration with ISIS. Furthermore, given the fluidity of combat, it seems that some of the AI allegations concerned villages the YPG did not even control at the time of the supposed ethnic cleansing. Finally, 40 percent of the fighters supporting the YPG were actually Arabs (as well as some Assyrians, Turkmen, and others) who had been folded into the new Syrian Democratic Forces (SDF) formally created by the PYD/YPG on October 10, 2015 and who would hardly be trying to ethnically cleanse themselves. Of course, if you are fighting against ISIS there is going to be some collateral damage, but the PYD and its YPG/YPJ fighting units have gone out of their way not to kill or displace the population.[16] Indeed, as David Romano and Mehmet Gurses have argued, "the Kurdish issue . . . may also offer a key to genuine democratic improvements in Turkey, Iran, Iraq, and Syria."[17]

In some cases, of course, the Arab population has been asked to leave during the fighting. But as soon as the fighting is over the PYD invites the Arab population to return, and it has returned. Indeed, that is what the democratic autonomy the Syrian Kurds are implementing is all about: Giving everybody the right, not just the Kurds, to administer themselves. On the other hand, we all know that ISIS even bragged about how much it destroyed cities and murdered people it disagreed with. Therefore, the Syrian Kurds argued it was ISIS that was causing most of the damage and killing, not the Syrian Kurds. In a misguided attempt to be politically correct, AI is faulting the little nuances of the Kurds, while implicitly ignoring the horrendous ones of ISIS.

Moreover, illustrating the law of unintended consequences, ISIS blowback had already led to the capture of 49 Turks when it overran Mosul in June 2014. They were only released after who knows what Turkey had to offer or threaten. Subsequently, Turkey came to blame ISIS for deadly attacks that mostly killed only ethnic Kurdish citizens in such Turkish cities as Suruc (Kobane's twin Turkish city) and Ankara in July and October 2015. These twin attacks furthered the Kurdish belief that the Turkish government could not or even did not want to protect them. Some actually claimed that Erdogan had turned a blind eye to such attacks in order to further the perception of Turkey under siege and thus increase his fortunes in the elections held on November 1, 2015. Such a wag-the-dog strategy might have helped Erdogan regain power in the short-run but would certainly hinder his chances to restart the peace process in the long-run.

In the summer of 2015, Turkey had finally claimed to have entered the struggle against ISIS by allowing the United States to use the Turkish Incirlik airbase to carry out bombing raids targeting

ISIS.[18] However, instead of Turkey striking ISIS, most of the Turkish air attacks hit the PKK bases in the Qandil Mountains along the border of the KRG and Iran and even on occasion Syrian Kurdish YPG forces in Rojava, leading some to conclude Turkey was simply using ISIS as a foil to really go after both the PKK and PYD.[19] The situation grew even more complicated on September 30, 2015 when Russia began air strikes against Syrian rebels, only to have a Turkish missile destroy one of its jets on November 24, 2015. Cemil Bayik, the co-head of the PKK's umbrella Kurdistan Communities Union (KCK), claimed that Turkey was really supporting ISIS and that Russia might begin directly supporting YPG/YPJ forces in Syria.[20] The Turkish action against Russia also had the potential to draw Turkey's U.S. NATO ally into a confrontation with Russia, which potentially would soon be supporting the U.S. bombing campaign against ISIS in the Syrian civil war that was close to becoming a Hobbesian struggle of all against all. For its part as 2015 came to a close, Turkey did begin to ramp up a domestic crackdown against ISIS by arresting several hundred suspects, action possibly too late given what earlier ignoring had allowed to proliferate and in 2016 came home with a vengeance as ISIS increased its bombings within Turkey.

In the autumn of 2015, the Syrian crisis exploded with yet another destabilizing dimension when more than a million Syrian refugees, among others, began entering Europe from Turkey. This sea of desperate humanity threatened the stability of the European Union (EU) and soon led the EU to offer Turkey $6.8 billion, progress toward visa liberalization, and a revitalization of Turkey's moribund EU accession process in return for Turkish help in stemming the refugee flood.[21] However, this deal had become problematic by the summer of 2016 as it risked the reputation of the EU given Erdogan's increasingly arrogantly autocratic behavior.[22]

In Turkey, violence against the pro-Kurdish HDP had already begun in the lead up to the June 7, 2015 elections and grew exponentially in the days heading toward the subsequent ones on November 1, 2015. Indeed HDP leaders blamed their loses in the second election on the violent atmosphere that prevented mass r allies as well as their party representatives from appearing in the mainstream mass media particularly following the deadly bombing of the HDP rally in Ankara on October 10, 2015. The International Crisis Group (ICG) concluded that:

> Following the ceasefire's collapse [in July 2015], most fighting has been concentrated in southeastern urban centres, where security forces have declared over 62 urban curfews, ranging in duration from several hours to two weeks. Between July and 15 December, violence claimed the lives of 194 security officials, at least 221 PKK insurgents and as many as 151 civilians. . . . Thousands of residents across the region have been displaced.[23]

By the end of 2015, the PKK-affiliated Kurdistan National Congress (KNK) summed up the situation by declaring:

> In short, everyone who is opposing the war is either being killed, imprisoned or forced to flee. Since August [2015] 300,000 Kurds have been forced to flee from their homes. The Turkish state is resuming its age-old policy of killing Kurds and emptying Kurdistan of its population while labelling those who resist this policy as terrorists or traitors.[24]

At the end of May 2016, a subsequent report stated that Turkey's continuing war against the PKK had cost it about $400 billion over the past three decades and added that since the new fighting had begun in July 2015 "about 5,000 rebels have been killed in the southeast and in airstrikes in northern Iraq in the period, while 438 security personnel, including 296 soldiers, have died, according to the state-run Anadolu news service."[25] Although Turkish state censorship prevented complete coverage of the on-going fighting, yet another report claimed that "more recently, Turkey deployed 20,000 soldiers and police officers to Mardin and Hakkari Provinces in March 2016 as part of a new wave of operations to expel the PKK from several district capitals."[26]

However, others argued that "by not distancing itself from the PKK and not criticizing its terrorist tactics, the HDP has delegitimized itself."[27] Specifically, "the Kurdish voters were disappointed by the actions of the HDP municipalities, such as declaring self-government and not recognizing the legitimacy of Ankara, not paying taxes or public-utility bills, and digging ditches around government buildings and along major roads against the police force."[28]

Further Developments

What does the breakdown of the Turkish-PKK peace process portend? Possibly the experiences and lessons learned to date will serve as a most important background for its eventual renewal. However, President Erdogan's attempt to criminalize the 1,128 Turkish and Kurdish academics who signed a petition to the Turkish government in January 2016 asking that it end its renewed violence in the southeast, his successful campaign to strip HDP co-leader Selahattin Demirtas and other HDP MPs of their parliamentary immunity so they can be tried for trumped up charges of treason, and, even more, the drastically changed country conditions that have followed in the wake of the failed coup attempt on July 15, 2016 are discouraging for a future peace process.[29] Thus, a nuanced analysis of the fluid situation follows.

The horrific Syrian civil war presented additional daunting obstacles for peace in Turkey. As of July 2016, 17 separate bombings connected in one way or another with Syria had killed more than 300 people in Turkey during the previous 12 months. The deadly bombing in Istanbul on January 12, 2016 that left 13 foreign tourists dead, followed by another on February 17, 2016 against a military bus filled with Turkish soldiers in what had been considered the most secure district in Ankara that killed 28 while wounding more than 60, and the tragic attack against the Istanbul Ataturk airport on June 28, 2016 that killed 45 and wounded 230, among several other such strikes, illustrated the deteriorating situation.

Turkey blamed ISIS for the Istanbul bombing, the PYD's YPG militia or the PKK offshoot Kurdistan Freedom Falcons (TAK) for the Ankara one, and ISIS for the Istanbul airport assault. Although the U.S.-backed Syrian Kurds denied any culpability, it was clear that all three of these attacks were at least partial blowback from the violence radiating out of Syria as well as the renewed Turkish-PKK fighting.[30] What is more, the February Ankara bombing elicited vituperative recriminations from Turkish president Erdogan against the United States for its aid to the YPG.[31] These denunciations of the United States increased exponentially when Turkey began to blame the United States for supporting what it termed the Fethullah Gulen Terrorist Organization (FETO), or parallel state, for backing the failed coup that occurred on July 15, 2016.[32]

For its part, the United States declared that the YPG was not a terrorist organization and urged Turkey to stop shelling the YPG in northern Syria, action that had begun when the Syrian Kurds crossed west of the Euphrates River in mid-February 2016 in their drive to join the isolated Kurdish canton of Afrin (Kurd Dagh) in Syria's west. itself under heavy attack from jihadists, with the already unified other two Syrian Kurdish cantons of Kobane and Hasaka (Jazira) to the east.[33] The PYD—now the lead organization in the Syrian Democratic Forces (SDF), a coalition of 13 Kurdish and Arab fighting groups from northeastern Syria that had been patched together on October 10, 2015 and become the main boots on the ground for the U.S.-led military campaign against ISIS—was seeking to eliminate the Manbij pocket that anchored ISIS's remaining 98-kilometer foothold on the Syrian-Turkish border and connected it with the Syrian headquarters of ISIS in Raqqa to the south. Turkey bitterly opposed the SDF because its success in eliminating the Manbij pocket would present Turkey with a unified, pro-PKK southern border that Turkey saw as an existential threat, especially after the renewal of its struggle against the PKK in Turkey.

Indeed, in March 2016, the PYD announced the establishment of an autonomous region based on federalism in Syria for the three Kurdish cantons of Jazira, Kobane, and Afrin, territory which also included large Arab minorities.[34] The area in question contained a large part of Syria's resources, including nearly two-thirds of its gas and oil reserves and important cotton and wheat-growing areas as well as almost two-thirds of the country's water resources, ten dams and much of Syria's livestock. Although all the inhabitants of this putative federal region would theoretically be represented in this supposedly decentralized bottom-up administration that would be divorced from the oppressive nation-state, stress women's rights, and be based on PKK leader Abdullah Ocalan's theory of democratic autonomy he took from the earlier writings of the late American anarchist Murray Bookchin,[35] it was clear that the actual power would be centralized and held by the PKK/PYD.

Both Turkey and the Assad regime (despite their mutual animosity) bitterly condemned this move, while the United States and Russia took a more neutral view. However, since Turkish-supported opponents of both ISIS and the Assad regime had already failed dismally in their attempt to push ISIS off Turkey's southern border so that Turkey could create a conflict-free zone there, the PYD was in a position to possibly prevail by default.

If Turkey continued to become more involved in Syria to counter both Rojava's expansion and Russia's support for Assad, things could quickly escalate into a greater confrontation that nobody would want. This could even include an indirect clash with the United States who supports the Syrian Kurds and now their SDF coalition as the most viable boots on the ground against ISIS, whom the United States views as the main peril. Turkey should remember how the United States had refused to support it regarding Cyprus in 1964 if the then-Soviet Union had threatened intervention.[36] Similarly, NATO is not guaranteed to support Turkey in a Syrian incursion that ends up clashing with Russia, much less the United States who supports the PYD/YPG/SDF. If a Turkish invasion of Syria goes badly, Turkey might even end up losing Hatay, the province Ataturk's patient and astute diplomacy added to the country in 1939, but which Syria has never recognized.

The Russian/Assad advance in the north that began early in 2016 clearly put them in a much stronger position concerning who would be invited to any future Syrian peace talks and under what conditions, but this did not yet mean that Assad had defeated the Turkish- and Saudi-backed rebels. The Syrian civil war continues challenging Turkish statecraft to avoid further immersion. In addition, Turkey should work closer with its U.S. and NATO allies instead of just pretending to—while actually supporting—jihadist oppositionists in Syria as a way to oust Assad and defeat the Syrian Kurds.

Furthermore, Turkey should get over its unreasonable fear of the Syrian Kurds and instead seek to embrace them similar to how Turkey successfully reversed its opposition to the Iraqi Kurds in 2007. Once the Syrian civil war ends, Turkey will remain the most powerful country in the region as well as the 16th largest economy in the world. Like the Iraqi Kurds, the Syrian Kurds will have no other alternative than to embrace Turkey to the mutual benefit of both. Meanwhile, Turkey should avoid confronting Russia (as well as the United States) in a senseless war that has no winner.

On the night of July 15, 2016 a failed coup in Turkey occurred whose aftermath has led to drastically changed country conditions that were likely to make the over-all situation in Turkey, including the Kurdish problem, much worse. At least 260 people were killed and more than 2,000 injured according to Turkish government reports. The actual death toll was probably higher. However, Erdogan himself declared to his supporters that the failed coup was a "gift from God."[37] This revealing confession meant that the failed coup gave him an excuse to further his own authoritarian ambitions, while purging his few remaining opponents. The future course of Turkey itself seemed challenged.

For example, Amnesty International (AI) reported that the Turkish government had fired or suspended at least 50,000 people from various institutions, including judges, teachers, soldiers, police and journalists.[38] Even the state-run Turkish Airlines had 211 employment contracts terminated. The government was calling anyone it did not like or agree with "terrorists." AI also reported that it had credible evidence that post-coup detainees, including generals, were being beaten, tortured, and raped/sodomized either digitally or by having gun barrels stuck up their anal opening, a method of degrading opponents Muammar Qaddafi reportedly had been subjected to with a bayonet just before he had been killed in October 2011. Turkish police were keeping detainees in stress positions for up to two days at a time, beating them and denying them food, water and medical treatment. The detainees were being held arbitrarily and denied access to lawyers and family, and were not properly informed of the charges against them. AI termed these reports of abuse including beatings and rape in detention as "extremely alarming, especially given the scale of detentions." In the vast majority of cases, lawyers added that no evidence establishing reasonable suspicion of criminal behavior was presented against their clients.

The Turkish government also declared a sweeping three-month state of emergency, which gave it the power to rule by decree and simply bypass the duly elected Turkish Parliament. Under one decree suspects could be detained for as long as 30 days without charge, and the government could listen in on all conversations they had with their attorneys. As already mentioned, opponents of the government, even peaceful ones, were freely being accused of "terrorism." This new state of emergency was in addition to the government-enforced curfews, discussed above, that had allowed its forces to roam freely against the civilian Kurdish population since the summer of 2015 when the Turkish-PKK cease-fire had broken down and heavy fighting resumed. If conditions had become so bad for many ethnic Turks, such as the military, judges, lawyers, journalists, and teachers, among others, what could hated and feared minorities such as the Kurds expect? As close friends of the Turkish Kurds concluded: "Kurds across the country are now threatened with suspension of their civil rights and freedoms by the widespread crackdown that Erdogan has launched in the wake of the attempted coup."[39]

Although Kurdish leaders in Turkey tried to disassociate themselves from the attempted coup—after all many of the military leaders now under arrest had been involved in the government's war against the PKK[40]—Erdogan still needed the PKK as an enemy to unite Turkey's nationalist vote behind him since the pro-Kurdish HDP had cost him an absolute majority in parliamentary elections held on June 7, 2015. Thus, even though the HDP's co-chair Salahattin Demirtas had denounced the coup when it first occurred, Erdogan chose not to thank and invite him to his presidential palace as he did with the two leaders of the Republican Peoples Party (CHP) and Nationalist Movement Party (MHP), the other two main parties in parliament who also had condemned the coup.[41] This exclusion clearly intended to isolate the peaceful pro-Kurdish party and its leaders as enemies and supporters of terrorism. While Erdogan's new prime minister Binali Yildirim had thanked the HDP for its support just after the coup had failed, a few hours later AKP supporters attacked three HDP offices in Osmaniye, Malatya, and Iskenderun.

Although he had done so only through the lens of the Kurdish struggle, Abdullah Ocalan, the founder and leader of the PKK, had been possibly the only participant in these events who had actually foreseen the possibly of a coup if the Turkish-PKK cease-fire and peace process failed: "If the resolution process [of the Kurdish question] comes to an end they are going to implement the coup mechanism. They are going to attempt a coup in Turkey. The resolution process is an obstacle in the way of a coup."[42] Whether the coup was the result of the Kurdish issue or other ones involving Erdogan's perceived authoritarianism, the result for the Kurds would likely be similar. The Kurdistan National Congress (KNK) —an arm of the PKK—for example, foresaw, that the reaction to the failed coup would lead to "a rise in anti-Kurdish sentiment and anti-democratic approaches. . . . This will lead to a deepening of genocidal policies against the Kurds. . . . It has also radicalized the sectarian nationalist circles close to the AKP."[43] New formations such as the *Osmanli Ocaklari* (Ottoman Hearths/Associations), paramilitary groups organized by Erdogan himself, could be expected to "step up their attacks against the Kurdish people." Thus, "the freedom forces of the Kurdish people and the democratic forces of the country should prepare themselves against these attacks."

New KRG Developments

Given the paradigm-altering conflicts involving the Kurds and ISIS discussed above, Iraq (and Syria even more) increasingly seemed to exist mainly in the minds of the U.S. State Department. However, the United States is so powerful that for the time being it still can keep an artificial state like Iraq more or less together despite its root problems. Buoyed by beltway groupthink, Iraq's growing disintegration still seems to elude U.S. policy makers who, when pondering the current predicament, might do well to remember that until the 20th century, Iraq and Syria (as well as Lebanon) were only geographical expressions, not states. Indeed, since antiquity the area that is now Iraq has largely had a tragic history of occupation and division. As French orientalist Georges Roux has documented, Iraq's north, south, and center have usually been in pitched battles against each other dating as far back as the ancient Sumerians in the south battling the Akkadians in the center and both fighting against the Assyrians in the north who in turn warred against the Babylonians.[44]

As for modern times, Adeed Dawisha has written how "from the early beginnings of the Iraqi state, the ruling elite and their British patrons recognized the potentially fissiparous nature of Iraqi society, divided as it was among Sunnis, Shiites and Kurds and exacerbated by a pronounced urban-rural divide," and concluded that the British had created a witches brew of Kurdish separatism, Shiite tribalism and Sunni assertiveness when they artificially crafted together today's disintegrating failed state.[45] In May 2016, for example, mobs loyal to Shiite cleric Muqtada al-Sadr on two separate occasions breached the heavily fortified government green zone in Baghdad and ransacked Iraq's parliament to protest the enfeebled government's inability to deal with corruption and sectarianism.[46] Such incidents indicated that even Joseph Biden's three-state solution for Iraq mentioned above might not satisfy Shiite disharmony in what would be their own state.

Moreover, it is true that during 2015 and 2016, the position of the Kurdistan Regional Government-Iraq (KRG) deteriorated for a variety of economic, political, security, and social reasons, resulting in the temporary suspension of immediate thoughts of independence. As a largely rentier state, the precipitous drop in oil prices during 2015 immediately reduced the KRG's available revenues, a problem compounded by Baghdad no longer remitting the constitutionally mandated 17 percent of its budget to the Kurds whose budget included a grossly bloated government payroll. Even the peshmerga ceased to be paid regularly despite the existential struggle against ISIS whose fighters remained threatening and near to the KRG border, a perilous situation that demanded continuing large monetary expenses.

Politically, the crisis also continued because of Massoud Barzani's refusal to step down from the presidency despite his extraordinary two-year extension that had ended in August 2015 on top of the earlier two four-year terms in office that had ended in August 2013. Instead Barzani had now arranged for a new, second two-year extension to maintain his position until August 2017. In October 2015, KDP prime minister Nechirvan Barzani dismissed Gorran cabinet members and even prevented Yousef Mohammed, the Gorran speaker of the KRG Parliament, from taking his seat in the legislature to protect the position of his presidential uncle, Massoud Barzani. The supposedly unified KRG still exhibited deep divisions between the various Kurdish parties and factions that would come back to haunt it when Massoud Barzani's referendum on independence failed to be accepted by regional neighbors and the United States in September 2017. Indeed, at one time or another, every major Kurdish political party has fought every other existing one.

The PUK's anti-terrorism force is currently run by Jalal Talabani's nephew Lahur, while the KDP's by Massoud Barzani's son Masrour, a situation that makes KRG unity even more difficult. In addition, Massoud Barzani's call in May 2016 for a referendum on independence[47] further added to the political problems as no state, friend or foe, supported such a demarche. Furthermore, the more than 2 million refugees and internally displaced persons (IDPs) dislocated by war and terrorism and now domiciled in Iraqi Kurdistan created enormous social problems. Even expatriates, who earlier had returned to Iraqi Kurdistan, were beginning to leave again.

Although Baghdad's collapse in the summer of 2014 when ISIS took Mosul allowed the KRG to occupy the disputed territories associated with Kirkuk, Baghdad would surely seek to win them back if and when it regained its strength, as occurred in October 2017. After all, Baghdad had an air force and heavy weapons, which the Kurds lacked. Indeed, since it is not independent, the KRG only receives its U.S.-supplied weapons through Baghdad, which, of course, is careful not to deliver the Kurds enough that would enable them to strike successfully for independence. As a result, the KRG peshmerga also lacked modern bomb disposal equipment to deal with ISIS-improvised explosive devices (I.E.D.s), a dearth that costs valuable Kurdish lives even though they are U.S. allies against ISIS. Baghdad, on the other hand, gets all it needs including heavy artillery and night-vision goggles.[48]

In the past the Kurds always had to remember the baleful maxim that they had no friends but the mountains. However, today, even though maybe 80 percent of the Iraqi Kurds live in urban areas and thus would not be sheltered by the mountains if invaded again, the Iraqi Kurds do have friends. Indeed, both the United States and Turkey appeared to indicate that they would reluctantly accept an independent KRG if it were declared, although Iran appeared to be adamantly opposed to such a development. Furthermore, who does not have on-going problems? With U.S. help, an independent KRG could work and give the United States a much-needed Middle East base in friendly, dependable territory, in contrast to the problematic situation with Turkey and the Arab statelets on the Gulf that currently house U.S. bases.

Problems Associated with KRG independence

Too often Kurds and others discuss independence as if it were the end of a process, rather than the beginning. Thus, it would be invaluable to suggest the likely problems associated with KRG independence.[49] In the first place, it should be clear that we are talking about sequenced or cascading independence for the KRG only, not some type of pan-Kurdish state that would also include the Kurdish portions of Turkey, Syria, and Iran. Although practically every Kurd dreams of a pan-Kurdish state, it is highly unlikely given the vastly different stages of Kurdish nationalist development in each state the Kurds inhabit.

Thus, as of 2016-17, the Kurds in Iraq seemed to be the ones most likely to soon become independent, followed by those in Syria. However, given the continuing strength of Turkey and Iran as viable states, the Kurds in those two countries appeared much less likely to follow suit, although those in Turkey were more likely to achieve some type of ethnic rights. Thus, the question arises, what would be the relationships between an independent KRG and the other constituent parts of Kurdistan still part of Syria, Turkey, and Iran? Would the KRG make irredentist claims on these other Kurdish areas? Would the KRG offer automatic citizenship for all Kurds like Israel does for all Jews? Would an independent KRG allow dual citizenship for Kurds living in other states?

As for the KRG, when Massoud Barzani finally did step down from the extraordinary and technically illegal extension of his presidential term, he was likely to continue being the president of the KDP, as occurred after the failed independence referendum in September 2017. Thus, the new president of the KRG or prime minister—if the KRG chose instead to become a parliamentary government instead of the de facto presidential one it was—would have less real power than the life-long president of the KDP. What kind of precedent would this constitute? More importantly, what would this mean for the constitutional development of a successful independent KRG?

What about other likely legal problems involving separate visa regimes and financial laws? How would an independent KRG organize its economy? Abdullah Ocalan's PKK still seems a staunch advocate of socialism (Marxism), while the KRG pursues a capitalist route. Would the gas-rich KRG share its oil resources with the gas-poor Kurds living in Turkey? In other words, would KRG oil be a pan-Kurdish resource or localized one? Similar problems exist among the Arab states and indeed were argued by Saddam Hussein as a justification for his invading Kuwait in 1990. Massoud Barzani's KDP has long seemed to put personal wealth accumulation ahead of pan-Kurdish largesse. On the other hand, as already broached, rentier states—such as the KRG—provide an unstable foundation for solid economic development as witnessed by the KRG's current economic problems.

In addition, what kind of economic infrastructure would an independent KRG have? At the present time, real banks are non-existent forcing many people to carry their life savings around in their pockets or keep them stashed at home. ATMs remain few. The KRG is largely a cash economy lacking a long-term sophisticated monetary policy, fiscal discipline, and sufficient reserves. Any attempt at creating a KRG currency would probably collapse. A possible compromise might be to create a symbolic currency pegged to the U.S. dollar or euro. A precedent for this already exists in Liberia, Panama, and East Timor which use the U.S. dollar. Furthermore, what about the large-scale crony capitalism and corruption prevalent today in the KRG? And in Turkey, what would be done with the Village Guards who still provide the income for some 50,000 Kurds and their families?

Early in 2016 the World Bank Group released a 219-page economic report on the KRG proposing reform options for fiscal adjustment and the diversification of the economy. The report addressed the high dependency on the oil sector, excessive role of the public sector in the economy, dependency on imports, weaknesses in the financial system and dependency on a cash economy.

Economic diversification could plausibly be affected by better utilizing land and water resources, expanding the private sector through available human resources and entrepreneurial spirit, exploiting the advantageous geographic location on east-west trade routes between highly productive industrialized economies, and taking advantage of foreign expertise. A World Bank study carried out in conjunction with the KRG ministry of planning estimated stabilization needs in 2015 at $1.4 billion.[50]

What about water resources? An independent Kurdistan in Turkey would inherit a large proportion of that state's fresh water supply and its ability to generate hydroelectric power which is an important reason that Turkey would continue to oppose Kurdish independence. The KRG and Rojava, on the other hand, obtain their fresh water supplies from upstream Turkey and are thus in a potentially much less advantageous position than their Kurdish brethren in Turkey. A lesser but still important symbolic problem involves choosing a flag and national anthem. Currently, many Kurds do share "Ey Raqip" (Hey Enemy) as a common anthem.

To repeat, Kurdish independence would not automatically be the solution to Kurdish problems but more likely the beginning of a host of new ones. Thus, it behoves all who hold a stake in the Kurdish future and its increasing importance for developments in the Middle East to be aware of these problems and to consider them sooner rather than later. However, these problems associated with putative KRG independence suddenly took a back seat following the failure of the referendum on independence that took place on September 25, 2017.

PERSONAL OBSERVATION

In my role as the secretary-general of the EU Turkey Civic Commission (EUTCC), I visit the PKK-affiliated Kurdish House or Kurdistan National Congress headquarters in Brussels at least twice a year to participate in meetings and help plan the annual Kurdish conference, sponsored by various leftist groups in the EU parliament. I have always been impressed by the gender equality I witness. Blending into the background, I have had the opportunity to watch women giving orders to men. All related groups function according to the co-chair rule, which requires joint male and female leaders to share the office. As inefficient as such a dual head might seem or actually be, it sets the stage for gender equality and is not mere window dressing. Both sexes have told me their duties in the Kurdish movement leave no time for marriage or other traditional gender roles. This is particularly true of the PKK and all its related organizations such as the Syrian Kurdish PYD/ YPG whose members I come in contact with while in Brussels.[51] Indeed as long ago as March 1998, when I visited Abdullah (Apo) Ocalan, the leader of the PKK, at his safe houses in and near Damascus, Syria, I watched gender equality or at least a lot more attempts at it within the PKK than among other groups and states within the Middle East.

In recent years, women's rights have become an important part of human rights. Nevertheless, like most traditional and Islamic societies, historically, Kurdish men have certain rights and responsibilities that are denied to women. Given the differences dictated by biology, men are supposed to govern, fight, and support their families. Women are supposed to bear and care for children, manage their households, and obey their husbands.

Nevertheless, compared to the other Islamic societies around them, Kurdish women have often exercised more freedom. Indeed, travelers have long noted how Kurdish women usually went unveiled, while also performing most of the hard manual labor. Even in marriage, Kurdish women could sometimes be wooed and won, although arranged marriages still persist. Wives, too, were treated more equally by their husbands than they were in most other Middle Eastern locales. Kurdish women have also held a more secure financial position than did their sisters in neighboring societies. Women, for example, could more easily succeed their husbands as the head of a family even when there were male children.

Kurdish women have also occasionally played prominent roles in politics and the military, among others.[52] Asenath Barzani (Asenat Barzani in Kurdish and Osnat Barzani in modern Hebrew) lived from 1590-

1670. She was renowned throughout Kurdistan for her knowledge of the Torah and Jewish law. In addition, she was the first female head of a yeshiva, a religious school where only men studied and was recognized as the first and only female rabbi in premodern Jewish history. Khanzad (or Xanzad in modern Kurdish) ruled over Harir and Soran in the present-day Irbil governorate during the reign of Ottoman sultan Murad IV (1623-1640). The KRG erected a statue in her honor in the city of Soran, near her former capital Rawanduz and thus adopted her as a national symbol. Mastureh Ardalan (1805-1848) was a noted female poet, philosopher, and historian. She too has become a national Kurdish symbol. The KRG held a festival commemorating the 200th anniversary of her birth in 2005.

Lady Kara Fatima of Marash won fame as a female warrior who led hundreds of Kurds against the Russians in the Crimean War (1853-1856) and represented the Kurds in the Ottoman court in Constantinople. The last autonomous ruler of the Hakkari region was a woman. The Ottoman army also had to face Pura Halima of Pizhdar, Kara Nargiz of the Shwan tribes in what is now Iraqi Kurdistan, and Persheng of the Milan tribe. Adila Khanem (1847-1924) was a famous and cultured chief of the Jaf tribe. She built a bazaar and gardens in the Persian style, presided over a court of justice, and saved the lives of several British soldiers stationed in Halabja during World War I, among other deeds.

Although actually an Assyrian, Margaret George (Shello) was a more recent example of a Kurdish female warrior. Hero Talabani, the wife of the late Jalal Talabani (died 2017), is a well-known personality in her own right. More than 30 percent of the KRG parliament elected on September 21, 2013 was female. Leyla Zana, a female Kurdish politician from Turkey, is famous for her advocacy of Kurdish human rights. On numerous occasions I have personally watched how she moves among men on an equal basis while holding their respect as one of their esteemed leaders.

In recent years, as already noted, Kurdish political parties in Turkey have mandated gender equality in their leadership roles. Abdullah Ocalan, the leader of the PKK, has been a very strong advocate of female equality.[53] Numerous women have occupied prominent positions and also fought in Kurdish militias. For example, Hevi Ibrahim was appointed prime minister of the Afrin canton in Rojava (Syrian Kurdistan), while Asia (Asya) Abdullah was co-chair of the ruling PYD in Rojava. Kongra Star is the confederation of organized women's structures in Rojava, and the Women's Defense Units (YPJ), a female military force. Rojda Felat, a YPJ member, was also the overall commander of the combined Syrian Kurdish-Arab forces (SDF), which took Raqqa from ISIS in October 2017. Figen Yuksekdag was the co-chair of the HDP, the leading pro-Kurdish party in Turkey, until she was convicted on charges of terrorism and lost her seat in parliament in February 2017.

In Rojava, women generally have the right to divorce, which previously was an entitlement reserved only for men, to inherit property on an equal basis with men, and to keep their children and their homes in a marital breakup. Polygamy and child and forced marriages have been banned. The Social Contract of the Democratic Federation of Northern Syria (Rojava) proclaims the elimination of discrimination against women in all spheres of life, while in the political sphere mandates a 40 percent quota of women from the federal administration to the small neighborhood communes. Shariah law provisions that gave a woman's testimony in court only half the weight of a man's have been eliminated.

Iraqi Kurdish parties and especially Iranian ones lag behind in such leadership roles. However, there are currently three gender-based studies centers in the Iraqi Kurdish region: 1.) The Gender and Violence Studies

Centre at the University of Sulaimani established in 2011, 2.) The Kurdistan Centre for Gender Studies at the Soran University established in 2014, and 3.) The Centre for Gender and Development Studies at the American University in Sulaymaniya (Sulaimani) established in 2016. Bayan Sami Abdul Rahman, the KRG representative in the United States, exudes a confident leadership role among her male Kurdish associates in Washington, DC. In private talks with her, she has told me that for the most part there is no gender discrimination against her, although she is sometimes left out of the loop during male social gatherings.

Despite these positive examples, women's rights, or the lack thereof, are increasingly issues in Kurdistan. Kurdish women in Turkey, for example, have sometimes been subjected to various forms of state violence including rape and sexual harassment, especially during the years of violence associated with the PKK in the 1980s and 1990s. The KRG in northern Iraq has recently sought to deal with honor killing, the murder of women by their own families because the women have somehow dishonored their families by infidelity or otherwise. Similar concern regarding honor killings has also been expressed in Turkey. Female genital mutilation (FGM) is a very important issue too often ignored or downplayed. Female Kurdish refugees and widows suffer more than their male counterparts. Despite progress, much clearly still remains to be done regarding women's rights in Kurdistan.

Back to Square One?

In May 2017, the University of Hewler in Irbil invited me to give the keynote address to a large scholarly gathering of around 700 people, including the prime minister of the Kurdistan Regional Government (KRG), Nechirvan Barzani. Indeed, Nechirvan Barzani was this particular Iraqi Kurdish university's patron. (Several universities in Iraqi Kurdistan have such patrons.) I considered my invitation an honor and went about preparing a serious, objective speech that would mostly stress the KRG's positive achievements, but also mention continuing problems such as KRG disunity, corruption, nepotism, and financial difficulties, among others. This proved to be a mistake in the eyes of those who had invited me. A minute into my brief criticism, the conference organizers tried to stop my speech, but I refused to halt. A couple of minutes later they tried again, but again I refused to stop. I noticed that the prime minister himself sitting in the center of the front row seemed to motion to let me continue, which I did somewhat shakenly.

My speech and the two attempts to bring it to a stop caused a sensation throughout the large auditorium and soon over the Kurdish media. Opponents of the ruling

Barzanis tried to use the attempt to stop me as ammunition to criticize the government; while for its part, the government media went after me.

The next speaker was a young, blind scholar who seemed to arouse great sympathy and respect. He certainly appeared to be very popular. He spoke well but then launched into a scathing critique of my previous comments, accusing me of plagiarism, among other sins. How was I to respond? This sympathetic-sounding, blind scholar's Philippic against my very academic integrity, and my inability to reply adequately reminded me how US president Lyndon Johnson once said of a political foe: I know he didn't have sex with a pig, but I surely would like to hear him deny it.

However, apparently even my critics seemed to recognize that the accusation of plagiarism had gone too far, and I never heard mention of it again. Indeed, the next speaker, a government official, was much kinder to me as he tried to explain how current circumstances made the problems I had mentioned more understandable. Although my longtime friend and current KRG representative to the United States, Bayan Sami Abdul Rahman, only half-tongue-in cheek called me the devil when I saw her during the break, another critic more sympathetically told me a Kurdish proverb that "friends can make you cry." In other words, I was still a friend but had made my Kurdish colleagues sad.

As I moved out of the auditorium, some praised me highly for saying what they told me they could not, while others told me how repugnant my comments had been. Within hours what had happened went viral throughout the land. Several different TV channels and other news media—all of which were partisan-owned— tried to interview me, but I realized that most of them were probably trying to use me as a weapon against their political opponents. Repressing the natural inclination to defend myself, I did not reply to the requests for interviews, some of which came from prominent sources.

A day later, Dr. Nahro Zagros—the vice president for research at Soran University near the Iranian border in the north and my friend—generously came to my aid by explaining to me honestly the implications of the entire contretemps. With my assent he then arranged for me to be interviewed by Rudaw TV, a Barzani outlet, but one that at least in this case gave me a fair platform. My impromptu interview proved largely successful as I tried to explain that as a friend of the Kurds who was also trying to be an objective scholar, I had felt it legitimate to make my few criticisms; indeed, that they might actually help the Kurds rather than if I had simply preached to the choir.

Little did I realize that a few months later, my untimely forebodings would prove a harbinger of the Kurdish disaster that followed the ill-timed KRG referendum on independence. A month or so after the KRG lost one-third of its territory, the conference organizer still told me that I should never had criticized the KRG as I did. I'm convinced that freedom of speech at the university improves the health of the institution and has increased enrollment. However, the university still unilaterally terminated my contract to write a monthly think piece for it, while not doing so to another scholar. Others told me that I would never be invited to the Kurdish region again, but a prominent spokesperson for the Patriotic-Union-of-Kurdistan (PUK)-affiliated American University/Sulaymaniya replied that her school would invite me. Kurdish disunity that had largely led to the referendum disaster remained.

———————

Although some 93 percent of the more than 70 percent of the voters who participated supported what was only an advisory, nonbinding referendum on independence held on September 25, 2017,[1] the hopes for an independent Kurdistan aborning in the guise of the KRG proved premature because of the negative interpretation Turkey, Iran, Iraq, and the United States gave it. On October 16, 2017, Iraqi forces with the strong support of the pro-Iranian, Shiite *Hashd al-Shaabi* or popular mobilizations units (PMUs),[2] with Turkish and U.S. acquiescence, occupied Kirkuk and other disputed territories, after already closing the KRG's two international airports in Irbil and Sulaymaniya and taking over the KRG's border crossings. The KRG lost approximately one-third of the territory and half of the oil that it had been controlling. Massoud Barzani resigned as KRG president, and the Kurdish region was thrown from the heights of ambition to the depths of failure. When Baghdad finally got around to reinstating the KRG budget that had been suspended since 2014, it reduced it from 17 to 12.5 percent.[3]

Despite its denunciations of the United States and others for this disaster,[4] surely the KRG was partially to blame. It had overreached and badly miscalculated by including Kirkuk and other disputed territories in the referendum in an overly ambitious attempt to unilaterally implement Iraqi Constitution Article 140 on the future of the disputed city.[5] The failure to put up even a fight for Kirkuk, also illustrated continuing Kurdish disunity despite the KRG's existence since 1992 and further that the Kurds had grossly over exaggerated their military power.[6] Despite the appearance of military strength based on its success against the Islamic State of Iraq and Syria (ISIS), the KRG peshmerga remained divided between Massoud Barzani's Kurdistan Democratic Party (KDP) and Jalal Talabani's Patriotic Union of Kurdistan (PUK), lacked heavy weapons since Baghdad controlled what material Irbil received from foreign states, and had achieved its recent victories only because of indispensable US air support, which was lacking when Baghdad reclaimed Kirkuk.

Turkish Opposition

The virulent degree of Turkish opposition to the referendum came as a disappointing surprise because the KRG had seemingly managed to create what was practically a de facto alliance with their powerful neighbor to the north. Indeed, as early as 2005, the peaceful, stable situation in the KRG began increasingly to attract Turkish business interests.[7] Turkish firms became heavily involved in such projects as building modern, international airports in Irbil and Sulaymaniya as well as cement plants, among other projects. Erdogan supported these economic initiatives for at least two reasons: First, such economic relations would help alleviate the economically depressed situation in southeastern Turkey and lessen Turkish Kurds' support for radical Kurdish groups such as the PKK; and second, Turkish-KRG economic relations would help bind the two, with Turkey, of course, as the senior partner. By the end of 2005, Turkish-Iraqi trade (much of it involving the KRG) had reached $2.6 billion.[8] On March 11, 2010, Turkey, in its own words, even opened a consul in the KRG capital Irbil "towards bolstering and advancing the friendly ties and cooperation between Turkey and KRG in every field."[9]

Turkey's inherent entrepreneurial spirit and the KRG's establishment of a business-friendly climate soon began to promote an "undeclared economic commonwealth"[10] between the two. In 2011, the KRG became the sixth largest export market for Turkey with exports of $5.1 billion. This expanded to $8 billion by 2013. The KRG had become Turkey's third largest market for exports. When Sinan Celebi, the KRG minister of trade and industry, visited Turkey in April 2012 he declared that 25 new Turkish companies were being launched every month in Iraqi Kurdistan, while more than half of all the foreign companies registered in the KRG were Turkish. The 485 Turkish companies in the KRG in 2009 had, by 2013, become approximately 1500. "From shopping centers to housing projects to furniture stores and ubiquitous consumer and commercial . . . goods, Turkish trademarks are to be seen every-where . . . including agriculture, banking and finance, construction, education, electrical power systems, health care, oil/gas extraction and services, telecommunication, transportation, tourism, and the water industry."[11] Turkish soft power seemed to promise a better life for both Turkey and the KRG.[12]

Economic cooperation inevitably began to lead to political co-operation. In 2013, Erdogan invited Massoud Barzani, the president of the KRG to Diyarbakir, Turkey's de facto Kurdish capital. There Barzani was addressed as the president of the KRG, instead of as a mere warlord from northern Iraq as previously described. Twice the then-Turkish prime minister also used the heretofore forbidden term Kurdistan while addressing his audience. Erdogan and Barzani appeared hand in hand on the podium before hundreds of thousands to declare "the brotherhood of Turks and Kurds,"[13] while Erdogan proclaimed: "'We are building a new Turkey,' dedicated to all ethnicities and faiths."[14]

What at the time seemed a historic rapprochement made the KRG one of Turkey's closest regional allies as well as third-largest export market after Germany and the United Kingdom. At the same time the Turkish-PKK peace process that had begun the previous March emphasized the concept of Turkey as the joint homeland of both Turks and Kurds. Turkey had become one of the main states supporting the KRG's economic independence, facilitating the KRG's selling oil and gas to the world market by bypassing Baghdad. Erdogan even went so far as to declare that KRG independence was an internal Iraqi affair.[15]

However, Erdogan's support for Barzani was, in part, a mere tactic to win conservative ethnic Kurdish support in Turkey against the PKK, not a full-blown backing of the KRG. A caveat that Erdogan was not fully on board with this seemingly new thinking concerning the KRG also came when the Turkish leader failed to send military aid to the KRG after it was suddenly attacked by ISIS in August 2014. Indeed, only timely U.S air support stopped the genocidal jihadists who had driven within 20 miles of Irbil. Earlier, Erdogan had allowed ISIS recruits to traverse Turkey to Syria to join ISIS.[16] Apparently the Turkish leader saw ISIS as a tool to combat the PKK and its affiliate, the PYD/YPG's Rojava, in the Syrian civil war as well as a means to help bring down the Assad regime.

Despite Barzani's strong opposition, the Syrian Kurds' campaign to establish Rojava as a new, de facto Kurdish state on Turkey's border with northeastern Syria possibly conflated Erdogan's inherent fear of any Kurdish state with the KRG.[17] Already, Devlet Bahceli, the leader of Turkey's rightwing, nationalist *Milliyetci Hareket Partisi* (MHP) or Nationalist Action Party, had decried Erdogan's Diyarbakir meeting with Barzani in November 2013: "The day Erdogan went on stage with the murderer Barzani was truly a day of historical high treason. We Turks have never seen such a betrayal in the history of the Turkish Republic."[18] Thus, it only remained for the pro-Kurdish HDP to help deny his AKP a ruling majority by entering the Turkish parliament in the elections of June 7, 2015, for Erdogan to feel it necessary to take up a strong Turkish nationalist role against the Kurds to regain his ruling majority. Kurdish politics in Turkey and Syria bit the KRG when it announced its intention to hold the referendum on independence on September 25, 2017.

Erdogan vs. the KRG

Although Barzani had long made his intentions clear about eventually seeking KRG independence, his announcement in June 2017 that an advisory referendum would be held at the end of September brought outrage on Erdogan's part as well as from many others including Baghdad and Tehran. Even the United States voiced its opposition, largely on the grounds that it would splinter the alliance against ISIS.[19]

Erdogan accused Barzani of committing a "betrayal,"[20] threatened to starve the KRG's population, and even found Israel's hand in the matter: "Once we put our sanctions in place, you'll be out in the cold. . . . If we turn off the [crude oil] valve, it's over. If trucks do not take stuff to northern Iraq, they won't find food or clothing. How will then Israel send them anything?"[21] At a forum in Istanbul, the seemingly enraged Turkish leader added: "After this, let's see through which channels the northern Iraqi regional government will send its oil, or where it will sell it."[22] Feisal al-Istrabadi, the former Iraqi ambassador to the United Nations, identified the ancient Turkish fear of the Kurds dividing and destroying their state when he added that particularly for Turkey, the KRG referendum was "an existential threat" because "how Turkey will deal with an independent . . . Iraqi Kurdistan, but deny their own Kurds independence is a problem requiring Solomonic wisdom."[23] Ali Cinar, the president of the Turkish Heritage Organization in Washington, D.C. and normally a voice of careful reason, added his support for Erdogan: "It's time that the Kurdish Regional Government listened to its neighbors and the international community and do what is right. The necessary action is to cancel the referendum vote in order to prevent bloodshed, a potential civil war and major destabilization of the region that can have catastrophic consequences."[24]

The Iraqi and Iranian governments also joined in the denunciations with Baghdad by closing the two KRG international airports in Irbil and Sulaymaniya, an action that immediately hurt the KRG's important international travel links and lucrative tourism. All three bordering states held military exercises along the KRG's borders.[25] As already noted, even the United States voiced its displeasure, a position that the KRG found particularly galling given how that country effectively had given rise to the KRG by destroying Saddam Hussein.[26] However, since Turkey was the KRG's largest trade partner as well as the transit country for the oil pumped out of the areas controlled by the Kurdish authorities to the international market, Erdogan's threats were paramount.

In pursuing his anti-Kurdish objectives, Erdogan tragically forsook the more promising road of cooperation that he had flirted with, which could have solved Turkey's Kurdish problem and even made Turkey the Kurds' senior partner and thus ultimate leader. Instead the Turkish president fell back upon Turkey's hoary, failed road of obstinate opposition. As Salih Muslim, a prominent Syrian Kurdish leader and frequent spokesman in Europe, reflected: "When I look back, I conclude that Turkey was never sincere about wanting to make peace with the Kurds. Had Turkey reached out to the Kurds, worked with the Kurds, it would have become the most powerful country in the Middle East."[27] Alas, this proved the road not taken.

US Opposition

Shortly before the new Trump administration came to office on January 20, 2017, the Atlantic Council, a prominent think tank in Washington, issued a detailed report chaired by former Ambassador Ryan Crocker, calling for the KRG to remain part of Iraq in the interests of future peace and stability.[28] Faced with the KRG advisory referendum on independence the Trump administration, in effect, opted to support this recommendation. Trump's then-secretary of state Rex Tillerson declared: "The United States does not recognize the Kurdistan Regional Government's unilateral referendum. . . . The vote and the results lack legitimacy, and we continue to support a united, federal, democratic and prosperous Iraq."[29] U.S. opposition to the referendum proved a major surprise and blow to the KRG.

Among the multitude of reasons for its position, the Trump administration specifically listed: 1.) maintaining unity in the fight against ISIS; 2.) shoring up the seemingly fragile Iraqi prime minister Haider al-Abadi ahead of upcoming elections scheduled for May 2018; 3.) the KRG overreach by including the disputed oil-rich Kirkuk in the referendum; 4.) the KRG failure to postpone the referendum in exchange for promised US support in negotiations with Baghdad; and 5.) the strong opposition of the neighboring, regional states of Iran, Turkey, Iraq, and Syria. Israel alone supported the referendum,[30] which was understandably yet another negative, among others.[31]

After the Iraqi forces, with considerable Iranian aid,[32] retook Kirkuk on October 16, 2017, a US Pentagon spokesman claimed that US commanders in the region were trying to mediate between the two sides in the city but did not allude to the ironic situation that both the US and Iran were on the same side. The US embassy in Baghdad asserted that: "We support the peaceful reassertion of federal authority, consistent with the Iraqi constitution, in all disputed areas, while Trump himself said: "We don't like the fact that they are clashing, but we're not taking sides."[33]

H.R. McMaster, Trump's then-national security advisor, ambiguously affirmed that the president's "sentiments are with both— with the Kurdish people and with the Iraqi people,"[34] and then elaborated that "what we need to do though is we have to work to mediate this conflict in a way that allows our Kurdish friends to enjoy the safety, security, and prosperity they built over so many years and not regress from that."[35] Six weeks later McMaster reiterated that bringing Baghdad and Erbil together "is a big priority for President Trump and for Secretary Tillerson and the whole [Trump] team."[36] In a telephone call between Rex Tillerson and Nechirvan Barzani, the KRG prime minister, Trump's then-secretary of state, "expressed his support for the democratic process . . . and hoped that the Kurdistan Regional Government will overcome the current challenges in the Region, for which he expressed his country's support."[37] As one post mortem found: "The KRG not only misread and misjudged the Trump administration's regional policy goals but consistently neglected to cultivate and groom the Kurdish-American diaspora . . . for a future beyond the military defeat of the Islamic State (IS)."[38]

However, in the end, probably the most important reason for the referendum disaster was KRG disunity. KRG president Massoud Barzani's historic Iraqi Kurdish enemy, the PUK, saw the referendum mainly as a ploy by Barzani to maintain his power at its expense, while both the Gorran movement and Islamists also opposed the referendum. Thus, when Baghdad sent its newly empowered forces with considerable Iranian support to retake Kirkuk on October 16, 2017, the Kurds could not agree on defending their position and simply melted away. "The failure to integrate and reform the KRG's security forces . . . weakened the position of the KRG vis-à-vis the Iraqi government. . . . A united Kurdish army receiving orders from one single source could strengthen the KRG's status against Baghdad."[39] As Bayan Sami Abdul Rahman, the KRG representative in Washington, concluded: "Disunity is definitely our Achilles heel. Kurdish disunity is our worst enemy. Whatever we think of our opponents and detractors, our disunity is our worst enemy."[40]

Aftermath

As an immediate consequence of the failed referendum, the KRG's once positive reputation as the other, peaceful and successful Iraq that had supported the United States in the war to remove Saddam Hussein in 2003. A decade later, this reputation played an important role in its moral stand in the struggle against ISIS and quickly disappeared in the aftermath of the referendum as a negative, demoralized persona took its place. For example, in December 2017, violent demonstrations broke out throughout the region, especially in Sulaymaniya and Halabja.[41] More than 600 people were arrested as protesters burned down the offices of political parties. These militants denounced: 1. The rampant corruption that had spawned a small elite of multimillionaires who dwelled in large mansions and possessed fleets of luxury cars; 2. The nepotism which had permitted President Massoud Barzani's son, Masrour Barzani, to become the intelligence chief and his nephew, Nechirvan Barzani, to serve as prime minister; 3. The kickbacks enjoyed by government officials from every deal made in the region; 4. The persecution of media outlets critical of the government; and 5. The delays in holding parliamentary and presidential elections. Before he finally resigned on November 1, 2017, Barzani had already extended his term in office on two separate occasions.

The financial crisis that had resulted from the fall of gas prices and Baghdad's discontinuation of its monthly stipend of 17 percent of the country's budget had sapped the KRG's strength. The loss of Kirkuk then reduced the KRG's oil exports by half. At the end of 2017, the KRG was more than $20 billion in debt,[42] the economy in freefall, and the citizenry demoralized. As one observer succinctly concluded: "The time is long gone when heads of states and foreign and defense ministers would stop over in Erbil to meet with KRG officials as equal 43

Yusuf Mohammed Sadiq—the speaker of the KRG parliament who had been prevented from assuming his position by Barzani's KDP since October 2015 and has now resigned—criticized the manner in which the referendum had been organized without properly involving the parliament. He declared that the parliament's role should be reestablished and preparations made for negotiations with Baghdad over all the disputed issues. "I want to see if parliament is able to do its work without any hindrance, with transparency to be brought into Kurdistan's financial process and with political parties stopping interference in the security forces."[44] When hundreds of club-wielding, pro-Barzani supporters trapped Gorran MPs criticizing Barzani during a parliamentary debate over what had occurred, Yusuf Mohammed blamed "thugs and anarchists" for the violence, while Abdul Wahid, the parliamentary leader of Gorran declared: "What happened this evening at parliament was a terror act and the K.D.P. is morally responsible for it. We are witnessing the destruction of our whole legislative establishment in the region."[45]

As of this writing in October 2018, the former powers of the

KRG president are being tenuously exercised by the prime minister, parliament, and the provincial authorities, among others. However, Massoud Barzani still retains some power through his
continuing leadership of the KDP, the chairmanship of the Political
Leadership Council comprising the KDP and a faction of the PUK,
as well as his family's control of key economic and political positions. Indeed, while resigning as president, he declared that he was
not resigning from politics: "I'm a pesh merga and will continue
to do whatever is needed and will be with my people in its struggle
for independence."[46] Nevertheless, within the KDP a power struggle looms between Barzani's nephew, Prime Minister Nechirvan
Barzani, and his son, Masrour Barzani—who is the Chancellor of
the KRG's Security Council and Parastin, the KDP's intelligence
agency.

The PUK suffered a much heavier blow due to its apparent collusion with Baghdad and Iran to pull out of Kirkuk and the death
of its founder and longtime leader Jalal Talabani on October 3,
2017 after a long, incapacitating illness. The PUK was now split
among its various members including Jalal Talabani's widow
Hero Talabani and her sons Bafel and Qubad, and longtime party
stalwarts Kosrat Rasul, Mala Bakhtiyar, and Barham Salih. In addition, Nawshirwan Mustafa's death on May 19, 2017 has dimin-
ished the Gorran party.

Barham Salih formally quit the PUK in January 2018 to form
his own new party, the Coalition for Democracy and Justice (CDJ),
only to rejoin the PUK in September 2018. On October 2, 2018,
the Iraqi parliament elected him to the largely ceremonial position
of president of Iraq, the same office his longtime mentor Jalal
Talabani had so prominently held. However, Fuad Hussein, the former chief of staff of KRG president Massoud Barzani, bitterly contested Salih's election, action that possibly boded ill for the future
of KRG unity. Nevertheless, Salih, as the new Iraqi president,
promised "to safeguard Iraq's unity and safety,"[47] a mere year after
the Kurds had voted for independence. Significantly, he also

immediately and astutely named Adel Abdul Mahdi, an Arab Shiite with wide parliamentary backing, as prime minister designate, ending several months of deadlock following the Iraqi national elections held on May 12, 2018.

Thus, the year 2017 not only saw the demoralizing failure of the independence referendum and the KRG's resulting isolation in regional and international politics, but the passing or removal of its three main political leaders: Massoud Barzani, Jalal Talabani, and Nawshirwan Mustafa. KRG elections originally scheduled for November 1, 2017 were first put on indefinite hold and then rescheduled for September 30, 2018. As Yusuf Mohammed Sadiq, the former speaker of the KRG initially concluded: "We first need to reorganize our own affairs at home," and then elaborated: "in addition, we need to re-establish good relations with the Iraqi federal government . . . [and] on the international level . . . with all neighboring countries and all of our friends—especially the United States."[48] Despite all these setbacks, the ruling KDP and PUK surprisingly gained seats in the Iraqi national elections held on May 12, 2018, while the opposition Gorran movement suffered losses, which it attributed to fraud.

In addition to the fear that an independent KRG might act as a magnet for ethnic Kurds living in Turkey, Iran, and Syria, as well as truncate Iraq, the possibility of another Israel also resonated among the regional neighbors. Indeed, Israel was the only regional state that supported the KRG referendum, probably in part as a way to divert Iranian resources away from itself. This was a continuation of a policy stretching back as far as 1931 to the days before Israel even existed when the Jewish Agency planted an operative in Baghdad.[49] From there, under journalistic cover, Reuven Shiloah, who later became the founder of the Israeli intelligence community, trekked through the mountains of Kurdistan and worked with the Kurds in pursuit of a "peripheral concept." Later, during the 1960s, Israeli military advisers trained Kurdish guerrillas as a way to reduce the potential military threat Iraq presented to the Jewish state and also to help Iraqi Jews escape to Israel. Basing his article on a CIA account, US reporter Jack Anderson wrote in 1972: "Every month . . . a secret Israeli envoy slips into the mountains in northern Iraq to deliver $50,000 to Mulla Mustafa al-Barzani. . . . The subsidy ensures Kurdish hostility against Iraq, whose government is militantly anti-Israel."[50] Clearly, Israeli support for the Kurds had a long pedigree.

This time, Ali Akbar Velayati, the former Iranian minister of foreign affairs and current senior adviser of Supreme Leader Ali Khamenei, declared: "With the defeat of the Kurds in Kirkuk, Barzani's conspiracy against the region's security was foiled. Barzani's aim and Israel's covert aim were to seize Kirkuk's oilfields to serve the Israeli interest. In the Kurdistan region, they raise the flag of Israel, and this means if Kurds gain independence in Iraq, we will share a border with Israel."[51] Nouri al-Maliki, the former Iraqi prime minister and still formidable presence in Baghdad, added that "we will not allow the creation of a second Israel in the north of Iraq."[52] This sentiment echoed former Iraqi defense minister Abd al-Aziz Uqayli's warning more than a half a century ago that the Iraqi Kurds were seeking to establish "a second Israel" in the Middle East.[53]

Despite these blows to the KRG, it did not necessarily mean that the Kurdish hopes for eventual independence were forever crushed. More likely it was simply another setback along the inevitable road to that eventual achievement which even strong Turkish supporters have recognized. For example, in the case of Turkey, M. Hakan Yavuz and Nihat Ali Ozcan recently suggested that Kurdish autonomy can be considered as a solution: "for the first time, some Turks are thinking about separating from the Kurdish minority,"[54] and that even "a Kurdish state seems to be inevitable, given the current political fragmentation throughout the Middle East."[55] Furthermore, it should be noted that before the economic crisis began, the Economist Intelligence Unit (EIU) had ranked the Iraqi Kurdistan Region 55th on a list of 158 countries in its Quality of Life Index and thus ahead of China (64), Turkey (71), India (76), Iran (85), Iraq (134), and Russia (142), among others.[56] Indeed, one might argue that given the textual ambiguity of the Iraqi constitution as well as Baghdad's failure to establish the constitutionally required supreme court to adjudicate constitutional disputes and implement the constitutionally required second chamber of the Iraqi legislature to protect the rights of regions and provinces, among others, the advisory referendum was not legally prohibited.[57]

When Baghdad retook Kirkuk in October 2017, as mentioned above, a Pentagon spokesman announced that US commanders in the region were trying to mediate between the two sides. US president Donald Trump added: "We don't like the fact that they are clashing, but we're not taking sides."[58] Although the Trump administration stopped payments for peshmerga salaries, it continued training the Kurdish force.[59] Indeed, illustrating its continuing long-term commitment to the KRG, the United States had already announced the construction of its new Consulate General in Irbil that would include a Chancery, marine residence, housing, and support facilities.[60] H.R. McMaster, the US national security advisor, declared that "we want to see . . . a strong Iraq emerge and of course part of a strong Iraq is a strong Kurdish region where we have very long-time partners whose partnership we value tremendously."[61] He explained that "we have to . . . mediate this conflict in a way that allows our Kurdish friends to enjoy the safety, security, and prosperity they built over so many years and not regress from that." Thus, concluded the U.S. national security advisor: our "sentiments are with both—with the Kurdish people and with the Iraqi people."

The current de-facto, anti-KRG alliance between Iran, Turkey, Iraq, and the United States makes for strange bedfellows and is not likely to last because of their inherent differences. This situation might even allow the KRG to use imaginative divide-and-rule-tactics against its opponents, which would be an ironic reversal of the tactics they often have used against the Kurds. For example, Sunni

Turkey is not likely to continue to countenance Shiite Iran dominating Iraq and the KRG region, especially after Turkey had earned a special position for itself in the Kurdish region. Nor is Sunni Saudi Arabia likely to look in favor upon its archenemy Shiite Iran fitting another piece into its jigsaw puzzle of building a Shiite crescent from Iran to the Mediterranean. Iraq, of course, remains divided between the ruling Shiites against the Sunni Arabs and the Kurds, while influential Iraqi Shiite leader Muqtada al-Sadr's recent turn from Iran to Saudi Arabia has further fragmented the de-facto, anti-KRG alliance by weakening Iranian control over Iraq. The United States will not continue to allow Iran to try to reduce Iraq into a satrapy, while also dominating the KRG. Finally, Israel will not permit Iran or Hezbollah on its borders in southern Syria.

So again, the current de-facto, anti-KRG alliance is not likely to last, which will facilitate the KRG's partial revival. In the meanwhile, despite these weighty problems and the accompanying demoralization, the KRG continues to play a vital role for its population including refugees and internally displaced persons (IDPs). Nevertheless, despite strong opposition from Turkey, the United States continues to support the ambitions of the Syrian Kurds in Rojava more than it does those of the Iraqi Kurds. This is in part because Damascus remains a US foe, while Baghdad is seen as a protégé. The overall pan-Kurdish issue involves many intricate, seemingly contradictory dimensions.

KRG Elections 2018

On September 30, 2018, new KRG parliamentary elections—originally scheduled for November 1, 2017, but postponed because of the fallout from the advisory independence referendum held on September 25, 2017—were finally held. A total of 111 seats were contested by 21 unequally matched parties.[62] The KDP led by KRG prime minister Nechirvan Barzani augmented its leading role by coming in first, winning approximately 45.6 per cent of the vote and 45 seats in the parliament, a gain of 7 from the previous election on September 21, 2013. The PUK, led by Kosrat Rasul Ali, partially righted its rot by winning approximately 21.2 per cent of the vote and elected 21 candidates, a gain of 3 over the previous election. The Gorran Party suffered a disastrous defeat by winning only 12.1 per cent and 12 seats in the parliament, a loss of 12, but still managed to come in third place. The New Generation Movement, a recently-created party trying to appeal to the youth and headed by businessman Shaswar Abdulwahid Qadir, came in fourth place with some 7.4 per cent of the vote and 8 seats. Two Islamic parties (the Kurdistan Islamic Group or Komal and the Kurdistan Islamic Union or Yekgrtu managed to garner about 12 per cent of the vote to win 12 seats, a loss of 5 from the previous election. Two other seats were won by minor groupings. Finally, a total of 11 seats were reserved for the Turkmen, Assyrian, and Armenian minorities.

Despite the recent disastrous setbacks and failure to establish new paths for more successful policies, the elections were a testimony to continuance and stability. However, only 57.3 per cent of the eligible voters participated, a falloff of about 16 per cent from the previous election in 2013. Although there were widespread allegations of fraud, the European Union (EU) urged acceptance of the results, which on balance did not seem unreasonable. Bilal Wahab, a Kurdish political analyst from the Washington Institute of Near East Policy, suggested that voting fatigue with a third election in just one year, disillusionment with the political and democratic process, last minute measures taken by the election commission, and the expectations of fraud were the main reasons for the disappointing voting turnout.[63] Nevertheless, the KRG's fifth parliamentary election since its establishment in 1992, must be deemed at least a partial success given the trials the Kurds had recently experienced and the prevailing situation in much of the Middle East

---

PERSONAL OBSERVATION

On December 17, 2016—after presenting a talk on the possibility of Iraqi Kurdish independence in the nearby new American University of Kurdistan—I also visited the Khanke/Khanki refugee camp in Iraqi Kurdistan just outside of the relatively large city Duhok, yet within some 50 miles from the ISIS (Daesh) frontlines in what was the still embattled city of Mosul. On that cold but clear day I found more than 16,000 internally displaced Yezidi Kurds from 2,850 families housed in 3,120 sturdy-looking tents. They all were from Sinjar (Shengal) to the west where a sudden ISIS attack in June 2014 had led to genocide, as an official UN report concluded, but comprised a small fraction of the almost 1.5 million internally displaced persons (IDPs) and refugees the KRG is providing for as of September 2018. Given their respective populations, that would be like the United States trying to absorb almost 100 million displaced persons!

The Yezidi Kurds are a religiously heterodox Kurdish group who have often, but incorrectly, been referred to by the pejorative title of "devil worshippers." In reality, they are a pre-Islamic Kurdish religious group that worship Malak Tawus or Lucifer before he was thrown out of heaven, a legend also in Christian mythology and the subject of John Milton's famous book, *Paradise Lost*.

Although a record 5,000 refugee seekers drowned in the Mediterranean Sea in 2016, these Yezidis I visited had fortunately survived. Indeed, for the most part those I saw strolling about looked reasonably healthy and clean, although I did not visit either of the two health centers (hospitals) with 9 doctors and a medical staff of 19 I was told the camp housed and thus did not see any of the sick and otherwise ailing.

Young people up through high-school age were on the way to a rather large, more permanent-looking school building (a prefab caravan) when I arrived in the morning. They all seemed reasonably well attired. I was told there were 6 other schools for a total of 5 primary and 2 secondary ones. Instruction was mostly in Kurdish, but Arabic was also used. There were more than 8,600 students and 176 teachers.

Although the streets were muddy, some camp inhabitants were even driving around in cars, some of which had helped them escape when ISIS originally attacked them. The camp director told me that funding for the camp had been supplied by a variety of organizations including the United Nations High Commissioner for Refugees (UNHCR), the United Nations Children's Fund (UNICEF), the Baghdad Iraqi Government, and the KRG. There were 1655 latrines, one for every 2 families, and 790 baths. An organization called Save the Children maintained the wash facilities and collected garbage.

On several occasions I stopped to talk to young and adult refugees and take photos of them with me. A number spoke reasonably good English, which some told me they had learned in school. Along my walk I also saw a number of tents that served as little stores selling food, but I did not have the opportunity to visit any larger eating structures. The little tent stores I entered were heated.

My visit was all too brief. However, I came away appreciating my own home back in the Cookeville, Tennessee much more, and at least satisfied that in this refugee camp at least the Kurdish authorities have made some successful efforts to deal with the many problems ISIS had wrought. And although my previously clean shoes were now very muddy, I wore this result as a badge of honor that enabled me to begin telling the story of what I had just witnessed for the next several days as I journeyed back to the United States through Kurdistan and Vienna.[64]

New Crisis in Syria

As the Kurdish crisis in Iraq gradually abated, the one in Syria suddenly exploded, threatening to actually pit US troops against those of its supposed North-Atlantic-Treaty- Organization (NATO) ally, Turkey. This was because the US had armed and continued to support the Syrian Kurdish-led and PKK-affiliated SDF/PYD/YPG forces against ISIS, Kurdish forces which Turkey viewed as an existential terrorist threat to its territorial integrity. With the victory of these US-supported Kurdish forces over ISIS by the end of 2017, the US drew further Turkish ire by announcing it would train and support some 30,000 SDF troops as border guards.[65] Even more tenuously than with the KRG and Iraq, the Trump administration was trying to square the circle with two of its allies strongly at odds with each other.

On January 20, 2018, Turkish troops with their Syrian-opposition allies (the Free Syrian Army) under the ironically-named Operation Olive Branch entered Afrin, the isolated third Syrian Kurdish canton on its border in northwestern Syria. No better illustration of the Trump administration's new problem could be given than the initial spectacle of Turkey, a US NATO ally, needing permission from Russia, NATO's main adversary, before acting. This was because Russia controlled the skies over the Kurdish enclave and in effect had been partially protecting it as part of its goal of preserving Syrian unity under Assad. However, now Russia decided not to oppose the Turkish incursion in support for Turkish backing for Russia's larger, overall aims in Syria such as weakening US influence in Syria, pushing the Kurds to negotiate with Damascus, and strengthening Russian-Turkish cooperation to the detriment of NATO.

Of course, Turkish animus toward the Syrian Kurds was nothing new as earlier, on August 26, 2016, Turkish troops had entered Syria to the east of Afrin to prevent the Syrian Kurds from crossing the Euphrates River and driving to the west to unite with Afrin.

At that time Operation Euphrates Shield managed to prevent these Kurdish ambitions. However, despite US promises, the Syrian Kurds did not retreat back to the east of the river. The SDF continued to hold the city of Manbij on the west side with US troops as advisors, whom the US said would stand their ground against any Turkish offensive.[66]

Therefore, this time, US troops could find themselves under direct attack from their NATO ally if Erdogan actually carried out his promise to "strangle . . . before it is born" the US-backed SDF border security force.[67] The Turkish president even threatened that "we will rid Manbij of terrorists, as was promised to us before. Our battles will continue until no terrorist is left right up to our border with Iraq."[68] Bekir Bozdag, the Turkish deputy prime minister, belligerently added that "those who support the terrorist organization will become a target in this battle," and advised that "the United States needs to review its soldiers and elements giving support to terrorists on the ground in such a way as to avoid a confrontation with Turkey."[69] Exuding outrage in reference to the US support for the SDF, the Turkish president asked rhetorically, "How can a strategic partner do such a thing to its strategic partner?"[70] He even threatened to give the US troops "an Ottoman slap,"[71] employing a Turkish idiom for a deadly or incapacitating blow.

Although Erdogan has been heavily criticized for these actions against the SDF/PYD/YPG in Afrin, in a damning report Roy Gutman, who had previously won a Pulitzer Prize for his international reporting, called the region under YPG control a 'mini-totalitarian state.'"[72] For example, "the story of the YPG is . . . the story of a governing authority that has arrested, tortured, and expelled rival political leaders; suppressed independent media and issued death threats against reporters . . . and has attempted to 'Kurdify' traditionally Arab towns." In addition, although "the two have fought ferocious battles against each other," the YPG and ISIS also "have often worked in tandem against moderate rebel groups." Furthermore, "the YPG was carrying out a series of assassinations. . . This and other such assaults, together with arrests of Kurdish party leaders opposed to the PYD, led to the flight of tens of thousands to Iraqi Kurdistan, where there are now some 300,000 Rojava Kurds; and to Turkey, where there are at least 200,000." Thus, "the story of the YPG . . . is also the story of a place so at loggerheads with two of its neighbors, Turkey and Iraqi Kurdistan, that both have closed access to Rojava."

A reply to Roy Gutman's accusations against the SDF/PYD/YPG described them as "a travesty of the truth," and claimed that "the author's biases for the Syrian opposition and Turkey . . . have been evident for years."[73] As for the calumny of Kurdish/ISIS collusion, "conspiracy theories . . . manpower issues, [and] the assessment of a particular location's strategic importance or lack thereof" largely explain why ISIS might have pulled out without fighting. What is more, as already noted in Chapter 8, the Syrian Kurds also have strongly objected to such negative reports against them.[74]

As for his threats to strike more SDF/YPG/ targets, of course, Erdogan did not want actually to attack US forces. His real aim was probably to end US support for the SDF, collect the weapons the group had received from the US, and force the Kurds to withdraw east of the Euphrates River. Likely even more importantly, his bellicose attitude was intended for domestic consumption to boost his support in Turkey for the snap presidential and parliamentary elections he suddenly called and won on June 24, 2018.

For its part, the Trump administration first sent US national security adviser H.R. McMaster to meet with his counterpart Ibrahim Kalin in Istanbul, and then on February 16, 2018, US secretary of state Rex Tillerson, to meet with Erdogan and his foreign minister Mevlut Cavusoglu in Ankara in an attempt to calm the atmosphere.[75] US defense secretary James Mattis also met with his Turkish counterpart Nurettin Canikli on the side lines of a NATO meeting. Although "a better atmosphere . . . emerged in both capitals," Turkey made it clear it still did not trust US promises. Cavusoglu declared in a press conference that "there were certain promises that were not kept, and there were certain issues that we could not resolve." So while the worst has so far been averted, it was obvious that the two largest NATO armies were playing with fire in this game of outrage and bluff. In addition, the US-Turkish standoff threatened to allow ISIS to begin reviving as well as emboldening such US and NATO adversaries as Russia, Iran, and Syria, among others.

In any event, Turkish troops finally took control of the city of Afrin on March 17, 2018. According to the Syrian Observatory for Human Rights, a British-based monitoring group, 1,500 Kurdish fighters died along with 289 civilians, while only 46 Turkish soldiers were killed.[76] The Kurds accused Turkey "of Turkification . . . after its occupation of Afrin city, to change the demography of Afrin Canton, and replace it with Turkish identity."[77] Erdogan quickly conflated his success in Afrin with the famous Turkish World-War-I victory of Gallipoli by bombastically declaring: "In Gallipoli they attacked us with the most powerful army," while "now that they do not have the courage to do so, they come at us with the world's basest, bloodiest, specially trained and equipped terrorist organisations."[78] The Turkish president added: "Now we will continue this process, until we entirely eliminate this corridor, including in Manbij, Ayn al-Arab [Kobane], Tel-Abyad, Ras al-Ayn (Sere Kaniyeh) and Qamishli."[79] Erdogan also warned that he might intervene in Sinjar, the Yezidi area in northwestern Iraq where the PKK had established a base in 2014 to help against ISIS even though the Kurdish militants had now reportedly withdrawn.[80]

In addition, the US-Turkish falling out exasperated other problems involving Turkey and NATO, the most flagrant of which was Turkey's agreement to purchase two batteries of advanced S-400 surface-to-air missiles from Russia. This system cannot be integrated into the NATO air-defense systems and will be operated by the Russians. Thus, unless Turkey is to be eliminated from NATO information sharing on counter measures aimed at defeating the

Russian air defense system, Russia will gain enormous intelligence concerning NATO defenses. Even more troubling, since Turkey is scheduled to receive 116 stealth F-35 fighter jets that will form the cornerstone of NATO's combat air resources for the next 30 years, Turkey will be in an excellent position to sharpen the S-400 air defense system against the F-35, intelligence that Russia will then be in a position to take advantage of to defeat the whole purpose of NATO's new generation of F-35 fighter jets.

Furthermore, to the extent that Trump's decision to continue supporting the Syrian Kurdish-led SDF mandated the US remaining in Syria, the danger of blundering into an unwanted confrontation with Russia persisted. Indeed, on February 7 and 8, 2018, four and perhaps dozens more Russian nationals apparently were killed in fighting between pro-Assad forces and the US-supported SDF in the vicinity of Deir al-Zour, a strategic, oil-rich territory in eastern Syria. Most of the deaths were attributed to a US air strike called in by SDF Kurdish fighters who thought they were being attacked.[81] Adding further uncertainty to the issue, at the end of March 2018, Trump suddenly declared that the United States might soon pull all its approximately 2,000 troops[82] out of Syria and ordered the State Department to suspend more than $200 million in civilian infrastructure and stabilization recovery funds for eastern (largely Kurdish) Syria.[83] This, of course, completely contradicted and confused the president's top advisors—both fired and newly hired—as well as US allies.

However, subsequent, alarming reports that ISIS might still have up to 14,000 fighters in Syria (and as many as 17,000 in Iraq, not to mention assets in many other states on five separate continents) led the Trump administration to reverse course. Brett McGurk, the Special Presidential Envoy for the Global Coalition to Counter ISIS, now simply told reporters on August 17, 2018: "We're remaining in Syria."

Moreover, in June 2018 the United States and Turkey reached an understanding for the SDF/YPG forces to begin pulling out of

Manbij and be replaced by separate, coordinated US and Turkish patrols in the western side of the area.[84] This agreement temporarily alleviated the possibility of a military clash between the two NATO allies. Of course, this would only be a beginning settlement as Turkey declared that the Manbij model eventually would also be applied to Syria's Raqqa, Kobane, and other important areas controlled by the Syrian Kurdish PYD/YPG, a proposed roadmap certain to be opposed and rejected by the Syrian Kurds. Thus, the onus would again fall upon the United States to decide whether to support its de facto Syrian Kurdish ally or de jure Turkish NATO ally. The long-term possibility of a US-Turkish military clash remained. Like the Iraqi Kurds, the future of the Syrian Kurds' hard-won autonomy looked particularly precarious and appeared increasingly dependent upon continuing US support.[85] Nearing the end of the second year of his presidency, Trump's fluctuating policies towards the Kurds not only had significant implications for their future security but also critically affected regional politics with Iraq, Iran, Syria, and Turkey, as well as NATO and Russia, among others.

Notes

Chapter 1

1. John Armstrong, *Nations before Nationalism* (Chapel Hill: University of North Carolina, 1982). I earlier published portions of this chapter in Michael M. Gunter, "The Modern Origins of Kurdish Nationalism," in Mohammed M. A. Ahmed and Michael M. Gunter, eds. *The Evolution of Kurdish Nationalism* (Costa Mesa, CA: Mazda Publishers, 2007), pp. 1-17.
2. Anthony D. Smith, *The Ethnic Origins of Nations* (Oxford: Blackwell, 1986).
3. Ernest Gellner, *Thought and Change* (London: Weidenfeld and Nicholson, 1964), p. 168.
4. Benedict Anderson, *Imagined Communities: Reflections on the Origin and Spread of Nationalism* (London: Verso, 1991).
5. Cited in Benyamin Neuberger, "State and Nation in African Thought," *Journal of African Studies* 4:2 (1977), p. 202.
6. Eugene Weber, *Peasants into Frenchmen: The Modernization of Rural France, 1870-1914* (Stanford, CA: Stanford University, 1976).
7. Edgar T. A. and W. A. Wigram, *The Cradle of Mankind: Life in Eastern Kurdistan*, 2nd ed. (London: A. & C. Black, 1922), p. vii.
8. Mehrdad R. Izady, *The Kurds: A Concise Handbook* (Washington, DC: Crane Russak: 1992), p. 24.
9. Ibid., p. 77.
10. Ibid., p. 23.
11. Ibid., p. 34.
12. Vladimir F. Minorsky, "Kurds, Kurdistan: Origins and Pre-Islamic History," in *The Encyclopedia of Islam,* New ed. Vol. 5. Leiden, Netherlands: Brill, 1981, p. 449.
13. Ibid.
14. Michael Eppel, "Historical Setting: The Roots of Modern Kurdish Nationalism," in Ofra Bengio, ed., *Kurdish Awakening: Nation Build-*

ing in a Fragmented Homeland (Austin: University of Texas Press, 2014), p. 40.

15. Ibid.
16. Ibid., p. 45.
17. Edith and E. F. Penrose, *Iraq: International Relations and National Development* (London: Ernest Benn, 1970), p. 276.
18. For a recent translation of part of this work, see Prince Sharaf al-Din Bitlisi (English translation and commentaries by M. R. Izady), *The Sharafnama: Or the History of the Kurdish Nation, 1597—Book One* (Costa Mesa, CA: Mazda, 2005).
19. The *khutba* is a religious ceremony read on Fridays. It used to consist of prayers for the Prophet, the first four (*Rashidun* or rightly guided) caliphs, the current caliph, and the ruler who was regarded as sovereign. Thus, to have one's name pronounced in the *khutba* was the equivalent of proclaiming full independence.
20. Cited in Martin van Bruinessen, *Agha, Shaikh and State: The Social and Political Structure of Kurdistan* (London: Zed, 1992), p. 267.
21. Cited in Amir Hassanpour, *Nationalism and Language in Kurdistan, 1918-1985* (San Francisco: Mellen Research University, 1992), pp. 53, 55.
22. Ferhad Shakely, *Kurdish Nationalism in Mam u Zin of Ahmad-iKhani* (Brussels: Kurdish Institute of Brussels, 1992), p. 64.
23. Amir Hassanpour, "The Making of Kurdish Identity: Pre-20th Century Historical and Literary Discourses," in Abbas Vali, ed., *Essays on the Origins of Kurdish Nationalism* (Costa Mesa, CA: Mazda, 2003), p. 112.
24. Ibid., p. 130.
25. Wadie Jwaieh, *Kurdish National Movement: Its Origins and Development* (Syracuse, NY: Syracuse University Press, 2006, p. 64.
26. Cited in David McDowall, *A Modern History of the Kurds* (London and New York: I. B. Tauris, 1996), p. 53.
27. John Hutchinson and Anthony D. Smith, eds., *Nationalism* (Oxford and New York: Oxford University, 1994), pp. 5ff., mention such other specific events as the first partition of Poland in 1775, the American Declaration of Independence in 1776, and Johann Fichte's *Address to the German Nation* in 1807. They also argue that "nationalism, as an ideological movement, did not emerge without antecedents" such as the printing press, classical humanism of some northern Italian cities, the growth of free towns as centers of capitalism, and the "disentangling of 'England' from 'France' at the end of the Hundred Years War

(1337-1453)," among numerous other events.

28. Martin van Bruinessen, "Ehmedi Xani's Mem u Zin and Its Role in the Emergence of Kurdish National Awareness," in Abbas Vali, ed., *Essays on the Origins of Kurdish Nationalism* (Costa Mesa, CA: Mazda, 2003), p. 44.

29. Hugh Seton-Watson, *Nations and States: An Enquiry into the Origins of Nations and the Politics of Nationalism* (Boulder,: Westview, 1977), p. 148.

30. Denise Natali, *The Kurds and the State: Evolving National Identity in Iraq, Turkey, and Iran* (Syracuse, NY: Syracuse University Press, 2005), p. 24.

31. Ibid., p. 160.

32. Hakan Ozoglu, *Kurdish Notables and the Ottoman State: Evolving Identities, Competing Loyalties, and Shifting Boundaries* (Albany: State University of New York, 2004), p. 117.

33. Ibid., p. 18. For further analyses of the Kemalist modernization project and state discourse toward the Kurds, see Mesut Yegen, "The Turkish State Discourse and the Exclusion of Kurdish Identity," *Middle Eastern Studies* 35 (April 1996), pp. 216-29.

34. M. Hakan Yavuz, "Five Stages of the Construction of Kurdish Nationalism in Turkey," *Nationalism & Ethnic Politics* 7 (Autumn 2001), p. 1.

35. Ibid., p. 2.

36. Ibid., p. 3. For further analyses, see M. Hakan Yavuz, "A Preamble to the Kurdish Question: The Politics of Kurdish Identity," *Journal of Muslim Minority Affairs* 18:1 (1998), pp. 9-18; and Robert Olson, "Five Stages of Kurdish Nationalism, 1880-1980," *Journal of Muslim Minority Affairs* 12:2 (1991), pp. 392-410.

37. Hamit Bozarslan, "Kurdish Nationalism in Turkey: From Tacit Contract to Rebellion (1919-1925)," in Abbas Vali, ed., *Essays on the Origins of Kurdish Nationalism* (Costa Mesa, CA: Mazda, 2003), p. 165.

38. Ibid.

39. For background, see C. J. Edmonds, *Kurds, Turks and Arabs: Politics, Travel and Research in North-Eastern Iraq, 1919-1925* (London: Oxford University, 1957); and Wadie Jwaideh, "The Kurdish Nationalist Movement: Its Origins and Development," Ph.D. dissertation, Syracuse University, 1960.

40. McDowall, *Modern History of the Kurds*, p. 158. For further discussions, see Edmonds, *Kurds, Turks and Arabs;* and Sa'ad Jawad, *Iraq and the Kurdish Question, 1958-1970* (London: Ithaca, 1981). Nev-

ertheless, Sheikh Mahmud did declare himself "king of Kurdistan" in 1922.

41. Cited in Dana Adams Schmidt, *Journey among Brave Men* (Boston: Little, Brown, 1964), pp. 109-10.

42. Gareth R.V. Stansfield, *Iraqi Kurdistan: Political Development and Emergent Democracy* (London and New York: RoutledgeCurzon, 2003).

43. Farideh Koohi-Kamali, *The Political Development of the Kurds in Iran: Pastoral Nationalism* (New York: Palgrave Macmillan, 2003).

44. On the Mahabad Republic of Kurdistan, see William Eagleton, Jr., *The Kurdish Republic of 1946* (London: Oxford University, 1963); and "The Republic of Kurdistan: Fifty Years Later," special issue, *International Journal of Kurdish Studies* 11, nos. 1-2 (1997).

45. Nelida Fuccaro, "Kurds and Kurdish Nationalism in Mandatory Syria: Politics, Culture and Identity," in Abbas Vali, ed., *Essays on the Origins of Kurdish Nationalism* (Costa Mesa, CA: Mazda, 2003), pp. 191-217. Also see Ismet Cheriff Vanly, "The Kurds in Syria and Lebanon," in Philip G. Kreyenbroek and Stefan Sperl, eds., *The Kurds: A Contemporary Overview* (London: Routledge, 1992), pp. 143-70. The late Vanly (1924-2011) was arguably the grand old academic activist of contemporary Kurdish nationalism.

46. Martin Strohmeier, *Crucial Images in the Presentation of a Kurdish National Identity: Heroes and Patriots, Traitors and Foes* (Leiden and Boston: Brill, 2003), p. 54.

47. Murat Somer, "Turkey's Kurdish Conflict: Changing Context, and Domestic and Regional Implications," *Middle East Journal* 58 (Spring 2004), p. 237.

48. Strohmeier, *Crucial Images in Kurdish National Identity*, p. 45.

49. Ibid., p. 61.

50. Ibid., p. 84.

51. Ibid., p. 104.

52. Martin van Bruinessen, "Shifting National and Ethnic Identities: The Kurds in Turkey and the European Diaspora," *Journal of Muslim Minority Affairs* 18 (April 1998), p. 39.

53. Murat Somer, "Failures of the Discourse of Ethnicity: Turkey, Kurds, and the Emerging Iraq," *Security Dialogue* 36 (March 2005), p. 114.

54. Natali, *Kurds and the State*, p. 161.

55. Ibid., pp. 164-65.

56. Ibid., p. 169.

57. For two separate collections of articles on these events, see Mo-

hammed M. A. Ahmed and Michael M. Gunter, eds., *The Kurdish Question and the 2003 Iraqi War* (Costa Mesa, CA.: Mazda, 2005); and Brendan O'Leary, John McGarry, and Khaled Salih, eds., *The Future of Kurdistan in Iraq* (Philadelphia: University of Pennsylvania, 2005).

Chapter 2

1. On why Kurdish nationalism presented such a minimal threat in Ottoman times, see Hakan Ozoglu, *Kurdish Notables and the Ottoman State: Evolving Identities, Competing Loyalties, and Shifting Boundaries* (Albany: State University of New York, 2004), p. 117; and Denise Natali, *The Kurds and the State: Evolving National Identity in Iraq, Turkey, and Iran* (Syracuse, NY: Syracuse University Press, 2005), p. 24.
2. For background, see Janet Klein, *The Margins of Empire: Kurdish Militias in the Ottoman Tribal Zone* (Stanford, CA: Stanford University Press, 2011).
3. On this point, see Bernard Lewis, *The Emergence of Modern Turkey* (2nd ed.; London: Oxford University Press, 1968), pp. 1-5.
4. Ismet Cheriff Vanly, *Le Kurdistan irakien: entite nationale* (Neuchatel: Editions de La Baconniere, 1970), p. 54; as cited in George S. Harris, "Ethnic Conflict and the Kurds," *Annals of the American Academy of Political and Social Science* 433 (September 1977), p. 115.
5. See Ismet G. Imset, "The PKK: Terrorists or Freedom Fighters?" *International Journal of Kurdish Studies* 10 (nos. 1 & 2; 1996), p. 53; and Robert Olson, "Kurds and Turks: Two Documents Concerning Kurdish Autonomy in 1922 and 1923," *Journal of South Asian and Middle Eastern Studies* 15 (Winter 1991), pp. 20-31.
6. For background, see Robert Olson, *The Emergence of Kurdish Nationalism and the Sheikh Said Rebellion, 1880-1925* (Austin: University of Texas Press, 1989); and Martin van Bruinessen, *Agha, Shaikh and State: The Social and Political Structures of Kurdistan* (London and New Jersey: Zed Books, 1992), pp. 265-305.
7. Derk Kinnane, *The Kurds and Kurdistan* (London: Oxford University Press, 1964), pp. 32-34; and Ismail Besikci, *Kurdistan & Turkish Colonialism: Selected Writings* (London: Kurdistan Solidarity Committee and Kurdistan Information Centre, 1991), p. 34.

8. National Foreign Assessment Center (US Central Intelligence Agency), *The Kurdish Problem in Perspective* (August 1979), p. 25.

9. See, for example, I. Giritli, *Kurt Turklerinin Gercegi* (Istanbul: Yeni Forum Yayincilik, 1989).

10. See *Turkish Daily News*, September 15, 2007. For background, see the monumental compilation by Peter A. Andrews, comp. and ed., *Ethnic Groups in the Republic of Turkey* (Wiesbaden: Dr. Ludwig Reichert Verlag, 1989), p. 18, in which Andrews states: "The popular view in Turkey is in fact quite realistic: . . . In Turkey there are seventy-two and a half peoples." The half refers to the Gypsies. Andrews also lists as ethnic groups in Turkey the Sunni Kurds, Alevi Kurds, Yezidi Kurds, Sunni Zazas, and Alevi Zazas.

11. For background, see Jacob M. Landau, ed., *Ataturk and the Modernization of Turkey* (Boulder, CO: Westview Press, 1984); and Feroz Ahmad, *The Making of Modern Turkey* (London and New York: Routledge, 1993). On the primitive state of the Kurdish national identity and language during the 1920s and 1930s, see Martin Strohmeier, *Crucial Images in the Presentation of a Kurdish National Identity: Heroes and Patriots, Traitors and Foes* (Leiden and Boston: Brill, 2003).

12. M. Hakan Yavuz, "Five Stages of the Construction of Kurdish Nationalism in Turkey," *Nationalism and Ethnic Politics* 7 (Autumn 2001), p. 1.

13. Ibid., p. 2.

14. Hamit Bozarslan, "Kurdish Nationalism in Turkey: From Tacit Contract to Rebellion (1919-1925)," in Abbas Vali, ed., *Essays on the Origins of Kurdish Nationalism* (Costa Mesa, CA: Mazda, 2003), p. 165.

15. "55 Landowners 'Exiled' from Towns," *Christian Science Monitor*, December 5, 1960, p. 14.

16. Marvine Howe, "Turks Imprison Former Minister Who Spoke Up on Kurds' Behalf," *New York Times*, March 27, 1981.

17. For more background on the PKK, see Aliza Marcus, *Blood and Belief: The PKK and the Kurdish Fight for Independence* (New York and London: New York University Press, 2007); and Ali Kemal Ozcan, *Turkey's Kurds: A Theoretical Analysis of the PKK and Abdullah Ocalan* (London and New York: Routledge, 2006).

18. For more on the legal, pro-Kurdish political parties in Turkey, see Nicole F. Watts, *Activists in Office: Kurdish Politics and Protest in Turkey* (Seattle and London: University of Washington Press, 2010).

19. For background, see Michael M. Gunter, "Turkey's Floundering EU

Candidacy and Its Kurdish Problem," *Middle East Policy* 14 (Spring 2007), pp. 117-23.

20. "Zana Reveals Details of Erdogan Meeting," *Hurriyet Daily News*, July 1, 2012. http://www.hurriyetdailynews.com/zana, accessed July 5, 2012.

21. *Briefing* (Ankara), October 2, 1989, p. 4.

22. Muserref Seckin and Ilter Sagirsoy, "Measures to Solve Kurdish Problem Proposed," *Nokta* (Turkey), June 3, 1990, pp. 17-22; as cited in *Foreign Broadcast Information Service—West Europe*, August 6, 1990, p. 38. Hereafter cited as *FBIS-WEU*.

23. Cited in *Hurriyet* (Turkey), April 1, 1990.

24. "The Southeast Report: What Does It Say?" *Briefing*, July 23, 1990.

25. Nicole and Hugh Pope, *Turkey Unveiled: A History of Modern Turkey* (Woodstock and New York: The Overlook Press, 1997), p. 265.

26. On this concept, see Irving L. Janis, *Victims of Groupthink: A Psychological Study of Foreign-Policy Decisions and Fiascoes* (Boston: Houghton Mifflin, 1972). Janis defines "groupthink" as a mode of thinking that people engage in when they are deeply involved in a cohesive in-group, when members' strivings for unanimity override their motivation to realistically appraise alternative courses of action." *Ibid.*, p. 9.

27. This figure and the following citation were taken from Mehrdad R. Izady, *The Kurds: A Concise Handbook* (Washington: Crane Russak, 1992), p. 119.

28. Cited in "MIT Report on Antiterror Struggle Revealed," *Milliyet*, December 18, 1996, p. 2; as cited in *FBIS-WEU*, December 18, 1996, p. 2.

29. Ankara TRT Television in Turkish, 1800 GMT, October 14, 1992; as cited in *FBIS-WEU*, October 15, 1992, p. 28.

30. Servet Mutlu, "Ethnic Kurds in Turkey: A Demographic Study," *International Journal of Middle East Studies* 28 (November 1996), pp. 532, 533.

31. "Kurdish Leader on Significance of Talks in Ankara," Ankara Anatolia in English, 1515 GMT, March 14, 1991; as cited in *Foreign Broadcast Information Service—Near East & South Asia*, March 15, 1991, p. 39.

32. Ibid.

33. "Kurdish Leader Wants 'Democratic Regime,'" Ankara Anatolia in Turkish, 1415 GMT, March 31, 1991; as cited in *FBIS-WEU*, April 1, 1991, p. 33.

34. Graham Fuller, "The Fate of the Kurds," *Foreign Affairs* 72 (Spring 1993), p. 114.
35. David McDowall, *A Modern History of the Kurds* (London and New York: I.B. Tauris, 1996), p. 430.
36. Henri J. Barkey and Graham E. Fuller, "Turkey's Kurdish Question: Critical Turning Points and Missed Opportunities," *Middle East Journal* 51 (Winter 1997), p. 72.
37. *Hurriyet*, April 28, 1992.
38. This and the following citation were taken from "Ozal Proposes Kurdish Camps in North Iraq," Ankara TRT Television Network in Turkish, 1700 GMT, April 16, 1991; as cited in *FBIS-WEU*, April 17, 1991, p. 29.
39. *Briefing*, June 29, 1992, p. 15.
40. Cited in "Iraqi Kurds Reportedly to Block Terrorist Attacks," Ankara TRT Television Network, 1600 GMT, April 8, 1992; as cited in *FBIS-WEU*, April 9, 1992, p. 43.
41. "Talabani Calls on PKK to End Armed Action," Ankara Anatolia in Turkish, 1415 GMT, October 18, 1991; as cited in *FBIS-WEU*, October 21, 1991, p. 58.
42. This and the following citation were taken from "Meets with Demirel," Ankara TRT Television Network in Turkish, 1600 GMT, June 9, 1992; as cited in *FBIS-WEU*, June 11, 1992, p. 42.
43. Cited in Ilter Sagirsoy and Nedret Ersamel, "We Created 10 Million Kurds," *Notka* (Turkey), February 10, 1991, pp. 20-27, as cited in *FIS-WEU*, March 6, 1991, p. 26.
44. "Reasons for Change Elaborated," Ankara Anatolia in English, 1510 GMT, January 28, 1991; as cited in *FBIS-WEU*, January 29, 1991, p. 56. As president, of course, Ozal had to resign as leader of the ANAP party. Subsequently, when a growing number of ANAP members became critical of his innovative position on the Kurdish question, Ozal considered establishing a new party that "would embrace the Kurds." *Hurriyet*, September 27, 1992.
45. Cited in "Ozal Interviewed on Kurdish Issue, Violence," *Milliyet*, August 23, 1992, p. 11; as cited in *FBIS-WEU*, September 3, 1992, p. 39.
46. Cengiz Candar, "Kurt Kimligini Kabul: Dil'e Saygi," *Radikal*, October 14, 2008.
47. "Demirel Warns on Effects of Kurdish Issue," *Cumhuriyet* (Istanbul), March 26, 1991; as cited in *FBIS-WEU, April 2, 1991, pp. 36-37.*
48. "Unbanning of Kurdish Discussed, Examined," *Nokta*, February 10,

1991, pp. 26-27; as cited in *FBIS-WEU*, March 6, 1991, p. 29.

49. Ilter Sagirsoy, "No, Despite Ozal," *Nokta*, February 24, 1991, pp. 28-29; as cited in *FBIS-WEU*, March 26, 1991, pp. 41-42.

50. The following citations were taken from Institut Kurde de Paris, *Information and Liaison Bulletin*, no. 70, January 1991, pp. 2-4. See also "Language Freedom to Herald Democracy Drive?" *Briefing*, February 11, 1991, pp. 6-9.

51. Cited in "Evren Regrets Ban on Public Use of Kurdish Language," *Today's Zaman*, November 11, 2007.

52. The following data and citations were taken from the two sources cited in endnote 50.

53. "Good-for-You to Ozal from Kurds," *Nokta*, February 17, 1991, pp. 26-29, as cited in *FBIS-WEU*, March 26, 1991, pp. 39-41.

54. Mehmet Ali Birand, "Interview with Abdullah Ocalan," *Milliyet*, March 25, 1991, p. 19; as cited in *FBIS-WEU*, April 2, 1991, p. 39.

55. This and the following citation were taken from "Kurdish Rebel Leader Proposes Talks with Ankara," Paris AFP in English, 1333 GMT, March 23, 1991; as cited in *FBIS-WEU*, March 25, 1991, pp. 44-45.

56. Cited in "Ocalan Spokesman Denies Report," *Hurriyet*, March 14, 1993, p. 22; as cited in *FBIS-WEU*, March 15, 1993, p. 43.

57. This and the following discussion and citations were taken from Kamran Qurrah Daghi, "Ocalan Explains Peace Overtures," *Al-Hayah*, March 17, 1993, p. 1, 4; as cited in *FBIS-WEU*, March 22, 1993, p. 42.

58. After crushing his rebellion, the Turkish authorities hanged Sheikh Said on 29 June 1925. See Olson, *The Sheikh Said Rebellion*, p. 127. Bedir Khan Beg ruled the powerful Kurdish emirate of Botan—which at its height included much of present-day southeastern Turkey and even parts of northern Iraq—from approximately 1821 to 1847, when the Ottomans forced him to surrender and sent him into exile, where he died. See Bruinessen, *Agha, Shaikh and State*, pp. 177-82.

59. "Government Caught Out by Apo's Offer," *Briefing*, March 22-29, 1993, p. 3.

60. This and the following citation were taken from "PKK Puts Shocking End to a 'Peace' Which Ankara Never Gave a Chance," *Briefing*, May 31-June 7, 1993, p. 6.

61. This and the following citations were taken from Ismet G. Imset, "Wiping Out the PKK Again and Again . . .," *Turkish Probe* (Turkey), July 6, 1993, pp. 4-7; as cited in *FBIS-WEU*, July 29, 1993, p. 52.

Imset was an objective observer of the entire Kurdish question who had published a great deal about the PKK during the 1980s and early 1990s until threats against his life led to his exile. For an example of his work, see Ismet G. Imset, *The PKK: A Report on Separatist Violence in Turkey (1973-1992)* (Istanbul: Turkish Daily News Publications, 1992).

62. Cited in "Talabani Interviewed on Ties with Turkey," *Ozgur Gundem*, December 19, 1993, p. 11; as cited in *FBIS-WEU*, December 27, 1993, p. 35. Talabani expressed similar sentiments concerning Ozal's intentions when I spoke with him at his home in Irbil in northern Iraq on 16 August 1993.

63. This and the following citation were taken from Rafet Balli, "The Way Ocalan Views Turkish Leaders," *Milliyet*, March 26, 1993, p. 20; as cited in *FBIS-WEU*, April 2, 1993, p. 65.

64. This and the following citation were taken from Ismet G. Imset, "PKK Leader Says Attacks Will Force Political Solution," *Turkish Daily News*, June 12, 1993, pp. 1, 11; as cited in *FBIS-WEU*, June 22, 1993, p. 75.

65. For background, see Michael M. Gunter, "Turkey: The Politics of a New Democratic Constitution," *Middle East Policy* 19 (Spring 2012), pp. 119-25.

66. Cited in "The Sun Also Rises in the South East," Briefing (Ankara), August 15, 2005.

67. For background, see Michael M. Gunter and M. Hakan Yavuz, "Turkish Paradox: Progressive Islamists versus Reactionary Secularists," *Critique: Critical Middle Eastern Studies* 16 (Fall 2007), pp. 289-301.

68. On Turkey's Deep State, see Michael M. Gunter, "Turkey, Kemalism and the 'Deep State,'" in *Conflict, Democratization and the Kurds in the Middle East* eds,. Mehmet Gurses and David Romano (New York: Palgrave Macmillan, 2014), pp. 17-39.

69. Cited in "Gul: Kurdish Problem is the Most Important Problem of Turkey," *Today's Zaman*, May 11, 2009.

70. Cited in *Today's Zaman*, August 12, 2009.

71. Author's contacts with Kurdish sources in Europe and the Middle East. For background, see Michael M. Gunter, *The Kurds Ascending: The Evolving Solution to the Kurdish Problem in Iraq and Turkey*, 2nd ed. New York: Palgrave Macmillan, 2011, pp. 155-88.

72. *Hurriyet*, issues of November 18, 2009; December 2, 2009; December 9, 2009; and December 14, 2009; as cited in Menderes Cinar, "The

Militarization of Secular Opposition in Turkey," *Insight Turkey* 12 (Spring 2010), p. 119.

73. Odul Celep, "Turkey's Radical Right and the Kurdish Issue: The MHP's Reaction to the 'Democratic Opening,'" *Insight Turkey* 12 (Spring 2010), p. 136.

74. Human Rights Watch, "Turkey Arrests Expose Flawed Justice System," November 1, 2011. Http://www.hrw.org/news/2011/11/01/turkey-arrests-expose. . . , accessed November 13, 2011.

75. Ibid.

76. "Turkey's Erdogan Calls for More Support for Peace Move," *Today's Zaman*, February 26, 2013. Http://www.todayszaman.com/news-308165-turkey's-Erdogan, accessed March 1, 2013.

77. The following data were taken from "Kongra-Gel Held Its 9th General Assembly," Firatnews.com, July 10, 2013. Http://en.firatnews.com/news/news/kongra-gel. . . , accessed July 11, 2013.

78. In reality, Karayilan had long held this position. As already noted, the KCK is an umbrella organization that supposedly includes the PKK. In practice, however, the two are the same.

79. Amberin Zaman, "Kurdish Rebel Group in Turkey Re-Focuses on Syria," Al-Monitor, July 17, 2013. Http://www.al-monitor.com/pulse/originals/2013/07/pkk-leadership-change. . . , accessed July 19, 2013.

80. This citation and the following information are largely taken from Guillaume Perrier, "Uneasy Truce Holds as Kurdish Guerrilla Forces Withdraw from Turkey," *The Guardian*, September 3, 2013. Http://www.mesop.de/2013/09/03/uneasy-truce-holds. . . , accessed September 5, 2013.

81. This citation and the following data were garnered from "PKK Plans 100 Protests a Day, Expecting Action from Gov't," *Today's Zaman*, August 25, 2013. Http://www.mesop.de/2013/08/25/pkk-plans-100-protests. . . , accessed August 25, 2013.

82. "PKK Stops Further Withdrawing from Turkey," MESOP, September 10, 2013. Http://www.mesop.de/2013/09/10/pkk-stops-further. . . , accessed September 10, 2013.

83. Chase Winter, "Turkey's Strained Kurdish Peace Process," Foreignpolicy.com, December 11, 2013. Http://www.foreignpolicy.com/posts/2013/12/11. . . , accessed December 13, 2013.

84. "Disillusioned and Divided," *The Economist*, May 24, 2014, p. 45.

85. Cited in Kadri Gursel, "Time Running Out for Turkey-PKK Peace Process," Al-Monitor, November 4, 2013. Http://www.al-monitor.com/pulse/originals/2013/11/akp-stall-kurd-peace-process.html, accessed November 11, 2013.

86. Cited in "Ocalan: This Process Has Three Components," Kurdish Info, December 8, 2013. Http://www.kurdishinfo.com/ocalan-process-three-components, accessed December 14, 2013.

87. "Celik Signals Turkey to Welcome Independent Kurdish State in Iraq," *Today's Zaman*, June 29, 2014. Http://www.mesop.de/2014/06/29/mesop-news-celik-signals. . . , accessed June 30, 2014.

88. Ulas Doga Eralp, "Turkey's Rapprochement with Iraqi Kurdistan: An Obstacle to Kurdish Peace Process?" Eurasiareview, November 28, 2013. Http://www.mesop.de/2013/11/28/turkeys-rapprochement. . . , accessed November 28, 2013.

89. "PYD Announces Constitution for Kurdish Regions," Kurdpress, July 22, 2013. Http://www.mesop.de/2013/07/22/pyd-announces. . . , accessed July 22, 2013.

90. "PYD 'Playing a Dangerous Game': PYD Has Authority Only on Regions 'Given by the al-Assad Regime': Iraqi Kurdish Leader Barzani," Anadolu Agency, November 14, 2013. Http://www.mesop.de/2013/11/14/pyd-playing -a-dangerous-game. . . , accessed November 14, 2013.

Chapter 3

1. For further detail, see Toby Dodge, *Inventing Iraq: The Failure of Nation-Building and a History Denied* (New York: Columbia University Press, 2003).

2. On Iraqi history see Phebe Marr, *The Modern History of Iraq*, 3rd ed. (Boulder, CO: Westview Press, 2012); Gareth Stansfield, *Iraq: People, History, Politics* (Cambridge, UK: Polity, 2007); and Charles Tripp, *A History of Iraq*, 3rd ed. (Cambridge, UK: Cambridge University Press, 2007).

3. For an extensive background analysis, see C. J. Edmonds, *Kurds, Turks and Arabs: Travel and Research in North-Eastern Iraq, 1919-1925* (London: Oxford University Press, 1957).

4. Before the breakup of the Soviet Union in 1991, its former republics languished under a similar type of quasi-colonial rule.

5. Three good analyses of these earlier years under Arab rule are David C. Adamson, *The Kurdish War* (New York: Praeger, 1964); Sa'ad Jawad, *Iraq and the Kurdish Question, 1958-1970* (London: Ithaca

Press, 1981); and Edgar O'Ballance , *The Kurdish Revolt, 1961-70* (London: Faber & Faber, 1973).

6. For three different interpretations, see Majid Khadduri, *Socialist Iraq: A Study in Iraqi Politics since 1968* (Washington, D.C.: The Middle East Institute, 1978); Samir al-Khalil, *Republic of Fear: The Inside Story of Saddam's Iraq* (New York: Pantheon Books, 1989); and Eric Davis, *Memories of State: Politics, History, and Collective Identity in Modern Iraq* (Berkeley: University of California Press, 2005).

7. For a collection of timely articles dealing with the evolution of pan-Kurdish nationalism, see Mohammed M. A. Ahmed and Michael M. Gunter eds., *The Evolution of Kurdish Nationalism* (Costa Mesa, CA: Mazda Publishers, 2007).

8. See, for example, Habibollah Atarodi, *Great Powers, Oil and the Kurds in Mosul (Southern Kurdistan/Northern Iraq), 1910-1925* (Lanham, MD: University Press of America, 2003); and D. K. Fieldhouse, ed., *Kurds, Arabs and Britons: The Memoir of Wallace Lyon in Iraq 1918-44* (London and New York, I. B. Tauris, 2002).

9. Cited in Ismet Sheriff Vanly, "Kurdistan in Iraq," in Gerard Chaliand, ed., *People without a Country: The Kurds and Kurdistan* (London: Zed Press, 1980), p. 161.

10. Peter J. Beck, "A Tedious and Perilous Controversy: Britain and the Settlement of the Mosul Dispute, 1918-1926," *Middle Eastern Studies* 17 (April 1981), pp. 256-76.

11. Cited in Vanly, "Kurdistan in Iraq," p. 162.

12. This and the previous citations were taken from Stephen H. Longrigg, *Iraq, 1900 to 1950: A Political, Social, and Economic History* (London: Oxford University Press, 1953), p. 196.

13. David McDowall, A *Modern History of the Kurds,* 3rd ed. (London and New York: I. B. Tauris, 2004), p. 158.

14. William Eagleton, Jr., *The Kurdish Republic of 1946* (London: Oxford University Press, 1963); and Archie Roosevelt, Jr., "The Kurdish Republic of Mahabad," *Middle East Journal* 1 (July 1947), pp. 247-69.

15. This and the following citation were taken from C. J. Edmonds, "The Kurds of Iraq," *Middle East Journal* 11 (Winter 1957), p. 61.

16. This and the following citation were taken from C. J. Edmonds, "The Kurds and the Revolution in Iraq," *Middle East Journal* 13 (Winter 1959), pp. 4 and 8.

17. Cited in Dana Adams Schmidt, *Journey among Brave Men* (Boston: Little, Brown, 1964), pp. 109-10.

18. For an excellent analysis, see Edmund Ghareeb, *The Kurdish Question*

in Iraq (Syracuse, NY: Syracuse University Press, 1981).

19. For details of Barzani's last days, see David A. Korn, "The Last Years of Mustafa Barzani," *Middle East Quarterly* 1 (June 1994), pp. 12-27.

20. For an analysis that contains much on the Kurdish struggle, see Uriel Dann, *Iraq under Qassem: A Political History, 1958-1963* (New York: Praeger, 1969).

21. For background, see Middle East Watch, *Genocide in Iraq: The Anfal Campaign against the Kurds* (New York: Human Rights Watch, 1993); Kanan Makiya, *Cruelty and Silence: War, Tyranny, Uprising and the Arab World* (New York and London: W. W. Norton & Company, 1993); Joost R. Hiltermann, *A Poisonous Affair: America, Iraq, and the Gassing of Halabja* (Cambridge: Cambridge University Press, 2007); and Choman Hardi, *Gendered Experiences of Genocide: Anfal Survivors in Kurdistan-Iraq* (Farnham Surrey, England: Ashgate Publishing Ltd, 2011).

22. Gareth R. V. Stansfield, *Iraqi Kurdistan: Political Development and Emergent Democracy* (London and New York: RoutledgeCurzon, 2003); Michael M. Gunter, *The Kurds Ascending: The Evolving Solution to the Kurdish Problem in Iraq and Turkey*, 2nd ed. (New York: Palgrave Macmillan, 2011); Mahir A. Aziz, *The Kurds of Iraq: Ethnonationalism and National Identity in Iraqi Kurdistan* (London and New York: I. B. Tauris, 2011); and Mohammed M. A. Ahmed, *Iraqi Kurds and Nation-Building* (New York: Palgrave Macmillan, 2012), among numerous others.

23. For background, see Reidar Visser and Gareth Stansfield, eds., *An Iraq of Its Regions: Cornerstones of a Federal Democracy?* (New York: Columbia University Press, 2008); and Brendan O'Leary, John McGarry, and Khaled Salih, eds., *The Future of Kurdistan in Iraq* (Philadelphia: University of Pennsylvania Press, 2005).

24. See, for example, Denise Natali, *The Kurdish Quasi-State: Development and Dependency in Post-Gulf War Iraq* (Syracuse, NY: Syracuse University Press, 2010).

25. For an incisive analysis, see Liam Anderson and Gareth Stansfield, *Crisis in Kirkuk: The Ethnopolitics of Conflict and Compromise* (Philadelphia: University of Pennsylvania Press, 2009).

26. I have met Nawshirwan Mustafa on several occasions, both in the United States and in the United Kingdom. When I visited him in his home in Sulaymaniya on a cold day in November 2006, I was struck by how there was no heat on in his house. Indeed, we all wore coats

for the meeting. The point that I think he was making is that, even though he was an important person in the KRG, he wanted to demonstrate that he enjoyed no special privileges as many others did.

27. Sherko Kirmanj, "Kurdish History Textbooks: Building a Nation-State within a Nation-State," *Middle East Journal* 68 (Summer 2014), pp. 367-84.

28. For further analysis, see Ofra Bengio, "Will the Kurds Get Their Way?" *American Interest*, November/December 2012. Http://www. mesop.de/2012/10/22/ofra-negio-moshe-dayan-center-will-the - kurds-get-their-way/, accessed October 22, 2012.

29. For more background, see Kamal Chomani and Jake Hess, "Pro-Democracy Demonstrations in Northern Iraq/South Kurdistan," MESOP.de, March 2, 2011. Http://www.mesop.de/2011/03/02/pro-democracy . . . , accessed March 3, 2011; and Kawa Hassan, "South Kurdistan 2011: Massive Political and Social Energies: No Fundamental Changes," *Kurdistan Tribune*, February 6, 2011, Http://kurdistantribune.com, accessed June 5, 2012.

30. Cited in Andrew Parasiliti, "Barham Salih: Bashar's Days Are Numbered," *Al Monitor,* September 12, 2012. Http://www.mesop.de/2012/09/13/barham-salih-bashars. . . , accessed September 13, 2012.

31. "Iraqi Kurdistan President Massoud Barzani Seeks Right to Self-Determination," Ekurd.net, December 11, 2011. Http://www.ekurd.net/mismas/articles . . . , accessed June 5, 2012.

32. For more background on this simmering conflict, see International Crisis Group, "Iraq and the Kurds: The High-Stakes Hydrocarbons Gambit," Middle East Report No. 120, April 19, 2012.

33. "US Senator McCain Expects Iraq Gov't to Collapse and Split into Three Different States," Ekurd.net, January 11, 2012. Http://www. ekurd.net/mismas/articles . . . , accessed June 5, 2012.

34. Joseph R. Biden and Leslie H. Gelb, "Unity through Autonomy in Iraq," *New York Times*, May 1, 2006.

35. Barry Malone, "Iraqi Calls Turkey 'Hostile State' as Relations Dim,' Reuters, April 20, 2012. Http://www.reuters.com/article/2012/04/21/us-iraq-turkey-id . . . , accessed June 5, 2012.

36. For further background, see Ofra Bengio, "Turkey: A Midwife for a Kurdish State?" *Jerusalem Post*, June 12, 2012; and Jonathan Spyer, "Say It Again: Kurdish Independence Now," *The Tower*, Issue #6, September 2013. Http://mosaicmagazine.com. . . , accessed November 18, 2013.

37. "Kurdistan's Barzani Suggests Iraq Might Use F-16s against Kurds,"

Ekurd.net, April 9, 2012. Http://www.ekurd.net/mismas/articles. . . , accessed June 5, 2012.

38. Lara Jakes, "Iraq's Kurdistan President Massoud Barzani Hints at Secession," Ekurd.net, April 25, 2012. Http://www.ekurd.net/mismas/articles. . . , accessed June 5, 2012.

39. "Before a Full-Blown War?" Aswataliraq.ingo, November 22, 2012. Http://www.mesop.de/2012/11/22/before-a-full-blown. . . , accessed November 24, 2012.

40. Micha'el Tanchum, "The Kurds' Big Year: The Political Conditions that Favor Kurdish Independence in Iraq," *Foreign Affairs,* January 12, 2015. Http:www.foreignaffairs.com/articles/142765, accessed March 11, 2015.

Chapter 4

1. The leading background source in English on the Kurds in Syria is Jordi Tejel, *Syria's Kurds: History, Politics and Society* (London and New York: Routledge, 2009). Also see Harriet Montgomery (Allsopp), *The Kurds of Syria: An Existence Denied* (Berlin: European Center for Kurdish Studies, 2005); and Kerim Yildiz, *The Kurds in Syria: The Forgotten People* (London: Pluto Press, 2005). For more recent sources, see International Crisis Group, "Syria's Kurds: A Struggle within a Struggle," Middle East Report No. 136, January 22, 2013; and Harriet Allsopp, *The Kurds of Syria: Political Parties and Identity in the Middle East* (London: I. B. Tauris, 2014). I published portions of this chapter earlier in Michael M. Gunter, *Out of Nowhere: The Kurds of Syria in Peace and War* (London: C. Hurst & Co., 2014).

2. For background, see Phillip Khoury, *Syria and the French Mandate: The Politics of Arab Nationalism* (London: I. B. Tauris, 1987); and Nelida Fuccaro, "Kurds and Kurdish Nationalism in Mandatory Syria: Politics, Culture and Identity," in Abbas Vali, ed., *Essays on the Origins of Kurdish Nationalism* (Costa Mesa, CA: Mazda Publishers, 2003), pp. 191-217.

3. On this point, see David McDowall, *A Modern History of the Kurds* (London and New York: I. B. Tauris, 1996), p. 4.

4. Wadie Jwaideh, *The Kurdish National Movement: Its Origins and Development* (Syracuse NY: Syracuse University Press, 2006), p. 143.

5. Tejel, *Syria's Kurds*, pp. 66 and 99.

6. For more on how nations are invented rather than existing since time

immemorial, see Benedict Anderson, *Imagined Communities: Reflections on the Origin and Spread of Nationalism* (London: Verso, 1991).

7. Martin Strohmeier, *Crucial Images in the Presentation of Kurdish National Identity: Heroes and Patriots: Traitors and Foes* (Leiden and Boston: Brill, 2003), p. 104. For the sake of brevity, the following page numerals in the text refer to the Strohmeier study so that repetitious endnotes may be avoided.

8. Tejel, *Syria's Kurds*, p. 46.

9. Jawad Mella, *The Colonial Policy of the Syrian Baath Party in Western Kurdistan* (London: Western Kurdistan Association, 2006).

10. On this point regarding dissimulation, "which is related to the religious term *taqiyya*" and is a strategy of group survival used by the Shiites and other minorities to avoid repression., see Tejel, *Syria's Kurds*, p. 83.

11. Cited in Maureen Lynch and Perveen Ali, "Buried Alive: Stateless Kurds in Syria," (Washington, DC: Refugees International, 2006), p. i. In addition, see Jordi Tejel, *Syria's Kurds: History, Politics and Society* (London and New York: Routledge, 2009), pp. 51-52; and Robert Lowe, "Kurdish Nationalism in Syria," in Mohammed M. A. Ahmed and Michael M. Gunter, eds., *The Evolution of Kurdish Nationalism* (Costa Mesa, CA: Mazda Publishers, 2007), pp. 294-96.

12. Cited in Lynch and Ali, "Buried Alive," pp. 1-2.

13. On the Baath Party, see Kamel S. Abu Jaber, *The Arab Ba'th Socialist Party: History, Ideology, and Organization* (Syracuse, NY: Syracuse University Press, 1966); John Devlin, *The Baath Party: A History from Its Origins to 1966* (Stanford, CA: Hoover Institution Press, 1976); and Gordon Torrey, "The Baath Ideology and Practice," *Middle East Journal* 23 (Autumn 1969), pp. 445-70.

14. The following excerpts were taken from an article published by the late famous Kurdish scholar Ismet Cheriff Vanly, in Mohammed M. A. Ahmed and Michael M. Gunter, eds., "The Oppression of the Kurdish People in Syria," *Kurdish Exodus: From Internal Displacement to Diaspora* (Sharon, MA: Ahmed Foundation for Kurdish Studies, 2001), pp. 55-56. The page numerals in the text above refer to those in the actual Hilal manuscript, which totaled 160 pages. For a full copy of this lengthy report, see Jawad Mella, *The Colonial Policy of the Syrian Baath Party in Western Kurdistan* (London: Western Kurdistan Association, 2006), pp. 63-267, and the extended critical replies that follow. Hilal subsequently served as minister of supplies from 1964 to 1970.

15. Tejel, *Syria's Kurds*, pp. 28-29.
16. On these points, see Wadie Jwaideh, *The Kurdish National Movement: Its Origins and Development* (Syracuse, NY: Syracuse University Press, 2006), p. 145.
17. For further analysis of these issues, see Peter Malanczuk, *Akehurst's Modern Introduction to International Law*, 7th revised ed. (London and New York: Routledge, 1997), pp. 169, 215.
18. Tejel, *Syria's Kurds*, p. 43.
19. Another difference was that no Kurdish party in Syria ever adopted an Islamist doctrine as has occurred in Turkey and Iraq. Alawite rule in Syria and the perceived Kurdish need to cooperate with it is probably one main reason for this position.
20. Christian Sinclair and Sirwan Kajjo, "The Evolution of Kurdish Politics in Syria," *Middle East Research and Information Project*, August 31, 2011. Http://www.merip.org/mero/mero083111?p. . . , accessed July 28, 2013.
21. Tejel, *Syria's Kurds*, p. 89.
22. For more on the multitude of Kurdish political parties in Syria, see KurdWatch. "Who Is the Syrian-Kurdish Opposition? The Development of Kurdish Parties, 1956-2011" (Berlin: European Center for Kurdish Studies, 2011), which contains a list of 14 Kurdish parties in Syria on pp. 13-15, including their names in English and Kurdish as well as their leaders; and Tejel, *Syria's Kurds*, pp. 48-49, 85-95, and finally 139-140, which contain a list of "Kurdish political parties in Syria." A total of 13 are listed with their names in Kurdish, Arabic, and English as well as their leaders, but only as of around 2008.
23. For earlier figures, see International Crisis Group (ICG), "Syria's Metastasizing Conflicts," Middle East Report No. 143, June 27, 2013, p. 1, n. 1 and n. 2.
24. Anne Barnard, "Syria Weighs Its Tactics as Pillars of Its Economy Continue to Crumble," *New York Times*, July 13, 2013.
25. Saeed Kamali Dehglan, "Syrian Army Being Aided by Iranian Forces," *The Guardian*, May 28, 2012. Http://www.guardian.co.uk/world/2012/may/28/syria . . . , accessed August 4, 2013.
26. Michael R. Gordon, "Iran Supplying Syrian Military via Iraqi Airspace,' *New York Times*, September 4, 2012.
27. Anne Barnard, "Leader of Hezbollah Warns It Is Ready to Come to Syria's Aid," *New York Times*, April 30, 2013.
28. Karim Emile Bitar (trans. Charles Goulden), "Syria: Proxy Theater of War," *Other Voices*, 16:6 (August 2013), pp. OV-3-Ov-5. This ar-

ticle originally appeared in *Le Monde diplomatique*, June 2013.

29. ICG, "Syria's Metastasizing Conflicts," p. 3, n. 14.

30. Peter Bouckaert, "Is This the Most Disgusting Atrocity Filmed in the Syrian Civil War?" *Foreign Policy*, May 13, 2013. Http://www. foreignpolicy.com/articles/2013/05/13/ most-disgusting-atrocity. . . , accessed August 5, 2013. Of course, the regime has committed its egregious atrocities, such as the massacre of as many as 100 civilians near the city of Baniyas, located on the Mediterranean Sea some 20 miles north of Tartus, on May 3, 2013. See "Syrian Dictator Assad 'Massacres Up to 100 men, Women and Children' with Knives and Guns as U.S. Says Arming Rebels Is Now an Option," *Daily Mail*, May 4, 2013. Http://www.dailymail.co.uk/ news/article-2318993/. . . , accessed May 29, 2013.

31. Mike Giglio, "Syria's Bashar Al-Assad Is Winning," *The Daily Beast*, May 17, 2013. Http://thedailybeast.cheapbabysclothes.co.uk/articles . . . , accessed August 5, 2013.

32. On May 11, 2013, for example, in what Turkey saw as blowback from Syria for Turkish support of the oppositionists, two bombings killed 51 and injured 140 in Reyhanli, a city on the Mediterranean coast just across the Syrian border.

33. Salih Muslim, email reply to Michael Gunter, July 10, 2013.

34. "Iraq-Syria: As Kurds Enter the Fray, Risk of Conflict Grows," IRIN: Humanitarian News and Analysis (UN Office for the Coordination of Humanitarian Affairs), August 2, 2012. Http://www.irinnews.org/Report/96007/IRAQ-Syria. . . , accessed August 2, 2012.

35. Alexander Shumilin, "Why Russia Will Not Abandon Assad: The Internal Dynamics behind Russia's Syria Policy," Center for Greater Middle East Conflicts at the Institute for the USA and Canada Studies (Russian Academy of Sciences), August 15, 2012. Http://www. mesop.de/2012/08/17/why-russia. . . , accessed August 17, 2012.

36. Cited in "Syrian Kurdish Leader: US Cannot Succeed in the Middle East without the Support of Kurds," Ekurd.net, June 20, 2008. Http://www.ekurd.net/mismas/articles/misc2008/6/syriakurdistan142. htm, accessed June 8, 2013.

37. Omar Hassino and Ilhan Tanir, "The Decisive Minority: The Role of Syria's Kurds in the Anti-Assad Revolution," A Henry Jackson Society Report, March 2012. Http://www.scpss.org/libs/spaw. . . , accessed June 6, 2012. Also see Denise Natali, "Syrian Kurdish Cards," Http://sharifbehruz.com. . . , accessed June 6, 2012.

38. Emrullah Uslu, "How Kurdish PKK Militants Are Exploiting the

Crisis in Syria. . .," *Terrorism Monitor*, April 9, 2012. Http://www. jamestown.org/. . . , accessed June 6, 2012.

39. Nabaz Shwany, "Is That Right to Accuse the PYD for Supporting Bashir Assad. . . " Ekurd.net, March 7, 2012. Http://www.ekurd.net/mismas/articles. . . , accessed June 6, 2012.

40. "Interview with Salih Muhammad, President of PYD." Firat News, February 2012. Http://en.firatnews.eu/index.php? . . . , accessed February 28, 2012.

41. Ibid.

42. Pydrojava.net, April 12, 2012.

43. One might note the similarity of this title to that of the PKK's *Hezen Parastina Gel* (HPG), or Peoples Defense Force (YPG).

44. Peter Hartling, "Arab Rebel-Kurd Tensions," Agence France Presse (AFP), October 31, 2012. Http://www.mesop.de/2012/10/31/arab-rebel-kurd-tensions. . . , accessed October 31, 2012.

45. Salih Muslim emphasized this fact in an email to me dated July 10, 2013.

46. Michael Weiss, "The Impending Syrian-Kurdish Conflict," Now Lebanon, November 2, 2012. Http://www.nowlebanon.com/NewsArticleDetails.aspx?ID=453196, accessed November 7, 2012; and Aymenn Jawad Al-Tamimi, "Kurdish Rivalries in Syria," *The American Spectator*, November 8, 2012. Http://www.meforum.org/3372/kurdish-rivalries-syria, accessed November 8, 2012.

47. Jordi Tejel, *Syria's Kurds: History, Politics and Society* (London and New York: Routledge, 2009), pp. 79 and 156, n. 17.

48. The Kurdish Union (Yekiti) Party, founded in 1992 and often a bitter foe of the PYD, also has some armed units, as do both branches of the Kurdish Freedom (Azadi) Party In addition, Massoud Barzani's Kurdistan Democratic Party (KDP) was training some units for the Kurdish Democratic Party of Syria (*el-Parti*), but was shocked at their incompetence. See Eva Savelsberg and Jordi Tejel, "The Syrian Kurds in 'Transition to Somewhere,'" in Mohammed M. A. Ahmed and Michael M. Gunter, eds. *The Kurdish Spring: Geopolitics Changes and the Kurds* (Costa Mesa, CA: Mazda Publishers, 2013), p. 214. Nevertheless, the PYD/YPG maintains the dominant armed Kurdish militia in Syria.

49. Wladimir van Wilgenburg, "Border Arrests Reveal Disunity, Conflict among Syrian Kurds," Al-Monitor, May 21, 2013. Http://www.al-monitor.com/pulse/originals/2013/05/pyd-arrests-syrian-kurds.html, accessed August 8, 2013.

50. "Protests of Kurdish Youth against PYD," MESOP, August 10, 2013. Http://www.mesop.de/2013/08/09/protests. . . , accessed August 10, 2013.

51. KurdWatch, "Press Release: On Our Own Behalf: KurdWatch Employee Threatened with Death," KurdWatch, August 13, 2013. Http://www.kurdwatch.org, accessed August 13, 2013.

52. Salih Muslim, email response to Michael Gunter, July 10, 2013.

53. "Turkey's Henchmen in Syrian Kurdistan Are Responsible for the Unrest Here," KurdWatch, November 8, 2011. Http://www.kurdwatch. org. . . , accessed June 6, 2012.

54. See, for example, Abdullah Ocalan, *Declaration on the Democratic Solution of the Kurdish Question* (London: Mesopotamian Publishers, 1999); Abdullah Ocalan, *Prison Writings: The PKK and the Kurdish Question in the 21st Century*, trans. and ed. Klaus Happel (London: Transmedia Publishing Ltd., 2011); and Abdullah Ocalan, *Prison Writings III: The Road Map to Negotiations*, trans. Havin Guneser (Cologne, Germany: International Initiative Edition, 2012). Also see Emre Uslu, "PKK's Strategy and the European Charter of Local Self-Government," *Today's Zaman*, June 28. 2010, Http://www.todayszaman.com/news-214416-109-pkks-strategy-and-the-european-charter-. . . , accessed November 26, 2010.

55. Cited in "Turkey's Henchmen. . . ," KurdWatch, November 8, 2011.

56. Cited in ibid.

57. Cited in Pydrojava.net, April 12, 2012.

58. Cited in "The Kurdish Patriotic Conference Is Nothing More Than a Name . . . ," KurdWatch, March 21, 2012. Http://kurdwatch.org.html/en/syria. . . , accessed June 6, 2012.

59. Tim Arango, "Kurds Prepare to Pursue More Autonomy in a Fallen Syria," *New York Times*, September 28, 2012; and Aymenn Al Tamimi, "Syria's Kurds Stand Alone after Rejecting Rebels and Regime," *The National*, July 23, 2012. Http://www.thenational.ae/thenationalconversation/comment/syrias-kurds. . . , accessed July 25, 2012.

60. Email interview with Eva Savelsberg, KurdWatch, European Center for Kurdish Studies, Berlin, Germany, August 26, 2013.

61. "Al-Nusra Commits to al-Qaeda, Deny Iraq Branch Merger," Agence France Presse, April 10, 2013. Http://www.naharnet.com/stories/en/78961-al-nusra-commits. . . , accessed August 10, 2013.

62. Cited in Ruth Sherlock, "Inside Jabhat al Nusra—The Most Extreme Wing of Syria's Struggle," *The Daily Telegraph*, December 2, 2012.

Http://www.telegraph.co.uk/news/worldnews/middleeast/syria/97165 45. . . , accessed August 10, 2013.

63. Jennifer Lang, "Turkey's Counterterrorism Response to the Syrian Crisis," *Terrorism Monitor* 11:4 (July 12, 2013). Http://www.mesop. de/2013/07/13/turkeys-counterterrorism-response. . . , accessed July 13, 2013.

64. Reina Faraj, "The Misogyny of Salafist Doctrine," *As-Safir* (Lebanon), April 15, 2013. Http://www.al-monitor.com/pulse/culture/2013/04/salafist. . . , accessed August 9, 2013.

65. "PYD Announces Constitution for Kurdish Regions," Kurdpress, July 22, 2013. Http://www.mesop.de/2013/07/22/pyd-announces. . . , accessed July 22, 2013.

66. Cited in Hemin Khoshnaw, "Salih Muslim's Ankara Visit Marks Major Policy Change," Rudaw, July 29, 2013. Http://rudaw.net/english/middleeast/syria/29072013, accessed August 2, 2013.

67. "Syrian Kurds Declare Autonomy on Eve of Geneva 2," RT News, January 21, 2014. Http://rt.com/news/syria-kurds-autonomy-geneva-989/, accessed April 2, 2014.

68. Abdullah Ocalan, *Prison Writings III: The Road Map to Negotiations*, trans. Havin Guneser (Cologne: International Initiative Edition, 2012). For further thoughts on these ideas, see Joost Jongerden and Ahmet Hamdi Akkaya, "Democratic Confederalism as a Kurdish Spring: The PKK and the Quest for Radical Democracy," in Mohammed M. A. Ahmed and Michael M. Gunter, eds., *The Kurdish Spring: Geopolitical Changes and the Kurds* (Costa Mesa: Mazda Publishers, 2013), 163-85.

Chapter 5

1. Human Rights Watch, *Iran: Freedom of Expression and Association in the Kurdish Regions* (New York: Human Rights Watch, 2009).

2. Amnesty International, *Iran: Human Rights Abuses against the Kurdish Minority* (New York: Amnesty International, 2008).

3. "Exorbitant Human Rights Violations in Iran," Voice of America, June 8, 2012. Http://www.mesop.de/2012/06/08/exorbitant . . . , accessed June 8, 2012.

4. Cited in David McDowall, *A Modern History of the Kurds* (London and New York: I. B. Tauris, 1996), p. 53.

5. Wadie Jwaideh, *The Kurdish National Movement: Its Origins and De-*

velopment (Syracuse, NY: Syracuse University Press, 2006), p. 80.

6. For background, see Farideh Koohi-Kamali, *The Political Development of the Kurds in Iran: Pastoral Nationalism* (New York: Palgrave Macmillan, 2003). For further analysis on the Kurds in Iran, see Kerim Yildiz and Tanyel Taysi, *The Kurds in Iran: The Past, Present and Future* (London: Pluto Press, 2007); Nader Entessar, "The Kurdish National Movement in Iran Since the Islamic Revolution of 1979," in Mohammed M. A. Ahmed and Michael M. Gunter, eds., *The Evolution of Kurdish Nationalism* (Costa Mesa, CA: Mazda Publishers, 2007), pp. 260-75; and A. R. Ghassemlou, "Kurdistan in Iran," in Gerard Chaliand, ed., *A People without a Country: The Kurds and Kurdistan* (New York: Olive Branch, 1993), pp. 95-121.

7. On the Mahabad Republic of Kurdistan, see William Eagleton, Jr., *The Kurdish Republic of 1946* (London: Oxford University, 1963); Archie Roosevelt, Jr., "The Kurdish Republic of Mahabad," *Middle East Journal* 1 (July 1947), 247-69; Jwaideh, *Kurdish National Movement*, pp. 243-66; McDowall, *Modern History of the Kurds*, pp. 231-46; and the special issue of *International Journal of Kurdish Studies* 11, nos. 1-2 (1997), entitled "The Republic of Kurdistan: Fifty Years Later."

8. David McDowall, *A Modern History of the Kurds*, 3rd revised ed. (London and New York: I. B. Tauris, 2004, reprinted 2007), p. 253.

9. In 2005, this motto was changed to "Kurdish national rights within the context of a democratic and federal Iran."

10. The following data were largely taken from Reese Erlich, *The Iran Agenda: The Real Story of U.S. Policy and the Middle East Crisis* (Sausalito, CA: PoliPoint Press, 2007).

11. Carol Prunhuber, *The Passion and Death of Rahman the Kurd* (New York: Universe Incorporated, 2010).

12. For further analysis, see Nader Entessar, "The Impact of the Iraq War on the Future of the Kurds in Iran," in Mohammed M. A. Ahmed and Michael M. Gunter, eds., *The Kurdish Question and the 2003 Iraqi War* (Costa Mesa, CA: Mazda, 2005), pp. 174-91.

13. These figures were taken from Bill Samii, "Iran: Country Faces Agitated Kurdish Population," *Radio Free Europe/RL*, July 23, 2005.

14. These data and the following were taken from "Iran Puts Pressure on Kurdish Cities in East Kurdistan," KurdishMedia.com, July 15, 2005.

15. Michael Howard, "Iran Sends In Troops to Crush Border Unrest," *Guardian*, August 5, 2005.

16. The following analysis is partially based on James Brandon, "Iran's

Kurdish Threat: PJAK," *Terrorism Monitor* 4:12 (June 15, 2006), Http://www.jamestown.org/programs/tm/single/. . . , accessed April 6, 2015; and Joshua Partlow, "Shelling Near Iranian Border Is Forcing Iraqi Kurds to Flee," *Washington Post Foreign Service*, September 13, 2007, Http://www.washingtonpost.com/wp-dyn. . . , accessed April 6, 2015.

17. Seymour M. Hersh, "The Next Act: Is a Damaged Administration Less Likely to Attack Iran, or More?" *The New Yorker*, November 27, 2006. Http://www.newyorker.com/magazine/2006/11/27/the-next-act. . . , accessed April 6, 2015.

18. Joanna Paraszczuk, "Iran Feature: Kurdish Movement PJAK Threatens President Rouhani with a 'Second Syria,'" *EA WorldView*, August 19, 2013. Http://eaworldview.com/2013/08/iran-today-kurdish-pjak-leader-threatens-rouhani/, accessed April 4, 2015.

19. Nasir Piroti, "Kurds in Iran Wary about Restart of Armed Conflict by PJAK," *Rudaw*, November 19, 2013. Http://rudaw.net/english/middleeast/iran/19112013, accessed April 4, 2015.

20. Behdad Bordbar, "Iranian Kurds Disappointed with Rouhani," *Al-Monitor*, December 23, 2013. Http://www.al-monitor.com/pulse/originals/2013/12/rouhani-disappoints . . . , accessed April 4, 2015.

21. Abdullah Mohtadi, "The Case of Iranian Kurds; Under Rouhani Government Kurds Continue to Suffer," Kurdish Policy Foundation, October 2, 2014. Http://kurdishpolicy.org/2014/10/02/the-case-of-iranian-kurds-under-rouhani. . . , accessed April 4, 2015.

22. Ibid.

23. Zuber Hawrami, "Iran's Rouhani and the Kurds: Don't Hold Your Breath," *Rudaw*, November 2, 2013. Http://rudaw.net/english/middleeast/iran/02112113, accessed April 4, 2015.

24. Cited in Mohtadi, "Case of the Iranian Kurds."

Chapter 6

1. James A. Baker III and Lee H. Hamilton (Co-Chairs), *The Iraq Study Group Report: The Way Forward—A New Approach* (New York: Vintage Books, 2006). I originally published portions of this chapter as "The Five Stages of American Foreign Policy towards the Kurds," *Insight Turkey* 13 (Spring 2011), pp. 93-106.

2. Kurdistan Regional Government, "President Barzani and Defense Secretary Gates in Erbil Reaffirm Long-Term KRG-US Relations,"

December 11, 2009. Http://www.krg.org/articles/detail.asp?1ngnr=
12&smap=o210100&rnr=223&anr=32969, accessed February 7,
2011.

3. Eli Lake, "U.S. Makes Political Pledge to Kurds in Iraq," *The Washington Times*, December 16, 2009.

4. For further background, see Marianna Charountaki, *The Kurds and
US Foreign Policy: International Relations in the Middle East since
1945* (London: Routledge, 2010).

5. See Samuel Flagg Bemis, *A Diplomatic History of the United States*
(5th ed,.; New York: Holt, Rinehart and Winston, Inc., 1965), p. 626.

6. On Ataturk and the Turkish War of Independence following World
War I, see Stanford J. Shaw and Ezel Kural Shaw, *History of the Ottoman Empire and Modern Turkey*, Vol. II, *Reform, Revolution and
Republic: The Rise of Modern Turkey, 1808-1975* (Cambridge: Cambridge University Press, 1977), pp. 340-72; Bernard Lewis, *The Emergence of Modern Turkey* (2nd ed.; London: Oxford University Press,
1968), pp. 239-93; and Erik J. Zurcher, *Turkey: A Modern History*
(London: I. B. Tauris, 1994), pp. 138-72.

7. For background, see C. J. Edmonds, *Kurds, Turks and Arabs: Travel
and Research in North-Eastern Iraq, 1919-1925* (London: Oxford
University Press, 1957).

8. For background, see David McDowall, *A Modern History of the Kurds*
(3rd ed.; London: I. B. Tauris, 2004); and Paul White, *Primitive
Rebels or Revolutionary Modernizers? The Kurdish National Movement in Turkey* (London and New York: Zed Books, 2000).

9. For further background, see Marlies Casier and Joost Jongerden, eds.,
*Nationalism and Politics in Turkey: Political Islam, Kemalism and
the Kurdish Issue* (London and New York: Routledge, 20110; Kerim
Yildiz and Susan Breau, *The Kurdish Conflict: International Human-
itarian Law and Post-Conflict Mechanisms* (London and New York:
Routledge, 2010); and Aliza Marcus, *Blood and Belief: The PKK and
the Kurdish Fight for Independence* (New York and London: New
York University Press, 2007).

10. For background, see Edmund Ghareeb, *The Kurdish Question in Iraq*
(Syracuse, NY: Syracuse University Press, 1981); and Michael M.
Gunter, *The Kurdish Predicament in Iraq: A Political Analysis* (New
York: St. Martin's Press, 1999).

11. Henry Kissinger, *White House Years* (Boston: Little, Brown and Co.,
1979), p. 1265.

12. The CIA Report the President Doesn't Want You to Read," *Village*

Voice, February 16, 1976, pp. 70-92. The part dealing with the Kurds is entitled "Case 2: Arms Support," and appears on pp. 85 and 87-88.

13. David A. Korn, "The Last Years of Mustafa Barzani," *Middle East Quarterly* 1 (June 1994), pp. 12-27.

14. Jonathan C. Randal, *After Such Knowledge, What Forgiveness? My Encounters with Kurdistan* (New York: Farrar, Straus and Giroux, 1997), p. 299.

15. Cited in "Iraq: KDP's Barzani Urges Arab-Kurdish Dialogue," *Al-Majallah* (London), October 5-11, 1997, p. 29, as cited in *Foreign Broadcast Information Service—Near East & South Asia* (97-283), October 10, 1997, p. 2.

16. The following discussion and citations are taken from the chapter on the "Kurdish Tragedy" in Henry Kissinger, *Years of Renewal* (New York: Simon and Schuster, 1999), pp. 576-96.

17. "Remarks to the American Association for the Advancement of Science," February 15, 1991; cited in *Public Papers of the Presidents of the United States: George Bush, 1991*, vol. 1 (Washington, DC: Government Printing Office, 1992), p. 145.

18. Cited in "United States Turns Down Plea to Intervene as Kirkuk Falls,' *International Herald Tribune*, March 30, 1991.

19. See US Congress, Senate, Committee on Foreign Relations, *Civil War in Iraq: A Staff Report to the Committee on Foreign Relations*, by Peter W. Galbraith, 102nd Congress, 1st session, May 1991.

20. Cited in Selim Caglayan, "Clinton Reprimands Barzani and Talabani," *Hurriyet* (Istanbul), January 28, 1995, p. 18; as cited in *Foreign Broadcast Information Service—West Europe*, February 1, 1995, p. 27.

21. Katherine A. Williams, "How We Lost the Kurdish Game," *Washington Post*, September 15, 1996, p. C1.

22. Cited in Tim Weiner, "Iraqi Offensive into Kurdish Zone Disrupts U.S. Plot to Oust Hussein," *New York Times*, September 7, 1996, p. 4.

23. Cited in Kevin Fedarko, "Saddam's Coup," *Time*, September 23, 1996, p. 44.

24. Cited in Harun Kazaz, "Ambiguity Surrounds N. Iraq Kurdish Agreement," *Turkish Probe*, October 11, 1998.

25. "Text: Clinton's Report on Iraq's Non-Compliance with UN Resolutions," *USIS Washington File*, November 6, 1998, GlobalSecurity.org, Http://www.globalsecurity.org, accessed February 28, 2011.

26. "Ozkok: Biggest Crisis of Trust with US," *Turkish Daily News*, July 7, 2003; and Nicholas Kralev, "U.S. Warns Turkey against Operations in Northern Iraq," *Washington Times*, July 8, 2003.

27. See endnote 1.

28. Kurdistan Regional Government, "President Barzani and Defense Secretary Gates in Erbil Reaffirm Long-Term KRG-US Relations," December 11, 2009.

29. Ibid.

30. Eli Lake, "U.S. Makes Political Pledge to Kurds in Iraq," *The Washington Times*, December 16, 2009.

31. For excellent background on this strategic issue, see Liam Anderson and Gareth Stansfield, *Crisis in Kirkuk: The Ethnopolitics of Conflict and Compromise* (Philadelphia: University of Pennsylvania Press, 2009).

32. Emrullah Uslu, "PKK Intensifies Violence to Bring Turkey into Confrontation with the European Union," 8 *Terrorism Monitor*, July 8, 2010. Http://www.jamestown.org/programs . . . , accessed March 1, 2011.

33. See, for example, US Department of State, Bureau of Democracy, Human Rights, and Labor, *Country Reports on Human Rights Practices—2009*, issued March 11, 2010. Http://www.state.gov . . . , accessed March 1, 2011.

34. Martin Indyk Statement, House International Relations Committee, June 8, *Iraq News*, June 11, 1999.

35. Cited in Toni Marshall, "Kurds Call Turkey Hypocritical," *Washington Times*, April 9, 1999.

36. Author interview with officials at the US State Department, Washington, DC, April 4, 1997.

37. Technically this is not true, as both the KDP and PUK were ludicrously classified as Tier III terrorist groups in 2001, apparently because of their opposition to the then-Iraqi government of Saddam Hussein. When this little known, embarrassing bureaucratic snafu was revealed, it caused a minicrisis in United States–KRG relations until the US Congress removed both Iraqi parties from the list in December 2014. See "US Removes Two Iraqi Kurdish Parties from Terrorist List, *Today's Zaman*, December 14, 2014. Http://www.todayszaman.com/anasayfa_us-removes-two-iraqi-kurdish-parties-from -terrorist-list_366977.html, accessed April 7, 2015.

38. The following data were taken from *Briefing* (Ankara), November 30, 1998, p. 16.

39. Cited in *Turkish Daily News*, December 25, 1998.

40. Cited in "U.S. Says Ocalan Should Be Brought to Justice," Reuters, February 1, 1999.

41. "Remarks by Ambassador Mark R. Parris to the American-Turkish Council's 18th Annual Conference on U.S.-Turkish Relations," May 6, 1999.
42. Gareth Jenkins, "A Military Analysis of Turkey's Incursion into Northern Iraq," 6 *Terrorism Monitor*, March 7, 2008. Http://www. jamestown.org/programs. . . , accessed March 1, 2011.
43. "US May Help Turkey Combat Kurdish Rebels: Gates," Agence France Presse, February 6, 2010. Http://www.google.com/hosted-news/afp/article . . . , accessed March 1, 2011.
44. For background, see US Congress. Senate. Committee on Foreign Relations. "Syria Transition Support Act of 2013," S. Rept. 113-79, 113th Congress, July 24, 2013. Http://beta.congress.gov/congressional-report/113th-congress/senate-report/79/1, accessed September 22, 2013.
45. There are reports that Jordan is serving as a base for the US Central Intelligence Agency (CIA) training Syrian rebels with support from Saudi Arabia. Patrick Cockburn, "How Action over Syria Risks Unsettling Fragile Balance of Power in the Middle East," *The Independent*, August 28, 2013. Http://www.independent.co.uk/voices/ commentators/how-action-over. . . , accessed August 28, 2013. In addition, US intelligence agencies are revamping and constructing air bases in the Kurdish areas of northern Iraq, despite official policy not to.
46. Wladimar van Wilgenburg, "Kurdish Party Rejects US Condemnation of 'PYD's Deadly Response,'" Rudaw, July 2, 2013. Http://rudaw. net/english. . . , accessed July 18, 2013; and "PYD Press Release: On Statement of U.S. Department of State Regarding Situation in Amuda, Syria," July 1, 2013. Http://peaceinkurdisatancampaign.worldpress. co. . . , accessed July 18, 2013.
47. "Salah Muslim's Press Conference before Going to Istanbul," Transnational Middle East Observer, July 26, 2013. Http://www.mesop.de /2013/07/salih-muslims. . . , accessed July 26, 2013.
48. The following citations and discussion are taken from Mutlu Civiroglu, "PYD's Salih Muslim: We Are Awaiting an Invitation for Talks with Washington," Rudaw, August 17, 2013. Http://www.mesop.de/ 2013/08/17/pyds-salih-muslim. . . , accessed August 17, 2013.

Chapter 7

1. See in the special issue on World War I, Mustafa Aksakal, "Introduction," 40 *International Journal of Middle East Studies* (November 2014), p. 653, the reference to "the momentous changes [in the Middle East] set in motion by the events of World War I." For a much fuller and current analysis of the rise of the Kurds, see my *Out of Nowhere: The Kurds of Syria in Peace and War* (London: Hurst Publishers, 2014); as well as the many relevant chapters in Mohammed M. A. Ahmed and Michael M. Gunter, eds., *The Kurdish Spring: Geopolitical Changes and the Kurds* (Costa Mesa, CA: Mazda Publishers, 2013); David Romano and Mehmet Gurses, eds., *Conflict, Democratization, and the Kurds in the Middle East: Turkey, Iran, Iraq, and Syria* (New York: Palgrave Macmillan, 2014); and Ofra Bengio, ed., *Kurdish Awakening: Nation Building in a Fragmented Homeland* (Austin: University of Texas Press, 2014). I originally published portions of this current chapter in Michael M. Gunter, "Iraq, Syria, ISIS and the Kurds: Geostrategic Concerns for the U.S. and Turkey," *Middle East Policy* 22 (Spring 2015), pp. 102-111.
2. Abdullah Ocalan, *Prison Writings III: The Road Map to Negotiations*, trans. Havin Guneser (Cologne: International Initiative Edition, 2012). For further thoughts on these ideas, see Joost Jongerden and Ahmet Hamdi Akkaya, "Democratic Confederalism as a Kurdish Spring: The PKK and the Quest for Radical Democracy," in Ahmed and Gunter, eds., *The Kurdish Spring*, pp. 163-85.
3. See, for example, the prescient writings of Jonathan Spyer, "Do 'Syria,' 'Iraq,' and 'Lebanon' Still Exist?" *The Tower*, February 19, 2014. Http://www.meforum.org/3715. . . , accessed October 7, 2014; Jonathan Spyer, "The Defense of Kobani," *The Jerusalem Post*, September 27, 2014. Http://www.meforum.org/4832. . . , accessed October 7, 2014; and Ofra Bengio, "Kurdistan Reaches toward the Sea," *Haaretz* (Jerusalem), August 3, 2012. Http://www.mesop.de/2012/08/03/kurdistan. . . , accessed August 8, 2012.
4. "The Rule of the Gunman: Why Post-Colonial Arab States Are Breaking Down," *The Economist*, October 11, 2014, p. 57.
5. Jihadism in the sense used here has come to mean a commitment to violent struggle against the perceived opponents of Islam. Frequently it involves transnational actions that tend to break down existing state borders, among other results.

6. Salafism is a movement critical of what it considers to be misguided additions to Islam, such as grave visitation, saint venerations, and monument preservations, among others. The doctrine calls for abolishing these unwanted accretions and returning to the actions of the original followers of the Prophet Muhammad, the *salaf* or predecessors. Sometimes, but not always hand in hand with Jihadism, Salafism too involves transnational actions that tend to break down existing state borders.

7. For background, see Vali Nasr, *The Shia Revival: How Conflicts within Islam Will Shape the Future* (New York and London: W. W. Norton & Company, 2006).

8. See, for example, David L. Phillips, "Research Paper: ISIS-Turkey List." Http://www.huffingtonpost.com/david-l-phillips/research-paper-isis-turke_b_6128950. html, November 9, 2014, which cites numerous sources. Accessed December 15, 2014. In addition, see Amberin Zaman, "Syrian Kurdish Leader: Ankara Supporting Jihadists," *Al-Monitor*, September 3, 2013. Http://www.al-monitor.com . . . , accessed October 7, 2014; Amberin Zaman, "Syrian Kurds Continue to Blame Turkey for Backing ISIS Militants," *Al-Monitor*, June 10, 2014. Http://www.al-monitor/ . . ., accessed October 7, 2014; and Liz Sly, "Biden Issues Second Apology, to United Emirates, over Comments," *Washington Post*, October 5, 2014. Http://www.washingtonpost.com. . . , accessed October 7, 2014, among many others. Amberin Zaman has been the Turkish correspondent for the prestigious British-based *The Economist* for the past 15 years.

9. Douglas A. Ollivant and Brian Fishman, "State of Jihad: The Reality of the Islamic State in Iraq and Syria," *War on the Rocks*, May 21, 2014. Http://warontherocks.com, accessed October 4, 2014.

10. One does not have to subscribe to the analyses of Daniel Pipes, who sees these violent attributes inherent in even mainline Islam, to admit that historically the very English word *assassin* is said to stem from the secretive Islamic organization that employed hashish to drug its adherents into launching suicide attacks against Crusader enemies more than 1000 years ago and that the Quran promises earthly sexual rewards for its fallen warriors. For a recent example of Daniel Pipes's work, see his "Explaining the Denial: Denying Islam's Role in Terror," *Middle East Quarterly* 20 (Spring 2013), pp. 3-12.

11. For further examples, see Alireza Doostdar, "How Not to Understand ISIS," *Jadaliyya Reviews*, October 2, 2014. Http://reviews.jadaliyya.com/pages/index/19485/how-not-to-understand-isis, accessed October 14, 2014.

12. For background, see Josh Rogin, "America's Allies Are Funding ISIS," *The Daily Beast*, June 14, 2014. Http://www.thedailybeast.com, accessed October 4, 2014; Martin Chulov, "How an Arrest in Iraq Revealed ISIS's $2bn Jihadist Network," *The Guardian*, June 15, 2014. Http://www.theguardian, accessed October 4, 2014; and Glen Carey, Mahmoud Habouch, and Gregory Viscusi, "Financing Jihad: Why ISIS Is a Lot Richer than Al-Qaeda," *Bloomberg News*, June 26, 2014. Http://www.bloomberg.com, accessed October 4, 2014.

13. This citation as well as the following analysis are largely based on Liz Sly, "How Saddam Hussein's Former Military Officers and Spies Are Controlling ISIS," *The Independent*, April 5, 2015. Http://www.independent.co.uk/news/world . . . , accessed April 8, 2015.

14. See Micahel Weiss and Hassan Hassan, *ISIS: Inside the Army of Terror* (New York: Regun Arts, 2015). Also see Joel Rayburn, *Iraq after America: Strongmen, Sectarians, Resistance* (Stanford, CA: Hoover Institution Press, 2014) on the links between ISIS and the Baathists.

15. Cited in Sly, "How Saddam Hussein's Former Military Officers and Spies Are Controlling ISIS."

16. Joost Jongerden and Bahar Simsek, "Turkey, the Islamic State, and the Kurdistan Liberation Movement," E-International Relations Publishing, November 24, 2014. Http://www.e-r.info/2014/11/24/turkey-the-islamic-state-and-the-kurdistan-liberation-movement, accessed December 2, 2014.

17. See Andrew Thompson and Jeremi Suri, "How America Helped ISIS," *International New York Times*, October 2, 2014, p. 7.

18. Terence McCoy, "ISIS Just Stole $425 million, Iraqi Governor Says, and Became the World's Richest Terrorist Group," *The Washington Post*, June 12, 2014. Http://www.washingtonpost.com, accessed October 4, 2014. However, others later expressed doubts about the authenticity of this event. See Borzou Daragahi, "Biggest Bank Robbery That Never Happened—$400m ISIS Heist," *Financial Times*, July 17, 2014. Http://www.ft.com, accessed October 4, 2014.

19. Patrick Goodenough, "Kurdish Gov't Alone in Fight against ISIS, Appeals for Airstrikes and Urgent Aid," *CNSNews.com*, August 7, 2014. Http://cnsnews.com, accessed October 4, 2014.

20. Wladimir Van Wilgenburg and Vager Saadullah, "Syrian Kurdish Factions Unite over Islamic State Threat," *Middle East Eye*, October 24, 2014. Http://www.middleasteye.net/news/syrian-kurdish-factions. . ., accessed October 24, 2014.

21. Mustafa Gurbuz, "US-PYD Rapprochement: A Shift in Washington's

Strategy?" *Rudaw*, October 24, 2014. Http://rudaw.net/english/opin-ion/241020141, accessed October 24, 2014; and "War-war, Not Jaw-jaw: Turkey and the Kurds," *The Economist*, October 18, 2014, p. 53.

Chapter 8

1. For background, see Michael M. Gunter, "Reopening Turkey's Closed Kurdish Opening," *Middle East Policy* 20 (Summer 2013), pp. 88-98; and Michael M. Gunter, "The Turkish-Kurdish Peace Process Stalled in Neutral," *Insight Turkey*, 16 (Winter 2014), pp. 19-26. I ear-lier published portions of this chapter as "The Kurdish Issue in Turkey: Back to Square One?" *Turkish Policy Quarterly* 14 (Winter 2016), pp. 77-86.

2. "We Will Not Make You the President, HDP Co-Chair Tells Erdogan," *Hurriyet Daily News*, March 17, 2015. http://www.hurriyetdailynews. com/we-will-not-make-you-the-president-hdp-co-chair-tells-erdogan-79792, accessed November 15, 2017.

3. Selcan Hacaoglu, "Siege at Edge of Fallen Empires Tests Erdogan's Hold on Turkey," May 26, 2016, http://www.bloomberg.com/news/ar-ticles/2016-05-26/turkey-s-kurdish-conflict-turns-once-great-town-into-deserted-battleground, accessed May 30, 2016.

4. Omer Tekdemir, "Politics of the Turkish Conflict: The Kurdish Issue," April 15, 2016, http://www.e-ir.ingo/2016/04/15/politics-of-the-turk-ish-conflict-the-kurdish issue/, accessed May 1, 2016. For background to various strategies both sides have used in the past, see Aysegul Aydin and Cem Emrence, *Zones of Rebellion: Kurdish Insurgents and the Turkish State* (Ithaca and London: Cornell University Press, 2015).

5. International Crisis Group, "A Sisyphean Task? Resuming Turkey-PKK Peace Talks" Crisis Group Europe Briefing No. 77 (Istanbul/ Brussels: International Crisis Group, 17 December 2015), p. 7.

6. M. Hakan Yavuz and Nihat Ali Ozcan, "Turkish Democracy and the Kurdish Question," *Middle East Policy* 22:4 (Winter 2015), p. 76.

7. Ibid., p. 78.

8. For background, see Peter Galbraith, *The End of Iraq: How American Incompetence Created a War without End* (New York: Simon & Schuster, 2006); and US vice president Joseph Biden's still very rel-evant three-state solution in Joseph R. Biden and Leslie H. Gelb, "Unity through Autonomy in Iraq," *New York Times*, May 1, 2006.

9. Among many other excellent studies on the KRG, see the relevant

sections of David Romano, *The Kurdish Nationalist Movement: Opportunity, Mobilization and Identity* (Cambridge: Cambridge University Press, 2006); and Denise Natali, *The Kurds and the State: Evolving National Identity in Iraq, Turkey, and Iran* (Syracuse: Syracuse University Press, 2005).

10. Among many other recent studies of ISIS, see Till F. Paasche and Michael M. Gunter, "Revisiting Western Strategies against ISIS," *Middle East Journal* 70 (Winter 2016), pp. 9-29; and Michael M. Gunter, "Iraq, Syria, ISIS and the Kurds: Geostrategic Concerns for the U.S. and Turkey," *Middle East Policy* 22 (Spring 2015), pp. 102-111.

11. On the Syrian Kurds, see Michael M. Gunter, *Out of Nowhere: The Kurds of Syria in Peace and War* (London: Hurst & Company, 2014); and the review essay on this book by Jonathan Steele, "The Syrian Kurds are Winning!" *New York Review of Books*, December 3, 2015, pp. 24-27.

12. See, for example, David L. Phillips, "Research Paper: ISIS-Turkey List," *Huffington Post*, November 9, 2014, http://www.huffingtonpost.com/david-l-phillips/research-paper-isis-turke_b_6128950.html, accessed December 1, 2014, which cites numerous sources. In addition, see by Amberin Zaman, "Syrian Kurdish Leader: Ankara Supporting Jihadists, *"Al-Monitor*, September 23, 2013, http://www.al-monitor.com/pulse/security/2013/09/pyd-leader-salih-muslim-turkey-support-jihadists-syria.html#, accessed January 2, 2016; and also in "Syrian Kurds Continue to Blame Turkey for Backing ISIS Militants," *Al-Monitor*, June 10, 2014, http://www.al-monitor.com/pulse/originals /2014/zaman-syria-kurds-rojava-ypg-muslim-pyd-turey-isis.html#, accessed January 2, 2016.

13. "ISID ne ise PKK da odur," Al Jazeera Turk, October 4, 2014, as cited in International Crisis Group, *Sisyphean Task?*, p. 4n10.

14. Alexander Sehmer, "Thousands of Arabs Flee from Kurdish Fighters in Syria's North," *Independent*, June 1, 2015. Also see similar claims in Amnesty International, "*We Had* Nowhere to *Go" - Forced Displacement and Demolitions in Northern Syria,"* (London: Amnesty International, 2015).

15. Amberin Zaman, "Amnesty International Accuses Kurdish YPG of War Crimes," *Al-Monitor*, October 13, 2015, http://www.al-monitor.com/pulse/originals/2015/10/syria-turkey-right-groups-accused-kurds-rojava-of-war-crimes.html#ixzz3v3WpsVTZ, accessed December 22, 2015.

16. Mehmet Gurses and David Romano, "Misguided Critiques of a Kurdish-centric Strategy against the Islamic State," Washington Kurdish Institute, April 6, 2016. Info@dckurd.org, accessed April 12, 2016.

17. David Romano and Mehmet Gurses, eds., *Conflict, Democratization, and the Kurds in the Middle East: Turkey, Iran, Iraq, and Syria* (New York: Palgrave Macmillan, 2014), p. 7.

18. Liz Sly and Karen De Young, "Turkey Agrees to Allow U.S. Military to Use Its Base to Attack Islamic State," *Washington Post*, July 23, 2015, https://www.washingtonpost.com/wpr;d/middle_east/turkey . . . , accessed January 3, 2016.

19. Tim Arango, "Turkey Confirms Strikes against Kurdish Militias in Syria," *New York Times*, October 27, 2015, http://www.nytimes.com/2015/10/28/world/europe/turkey-syria-kurdish-militias.html, accessed January 3, 2016.

20. "KCK's Bayik: Turkey Downed the Russian Plane to Protect IS," Kurdish Info (Firat News Agency), November 26, 2015, www.kurdishinfo.com/kcks-bayik-turkey-downed-the-russian-plane-to-protect-isis, accessed January 3, 2015.

21. "EU Reaches $3bn Deal with Turkey to Curb Refugee Crisis," Al Jazeera, November 30, 2015, http://www.aljazeera.com/news/2015/11/eu-seeks-deal-turkey-curb-refugee-crisis-151129152134803.html, accessed January 3, 2015.

22. "Europe's Murky Deal with Turkey," *The Economist*, May 28, 2016, p. 43.

23. International Crisis Group, *Sisyphean Task?* p. 8.

24. Kurdistan National Congress, "The Turkish State Continues Its Attacks in Kurdistan," December 30, 2015.

25. Selcan Hacaoglu, "Siege at Edge of Fallen Empires Tests Erdogan's Hold on Turkey." See endnote 3 for the full citation.

26. Genevieve Casagrande, Christopher Kozak, and Franklin Holcomb, "Russia & Turkey Escalate: Russia's Threat to NATO Goes beyond Eastern Europe/The PKK Participation against Europe," May 23, 2016, http://www.mesop.de/russia-turkey-escalate-russias-threat-to-nato . . . accessed May 27, 2016.

27. Yavuz and Ozcan, "Turkish Democracy and the Kurdish Question," p. 82.

28. Ibid., p. 81.

29. A. Kadir Yildirim, "Why Turkey's Government Is Threatening Academic Freedom," *Washington Post*, January 16, 2016, https://www.washingtonpost.com/news/monkey-cage/wp/2016/01/16/why-

turkeys-growing. . . , accessed January 26, 2016; and Amnesty International, "Turkey Crackdown by the Numbers: Statistics on Brutal Backlash after Failed Coup," July 26 (updated on July 28), 2016, https://www.amnesty.org/en/latest/news/2016/07/turkey-crackdown . . . , accessed July 29, 2016.

30. Michael Cruickshank and Gissur Simonarson, "A Kurdish Convergence in Syria," *New York Times*, February 25, 2016, http://www.nytimes.com/2016/02/26/opinion/a-kurdish-convergence-in-syria.html, accessed February 26, 2016.

31. "Turkish President Accuses US of Supporting Terrorism," *Today's Zaman*, February 23, 2016, http://www.todayszaman.com/diplomacy_turkish-president -accuses-us-of-supporting-terrorism_ 413109 .html, accessed February 26, 2016.

32. Tim Arango and Ceylan Yeginsu, "Turks Can Agree on One Thing: U.S. Was Behind Failed Coup," *New York Times*, August 2, 2016. Fethullah Gulen is an important interfaith Islamic scholar and imam who heads the Gulen or *Hizmet* (Service) Movement, which is an international network of universities, hospitals, charities, business associations, news outlets, and schools spread across more than 150 countries. He has lived in exile in the United States since 1999. Some dismiss him as a dangerous cult leader infiltrating existing state structures such as those of Turkey, while others hail him as an enlightened beacon of interfaith ecumenicism. Formerly an ally, he became a bitter political enemy of Erdogan in 2013. Erdogan accused him of masterminding the failed coup and demanded that the United States extradite him. The United States refused on the grounds that there was no credible evidence indicating he was guilty. Gulen has been ambiguous toward the Turkish-PKK peace process. For background, see M. Hakan Yavuz and Bayram Balci, eds., *Turkey's July 15th Coup: What Happened and Why* (Salt Lake City: The University of Utah Press, 2018).

33. "US Calls on Turkey to Stop Shelling PYD, Citing Syria Cease-fire," *Today's Zaman*, February 24, 2016, http://www.todayszaman.com/ diplomacy_us-calls-on-turkey-to-stop-shelling-pyd-citing-syria-cease-fire_413216.html, accessed February 26, 2016.

34. "Syria: Opinions and Attitudes on Federalism, Decentralization, and the Experience of the Democratic Self-Administration," The Day After, May 19, 2016, http://tda-sy.org/federalism%d9%80decentralization%9%80report/ , accessed June 7, 2016.

35. Abdullah Ocalan, *Prison Writings III: The Road Map to Negotiations*, trans. by Havin Guneser (Cologne: International Initiative Edition,

2012). For further thoughts on these ideas, see Joost Jongerden and Ahmet Hamdi Akkaya, "Democratic Confederalism as a Kurdish Spring: The PKK and the Quest for Radical Democracy," in Mohammed M.A. Ahmed and Michael M. Gunter, eds., *The Kurdish Spring: Geopolitical Changes and the Kurds* (Costa Mesa, CA: Mazda Publishers, 2013), pp. 163-85.

36. George S. Harris, *Troubled Alliance: Turkish-American Problems in Historical Perspective, 1945-1971* (Washington D.C., American Enterprise Institute for Public Policy Research, 1972), pp. 114-15.

37. Cited in "After the Coup, the Counter-coup," *The Economist*, July 23, 2016, p. 14.

38. The previous and following discussion is based largely on Merrit Kennedy, "Amnesty International: After Turkey's Failed Coup, Some Detainees Are Tortured, Raped," National Public Radio (NPR), July 25, 2016, http://www.npr.org/sections/thetwo-way/2016/07/25/487254277/amnesty-nternational-after . . ., accessed July 29, 2016; "Amnesty International Reports 'Credible Evidence' Turkey Torturing Post-coup Detainees," *Haaretz*, July 29, 2016, http://www.haaretz.com/middle-east-news/turkey/1.733018, accessed July 29, 2016; Jason Hanna and Tim Hume, "Turkey Detainees Tortured, Raped after Failed Coup, Rights Group Says," CNN, July 27, 2016, http://www.cnn.com/2016/07/26/europe/turkey-coup-attempt-aftermath/, accessed July 29, 2016; William Reed, "Turkish Police Torture, Rape Own Soldiers, Officers, Judges," The Clarion Project, July 25, 2016, https://www.clarionproject.org/analysis/turkish-police-rape-own-soldiers-officers-judges, accessed July 29, 2016; Elizabeth Redden, "Turkey's Fraying International Ties," Inside Higher Ed, July 29, 2016, https://www.insidehighered.com/news/2016/07/29/how-crackdown . . . , accessed July 29, 2016; and interviews with various sources who asked to be anonymous given the fluid, dangerous situation prevailing in Turkey.

39. Peace in Kurdistan Campaign, "Neither Coup nor State of Emergency Turkey Needs Peace and Democracy," July 25, 2016, https://peaceinkurdistancampaign.com/2016/07/25/neither-coup-nor-state-of emergency. . . , accessed July 29, 2016.

40. For example, General Akin Ozturk had been responsible for the 2011 massacre of some 34 Kurdish civilians at Roboski, while General Adem Huduti had been a leader of the more recent bloody attacks on such Kurdish cities as Cizre and Diyarbakir carried out under the guise

of curfews instituted subsequent to the collapse of the cease-fire in July 2015. Now these two military figures had been swept up by the post-coup reactions as detainees exhibited before the cameras. Djene Rhys Bajalan, "With Blood They Consecrate a New Order: Erdogan's 'Revolution,'" Jadaliyya, July 25, 2016, http://www.jadaliyya.com /pages/index/24820/with-blood . . . , accessed July 28, 2016.

41. Alex MacDonald, "Erdogan Excludes Pro-Kurd Party from First Meeting with Opposition after Coup," Middle East Eye, July 25, 2016, http://www.middleeasteye.net/news/hdp-co-leader-hits-out . . . , accessed July 29, 2016.

42. Cited in Yeghia Tashjian, "Where Does the Attempted Coup Leave Turkey's Kurds?" The New Arab, July 18, 2016, https://www.alaraby. co.uk/english/Comment . . . , accessed July 29, 2016. Also see Michael Rubin, "Could There Be a Coup in Turkey?" AEI [American Enterprise Institute], March 21, 2016, https://www.aei.org/publica-tion/could-there-be-a coup-in-turkey . . ., accessed August 3, 2016. Rubin more accurately saw the possible coup in terms of an Erdogan "out-of-control . . . imprisoning opponents, seizing newspapers left and right, and building palaces at the rate of a mad sultan or aspiring caliph, " not because of the collapse of the Kurdish peace process.

43. This and the following citations were taken from Kurdistan National Congress (KNK), "Turkey's Failed Coup and Erdogan's Anti-Kurdish Agenda," July 19, 2016, http://www.kongrakurdistan.org, accessed July 29, 2016.

44. Georges Roux, *Ancient Iraq* (London: Allen & Unwin, 1964).

45. Adeed Dawisha, *Iraq: A Political History from Independence to Occupation* (Princeton: Princeton University Press, 2009), p. 5.

46. "Fallujah, Again," *The Economist*, May 28, 2016, p. 41.

47. Roy Gutman, "Iraqi Kurdish Leader Calls for Redrawing Regional Borders – And Attacks Fellow Kurds," *The Nation*, May 18, 2016.

48. Charles Glass, "Disunited Front: The Chaotic, Underfunded Battle against the Islamic State," *Harper's*, February 2016.

49. The following discussion owes much to Michael Rubin, *Kurdistan Arising? Considerations for Kurds, their Neighbors, and the Region* (Washington, D.C., American Enterprise Institute, 2016).

50. World Bank Group, *Kurdistan Region of Iraq: Reforming the Econ-omy for Shared Prosperity and Protecting the Vulnerable* (Washing-ton, D.C.: World Bank Group, 2016).

51. The most recent issue of the scholarly journal *Kurdish Studies* 6 (May

2018) was entirely devoted to women's issues. See in particular Nazand Begikhani, Wendelmoet Hamelink, and Nerina Weiss, "Theorising Women and War in Kurdistan: A Feminist and Critical Perspective" pp. 5-30, which connects "our topic to feminist theory, to anthropological theory on war and conflict and their long-term consequences, and . . . also their resistance and agency as female combatants and women activists," p. 5.

52. The discussion in this paragraph, is largely based on Ofra Bengio, "Game Changers: Kurdish Women in Peace and War," *Middle East Journal* 70 (Winter 2016), pp. 30-46.

53. Abdullah Ocalan, *Liberating Life: Woman's Revolution* (Cologne, Germany: International Initiative Edition in cooperation with Mesopotamian Publishers, Neuss, 2013).

Chapter 9

1. "92.7% 'Yes' for Independence: Preliminary Official Results," *Rudaw*, September 27, 2017, http://www.rudaw.net/english/kurdistan/270920174, accessed October 1, 2017.

2. Fazel Hawramy, "Iran Willing To Normalize Ties with KRG, but Not without Change," *Iran-Business News*, December 23, 2017, www.iran-bn.com/2017/12/23/iran-willing-to-normalize-ties-with-krg/, accessed December 26, 2017; and Baxtiyar Goran, "Najmaldin Karim: Warns of Resurgence of Islamic State, Says US Supports Strong Kurdistan," Kurdistan 24, April 6, 2018, www.kurdistan24.net/en/news/eb87beb8-e379-4233-beee-b22bebf88a0d, accessed April 10, 2018.

3. Omar Sattar, "Iraqi Budget Drives Another Wedge between Baghdad, Kurds," *Al-Monitor*, March 9, 2018, https://www.al-monitor.com/pulse/originals/2018/03/iraq-budget-kurdistan.html, accessed March 12, 2018.

4. See, for example, "Barzani No US 'Support' for Kurdish Referendum if Postponed," *Rudaw*, November 11, 2017, http://www.rudaw.net/english/kurdistan/11112017, accessed November 15, 2017.

5. For background on Kirkuk—which is both a city of some 1 million shared by Kurds (45 percent), Arabs (38 percent), Turkmens (15 percent), and Christians (2 percent) and also the surrounding governorate (province)—see Liam Anderson and Gareth Stansfield, *Crisis in Kirkuk: The Ethnopolitics of Conflict and Compromise* (Philadelphia: University of Pennsylvania Press, 2009). The recent "rough" popula-

tion percentages were taken from David Zucchino, "Iraqi Forces Retake All Oil Fields in Disputed Areas as Kurds Retreat," *New York
Times*, October 17, 2017, https://www.nytimes.com/2017/10/17/
world/middleeast/iraq-kurds-kirkuk.html, accessed November 2,
2017. While the Kurds complain about Saddam Hussein's Arabization, the Arabs accuse the Kurds of Kurdification. Najmaldin Karim,
who had been the Kurdish governor of Kirkuk since March 2011, was
forced to flee when Baghdad retook the city in October 2017. Despite
Barzani's claim of wide 92 percent support for his referendum, he did
not release a complete report of turnout by district. Thus, in areas disputed between the KRG and Baghdad, the turnout was actually very
small as many minorities opposed KRG independence. Michael
Rubin, "Is the Kurdish Spring Here?" December 20, 2017, http://
www.mesop.de/is-the-kurdish-spring-here-by-michael-rubin-ameri-
can-enterprise/, accessed December 23, 2017.

6. For further penetrating thoughts on the KRG's miscalculations, see
Denise Natali, "Iraqi Kurdistan Was Never Ready for Statehood,"
Foreignpolicy.com, October 31, 2017, http://foreignpolicy.com/
2017/10/31/iraqi-kurdistan-was-never-ready-for-statehood, accessed
November 15, 2017; Aymenn Jawad al-Tamimi, "Iraq Kurdistan's Crisis: A Failure of Strategy," *The American Spectator*, October 22, 2017,
http://www.meforum.org/6976/iraqi-kurdistan-crisis-a-failure-of-
strategy, accessed November 15, 2017; and Michael Eppel, "A Future
for Kurdish Independence?" *Middle East Quarterly*, Spring 2018,
http://www.meforum.org/7226/kurdish-independence, accessed
March 3, 2018. For background, see Ofra Bengio, *The Kurds of Iraq:
Building a State within a State* (Boulder and London: Lynne Rienner
Publishers, 2012), among numerous other sources.

7. For background to this situation, see Michael M. Gunter and M.
Hakan Yavuz, "The Continuing Crisis in Iraqi Kurdistan," *Middle
East Policy* 12 (Spring 2005), pp. 122-133.

8. See www.Kurdishmedia.com, May 2, 2006.

9. Cited in "Erbil Turkish Consulate," http://erbil.co/listing/erbil-turk-
ish-consulate, accessed October 5, 2017.

10. This citation and the following data were gleaned from Soner Cagap-
tay et al., "Turkey and the KRG: An Undeclared Economic Commonwealth," The Washington Institute for Near East Policy, Policy Watch
2387, March 16, 2015, http://www.washingtoninstitute.org/policy-
analysis/view/turkey-and-the-krg-an-undeclared-economic-
commonwealth, accessed October 5, 2017.

11. Ibid.
12. For background, see Mesut Yegen, "The Kurdish Question in Turkey: Denial to Recognition," In Marlies Casier and Joost Jongerden, eds., *Nationalisms and Politics in Turkey: Political Islam, Kemalism and the Kurdish Issue* (London and New York: Routledge, 2011), pp. 67-84.
13. Mehmet Umit Necef, "Barzani and Erdogan Meet in Diyarbakir: A Historical Day," Center for Mellemoststudier, December 2013, https://static.sdu.dk/mediafiles. . . , accessed October 4, 2017.
14. Cited in Asli Aydintasbas, "Why the Kurdish Referendum Is None of Turkey's Business," *Washington Post*, October 2, 2017, https://www. washingtonpost.com/news/global-opinions/wp/2017/10/02/why-the-kurdish-referendum-is-none-of-turkey's-business/?utm term=.497dd6d9e372, accessed October 2, 2017.
15. Galip Dalai, "After the Kurdish Independence Referendum: How to Prevent a Crisis in Iraq," *Foreign Affairs*, October 2, 2017, https://www.foreignaffairs.com/articles/middle-east/2017-10-02/after-kurdish-independence-referendum?cid=int-now&pgtype=qss, accessed October 2, 2017.
16. Monica Marks, "ISIS and Nusra in Turkey: Jihadist Recruitment and Ankara's Response," Institute for Strategic Dialogue, 2016. See also the comments of Marc Pierini, the former EU ambassador to Turkey, and John Kerry, the former US secretary of state, in John Vandiver, "Europe's Fear: Turkey's Porous Border Serves as Gateway for ISIS's Spread," *Stars and Stripes,* July 5, 2014; and the comments of Joe Biden, the former US vice president, in Deborah Amos, "A Smuggler Explains How He Helped Fighters Along 'Jihadi Highway,'" NPR, October 7, 2014, http://www.npr.org/sections/parallels/2014/10/07/354288389/a-smuggler-explains-how-he-helped-fighters-along-jihadi-highway, accessed January 8, 2017. See also Tim Arango and Eric Schmitt "A Path to ISIS, Through a Porous Turkish Border," *New York Times*, March 9, 2013, http://www.nytimes.com/2015/03/10/world/europe/despite-crackdown-path . . ., accessed January 9, 2017; Emrullah Uslu, "Jihadist Highway to Jihadist Haven: Turkey's Jihadi Policies and Western Security," *Studies in Conflict and Terrorism* 39:9 (2016); and Hardin Lang and Mutah Al Wari, "The Flow of Foreign Fighters to the Islamic State," Center for American Progress, March 2016.
17. See, for example, Hande Firat, "We Will Not Allow a Kurdish State on Our Borders: Erdogan," *Hurriyet Daily News*, August 24, 2017,

http://www.hurriyetdailynews.com/we-will-not-allow-a-kurdish-state-on-our-borders erdogan.aspx?pageID=517&nID=117059& NewsCatID=352, accessed August 30, 2017, where Erdogan was quoted declaring that the term "Kurdish state" is an "insult to my Kurdish brothers. . . . We will send those who want to break this nation [Turkey] apart to the grave."

18. Cited in Necef, "Barzani and Erdogan Meet in Diyarbakir," p. 3.

19. U.S Department of State, "Iraqi Kurdistan Regional Government's Planned Referendum," September 20, 2017 https://www.state.gov/r/pa/prs/ps/2017/09/274324.htm, accessed October 8, 2017.

20. Cited in Mustafa Gurbuz, "Does Turkey Really Want to Punish Iraqi Kurdistan?" October 3, 2017. Arabcenterdc.org/policy-analyses/does-turkey-really-want-to-punish-iraqi-kurdistan/, accessed October 4, 2017.

21. Cited in Aydintasbas, "Why the Kurdish Referendum is None of Turkey's Business."

22. Cited in "Iraqi Kurds Vote in Independence Referendum," Al-Jazeera, September 25, 2017, http://www.aljazeera.com/news/2017/09/iraqi-kurds-vote-independence-referendum-170925032733525.html, accessed September 27, 2017.

23. Cited in Ibid.

24. Cited in Ali Cinar, "The Kurdish Referendum Will Destabilize the Region More." September 24, 2017, http://augustafreepress.com/kurdish-referendum-will-destablize-region/, accessed September 27, 2017.

25. Dalai, "After the Kurdish Independence Referendum." The two KRG airports were finally reopened for regular international travel in March 2018.

26. Interview with Bayan Sami Abdul Rahman, KRG representative to the United States, September 27, 2017. However, once the referendum was held, the United States made it clear that it would take no sanctions against the KRG. David Ignatius, "The U.S. Owes It to the Kurds to Help De-escalate Tensions after the Independence Referendum," *Washington Post*, September 28, 2017, https://www.washingtonpost.com/blogs/post-partisan/wp. . . , accessed October 8, 2017.

27. Cited in Amberin Zaman, "Salih Muslim: Syria's Kurdish Problems Will Be Solved by Syrians, Not Turkey," *Al-Monitor*, February 26, 2018, https://www.al-monitor.com/pulse/originals/2018/02/salih-muslim-syria-kurds-turkey-arrest.html#xzz58MJtXsVD, accessed March 1, 2018.

28. Atlantic Council, "Report of the Task Force on the Future of Iraq: Achieving Long-Term Stability to Ensure the Defeat of ISIL," Washington, D.C., November 2016.

29. Cited in Andrew Bernard, "Tillerson: The United States Does Not Recognize the Kurdish Referendum," *The American Interest*, https://www.the-american-interest.com/.../tillerson-the-united-states-does-not-recognize, September 30, 2017, accessed January 8, 2018. Also see Rhys Dubin and Emily Tamkin, "Iraqi Kurds Vote for Independence over U.S. Objections," *Foreign Policy*, September 25, 2017, http://foreignpolicy.com/2017/09/25/iraqi-kurds-vote-for-independence-over-u-s-objections, accessed January 8, 2018; and Katrina Manson, "US Warns Kurdistan over Independence Referendum," *Financial Times*, September 20, 2017, https://www.ft.com/content/69b5b776-9e58-11e7-8cd4-932067fbf946, accessed January 8, 2018.

30. On the Israeli-KRG relationship, see Ofra Bengio, "Surprising Ties between Israel and the Kurds," *Middle East Quarterly* 21 (Summer 2014); and Michael B. Bishku, "Israel and the Kurds: A Pragmatic Relationship in Middle Eastern Politics," *Journal of South Asian and Middle Eastern Studies* 41 (Winter 2018), pp. 52-72.

31. Loveday Morris, "How the Kurdish Independence Referendum Backfired Spectacularly," *Washington Post*, October 20, 2017, https://www.washingtonpost.com/world/how . . ., accessed January 8, 2018; and Seth J. Frantzman, "Why the US Chose to Oppose the Kurdish Independence Referendum," *Jerusalem Post*, September 19, 2017, http://www.jpost.com/International/Why-the-US-chose-to-oppose-the-Kurdish-independence-referendum-505498, accessed January 8, 2018.

32. On Iran, see Nader Entessar, "Uneasy Neighbors: Iran and the Kurdish Regional Government," *Journal of South Asian and Middle Eastern Studies* 41 (Winter 2018), pp. 73-84.

33. Martin Chulov, Julian Borger, and Saeed Kamali Dehghan, "US Military Rushes to Defuse Looming Crisis in Kirkuk after Iraqi Army Advances," *The Guardian*, October 16, 2017, https://www.theguardian.com/world/2017/oct/16/iraq-kurdish-forces-army-us-military, accessed January 9, 2018.

34. Cited in "McMaster: Iraq Must Not Align with Iran, Kurds Must Enjoy Security," *Rudaw*, October 25, 2017, http://www.rudaw.net/english/kurdistan/241020175, accessed January 10, 2018.

35. Cited in Ibid.

36. Cited in Laurie Mylroie, "White House National Security Adviser:

US Is 'Very Committed' to Kurds' Success in Iraq," Kurdistan 24, December 14, 2017, http://www.kurdistan24.net/en/news/e46c9260-0543-4527-9c64-eOa86ad58ba11, accessed January 10, 2018.

37. Cited in Kurdistan Regional Government Representation in the United States, Readout of Telephone Call between KRG Prime Minister Nechirvan Barzani and US Secretary of State Rex Tillerson," January 17, 2018.

38. Vera Eccarius-Kelly, "The Kurdistan Referendum: An Evaluation of the Kurdistan Lobby," *Journal of South Asian and Middle Eastern Studies* 41 (Winter 2018), pp. 20-21.

39. Hawre Hasan Hama, "Partisan Armed Forces of Kurdistan Regional Government," *Journal of South Asian and Middle Eastern Studies* 41 (Winter 2018), p. 47.

40. Cited in Krishnadev Calamur, "Why Doesn't the U.S. Support Kurdish Independence?" *The Atlantic*, October 20, 2017, https://www.the-atlantic.com/international/archive/2017/10/us-kurdish-independence/543540/, accessed January 9, 2018. For historical background, see Michael M. Gunter, "The Bane of Kurdish Disunity." *Orient* 42 (December 2001), pp. 605-616.

41. The following discussion is based on interviews with KRG citizens and Zvi Bar'el, "Kurdistan's at a Breaking Point, but Will It Be a 'Kurdish Spring' or a Civil War?' *Haaretz Israel*, December 25, 2017, http://www.mesop.de/mesop-news-today's-genreral-opinion-analy-sis-kurdistans-at-a-breaking-point-but-will-it-be-a-kurdish-spring-or-a-civil-war/, accessed January 3, 2018.

42. Ibid., and Rubin, "Is the Kurdish Spring Here?"

43. Cited in Fazel Hawramy, "Is the Sun Setting on KDP-PUK Dominance in Iraqi Kurdistan? *Al-Monitor*, February 13, 2018, www.kurdpress.com/en/details.aspx?id=490, accessed February 15, 2018.

44. Cited in Dana Taib Menmy, "KRG Parliament Speaker Calls for Rethinking Strategy in Baghdad Talks," *Al-Monitor*, December 14, 2017, www.kurdpress.com/en/details.aspx?id=83, accessed December 20, 2017.

45. Cited in Margaret Coker, "Kurdish Leader Quits, Latest Fallout from Much-Criticized Independence Vote," *New York Times*, October 29, 2017, https://www.nytimes.com/2017/10/29/world/middleeast/iraq-kurds-massoud-barzani.html, accessed November 3, 2017.

46. Cited in Ibid.

47. Cited in "Iraq Names New President and Prime Minister, Ending

Deadlock," *New York Times*, October 2, 2018, https://www.nytimes.com/reuters/2018/10/02/world/middleeast/iraq-president-prime-minster.html, accessed October 3, 2018. The author of this book has known Barham Salih, 58, since 1993 as an intelligent, honest, energetic and moderate Kurdish patriot who holds a PhD in statistics and computer applications in engineering from the University of Liverpool in the UK. Previously he had served as the deputy prime minister of Iraq and then as the prime minister of the KRG. Given the innumerable problems Iraq and the KRG are currently experiencing, Salih is in a unique position to play a positive role.

48. Cited in Menmy, "KRG Parliament Speaker Call for Rethinking Strategy in Baghdad Talks."

49. The following information was taken from Dan Raviv and Yossi Melman, *Every Spy a Prince: The Complete History of Israel's Intelligence Community* (Boston: Houghton Mifflin Company, 1990), pp. 21 and 82; Ian Black and Benny Morris, *Israel's Secret Wars: A History of Israel's Intelligence Services* (New York: Grove Weidenfeld, 1991), pp. 184-85 and 327-30; and Andrew Cockburn and Leslie Cockburn, *Dangerous Liaison: The Inside Story of the US-Israeli Covert Relationship* (New York: Harper Collins, 1991), pp. 104-105.

50. Jack Anderson, "Israelis Infiltrate Arab Regimes," *Washington Post*, September 17, 1972, p. B7.

51. Cited in Martin Chulov, Julian Borger, and Saeed Kamali Dehghan, "US Military Rushes to Defuse Looming Crisis in Kirkuk after Iraqi Army Advances," *The Guardian*, October 16, 2017, https://www.theguardian.com/world/2017/oct/16/iraq-kurdish-forces-army-us-military, accessed October 20, 2017.

52. Cited in Adam Mirani, "Why Does Israel Support an Independent Iraqi Kurdistan?" Telesur, September 16, 2017, https://www.telesurtv.net/english/news/Why-Does-Israel-Support-an-Independent-Iraqi-Kurdistan—20170923-0023.html, accessed March 29, 2018.

53. Bilal Wahab, "Why Israel Is Cheering On Iraqi Kurds' Push for Independence," *World Politics Review*, October 4, 2017, http://www.washingtoninstitute.org/policy-analysis/view/why-Israel-is-cheering-on-iraqi-kurds-push-for-independence, accessed March 29, 2018.

54. M. Hakan Yavuz and Nihat Ali Ozcan, "Turkish Democracy and the Kurdish Question," *Middle East Policy*, 22 (Winter 2015), p. 76.

55. Ibid., p. 78.

56. The Economist Intelligence Unit (EIU), "Benchmarking the Kurdistan Region," May 2014, http://en.calameo.com/read/0003488705c1e4c15ff08, accessed March 10, 2018.

57. For further thoughts on this, see the opinion piece by Masoud Barzani, "The Time Has Come for Iraqi Kurdistan to Make Its Choice on Independence," *Washington Post*, June 28, 2017, https://www.washingtonpost.com/news/democracy-post/wp/2017/06/28/the-time-has-come-for-iraqi-kurdistan-to-make-its-choice-on-independence/?u, accessed July 7, 2017.

58. Cited in Chulov, Borger, and Kamali, "US Military Rushes to Defuse Looming Crisis in Kirkuk after Iraqi Army Advances."

59. Jack Detsch, "Pentagon Stops Budgeting for Peshmerga Salaries," *Al-Monitor*, February 20, 2018, https://www.al-monitor.com/pulse/originals/2018/02/pentagon-stop-budgeting-peshmerga-salaries-iraq.html, accessed February 25, 2018.

60. "Two Firms Win Bids on New $600 Million US Consulate Project in Erbil," *Rudaw*, July 8, 2017, http://www.rudaw.net/english/kurdistan/080720171, accessed February 2, 2018.

61. This and the following citations were taken from "McMaster: Iraq Must Not Align with Iran, Kurds Must Enjoy Security," *Rudaw*, October 25, 2017, http://www.rudaw.net/english/kurdistan/241020175, accessed October 28, 2018.

62. The following figures were mainly taken from *Rudaw*—a respected KDP-affiliated media group in the Iraqi Kurdish region—in its Kurdish issue of October 3, 2018. They also were verified by an official at the KRG representative's office in Washington, D.C. Although these figures were preliminary, they were not expected to change significantly.

63. Karwan Faidhi, "KRG Election: Why Such a Low Turnout?" *Rudaw*, October 3, 2018, http://www.rudaw.net/mobile/english/analysis/0310218, accessed October 3, 2018. The three elections Iraqi Kurds voted in during the past year were the advisory independence referendum on September 25, 2017, the Iraqi national elections held on May 12, 2018, and the KRG parliamentary elections held on September 30, 2018.

64. For a lengthy KRG report of 144 pages, including many photos on IDPs and refugees throughout Iraqi Kurdistan, see Kurdistan Region Government (KRG), Duhok Governorate, Board of Relief and Humanitarian Affairs, B.R.H. A. – Executive Directorate, *IDPs and Refugees in Duhok Governorate: Profile and General Information*, February 2016. The Khanky Camp I visited is profiled on pp. 109-110. "The KRG Joint Crisis Coordination Center estimates that the

annual cost of hosting the 1.4 million displaced Iraqis and Syrians currently in Kurdistan is $1.9 billion." Kurdistan Regional Government Representation in the United States, email to author, January 12, 2018.

65. Aymen Jawad al-Tamimi, "Dispatch: The Syrian Democratic Forces' Border Guards," Middle East Forum, January 20, 2018, http://www.meforum.org/blog/2018/01/the-syrian-democratic-forces-border-guards, accessed January 22, 2018.

66. Emre Peker and Julian E. Barnes, "NATO to Try 'Kitchen Table' to Soothe U.S.-Turkey Dispute," Wall Street Journal, February 11, 2018, http://www.wsj.com/articles/nato-to-try-kitchen-table-to-soothe-u-s-turkey-dispute-1518354000, accessed February 13, 2018.

67. Cited in "An Unhappy Marriage," The Economist, February 3, 2018, p. 43.

68. Cited in "Turkish Operations in Syria to Reach up to Manbij and Iraqi border: Erdogan," Hurriyet Daily News, January 26, 2016, http://www.hurriyetdailynews.com/turkish-operations-in-syria-to-reach-up-to-manbij-and-iraqi-border-erdogan-126331, accessed January 28, 2018.

69. Cited in "MESOP NEWS: - End Support for Kurds Militia YPG or You're a Target / Nearer to 3rd World War?" February 1, 2018, http://www.mesop.de/mesop-news-end-support-for-kurds-militia-ypg-or-youre-a-target-nearer-to-3rd-world-war/, accessed February 3, 2018.

70. Cited in "Turkish Operations in Syria to Reach up to Manbij and Iraqi Border."

71. Cited in "Muzzling the Fourth Estate," The Economist, March 3, 2018, p. 45. Some 16 Turkish newspapers featured this warning on their front pages the next day! Ibid. "While unlikely, it is no longer inconceivable that Turkey and the United States would one day be shooting at each other." Michael Rubin, "The US and Turkey Could Go To War," Washington Examiner, April 17, 2018, https://www.washingtonexaminer.com/opinion/the-us-and-turkey-could-go-to-war, accessed April 15, 2018.

72. This and the following citations were taken from Roy Gutman, "Have the Syrian Kurds Committed War Crimes? The Nation, February 7, 2017, https://www.thenation.com/articles/have-the-syrian-kurds-committed-war-crimes/, accessed June 2, 2017. Amnesty International has made similar claims. See "Syria: 'We Had Nowhere to Go' – Forced Displacement and Demolitions in Northern Syria," Amnesty International, October 12, 2015, https://www.amnesty.org/en/documents/mde24/2503/2015/en/, accessed November 4, 2015.

73. This and the following citation were taken from Aymenn Jawad Al-Temimi, "A Response to Roy Gutman's 'Have the Syrian Kurds Committed War Crimes?'" *Syria Comment*, February 11, 2017, http://www.joshualandis.com/blog/response-roy-gutmans-syrian-kurds-committed-war-crimes/, accessed June 2, 2017.

74. Amberin Zaman, "Amnesty International Accuses Kurdish YPG of War Crimes," *Al-Monitor*, October 13, 2015, www.mesop.de/amnesty-international-accuses-kurdish-ypg-of-war-crimes-by-author-amberin-zaman-al-monitor/, accessed November 1, 2015.

75. The following discussion and citations were taken from Samih Idiz, "Despite Progress on Paper, Turkey, US Still Leagues Apart," *Al Monitor*, February 20, 2018, http://www.mesop.de/despite-progress-on-paper-turkey-us-still-leagues-apart/, accessed February 22, 2018.

76. "Where Next? Turkey Takes Afrin," *The Economist*, March 24, 2019, p. 42. Jonathan Spyer, an astute Israeli journalist, gave slightly different figures from the Syrian Observatory: 78 Turkish soldiers and 437 pro-Turkish Syrian Sunni rebels had been killed. He agreed that 1,500 Kurdish fighters had died. Jonathan Spyer, "The Sultan's Pleasure: Turkey Expands Its Operations in Syria and Iraq," *The Jerusalem Post*, March 31, 2018, https://www.meforum.org/articles/.../the-sultan's-pleasure-turkey-expands-its-operation, accessed April 2, 2018.

77. Cited in Democratic Self-Administration in Rojava, North Syria, "The Turkish Occupation Policy of Turkification and Demographic Change in Afrin," April 23, 2018, www.kuridshinstitute.be/wp-content/uploads/2018/05/Turkification-of-Afrin-pdf, accessed May 2, 2018.

78. Cited in "Where Next? Turkey Takes Afrin."

79. Cited in Spyer, "The Sultan's Pleasure."

80. Fehim Tastekin, "Erdogan Keeps Finger on Trigger as PKK Exits Sinjar," *Al-Monitor*, March 26, 2018, https://www.al-monitor.com/pulse/originals/2018/03/turkey-iraq-sinjar-pkk-withdraw-from-yazidi-region.html, accessed April 2, 2018.

81. Ivan Nechepurenko, Neil MacFarquhar, and Thomas Gibbons-Neff, "Dozens of Russians Are Believed Killed in U.S.-Backed Syria Attack," *New York Times*, February 13, 2018, http://www.nytimes.com/2018/02/13/world/europe/russia-syria-dead.html, accessed February 13, 2018.

82. Jonathan Spyer, the well-informed Israeli journalist/scholar, claims that "the real number is probably twice that" or 4,000. Jonathan Spyer, "The Future of Eastern Syria and the Israeli Interest," *The Jerusalem*

Post, August 15, 2018, https://www.jpost.com/Opinion/The-future-of-eastern-Syria-and-the-Israeli-interest, accessed August 20, 2018.

83. Eric Schmitt, Helene Cooper, and Alissa J. Rubin, "Trump Orders State Dept. to Suspend Funds for Syria Recovery," *New York Times*, March 30, 2018, https://www.nytimes.com/2018/03/30/world/middleeast/syria-us-coaltion-deaths.html, accessed April 2, 2018.

84. "YPG Confirms Withdrawal from Syria's Manbij after Turkey-US Deal," Aljazeera, June 5, 2018, https:///aljazeera.com/news/2018/06/ypg-confirms-wthdrawal-syria-manbij-turkey-deal-180605142952090.html, accessed June 7, 2018; and "Turkish Army Conducts 10th Round of Patrols in Manbij," *Hurriyet Daily News*, July 6, 2018, http://www.hurriyetdailynews.com/turkish-army-conducts-10th-round-of-patrols-in-manbij-134252, accessed July 7, 2018.

85. Sirwan Kaijo, "Kurds Tie Northern Syria Stability to Continued US Military Presence," *The Defense Post*," August 31, 2018, https://thedefensepost.com/2018/08/31/kurds-northern-stability-us-military-presence/, accessed September 2, 2018.

Selected Bibliography

Please consult my extensive endnotes at the end of each chapter for the various, mostly online news and other sources that I have used in this book but not listed in this bibliography. For a much more detailed bibliography on the Kurds, see the third edition of my *Historical Dictionary of the Kurds* (Lanham, MD: Rowman & Littlefield, 2018). For an even larger bibliography on the Kurds (but before 1997), see Lokman I. Meho, com., *The Kurds and Kurdistan: A Selective and Annotated Bibliography* (Westport, CT: Greenwood Press, 1997); and Lokman I. Meho and Kelly L. Maglaughlin, coms., *Kurdish Culture and Society: An Annotated Bibliography* (Westport, CT: Greenwood Press, 2001).

Abu Jaber, Kamel S. *The Arab Ba'th Socialist Party: History, Ideology, and Organization.* Syracuse: Syracuse University Press, 1966.

Acikyildiz, Birgul. *The Yezidis: The History of a Community, Culture and Religion.* London: I.B. Tauris, 2010.

Ahmed, Mohammed M. A. *America Unravels Iraq: Kurds, Shiites and Sunni Arabs Compete for Supremacy.* Costa Mesa, CA: Mazda Press, 2010.

_____. *Iraqi Kurds and Nation-Building.* New York: Palgrave Macmillan, 2012.

Ahmed, Mohammed M. A., and Michael M. Gunter, eds. *The Kurdish Question and International Law.* Oakton, VA: Ahmed Foundation for Kurdish Studies, 2000.

_____. *Kurdish Exodus: From Internal Displacement to Diaspora.* Sharon MA: Ahmed Foundation for Kurdish Studies, 2002.

_____. *The Kurdish Question and the 2003 Iraqi War.* Costa Mesa, CA: Mazda Press, 2005.

_____. *The Evolution of Kurdish Nationalism.* Costa Mesa, CA: Mazda Press, 2007.

_____. *The Kurdish Spring: Geopolitical Changes and the Kurds.* Costa Mesa, CA: Mazda Press, 2013.

Alkadiri, Raad. "Oil and the Question of Federalism in Iraq." *International Affairs* 86:6 (2010), pp. 1315-28.

Allsopp, Harriet. *The Kurds of Syria: Political Parties and Identity in the Middle East.* London: I.B. Tauris, 2014.

Amnesty International. *Document - Syria: Kurds in the Syrian Arab Republic One Year after the March 2004 Events.* 2005. Http://www.amnesty.org/en/library/asset. . . , accessed September 26, 2013.

_____. *Iran: Human Rights Abuses against the Kurdish Minority.* New York: Amnesty International, 2008.

Anderson, Benedict. *Imagined Communities: Reflections on the Origin and Spread of Nationalism.* London: Verso, 1991.

Anderson, Liam, and Gareth Stansfield. *Crisis in Kirkuk: The Ethnopolitics of Conflict and Compromise.* Philadelphia: University of Pennsylvania Press, 2009.

Atlantic Council. "Report of the Task Force on the Future of Iraq: Achieving Long-Term Stability to Ensure the Defeat of ISIL," Washington, D.C., November 2016.

Aydin, Aysegul, and Cem Emrence. *Zones of Rebellion: Kurdish Insurgents and the Turkish State.* Ithaca and London: Cornell University Press, 2015.

Aziz, Mahir. *The Kurds of Iraq: Nationalism and Identity in Iraqi Kurdistan,* rev. ed. London and New York: I.B. Tauris, 2015.

Baker III, James A., and Lee H. Hamilton (Co-Chairs). *The Iraq Study Group Report: The Way Forward—A New Approach.* New York: Vintage Books, 2006.

Barkey, Henri J., and Graham E. Fuller. *Turkey's Kurdish Question.* New York: Rowman & Littlefield, 1998.

Bengio, Ofra. *The Kurds of Iraq: Building a State within a State.* Boulder and London: Lynne Rienner Publishers, 2012.

_____, ed. *Kurdish Awakening: Nation Building in a Fragmented Homeland.* Austin: University of Texas Press, 2014.

_____. "Game Changers: Kurdish Women in Peace and War," *Middle East Journal* 70 (Winter 2016), pp. 30-46.

Bilgin, Fevzi, and Ali Sarihan, eds. *Understanding Turkey's Kurdish Question.* Plymouth, UK: Lexington Books, 2013.

Bishku, Michael B. "The Geopolitics of the Kurds since the First World War: Between Iraq and Other Hard Places." In *Routledge Handbook on the Kurds,* ed. Michael M. Gunter. London and New York: Routledge, 2019.

Bitar, Karim Emile. "Syria: Proxy Theater of War." trans. by Charles Goulden. *Other Voices* 16:6 (August 2013), pp. OV-3-Ov-5.

Bookchin, Murray. "Libertarian Municipalism: An Overview." *Green Perspectives*, No. 24 (1991).

_____. "The Meaning of Confederalism." *Green Perspectives*, No. 20 (1990).

Bozarslan, Hamit. "Kurdish Nationalism in Turkey: From Tacit Contract to Rebellion (1919-1925)." in Vali Abbas, ed. *Essays on the Origins of Kurdish Nationalism*. Costa Mesa, CA: Mazda Publishers, 2003, pp. 14-39.

_____. "Political Crisis and the Kurdish Issue in Turkey." in Robert Olson, ed. *The Kurdish Nationalist Movement in the 1990s: Its Impact on Turkey and the Middle East*. Lexington: University Press of Kentucky, 1996, pp. 135-153.

Brandon, James. "The PKK and Syria's Kurds." *Terrorism Monitor* 5:3 (February 21, 2007), pp. 4-6. Http://www.jamestown.org. . . , accessed July 25, 2013.

Bruinessen Martin van. "From Adela Khanum to Leyla Zana: Women as Political Leaders in Kurdish History." in Shahrzad Mojab, ed. *Women of a Non-State Nation: The Kurds*. Costa Mesa, CA: Mazda Publishers, 2001, pp. 95-112.

_____. "Matriarchy in Kurdistan? Women Rulers in Kurdish History." *International Journal of Kurdish Studies* 6 (Fall 1993), pp. 25-39.

_____. *Agha, Shaikh and State: The Social and Political Structure of Kurdistan*. London and New Jersey: Zed Books, 1992.

Casier, Marlies, and Joost Jongerden, eds. *Nationalism and Politics in Turkey: Political Islam, Kemalism and the Kurdish Issue*. London and New York: Routledge, 2011.

Casier, Marlies, Joost Jongerden, and Nic Walker. "Fruitless Attempts? The Kurdish Initiative and Containment of the Kurdish Movement in Turkey." *New Perspectives on Turkey* No. 44 (Spring 2011), pp. 103-127.

Celep, Odul. "Turkey's Radical Right and the Kurdish Issue: The MHP's Reaction to the 'Democratic Opening.'" *Insight Turkey* 12 (Spring 2010), pp. 125-142.

Chaliand, Gerard, ed. *A People without a Country: The Kurds and Kurdistan*. New York: Olive Branch Books, 1993.

Charountaki, Marianna. *The Kurds and US Foreign Policy: International Relations in the Middle East since 1945*. London: Routledge, 2010.

Chyet, Michael L. *Kurdish-English Dictionary/Ferhenga Kurmanci-Inglizi*. New Haven and London: Yale University Press, 2003.

Cicek, Cuma. *The Kurds of Turkey: National, Religious and Economic Identities*. London and New York: I.B. Tauris, 2017.

Cizre, Umit, ed. *Secular and Islamic Politics in Turkey: The Making of the Justice and Development Party*. London: Routledge, 2007.

Clarry, Stafford. "Roaming Iraqi Kurdistan." In *Routledge Handbook on the Kurds*, ed. Michael M. Gunter. London and New York: Routledge, 2019.

Connor, Walker. *Ethnonationalism: The Quest for Understanding*. Princeton: Princeton University Press, 1994.

Dawisha, Adeed. *Iraq: A Political History from Independence to Occupation*. Princeton: Princeton University Press, 2009.

Devlin, John. *The Baath Party: A History from Its Origins to 1966*. Stanford, CA: Hoover Institution Press, 1976.

Dodge, Toby. *Inventing Iraq: The Failure of Nation Building and a History Denied*. New York: Columbia University Press, 2003.

Eccarius-Kelly, Vera. *The Militant Kurds: A Dual Strategy for Freedom*. Westport, CT: Praeger Security International, 2010.

Edmonds, C. J. *Kurds, Turks and Arabs: Travel and Research in North-Eastern Iraq, 1919-1925*. London: Oxford University Press, 1957.

Eppel, Michael. *A People without a State: The Kurds from the Rise of Islam to the Dawn of Nationalism*. Austin: University of Texas Press, 2016.

Entessar, Nader. *Kurdish Politics in the Middle East*. Lanham, MD: Lexington Books, 2010.

EU Turkey Civic Commission (EUTCC). "The Kurdish Question in Turkey: Time to Renew the Dialogue and Resume Direct Negotiations." December 5-6, 2012, European Parliament, Brussels, Belgium. For some of these proceedings, see http://www.mesop.de.

Fuccaro, Nelida. "Kurds and Kurdish Nationalism in Mandatory Syria: Politics, Culture and Identity." in Abbas Vali, ed. *Essays on the Origins of Kurdish Nationalism*. Costa Mesa, CA: Mazda Publishers, 2003, pp. 191-217.

Galbraith, Peter W. *The End of Iraq: How American Incompetence Created a War without End*. New York: Simon & Schuster, 2006.

Gelie, Alessandra, and Kerim Yildiz. *Development in Syria: A Gender and Minority Perspective*. London: Kurdish Human Rights Project, 2005.

Gellner, Ernest. *Nations and Nationalism*. Ithaca: Cornell University Press, 1983.

Ghareeb, Edmund. *The Kurdish Question in Iraq*. Syracuse: Syracuse University Press, 1981.

Grabolle-Celiker, Anna. *Kurdish Life in Contemporary Turkey: Migration, Gender and Ethnic Identity*. London and New York: I.B. Tauris, 2013.

Gunes, Cengiz. *The Kurdish National Movement in Turkey: From Protest to Resistance*. London and New York: Routledge, 2012.

Gunter, Michael M. *The Kurds in Turkey: A Political Dilemma*. Boulder, CO: Westview Press, 1990.

_____. *The Kurds of Iraq: Tragedy and Hope*. New York: St. Martin's Press, 1992.

_____. *The Kurds and the Future of Turkey*. New York: St. Martin's Press, 1997.

_____. *The Kurdish Predicament in Iraq: A Political Analysis*. New York: St. Martin's Press, 1999.

_____. *The Kurds Ascending: The Evolving Solution to the Kurdish Problem in Iraq and Turkey*, 2nd ed. New York: Palgrave Macmillan, 2011.

_____. *Out of Nowhere: The Kurds of Syria in Peace and War*. London: C. Hurst & Co., 2014.

_____, ed. *Kurdish Issues: Essays in Honor of Robert W. Olson*. Costa Mesa, CA: Mazda Publishers, 2016.

_____, ed. *Routledge Handbook on the Kurds*. London and New York: Routledge, 2019.

_____. "Erdogan's Backsliding: Opposition to the KRG Referendum." *Middle East Policy* 25 (Spring 2018), pp. 96-103.

_____. "Trump, Turkey and the Kurds." *Middle East Policy* 24 (Summer 2017), pp. 78-86.

_____. "Erdogan and the Decline of Turkey." 23 *Middle East Policy* (Winter 2016), pp. 123-135.

_____. "Iraq, Syria, ISIS and the Kurds: Geostrategic Concerns for the U.S. and Turkey." *Middle East Policy* 22 (Spring 2015), pp. 102-111.

_____. "US Middle East Policy and the Kurds," *Orient* 58:2 (2017), pp. 43-51.

_____. "Unrecognized De Facto States in World Politics: The Kurds," *Brown Journal of World Affairs* 20 (Spring/Summer 2014), pp. 147-64.

_____. "Reopening Turkey's Closed Kurdish Opening?" *Middle East Policy*, 20 (Summer 2013), pp. 88-98.

_____."The Kurdish Spring," *Third World Quarterly*, 34:3 (2013), pp. 441-57.

_____. "Murder in Paris: Parsing the Murder of Female PKK Leader." *Militant Leadership Monitor* 4 (January 2013), pp. 12-13.

_____. "Arab-Kurdish Relations and the Future of Iraq." *Third World Quarterly* 32:9 (2011), pp. 1623-35.

_____. "The Continuing Kurdish Problem in Turkey after Ocalan's Capture." *Third World Quarterly* 21 (October 2000), pp. 849-69.

_____. "Turkey: The Politics of a New Democratic Constitution." *Middle East Policy* 19 (Spring 2012), pp. 119-25.

_____. "The Connection between Turkey's Intelligence Community and Organized Crime." *International Journal of Intelligence and CounterIntelligence* 11 (Summer 1998): 119-41.

_____. "Abdullah Ocalan: We Are Fighting Turks Everywhere." *Middle East Quarterly* 5 (June 1998): 79-85.

Gunter, Michael M., and M. Hakan Yavuz. "Turkish Paradox: Progressive Islamists versus Reactionary Secularists." *Critique: Critical Middle Eastern Studies*. 16 (Fall 2007), pp. 289-301.

Gurbuz, Mustafa, "Turkey's Kurdish Question and the Hizmet Movement," Rethink Paper 22, Rethink Institute, Washington, DC. March 2015, www.rethinkinstitute.org/wp-content/uploads/2015/03/Gurbuz-Turkey's Kurdish-Question-and-Hizmet.pdf, accessed August 30, 2016.

_____. "Recognition of Kurdish Identity and the Hizmet Movement," Gulen Movement, http://www.gulenmovement.us/recognition-of-kurdish-identity-and-the-hizmet-movement.html, accessed August 30, 2016.

Hardi, Choman. *Gendered Experiences of Genocide: Anfal Survivors in Kurdistan-Iraq*. Farnham, UK: Ashgate, 2011.

Hassanpour, Amir. *Nationalism and Language in Kurdistan, 1918-1985*. San Francisco: Mellen Research University Press, 1992.

Hassino, Omar, and Ilhan Tanir. "The Decisive Minority: The Role of Syria's Kurds in the Anti-Assad Revolution." A Henry Jackson Society Report, March 2012. Http://www.scpss.org/libs/spaw. . . , accessed June 6, 2012.

Hechter, Michael. *Alien Rule*. Cambridge: Cambridge University Press, 2013.

Heper, Metin. *The State and Kurds in Turkey: The Question of Assimilation*. New York: Palgrave Macmillan, 2007.

Houston, Christopher. *Islam, Kurds and the Turkish Nation State*. Oxford and New York: Berg, 2001.

_____. *Kurdistan: Crafting of National Selves*. Bloomington and Indianapolis: Indiana University Press, 2008.

Human Rights Watch. *Iran: Freedom of Expression and Association in the Kurdish Regions*. New York: Human Rights Watch, 2009.

Ihsan, Mohammed. *Nation Building in Kurdistan: Memory, Genocide and Human Rights*. London and New York: Routledge, 2017.

Imset, Ismet G. "The PKK: Terrorists or Freedom Fighters?" *International Journal of Kurdish Studies* 10 (nos. 1 & 2; 1996), pp. 45-100.

_____. *The PKK: A Report on Separatist Violence in Turkey (1973-1992)*. Istanbul: Turkish Daily News Publications, 1992.

International Crisis Group. "Winning the Post-ISIS Battle for Iraq in Sinjar." Report No. 183. Middle East & North Africa. February 20, 2018.

_____. "Turkey's Syrian Refugees: Defusing Metropolitan Tensions." Report No. 248. Europe & Central Asia. January 29, 2018.

_____. "Post-ISIS Iraq: A Gathering Storm." Middle East & North Africa. October 26, 2017.

_____. "Oil and Borders: How to Fix Iraq's Kurdish Crisis." Briefing No. 55. Middle East & North Africa. October 17, 2017.

_____. "Turkey's PKK Conflict Kills Almost 3,000 in Two Years." July 20, 2017.

_____. "Arming Iraq's Kurds: Fighting IS, Inviting Conflict." Report No. 158. Middle East & North Africa. May 12, 2015.

_____. "Flight of Icarus? The PYD's Precarious Rise in Syria." Middle East Report No. 151. May 8, 2014.

_____. "Syria's Kurds: A Struggle within a Struggle." Middle East Report No. 136. January 22, 2013.

_____. "Syria's: Metastasizing Conflicts." Middle East Report No. 143. June 27, 2013.

_____. "Syria's Mutating Conflict." Middle East Report No. 128. August 1, 2012.

_____. "Iraq and the Kurds: The High-Stakes Hydrocarbons Gambit." Middle East Report No. 120. April 19, 2012.

_____. "Iraq's New Battlefront: The Struggle over Ninewa." Middle East Report No. 90. Mosul/Brussels: International Crisis Group. September 28, 2009.

_____. "Iraq and the Kurds: Trouble along the Trigger Line." Middle East Report No. 88. Baghdad/Erbil/Brussels: International Crisis Group. July 8, 2009.

_____. "Turkey and Iraqi Kurds: Conflict or Cooperation?" Middle East Report No. 81. Istanbul/Brussels: International Crisis Group. November 13, 2008.

_____. "Oil for Soil: Toward a Grand Bargain on Iraq and the Kurds." Middle East Report No. 80. Kirkuk/Brussels: International Crisis Group. October 28, 2008.

_____. "Iraq and the Kurds: Resolving the Kirkuk Crisis." Middle East Report No. 64. Kirkuk/Amman/Brussels: International Crisis Group. April 19, 2007.

Izady, Mehrdad R. *The Kurds: A Concise History*. Washington: Crane Russak, 1992.

Jabar, Faleh A., and Renad Mansour eds. *The Kurds in a Changing Middle East: History, Politics and Representation*. London: I.B. Tauris, 2018.

Jabar, Faleh A., and Hosham Dawod, eds. *The Kurds: Nationalism and Politics*. London: Saqi, 2006.

Jongerden, Joost. *The Settlement Issue in Turkey and the Kurds: An Analysis of Spatial Policies, Modernity and War*. Leiden and Boston: Brill, 2007.

Jongerden, Joost, and Ahmet Hamdi Akkaya. "Democratic Confederalism as a Kurdish Spring: The PKK and the Quest for Radical Democracy." in Mohammed M.A. Ahmed and Michael M. Gunter, eds. *The Kurdish Spring: Geopolitical Changes and the Kurds*. Costa Mesa, CA: Mazda Publishers, 2013.

Jwaideh, Wadie. *The Kurdish National Movement: Its Origins and Development*. Syracuse N.Y.: Syracuse University Press, 2006.

King, Diane E. *Kurdistan on the Global Stage: Kinship, Land, and Community in Iraq*. New Brunswick and London: Rutgers University Press, 2014.

Kirisci, Kemal, and Gareth M. Winrow. *The Kurdish Question and Turkey: An Example of a Trans-state Ethnic Conflict*. London: Frank Cass, 1997.

Kirmanj, Sherko. "Kurdish History Textbooks: Building a Nation-State within a Nation-State." *Middle East Journal* 68 (Summer 2014), pp. 367-384.

Kissinger, Henry. *White House Years*. Boston: Little, Brown and Co., 1979.

_____. *Years of Renewal*. New York: Simon and Schuster, 1999.

Klein, Janet. *The Margins of Empire: Kurdish Militias in the Ottoman Tribal Zone*. Stanford, CA: Stanford University Press, 2011.

Koohi-Kamali, Farideh. *The Political Development of the Kurds in Iran*. New York: Palgrave Macmillan, 2003.

Korn, David A. "The Last Years of Mustafa Barzani." *Middle East Quarterly* 1 (June 1994), pp. 12-27.

Kurdish Human Rights Project. *Enforcing the Charter for the Rights and Freedoms of Women in the Kurdish Regions and Diaspora*. London: Kurdish Human Rights Project, 2004.

Kurdistan Regional Government. *The Kurdistan Region: Invest in the Future*. Washington, DC: Newsdesk Media Inc., 2007.

KurdWatch. "Who is the Syrian-Kurdish Opposition? The Development of Kurdish Parties, 1956-2011." Berlin: European Center for Kurdish Studies, 2011.

Lang, Jennifer. "Turkey's Counterterrorism Response to the Syrian Crisis." *Terrorism Monitor* 11:14 (July 12, 2013). Http://www.refworld.org . . . , accessed July 22, 2013.

Lawrence, Quil. *The Invisible Nation: How the Kurds' Quest for Statehood Is Shaping Iraq and the Middle East*. New York: Walker and Company, 2008.

Lewis, Bernard. *The Emergence of Modern Turkey*, 2nd ed. London: Oxford University Press, 1968.

Lowe, Robert, and Gareth Stansfield, eds. *The Kurdish Policy Imperative*. London: Chatham House, 2010.

Lowe, Robert. "Kurdish Nationalism in Syria." in Mohammed M.A. Ahmed and Michael M. Gunter, eds. *The Evolution of Kurdish Nationalism*. Costa Mesa, CA: Mazda Publishers, 2007, pp. 287-308.

_____. "The *Serhildan* and the Kurdish National Story in Syria." in Robert Lowe and Gareth Stansfield, eds. *The Kurdish Policy Imperative*. London: Royal Institute of International Affairs, 2010, pp. 161-179.

Lundgren, Asa. *The Unwelcome Neighbour: Turkey's Kurdish Policy*. London and New York: I.B. Tauris, 2007.

Makiya, Kanan (Samir Al-Khalil). *Cruelty and Silence: War, Tyranny, Uprising and the Arab World*. New York and London: W. W. Norton & Company, 1993.

Marcus, Aliza. *Blood and Belief: The PKK and the Kurdish Fight for Independence*. New York and London: New York University Press, 2007.

Marr, Phebe. *The Modern History of Iraq*, 3rd ed. Boulder CO: Westview Press, 2012.

McDowall, David. *A Modern History of the Kurds*. London and New York: I.B. Tauris, 1996.

McKiernan, Kevin. *The Kurds: A People in Search of Their Homeland*. New York: St. Martin's Press, 2006.

Mella, Jawad. *The Colonial Policy of the Syrian Baath Party in Western Kurdistan*. London: Western Kurdistan Association, 2006.

Mojab, Shahrzad, ed. *Women of a Non-State Nation: The Kurds*. Costa Mesa, CA: Mazda Publishers, 2001.

Montgomery (Allsopp), Harriet. *The Kurds of Syria: An Existence Denied*. Berlin: European Center for Kurdish Studies, 2005.

Mutlu, Servet. "Ethnic Kurds in Turkey: A Demographic Study." *International Journal of Middle East Studies* 28 (November 1996): 517-41.

Natali, Denise. *The Kurdish Quasi-State: Development and Dependency in Post-Gulf War Iraq*. Syracuse, NY: Syracuse University Press, 2010.

_____. *The Kurds and the State: Evolving National Identity in Iraq, Turkey, and Iran*. Syracuse: Syracuse University Press, 2005.

O'Leary, Brendan. "The Kurds, the Four Wolves, and the Great Powers." *Journal of Politics* 80 (January 2018), pp. 353-66.

O'Leary, Brendan, John McGarry, and Khaled Salih, eds. *The Future of Kurdistan in Iraq*. Philadelphia: University of Pennsylvania Press, 2005.

Ocalan, Abdullah. *Declaration on the Democratic Solution of the Kurdish Question*. London: Mesopotamian Publishers, 1999.

_____. *Prison Writings: The Roots of Civilisation*, trans. by Klaus Happel. London: Pluto Press, 2007.

_____. *Prison Writings: The PKK and the Kurdish Question in the 21st Century*, trans. and edited by Klaus Happel. London: Transmedia Publishing Ltd., 2011.

_____. *Prison Writings III: The Road Map to Negotiations*, trans. by Havin Guneser. Cologne, Germany: International Initiative Edition, 2012.

Olson, Robert. *The Emergence of Kurdish Nationalism and the Sheikh Said Rebellion, 1880-1925*. Austin: University of Texas Press, 1989.

_____. *Turkey's Relations with Iran, Syria, Israel, and Russia, 1991-2000*. Costa Mesa, CA: Mazda Press, 2001.

_____. *Turkey-Iran Relations, 1979-2004: Revolution, Ideology, War, Coups and Geopolitics*. Costa Mesa, CA: Mazda Press, 2004.

_____. *The Goat and the Butcher: Nationalism and State Formation in Kurdistan-Iraq since the Iraqi War*. Costa Mesa, CA: Mazda Press, 2005.

_____. *Blood, Beliefs and Ballots: The Management of Kurdish Nationalism in Turkey, 2007-2009*. Costa Mesa, CA: Mazda Press, 2009.

Orhan, Mehmet. *Political Violence and Kurds in Turkey*. London: Routledge, 2015.

Ozcan, Ali Kemal. *Turkey's Kurds: A Theoretical Analysis of the PKK and Abdullah Ocalan*. London and New York: Routledge, 2006.

Ozoglu, Hakan. *Kurdish Notables and the Ottoman State: Evolving Identities, Competing Loyalties, and Shifting Boundaries*. Albany: State University of New York Press, 2004.

Paasche, Till, and Michael M. Gunter, "Revisiting Western Strategies against the Islamic State in Iraq and Syria," *Middle East Journal* 70 (Winter 2016), pp. 9-29.

Park, Bill. "Turkey's Kurdish Problems, the Kurds' Turkish Problems." In *The Kurdish Question Revisited*, eds. Gareth Stansfield and Mohammed Shareef, 199-209. London: Hurst and Company, 2017.

Phillips, Christopher. *The Battle for Syria: International Rivalry in the New Middle East*. New Haven, CT: Yale University Press, 2018.

Phillips, David. *The Kurdish Spring: A New Map of the Middle East*. New Brunswick and London: Transaction Publishers, 2015.

_____. *Losing Iraq: Inside the Postwar Reconstruction Fiasco*. Boulder, CO: Westview Press, 2005.

Prunhuber, Carol. *The Passion and Death of Rahman the Kurd*. New York and Bloomington: iUniverse Inc., 2009.

Rand Corporation. *Regional Implications of an Independent Kurdistan*. Santa Monica, CA: Rand Corporation, 2016.

Randal, Jonathan C. *After Such Knowledge, What Forgiveness? My Encounters with Kurdistan*. New York: Farrar, Straus and Giroux, 1997.

Romano, David. *The Kurdish Nationalist Movement: Opportunity, Mobilization and Identity*. Cambridge: Cambridge University Press, 2006.

_____. "Iraqi Kurdistan and Turkey: Temporary Marriage?" *Middle East Policy* 22 (Spring 2015), pp. 89-101.

_____. "Iraq's Descent into Civil War: A Constitutional Explanation." *Middle East Journal* 68 (Autumn 2014), pp. 547-566.

_____. "An Outline of Kurdish Islamist Groups in Iraq." *Jamestown Occasional Papers Series*. Washington, D.C.: Jamestown Foundation, September 17, 2007.

Romano, David, and Mehmet Gurses, eds., *Conflict, Democratization, and the Kurds in the Middle East: Turkey, Iran, Iraq, and Syria.* New York: Palgrave Macmillan, 2014.

Roux, Georges. *Ancient Iraq.* London: Allen & Unwin, 1964.

Rubin, Michael. *Kurdistan Rising: Consideration for Kurds, Their Neighbors, and the Region.* Washington, D.C.: American Enterprise Institute, 2016.

Saeed, Seevan. *Kurdish Politics in Turkey: From the PKK to the KCK.* London and New York: Routledge, 2017.

Savelsberg, Eva. "The Kurdish PYD and the Syrian Civil War." In *Routledge Handbook on the Kurds,* ed. Michael M. Gunter. London and New York: Routledge, 2019.

Sinclair, Christian, and Sirwan Kajjo. "The Evolution of Kurdish Politics in Syria." *Middle East Research and Information Project,* August 31, 2011. Http://www.merip.org/mero/mero083111?p. . . , accessed July 28, 2013.

Stansfield, Gareth. *Iraqi Kurdistan: Political Development and Emergent Democracy.* London: RoutledgeCurzon, 2003.

_____. *Iraq: People, History, Politics.* Cambridge and Oxford: Polity, 2007.

Stansfield, Gareth, and Liam Anderson. "Kurds in Iraq: The Struggle between Baghdad and Erbil." *Middle East Policy* 16 (Spring 2009), pp. 134-45.

Stansfield, Gareth, and Mohammed Shareef, eds. *The Kurdish Question Revisited.* London: Hurst & Company, 2017.

Strohmeier, Martin. *Crucial Images in the Presentation of Kurdish National Identity: Heroes and Patriots: Traitors and Foes.* Leiden and Boston: Brill, 2003.

Tahiri, Hussein. *The Structure of Kurdish Society and the Struggle for a Kurdish State.* Costa Mesa, CA: Mazda Press, 2007.

Taspinar, Omer. *Kurdish Nationalism and Political Islam in Turkey: Kemalist Identity in Transition.* New York and London: Routledge, 2005.

Tejel, Jordi. *Syria's Kurds: History, Politics and Society.* London and New York: Routledge, 2009.

Tezcur, Gunes Murat. "Ordinary People, Extraordinary Risks: Participation in an Ethnic Rebellion." *American Political Science Review* 110 (May 2016), pp. 247-264.

Toperich, Sasha, Tea Ivanovic, and Nahro Zagros, eds. *Iraqi Kurdistan Region: A Path Forward.* Washington, D.C.: Center for Transatlantic Relations/Johns Hopkins University, 2017.

Tripp, Charles. *A History of Iraq*, 3rd ed. Cambridge, UK: Cambridge University Press, 2007.

Turkish Economic and Social Studies Foundation (TESEV). *A Roadmap for a Solution to the Kurdish Question: Policy Proposals from the Region for the Government*. Istanbul: TESEV, 2008.

_____. *Towards a Solution of the Kurdish Question: Constitutional and Legal Recommendations*. Istanbul: TESEV, 2010.

Unal, Mustafa Cosar. *Counterterrorism in Turkey: Policy Choices and Policy Effects toward the Kurdistan Workers' Party (PKK)*. London and New York: Routledge, 2012.

Uslu, Emrullah. "How Kurdish PKK Militants are Exploiting the Crisis in Syria to Achieve Regional Autonomy." 10:7 *Terrorism Monitor*, April 6, 2012, pp. 8-11. Http://www.jamestown.org/. . . , accessed June 6, 2012.

Vali, Abbas, ed. *Essays on the Origins of Kurdish Nationalism*. Costa Mesa, CA: Mazda Press, 2003.

_____. *Kurds and the State in Iran: The Making of Kurdish Identity*. London: I.B. Tauris, 2014.

Vanly, Ismet Cheriff. "The Kurds in Syria and Lebanon." in Philip G. Kreyenbroek and Stefan Sperl, eds. *The Kurds: A Contemporary Overview*. London: Routledge, 1992, pp. 143-70.

_____. "The Oppression of the Kurdish People in Syria." in Mohammed M.A. Ahmed and Michael M. Gunter, eds. *Kurdish Exodus: From Internal Displacement to Diaspora*. Sharon, Mass.: Ahmed Foundation for Kurdish Studies, 2002, pp. 49-62.

Visser, Reidar, and Gareth Stansfield, eds. *An Iraq of Its Regions: Cornerstones of a Federal Democracy?* New York: Columbia University Press, 2008.

Watts, Nicole F. *Activists in Office: Kurdish Politics and Protest in Turkey*. Seattle: University of Washington Press, 2010.

White, Damian F. *Bookchin: A Critical Appraisal*. London: Pluto Press, 2008.

White, Paul. *Primitive Rebels or Revolutionary Modernizers? The Kurdish National Movement in Turkey*. London and New York: Zed Books, 2000.

_____. *The PKK: Coming Down from the Mountains*. London: Zed Books, 2015.

Wigram, Edgar T. A., and W. A. Wigram. *The Cradle of Mankind: Life in Eastern Kurdistan*, 2nd ed. London: A. & C. Black Ltd., 1922.

World Bank Group. "Kurdistan Region of Iraq: Reforming the Economy for Shared Prosperity and Protecting the Vulnerable." Washington, D.C., May 30, 2016. Http://documents.worldbank.org/curated/en/708441468196727918/Executive-summary

Yadirgi, Veli. *The Political Economy of the Kurds of Turkey: From the Ottoman Empire to the Turkish Republic*. Cambridge: Cambridge University Press, 2017,

Yavuz, M. Hakan. *Islamic Political Identity in Turkey*. Oxford: Oxford University Press, 2003.

_____. *Secularism and Muslim Democracy in Turkey*. New York: Cambridge University Press, 2009.

_____. *Toward an Islamic Enlightenment: The Gulen Movement*. Oxford: Oxford University Press, 2013.

_____. "Five Stages of the Construction of Kurdish Nationalism in Turkey." *Nationalism & Ethnic Politics* 7 (Autumn 2001), pp. 1-24.

_____. "A Preamble to the Kurdish Question: The Politics of Kurdish Identity." *Journal of Muslim Minority Affairs* 18:1 ((1998), pp. 9-18.

Yavuz, M. Hakan, and Bayram Balci, eds. *Turkey's July 15th Coup: What Happened and Why*. Salt Lake City: The University of Utah Press, 2018.

Yildiz, Kerim. *The Kurds in Syria: The Forgotten People*. London: Pluto Press, 2005.

_____. *The Kurds in Iraq: The Past, Present and Future*. London: Pluto Press, 2004.

_____. *The Kurds in Turkey: EU Accession and Human Rights*. London: Pluto Press, 2005.

Yildiz, Kerim, and Susan Breau. *The Kurdish Conflict: International Humanitarian Law and Post-Conflict Mechanisms*. London and New York: Routledge, 2010.

Yildiz, Kerim, and Tanyel Taysi. *The Kurds in Iran: The Past, Present and Future*. London: Pluto Press, 2007.

Yuksel, Metin. "The Encounter of Kurdish Women with Nationalism in Turkey." *Middle Eastern Studies* 42 (September 2006), pp. 777-802.

Zaken, Mordechai (Moti). *Jewish Subjects and Their Tribal Chieftains in Kurdistan: A Study in Survival*. Leiden and Boston: Brill, 2007.

Zurcher, Erik J. *Turkey: A Modern History*, 3rd revised ed. London: I. B. Tauris, 2004.

Index

Abadi, Haider al- 219
Abdal Khan 7
Abdul Hamid II (Sultan) 27
Abdul Salam II, Sheikh (Barzani) 67
Abu al-Fida 9
Aflaq, Michel 100
Afrin (Kurd Dagh/Syria) 88, 121,
    125, 126, 129, 130, 195, 196, 209,
    231, 232, 234, 283
Ahl-i Haqq 133
Ahmad, Ibrahim 17, 68
Ahmadi Khan 7-9, 14
Ahmadinejad, Mahmoud 145, 146,
    149
Ahmedi, Abdul Rahman Haji 148
Ajanib (Syria) 97, 98, 115, 125
Ak Koyunlu 5
Akrad 3
AKP (*Adalet ve Kalkinma Partisi/*
    Turkey) 34, 49-51, 185, 186, 199,
    200, 217
Alawites 93, 110
Albright, Madeleine 160
Aleppo 88, 89, 90, 92, 107, 114, 120,
    125, 128, 129, 130, 173
Alevi xv, 134, 242
Alp Arslan 4
Al-Qaeda 58, 110, 112, 113, 127,
    130, 159, 167, 169, 172
American University of Kurdistan
    229
Amnesty International (AI) 190, 191,
    198
Amuda theater (Syria) 96
Anfal 62, 70, 144, 250
Ankawa (Iraq) 85
Anti-Terrorism Law (Turkey) 47
Arab Belt (Syria) 98, 99, 102

Arab Spring 80, 110, 114, 115, 119
Ararat Rebellion (Turkey) 28, 92
Ardalan xv, 6, 12, 133, 208
Armenia (Armenians) xvii, xviii, xix,
    13, 20
Article 140 (Iraqi Constitution) 84,
    163
Article 301 (Turkish Penal Code) 47
Article 312 (Turkish Penal Code) 47
Asayesh (security forces of PYD)
    122
Assad, Bashar al- 111, 112, 114, 115,
    116, 117, 118, 119, 120, 121, 122,
    123, 124, 125, 127, 128, 168, 169,
    172, 173, 177, 182
Assad, Hafeez al- 100, 107, 108
Assyrians xv, 13, 61, 67, 76, 137,
    190, 201
Ataturk, Kemal 16, 19, 27, 33
Atlantic Council (US) 219, 278
Ayyubids 5, 7
Azadi Party (Syria) 122, 256

Baath Party (Iraq) 62, 69, 178, 179,
    183
Baath Party (Syria) 96, 98, 100, 111,
    253
Baban 6
Baghdad Pact (1955) 25
Baghdadi, Abu Bakr al- 179.
    See also ISIS
Bahceli, Devlet 217
Bakdash, Khalid 91, 104
Baker-Hamilton Report 152
Bakhtiyar, Mala 223
Baradust 9
Barazi, Muhsen 95
Barzan 66, 69

Barzani, Asenath 207
Barzani, Masrour 221, 223
Barzani, Massoud 32, 38, 57, 67, 70, 73, 76, 79, 81, 83, 84, 108, 117, 119, 122, 143, 144, 146, 148, 152, 156, 157, 163, 180, 202, 204, 214, 216, 221, 223, 224, 251, 252, 256
Barzani, Mulla Mustafa 16, 17, 20, 65, 66, 70, 91, 101, 105, 139, 140, 154, 155
Barzani, Nechirvan Idris 76, 79
Barzani, Sheikh Ahmad 67
Barzinji, Sheikh Mahmud 16, 63, 65, 137
Baydemir, Osman 34
Bayik, Cemil 34, 53, 148, 192
Bayti Dimdim (epic book) 9
BDP (*Baris ve Demokrasi* Partisi/ Turkey) 33, 51, 56.
    See also HDP
Bedir Khan 13-14, 18, 91, 245
Bedir Khan, Celadet (Jaladet) 19-20, 91, 92, 104
Bedir Khan, Kamuran 18, 20, 91
Bedir Khan, Rewshen 104
Bedir Khan, Tureyya (Thurayya) 18, 19, 91
Biden, Joseph 82, 201, 251, 268
Birand, Mehmet Ali 43, 245
Bitlis 6, 7
Bitlisi, Idris 6, 9
Bookchin, Murray 196
Botan 6, 9, 13, 18, 88, 91, 245
Britain 12, 13, 25, 76, 115, 127, 135, 137, 249
Bush, George H.W. 157
Bush, George W. 109, 157-58, 163

Camp Bucca (Iraq) 179
Candar, Cengiz 42, 244
Cavusoglu, Mevlut 233
Cegerxwin, Sexmus Hesen 12, 93
Cello, Shahin 126
Chaldiran, Battle of (1514) 6
Chechnya 112, 127, 177
Chelebi, Evliya 7
China 11, 110, 117, 226

CHP (*Cumhuriet Halk Partisi*) 50, 199
CIA (Central Intelligence Agency/ USA) 156, 261
Ciller, Tansu 26, 46
Cizre 5, 13, 88, 91, 187, 272
Clausewitz, Carl von 183
Clinton, Bill 159
Coalition for Democracy and Justice (KRG) 223
Constructionists 1
Copenhagen Criteria 33
Crocker, Ryan 219
Cyprus 197

Daesh 175, 229. *See also* ISIS
Dalanpar, Mount 139
Darwish, Hamid Haj 105
Davutoglu, Ahmet 188
Decree 93 (Syria) 97, 115
Demirel, Suleyman 26, 41, 42, 46
Demirtas, Selahattin 56, 186, 194.
    See also HDP
Democratic Autonomy 51, 122, 132, 175, 187, 191, 196. *See also* Ocalan, Abdullah
Democratic Union Party (Syria) 190.
    See PYD
Derek (Al-Malikiyah/Syria) 99
Dijla Operations Command (Iraq) 82
Dimdim (Dumdum) 8-9
Dimili 10. *See also* Zaza
Diyarbakir (Amed) 4, 6, 7, 34, 57, 74, 187, 216, 217, 272, 276, 277
Dogan, Gulistan 148
Dohuk (Iraq) 71, 78, 181
Dolmabahce consensus
Druzes 93
DTP (*Demokratik Toplum Partisi*) 33, 49, 50, 51

Egypt 5, 96, 110, 127, 171, 176
Elci, Serafettin 31
Emirates (Kurdish) 5, 6-7, 8, 9, 12, 13, 136, 266
Erdogan, Recep Tayyip 26, 34, 49, 52, 82, 185, 186

Erzurum Congress (1919/Turkey) 28
Ethnie 1
EU (European Union) 21, 30, 33, 34, 47, 59, 60, 117, 165, 192, 206, 228, 242, 256, 270, 276
Evren, Kenan 43

F-35 Fighter Jets 235
Fadluyids 7
Faisal I, King 61, 65, 89
Fatima, Lady Kara 208
Felat, Rojda 209
Female Genital Mutilation (FGM) 77, 210
FETO (Fethullah Gulen Terrorist Organization) 195
Firat, Abdulmelik 31
Fourteen Points 27, 62, 154. *See also* Wilson, Woodrow
Free Syrian Army (FSA) 112, 120, 121, 128, 231

GAP (Southeast Anatolia Project/ Turkey) xxi, 185
Gates, Robert 152, 163, 166
Geneva II Peace Process (Syria) 181
George (Shello), Margaret 208
Germany xix, 34, 180, 216, 257, 274
Gezi Park Demonstrations (Turkey) 34
Ghassemlou, Abdul Rahman 138, 143, 144, 146
Ghouta (Syria) 167
Golani, Abu Mohammad al- 127. *See also* Jablat al-Nusra
Gorran (Change) Party 77, 79, 80, 83, 223, 228
Gul, Abdullah 49
Gulen, Fethullah 195
Gulnawaz, Abdulsalm 149
Gurani 10, 12, 134
Gursel, Cemal 29
Gutman, Roy 232, 233, 273, 282, 283

Haji, Mir 139
Hajo Agha 92, 93

Hajo, Siamend 122
Hakkari (Turkey) 4, 6, 137, 194, 208
Halabja (Iraq) 62, 70, 71, 144, 168, 208, 221, 250
Halima, Pura of Pizhdar 208
Hamidiye 27
Hasankeyf (Turkey) 5, 6
Hasanwahid 4
Hashemi, Tariq al- 81
Hasht Bihisht 7, 9. *See also* Bitlisi, Idris
Hawar (journal) 93, 94
Hayy al-Akrad (Syria) 104
HDP (*Halklarin Demokratik Partisi*/ Turkey) 33, 60, 186, 188, 192-194, 199, 209, 217, 268, 186, 188, 192-194, 199, 209, 217, 268. *See also* BDP
Hejri, Mostafa 141-143, 144
Heverkan tribal confederation (Syria) 92, 93
Hezbollah (Lebanon) 110, 111, 112, 113, 116, 227, 254
Hilal, Muhammad Talab 101-102
Hisso, Isa 130
Hiwa Party (Iraq) 139
HPG (Hezen Parastina Gel) 54. *See also* PKK
Hussein, Fuad 223
Hussein, Saddam xx, 17, 22, 33, 39, 41, 61, 62, 66, 69, 70, 73, 75, 77, 81, 95, 108, 109, 127, 143, 151, 154, 156-158, 160-162, 166-168, 171, 178, 179, 183, 188, 204, 218, 221, 263, 267, 275
Husseini, Izziddin Sheikh 141

Ibn al-Athir 4, 9
Ibrahim, Hevi 209
Ibrahim Pasha 103
IDPs (Internally Displaced Persons) 110, 176, 202, 227, 229, 281. *See also* Refugees
Ihsan Nuri Pasha 92
Incirlik Airbase
Inonu, Erdal 42
Inonu, Ismet 28

Institut Kurde de Paris 43, 245
Iran xv, xvii, xviii, xix, xxi, 4, 10, 11,
    15-18, 21-23, 25, 34, 63, 67, 69,
    69, 70, 73, 76, 84, 92, 104, 105,
    110, 111, 112, 116, 133-150, 151,
    152, 154, 155, 156, 157, 158, 160,
    167, 169, 171, 172, 173, 176, 180,
    181, 185, 188, 191, 192, 203, 204,
    214, 220, 223, 224, 226, 227, 234,
    236, 239-241, 254, 258-260, 265,
    269, 270, 274, 278, 281
Iran-Iraq War (1980-88) 39, 70, 143,
    144
Iraq xv, xvii, xviii, xix, xx, 2, 4, 5,
    10, 13, 15, 16, 17, 18, 21, 22, 23,
    25, 26, 32, 33, 34, 38, 39, 40, 41,
    43, 45, 54, 57, 58, 61-86, 87, 88,
    90, 97, 98, 101, 102, 104, 105,
    108, 109, 110, 111, 116, 118, 127,
    133, 134, 137, 139, 140, 141, 143,
    144, 146, 151, 152, 153, 154, 155,
    157, 158, 160, 162, 163, 164, 166,
    167, 169, 171, 175, 176, 178, 179,
    180, 181, 182, 183, 185, 186, 188,
    191, 194, 200, 201, 204, 210, 214,
    216, 218-221, 223-227, 231, 232,
    234-236, 238-241, 244-246, 248-
    252, 254, 257, 259-270, 273, 275,
    276, 278-281, 283
Iraqi Kurdistan Front 70, 144
Iraqi National Council (INC) 160,
    261
Irbil (Arbil/Erbil/KRG) xx, 71, 73,
    74, 75, 76, 78, 80, 81, 82, 84, 85,
    117, 119, 163, 208, 211, 214, 215,
    217, 218, 226, 246
ISIL (Islamic State of Iraq and the
    Levant). 278. See ISIS
ISIS (Islamic State of Iraq and Syria/
    Levant) xx, xxi, 57, 58, 78, 84,
    85, 110, 113, 127, 130, 151, 153,
    154, 161, 167, 169, 172-175, 177-
    183, 186, 189-192, 195-197, 200-
    203, 209, 214, 216, 217, 219, 221,
    229-235, 265-267, 269, 276.
    See also Jihadists; Salafists
Islamic State (IS) 186, 214, 220, 266,

    267, 270, 273, 274, 276. See ISIS
Israel 87, 101, 102, 112, 117, 128,
    155, 164, 166, 167, 169, 170, 171,
    204, 218, 220, 224, 225, 227,
    278-280

Jablat al-Nusra 58, 172, 257
Jazira (Hasaka/Syria) 58, 88, 89, 91,
    92, 93, 99, 101, 102, 103, 126,
    195, 196
Jihadists 58, 120, 127, 128, 129, 130,
    170, 173, 177, 178, 179, 182, 189,
    195, 217, 266, 269. See also ISIS;
    Salafists
Jongerden, Joost 142, 258, 261, 265,
    267, 272, 276
Jordan 87, 110, 117, 127, 176, 264
Josh xviii, 16, 267

Kaboglu, Ibrahim Ozden 30
Kahveci, Adnan 36 -
Kandal Mountains. See Qandal
    Mountains
Kara Koyunlu 5
Karayilan, Murat 34, 54
Kardouchoi 2, 3
Karim, Najmaldin O., Dr. 74, 76
Kassem, Abdul Karim General 69
Kawa 3, 251
KCK (Koma Civaken Kurdistan) 34,
    51, 52, 53, 54, 55, 148, 192, 247,
    270. See also PKK
KDP (Kurdistan Democratic Party)
    32, 38, 40, 57, 60, 67, 70, 73-81,
    83, 105, 122, 130, 143, 144, 157,
    159, 160, 165, 202, 204, 214, 222-
    224, 227, 256, 262, 263. See also
    Barzani, Massoud; Barzani, Mulla
    Mustafa; KRG
KDPI (Kurdistan Democratic Party of
    Iran) 139, 140, 141, 142, 143,
    149, 150
Khalkhali, Sadiq Ayatollah 141
Khan Yakdas 9
Khanaqin (Iraq) 72, 80
Khanke/Khanki Refugee Camp 229
Khanzad 208

Khasnawi, Sheikh Mashouq 107, 109
Khatami, Mohammad 145
Khatib, Moaz al- 113
Khoybun 92-93, 103, 104
Khomeini, Ruhollah Ayatollah 141
Khutba 7, 238
Kirkuk (Iraq) 65, 70, 72, 74, 79, 80,
81, 84, 153, 162, 161, 162, 163,
164, 183, 202, 214, 219-223, 225,
226, 250, 262, 263, 274, 275, 278,
280, 281. Kissinger, Henry 155,
261, 262
KNK (Kurdistan National Congress)
193, 200
Kobane (Ain al-Arab/Syria) xxi, 58,
88, 99, 122, 125, 126, 130, 174,
181, 182, 186, 189, 191, 195, 196,
234, 236
Koma Civaken Kurdistan. See KCK
Komala (J.K.) 138-139
Komala (Marxist Party) 140, 141,
142, 149, 150
Kongra Star 209
Kordestan (Iranian province) 133,
145
KRG (Kurdistan Regional Government) xx, xxi, 2, 10, 26, 40, 57,
59, 60, 61, 62, 63, 65, 67, 69, 71-
85, 108, 109, 116, 117, 119, 122,
124, 126, 133, 141, 142, 144, 146,
147, 148, 150-153, 154, 157, 158,
161-164, 166, 169, 174, 175, 176,
180, 181, 189, 192, 200-206, 208,
210-231, 251, 260, 261, 263, 268,
274, 275, 277, 279-282
KRG Elections (September 30, 2018)
224, 227, 281
KRG Independence, problems
KRG Independence Referendum
(September 25, 2017) 206, 213,
217, 227, 277, 278, 281
Kuftaru, Sheikh Ahmad 91
Kurd Ali, Muhammad Farid 12
Kurd Dagh (Afrin/Syria) 88, 126
Kurdayeti 8, 15, 21
Kurdish Democratic Party in Syria
(KDPS/*el-Party*) 92, 96, 104, 106

Kurdish Democratic Progressive
Party in Syria 106
Kurdish diaspora xix, 22
Kurdish Future Movement 114
Kurdish languages (dialects) 9, 10-
11, 29, 93-94. *See also* Dimili
(Zaza); Kurmanji; Gurani; Sorani
Kurdish League (Syria) 104
Kurdish literature 7-9, 12, 91
Kurdish National Coalition
(KNC/Syria) 106
Kurdish Opening (Turkey) 26, 49-51,
268
Kurdish population xv, xvi, xvii, xix,
xx, 28, 29, 33, 37, 40, 73, 76, 89,
95, 97, 133, 158, 199, 259
Kurdistan (journal) 12, 94
Kurdistan 185, 187, 189, 191-193,
195, 197, 199-211, 214-216, 218-
220, 222, 224, 225, 228-230, 233,
237, 238, 240, 241, 248-253, 256,
257, 259, 260, 262, 263, 265, 267,
270, 272-275, 277-282
Kurdistan Democratic Party (KDP)
202, 204, 214, 222-224, 227, 256,
262, 263. *See* KDP
Kurdistan Democratic Party of Iran.
See KDPI
Kurdistan Regional Government 189,
192, 200-206, 208, 210-231, 251,
261, 263, 268, 274, 275, 277,
279-281. *See* KRG
Kurdistan Workers Party 185.
See PKK
Kurmanji 8, 10, 89. *See also* Kurdish
languages (dialects)
Kuwait 70, 157, 204

Lausanne, Treaty of (1923) 27, 43,
63
Law 2932 (Turkey) 41, 43
League of Nations 61, 62, 63, 89, 90
Lebanon 87, 92, 99, 110, 111, 112,
116, 117, 127, 167, 176, 200, 240,
256, 258, 265
Libya 110, 127, 176

Mahabad Republic of Kurdistan
(Iran) 17, 18, 67, 68, 139, 240,
259. *See also* Muhammad, Qazi
Mahdi, Adel Abdul 224
Maktoumeen (Syria) 97, 98, 115
Malazgird, Battle of (1071) 4
Maliki, Nouri al- 81, 82, 83
Manbij (Syria) 196, 232, 234, 236,
282, 284
Mandela, Nelson 56
Mar Shimun 137
March Manifesto (1970) 68, 70
Marwanid 4, 5
Masum, Fuad 72, 73
Mattis, James 233
McCain, John 81
McGurk, Brett 235
McMaster, H.R. 220, 226, 233
Medes 3
Melaye Cizri 9
Mem u Zin (epic book) 8, 9, 14, 239
MHP (*Milliyetci Hareket Partisi-*
Turkey) 50, 199, 217, 247
Milli confederation 103
Miri Kor (Mir Muhammad Pasha)
13
Mir (prince) 7, 9, 13, 91
Morsi, Mohammed 171
Mosul (Iraq) 4, 57, 61, 63, 84, 89,
155, 162, 180, 182, 183, 191, 202,
229, 249
Mountain Turks 29
Muhammad Sherif Pasha 19
Muhammad, Kamuran 121
Muhammad, Qazi 139-140. *See also*
Mahabad Republic of Kurdistan
Muhtadi, Abdullah 150
Mujahedin-e Khalq 148
Mumcu, Ugur 43
Muslim, Salih 58, 59, 116, 117-120,
122-124, 131, 143, 173, 174, 219,
255-258, 264, 277. *See also* PYD
Mustafa, Nawshirwan 76, 79, 83,
223, 224, 250. *See also Gorran*
(Change) Party
Mustafa, Nawshirwan 76, 79, 83,
223, 224, 250

Mykonos Restaurant 144.
See also Sharafkindi, Sadiq
Mythomoteur 1

Naqshbandi Sufi Order 66, 133, 136
Nargiz, Kara 208
Nasrallah, Hassan 112. *See also*
Hezbollah (Lebanon)
Nasser, Gamal Abdul 96
National Coalition for Syrian
Revolutionary and Opposition
Forces 112
National Intelligence Organization
(MIT/Turkey) 38
National Security Council
(MGK/Turkey) 37, 45, 46
NATO (North Atlantic Treaty Organi-
zation) 32, 110, 111, 112, 117,
155, 161, 162, 164, 173, 189, 190,
192, 197, 231-236, 270, 282
Newroz (Nevruz) xv, 3, 29, 109
New Generation Movement 228
Nezan, Kendal 43
Nishtiman (journal) 139
Nixon, Richard 155
Nizam al-Din, Tawfiq General 97
No-Fly Zone (Iraq) 22, 40, 70, 71,
73, 158, 160

Obama, Barack 81, 168, 170-172
Ocalan, Abdullah (Apo) 16, 32,
36, 44, 47, 50, 53, 59, 118,
122, 126, 143, 146, 165, 175, 185,
196, 199, 204, 207, 209, 242, 245,
257, 258, 265, 271, 274. *See also*
PKK; KCK
OHAL (*Olaganustu Hal Bolgesi/*
Emergency Rule/Turkey) 35
Oil xx, xxi, 17, 23, 71, 72, 77, 81, 83,
87, 98, 130, 155, 163, 167, 183,
196, 201, 204, 205, 214, 216, 218,
222, 249, 275
Omar, Fuad 118
Operation Euphrates Shield 232
Operation Olive Branch 231
Operation Provide Comfort
(OPC/Iraq) 40, 73, 158, 159

Oran, Baskin 30
Oslo Talks (2009-2011) 56.
    See also Kurdish Opening
Ottoman Empire xv, 6, 7, 12-13, 14,
    15, 16, 27, 31, 62, 87, 88, 96, 133,
    135, 136, 154, 261
Ozal, Turgut 26, 35-46

Pahlavi, Muhammad Reza (The Shah)
    138, 140, 156
Pahlavi, Reza Shah 137, 138, 172
Pamuk, Orhan 47
Partiya Yekitiya Demokrat (Syria).
    See PYD
People's Council of Western Kurdis-
    tan (Syria) 116. *See also* PYD
Peoples Defense Units 190. *See*
    YPG; PYD
Persheng 208
Persian Empire 4, 133, 134, 135
Peshmergas 72, 163, 180
Peyamiani sei Sanowar (Three
    Borders Meeting) 139
PJAK (Free Life Party of
    Kurdistan/Iran) 147, 148, 149,
    260
PKK (Kurdistan Workers Party) 16,
    19, 26, 32-35, 36, 37, 38, 39, 44-
    46, 47, 48, 50-60, 100, 107, 116,
    118, 119, 120, 121, 122, 124, 126,
    132, 143, 144, 147, 148, 149, 150,
    153, 154, 155, 158, 159, 162, 163,
    164-166, 175, 177, 180, 181, 182,
    185-190, 192-196, 199, 200, 204,
    207, 209, 210, 215-217, 234, 241,
    242, 244-247, 255-258, 261, 263,
    265, 269, 270, 272, 283. *See also*
    KCK; Ocalan, Abdullah
Primordialists (Essentialists) 1, 2
PUK (Patriotic Union of
    Kurdistan/Iraq) 38, 70, 73, 74, 76,
    77, 78, 79, 80, 83, 106, 143, 144,
    157, 159, 165, 202, 213, 214, 221,
    223, 224, 228, 263. *See also*
    Talabani, Jalal
PYD (*Partiya Yekita ya Demokratik*/
    Democratic Union Party/Syria)

58, 59, 106, 107, 116-126, 130,
    131, 143, 159, 173-174, 175, 180,
    181, 182, 190-192, 195-197, 207,
    209, 217, 231-233, 236, 248, 256-
    258, 264, 271. *See also* Muslim,
    Salih; YPG; YPJ

Qadiri, Shivan 146, 147
Qamishli (Syria) 59, 89, 107-109,
    114, 122, 124, 125, 129, 130, 131,
    187, 234
Qamishli Uprising (*Serhildan*) 107-
    109, 124
Qandil (Kandal) Mountains (Iraq) 34,
    58, 126, 147, 148, 166, 181, 192
Qarachok (Syria) 98
Qatar 110, 111, 113, 178

Rahman, Bayan Sami Abdul 153,
    210, 212, 221, 277
Ramazanzadeh, Abdollah 145
Raqqah (Syria) 113, 130, 196, 209,
    236. *See also* ISIS
Ras al-Ayn (Syria). *See* Serekaniye
Rasul, Kosrat 223, 228
Refugees 39, 66, 73, 77, 110, 134,
    158, 176, 182, 190, 192, 202,
    210, 227, 229, 230, 253, 281.
    See also IDPs
Rekeftin 121
Remilan (Syria) 99
Reyhanli (Turkey) 255
Roboski (Turkey) 272
ROJ TV 35
Rojava (Syrian/Western Kurdistan)
    59, 87, 181, 189, 192, 196, 206,
    209, 217, 227, 233, 283
Rouhani, Hassan 149
Rudaw TV (KRG) 213
Russia 10, 12, 13, 15, 110, 111, 112,
    117, 137, 165, 168, 169, 172, 192,
    196, 197, 226, 231, 234-236, 255,
    270. *See also* Soviet Union

S-400 Air Defense System 235
Saadabad, Treaty of (1937) 25
Sabri, Osman 92, 96, 105, 106

Sadiq, Yusuf Mohammed 222, 224
Sadr, Muqtada al- 201, 227
Safavid dynasty (Persia) 133
Said, Sheikh 19, 25, 28, 31, 89, 94,
    241, 245
Saladin (Salah al-Din) 5, 7, 88
Salafists 58, 121, 126, 128, 129, 130,
    170, 178. *See also* ISIS; Jihadists
Salih, Barham 72, 74, 79, 81, 83,
    223, 251, 280
SALSRA 166, 167. *See also* Lebanon
Saudi Arabia 110, 111, 113, 117, 118,
    127, 178, 227, 264
SDF (Syrian Democratic Forces)
    190, 195-197, 209, 231-233, 235
Selo, Fawzi 95
Serekaniye (Ras al-Din/Syria) 99,
    125, 126, 129, 130
Serhildan (Syria) 107, 108, 124.
    See also Qamishli Uprising
Serok (president) 54, 118
Sevres, Treaty of (1920) 27, 62, 158
Seyahatname (Book of Travels) 7.
    See also Chelebi, Evliya
Sezer, Ahmet 26
Shabiha (Syria) 118
Shaddadid (Kurdish dynasty) 4
Shahin, Kamal 121
Shammar tribe (Arab/Syria) 103
Sharaf Khan Bitlisi 7, 66.
    See also Sharafnama
Sharafkindi, Sadiq 143, 144.
    See also Mykonos Restaurant
Sharafnama (epic book) 5, 7, 8, 66,
    238. *See also* Sharaf Khan Bitlisi
Shia (Shiites) 57, 65, 70, 81, 84, 116,
    134, 150, 157, 158, 176, 180, 201,
    227, 253, 266
Shingali, Fawzi 121
Shishakli, Adib al- 95
Simko, Ismail Agha 136
Sinjar (Shingal/Iraq) 72, 181, 229,
    234, 283
Sivas Congress (1919/Turkey) 28
Sorani 10, 11, 12, 134. *See also*
    Kurdish languages (dialects)
Soviet Union 10, 17, 67, 68, 137,

139, 140, 155, 180, 248. *See also*
    Russia
Sulaymaniya (KRG) 63, 65, 71, 76,
    77, 78, 80, 121, 141, 162, 210,
    213-215, 218, 221, 250
Sun-Language Theory (Turkey) 29
Supreme Kurdish Council (Syria)
    117, 120, 125
Sykes-Picot Agreement 89, 96, 175,
    189
Syria 5, 10, 18, 19, 21, 22, 23, 26,
    32, 44, 48, 57, 58-59, 63, 73, 84,
    86-132, 133, 143, 151, 154, 157,
    159, 161, 165, 166-174, 176, 177,
    180, 181, 182, 183, 185-189, 191,
    192, 195-197, 200, 203, 204, 207,
    209, 214, 217, 220, 224, 227, 231,
    234-236, 240, 247, 252-258, 260,
    264-266, 269-271, 277, 282-284
Syrian Communist Party (SCP) 91,
    104, 105
Syrian National Council (SNC) 113,
    114, 116, 119, 120, 121, 123
Syrian Observatory for Human Rights
    234

Taha of Nehri, Sheikh 136, 137
Takfiri (apostates to Islam) 58, 112,
    128, 129
Talabani, Hero 208, 223
Talabani, (Mam) Jalal 17, 38, 41, 44,
    46, 68, 70, 72, 73, 75, 76, 82, 83,
    105, 143, 144, 157, 202, 208, 214,
    223, 224. *See also* PUK
Talabani, Lahur 202
Talabani, Qubad 153
Tammo, Mishaal al- 114-115
Tartus (Syria) 88, 112, 255
Terrier Plan 103
TEV-DEM 125. *See also* PYD
Tewfiq, Haji (Piremerd) 12.
    See also Kurdish literature
Tillerson, Rex 219, 220, 233, 279
Transnational Administrative Law
    (TAL/Iraq) 109
Tribes 3, 4, 14, 16, 27, 67, 89, 90, 92,
    102, 103, 106, 137, 138, 176, 208

Truman Doctrine 161
Trump, Donald 226
Tudeh (Iranian Communist Party)
    140
Tunisia 110, 120, 127
Turkey xv, xvii, xviii, xix, xx, xxi, 4,
    5, 6, 10, 13, 15, 16, 18, 19, 21, 22,
    23, 25-60, 62, 63, 73, 74, 76, 77,
    78, 80, 82, 84, 87, 88. 89, 90, 91,
    92, 94, 97, 98, 99, 100, 102, 103,
    104, 105, 108, 110, 111, 116, 119,
    121. 122, 123, 124, 125, 126, 127,
    129, 130, 131, 133, 137, 139, 140,
    143, 144, 151, 152, 153, 154, 155,
    157, 158, 159, 161, 162, 164, 165,
    166, 173, 175, 176, 177, 181, 182,
    183, 185, 188-200, 203-206, 208-
    210, 214-220, 224-227, 231-236,
    239-248, 250, 251, 254, 255, 257,
    258, 260-273, 275-277, 282, 283
Turkey, failed coup (July 15, 2016)
    194, 195, 197
Turkish Historical Thesis 29
Turkish-Kurdish peace process,
    failure 187, 194
Turkomans 61, 76, 84

Ubeydullah of Nehri, Sheikh 14, 135
UN Security Council Resolution 688
    (1991) 95, 158

UN Security Council Resolution 986
    77
United Arab Emirates (UAE) 111,
    178
United Arab Republic (UAR) 96, 105
United Nations (UN) 40, 62, 71, 73,
    77, 78, 91, 95, 112, 115, 127, 158,
    168, 169, 172, 178, 218, 229, 230,
    255, 262
United States (US) 22, 23, 33, 34, 35,
    38, 40, 48, 69, 70, 71, 73, 74, 76,
    82, 83, 84, 110, 111, 112, 117,
    120, 127, 128, 141, 148, 151-174,
    179, 180, 181, 182, 183, 189, 191,
    195-197, 200, 202, 203, 210, 212,
    214, 217-219, 221, 224, 226, 227,

229, 230, 232, 235, 236, 250, 261,
    263, 271, 277-279, 282
Uzun Hasan 5

Vanly, Ismet Cheriff 75

Wahabi 178
Weber, Max 183
Wifaq (Syrian Democratic Concord
    Party) 121
Wilson, Woodrow 27, 62, 154
Women 20, 53, 76, 77, 79, 120, 124,
    129, 130, 134, 147, 148, 150, 173,
    190, 196, 206, 207, 209, 210, 255,
    274

Xenophon 2, 3

Yekiti (Union) Party (Syria) 124,
    127, 256
Yezidi Kurds 181, 183, 229, 242
YPG (Peoples Defense Units/PYD)
    120, 122, 124, 125, 126, 130, 190,
    192, 195, 197, 207, 217, 231-233,
    235, 236, 256, 269, 282-284. See
    also PYD; YPJ
YPJ (Women's Defense Units/PYD)
    120, 130. See also PYD; YPG
Yuksekdag, Figen 209
Yusif, Nadeem 121

Zab River xvii
Zagros mountains xvii, 4
Zaim, Husni Colonel 95, 172
Zana, Leyla 35, 208
Zarqawi, Abu Musab al- 127
Zawahiri, Ayman al- 127
Zaza 10, 105, 106. See also Dimili;
    Kurdish languages (dialects)
Zaza, Nureddin 105, 106
Zebari (Zibari), Hoshyar 40, 72, 76,
    111
Zionist movement 101, 102
Zoroastrianism 20
Zuhab, Treaty of (1639) 6

9 781558 766419